The World of Damon Runyon

The World Of DAMON RUNYON

TOM CLARK

With illustrations by the author

HARPER & ROW, PUBLISHERS
New York · Hagerstown · San Francisco · London

Grateful acknowledgment is made to King Features for permission to reprint twelve columns by Damon Runyon. © King Features Syndicate, Inc., 1946 and 1964.

FIRST EDITION

Designed by Stephanie Tevonian

Library of Congress Cataloging in Publication Data

Clark, Tom, 1941–
  The world of Damon Runyon.

  Bibliography: p.
  1. Runyon, Damon, 1880–1946. 2. Authors, American—
20th century—Biography. I. Title.
PS3535.U52Z6   818'.5'209 [B]   78-2122
ISBN 0-06-010771-5

78   79   80   81   82   10   9   8   7   6   5   4   3   2   1

Acknowledgments and Dedication

The author owes a special debt of thanks to Ed Lawson; Gerry McCauley, Fran McCullough, Patti Fairfield, Rita Clark, John Clark, Ralph Gutlohn, George Kelly, Sue Friedland, Vaughn Stewart, and Chrisann Gniechwitz also helped. John Kinney played a major role in the early going. Juliet Clark was patient. Angelica Clark assisted with the research and writing, typed the manuscript and put up with it all. The book is dedicated to her.

Contents

Preface

Damon Runyon was a listener and a watcher, a peripatetic student of life who possessed a diamond cutter's powers of attention, the dispassionate curiosity of a scientist, the investigative energy of a great reporter, and the local knowledge of a denizen of the streets. He was a kind of Broadway Boswell, a bright reflector of the Golden Age of guys and dolls, gangsters and stars—many of whom were first glamorized and made into legend by his writings. Everywhere he went (and that was almost everywhere) he cultivated new acquaintances and friends and collected material for his writing the way a field zoologist collects specimens.

It was a method that required a "candid camera" approach, a natural blending, or (to extend the zoologist metaphor) an assumption of protective coloration: Runyon spoke and looked and acted in much the same way as those strange and rare creatures he stalked through the Broadway jungles. This was perhaps partially a conscious choice on his part, and as such it could be called hypocritical—except for two things. One, Runyon truly cared for and respected those people whose lives he hunted down and mounted in the glass cases of his columns and stories; two, there was no other way to get near them.

> One of the odd things about Damon was that he was a very cultured man. He pretended he wasn't. He concealed his culture and much of his knowledge. I have no idea why—but I think Damon wanted to get as close to the people he wanted to write about as he could. He wrote about mugs because they were interesting people.
> —Jimmy Cannon

The phrase "Damon Runyon character," in the common parlance, denotes some New York-talking guy whose grammar is rough and purpose slightly shady. Damon Runyon himself was never arrested, but many of his chums seemed to have done little else. If his name has passed into common speech as a generic term for the thugs and mugs who once inhabited the paralegal grey areas of one corner of American society, it is only a case of guilt by association. Biography by association, one might say, is the way Damon will be treated here.

* * *

Preface

Whenever the Demon could not balance his books, he would set down the amount needed to get him out of the red, and then explain it with the phrase, "Spent while going around and about."

One day Bugs Baer found that he had squandered fifteen dollars more than he could justify in his itemized account. So he wrote, "Fifteen dollars, for going around and about like Damon Runyon." The auditor flatly refused to honor the claim.   —Gene Fowler

The Damon Runyon world into which one steps in the first line of one of his stories usually consists of a street corner, all-night restaurant, racetrack, or sports arena where the narrator—who is a close relative of the author—has paused in his daily rounds.

> One evening along about seven o'clock I am sitting in Mindy's restaurant putting on the gefillte fish, which is a dish I am very fond of, when in comes three parties from Brooklyn wearing caps as follows: Harry the Horse, Little Isadore and Spanish John . . .
>
> I am really much surprised to see these parties on Broadway, as it is well known that the Broadway coppers just naturally love to shove such parties around, but here they are in Mindy's, and there I am, so of course I give them a very large hello . . .
>   —"Butch Minds the Baby"
>
> One night I am passing the corner of Fiftieth Street and Broadway, and what do I see but Dave the Dude standing in a doorway talking to a busted-down old Spanish doll by the name of Madame La Gimp . . .   —"Madame La Gimp"
>
> It comes on springtime, and the little birdies are singing in the trees in Central Park, and the grass is green all around and about, and I am at the Polo Grounds on the opening day of the baseball season, when who do I behold but Baseball Hattie . . .
>   —"Baseball Hattie"

If Damon hadn't been continuously "around and about," he'd have been minus his best material. He's always drawn into a story in the same way—as the detached observer or innocent bystander to whom life has a way of just happening. The unnamed narrator in Runyon's Broadway tales is a noninvolved, nonjudging, live-and-let-live spectator of the passing scene. It may have been a disingenuous pose—surely Damon had a great deal more intention than his fictional narrator ever admits to—but there is also evidence to suggest that the man Runyon, who took no stand in family matters and hated politics, was indeed as detached a guy as ever dwelt on the isle of Manhattan. A kind of Broadway Buddhist, he had an ironic and semicomic view of reality that allowed him to care very much for it without at all committing himself to it. This ability made him a great, clear-eyed newspaper reporter. Newspaper writing proved to be his most enduring talent, no matter the honors and sums fiction and movies won him. In his own mind he was always a newspaperman above and before all else. And it is by newspapermen that his work is most revered and

Preface

his memory most cherished. He saw the truth as it was and told it in accurate and revealing word-pictures that had a way of containing his feelings without ever letting them get in the way.

The two most famous and respected New York newspaper editors of the first half of the twentieth century, Arthur Brisbane of Hearst's *Journal* and *American* and Herbert Bayard Swope of Pulitzer's *World,* were rivals in their business life and agreed personally about very few things. But one belief they held in common was that Damon Runyon was the greatest newspaper reporter in the country.

As a columnist and reporter for three and a half decades, Runyon lived through and recorded what Frederick Lewis Allen called the Big Change, the great social transition that was to result in a modern America. Many of the prime movers (for better or worse) of this change were the principals of Damon's newspaper and fiction pieces—the stars and killers, the bosses and the beautifuls. In the period after the first World War, as Allen wrote, "gradually military affairs and foreign affairs and politics began to yield first place in newspaper coverage to scandals, crimes, disasters, human dramas, and sports . . . Something like a World Series-week spirit—a contagion of delighted concern over things that were exciting but didn't matter profoundly—was dominant." There was an expansion of public interest in areas of achievement that had previously been considered vulgar, trivial, or undignified. New heroes—Dempsey, Lindbergh, Ruth—were affecting people's lives dramatically. It was an age in which the prospects of any person— a Colorado urchin like Dempsey or a New York urchin like Al Capone—were limited only by his energy and talents as an individual.

Everyone could be a hero. To his readers, Runyon's glory as a man and writer was the reflected glory of those whose lives he watched and listened to and sooner or later made into stories that were as vivid and actual as the real thing (and usually much more permanent). The scribe of Broadway spent his adult life "around and about" in a social and sociable universe, a world governed not by thoughts or ideas or symbols but by men and women and their actions. The daily intensity of this world was like a magnet that tugged at his shoes and kept him moving when others would have flagged.

Perhaps more than any other writer's of his time, Damon's *was* the life of his time. For this reason I have chosen to focus on his story through the "looking glass" of those whose deeds he wrote: John McGraw, Jack Dempsey, Arnold Rothstein, Jimmy Walker, Al Capone. Runyon disdained to attempt an autobiography, claiming that his personal life was of no unusual interest: "I have accomplished no great deeds," he said. Certainly he was underestimating himself, but his point—that as a writer he had been a mirror to great deeds rather than performing them himself—was quite accurate. Taking his point, I have tried to write Damon's "life" as he would have wished it. Not, that is, as his story alone, but as that of his times, as he experienced them and committed them to prose.

The Runyon story took place in a wild variety of milieus. There were the rough-and-tumble streets of his native Wild West; the equally rough but more worldly-wise regions of Broadway and the fight ring, the Garden and Stillman's gym; the uproarious press boxes of the Polo Grounds and Ebbets Field and Yankee Stadium; the bettors' paradises like Jack Doyle's billiard parlor; the talk and good meals at Reuben's and Churchill's and at Jack Dunstan's all-night Broadway eatery in the prewar days; the Club Durant and the Club Richman, the Parody and the Silver Slipper, and Billy LaHiff's Tavern in the amazing twenties; floating card games and speakeasies; Lindy's and Toots Shor's and the Colony and the Stork Club later on; polo fields and penthouses at the Parc Vendome; packed courtrooms in Queens and Jersey, and all-white mansions next door to gangsters on Florida isles; the ten-dollar windows at Pimlico and Hialeah and Saratoga; and then, still later, the new, more affluent West: Hollywood, Romanoff's, Gertrude Neisen's villa in Holmby Hills, where Damon put in a few years making his tales into movies before returning to his Broadway stamping grounds to die, voiceless yet turning out a daily column until the very end.

Runyon wrote, by his own estimate, 80 million words. The subject of all of them is the omnipresent interest of his life: people. The characters of the courtroom and the ring, the nightclub and the track, were the "family" of Damon Runyon more truly than his estranged children and departed wives. Runyon's story is in the Mathewsons and McGraws and Stengels and Dempseys and Ruths; the Lou Claytons and Tad Dorgans and Hype Igoes and Texas Guinans; the Rothsteins and Costellos and Capones; the Jimmy Walkers and Slim Lindberghs and Tex Rickards and Ring Lardners and Walter Winchells and Abba Dabba Bermans and Shoeless Joe Jacksons and Nick the Greeks and all the rest of the endless stream of large and small personages, the "Damon Runyon characters" whose lives Runyon shaped into a body of work that earned him a fortune and made him one of the most popular and successful writers of his time. The comic irony he brought to his treatment of them all—big shots and small—was a great equalizer. Runyon's characters exist in his writing in a democracy of importance that places ragtag souls like Unser Fritz (a petty, defeated horseplayer) shoulder to shoulder with gambling

Preface

bosses and show girls and mob kings and playboys and board members of the Jockey Club. All of their stories interested him equally, as long as they contained something of that "roar" he once told his newspapering protégé Gene Fowler he heard along Broadway—that great pulse of life and action which was his only and constant subject.

Their stories also tell the story of America in the early part of this century, as lived in a particular locale called Broadway—which is not so much a street as a state of the spirit, a name signifying an epoch that was already gone by the time Damon ceased to walk its mundane pavements. Runyon's Broadway was strolled by the Babe and by Jack Dempsey and Mae Murray and Jimmy Walker but never by Barbara Walters or Joe Namath or Mickey Mantle or John Lindsay. By that latter time the memory alone remained, mainly inside the covers of Runyon collections and in the stage production and film of *Guys and Dolls*.

In the lives and stories of the people who made up Damon Runyon's Broadway Era, the real Runyon story lies. The book that follows is a search for it.

The World of Damon Runyon

1

Trials of Transportation

Damon Runyon was a poor boy from the West who went to the East and struck it rich as a writer. He had been a loner as a boy, and for all his love of good company in later years, he remained a loner, a traveler in life who had many regular stops but called none of them home. Simple movement ("around and about") always pleased him. He hated staying home, preferring even in his dying days to drown his aloneness in a crowd.

As an adult Runyon had thousands of friends, none of whom—according to Gene Fowler, who along with Bugs Baer probably got as close to Damon as any of his newspaper associates—knew him well. His affections for his friends were genuine, and theirs for him. Yet his sensitivity and his sharp tongue were notorious, and they often made friendship difficult. He was said to be vain, cynical, and sour. His black moods became famous. He was always aloof, around friends and particularly around his family. "He had what amounted to a phobia against relationships, particularly family," his son, Damon, Jr., wrote. Bill Corum, a good friend, admitted that his and Damon's was a friendship that demanded a lot of understanding on both sides. "He was self-conscious, suspicious and so sensitive that you could almost make him mad by just poking your finger at him."

And yet Damon was a man to whom his friends meant everything, as the great conviviality and warmth of his later columns show. For every anecdote of his "touchiness" or "coolness" there are two concerning his generosity to everybody from two-bit drifters to fellow sportswriters. Men like Fowler, Baer, and Bob Considine owed their first New York newspaper jobs to Runyon's efforts on their behalf. His assistance to young writers was legendary; Dan Parker, Jimmy Cannon, Ford Frick were others among the dozens in whose professional careers Damon's influence and advice played a significant role. "A lot of people talk of Damon as a cold, remote man," Jimmy Cannon said. "But he was kind and generous to me . . . He treated me as a kid brother."

Marshall Hunt, another young sportswriter, noticed that the "touchy" Runyon soon gave way to a kinder man once you got

1

past the stiffness of introductions. Hunt tells of talking Runyon into a breakfast date and then breaking the ice. "He looked up at me and then grinned and for the first time he seemed to mean that grin, and from then on we hit it off."

Fred Lieb, Runyon's press box contemporary, found Damon sympathetic, "an inherently honest and decent person" with a "sharp sense of humor"—not the "iconoclast . . . who liked to demolish tin gods and hallowed traditions" that others among their peers saw in him. Although it was true, Lieb writes in *Baseball As I Have Known It,* that when Damon "peered out at the world through glasses that made him look studious, there was a suggestion that he was mildly amused at the foolishnesses he saw," this was simply Runyon's style. Lieb did not consider Damon unkind. "I thought he liked most of all to stand quietly in the background watching and half laughing at the people who passed his vision. But destructive or bitter—never."

Others remember only a harsh, severe man. Runyon's strict teetotaling obviously bothered some of his younger colleagues. Abe Kemp, a writer from the Coast who'd come to town as a Runyon worshiper ("he was what I aspired to be—a character writing about characters"), was scared half to death by the real Damon who interviewed him for a job on the sports staff of the *American* in 1922. "This was when Runyon had switched from becoming a drunkard to becoming a teetotaler," Kemp recalled. "He asked me so God damn many questions I got terrified. How much do you drink? How much do you smoke? I got scared. I thought to myself, 'Holy Jesus, I don't want to work for any sonuvabitch like that.'"

Not surprisingly, Runyon's relations with many of his fellow newspapermen were complicated by natural feelings of competition and envy, usually on the fellow scribe's part. Many a young writer whom Runyon helped get his start later became a Runyon foe. It was hard to avoid this in so competitive a business. And we are told that Damon had a fantastically thin skin. When the pedantic columnist F.P.A. (Franklin Pierce Adams) criticized Damon's grammar, he became an enemy. Bill Corum said Runyon had "rabbit ears" when it came to criticism. Real or imagined slights often did permanent damage to his relations with other journalists. Bob Considine, a man he'd brought to the *American* sports department, became an enemy when Runyon sensed Considine was "after his job." An insulting remark made by Mark Hellinger in the lobby of the 48th Street Theatre on the opening night of Damon's play *A Slight Case of Murder* ("This will be a slight case of getting out of here as quick as I can," Hellinger cracked to a chum) was overheard by Runyon, and from that evening he never looked on the fellow columnist with anything but contempt.

Trials of Transportation

Even Gene Fowler, who might never have left Colorado had it not been for Runyon's generous sponsorship, apparently never quite got over certain critical comments Damon made about his behavior and apparel on his arrival in New York in 1918. ("Damon, you're like Powder River—a mile wide and an inch deep," Fowler once shouted at his friend.) And as friendly as Damon and Bugs Baer were (they shared an office for nearly two decades and in the twenties were apartment-mates for a while in a flat above Billy LaHiff's Tavern), when Bugs looked back on Damon in the fifties it was with the thin kindness of distance. "There wasn't a time when Runyon wouldn't throw a drowning man both ends of the rope," Bugs said.

(Baer had once griped about Damon's penchant for "writing everybody else out of the paper"—a comment on the Demon's vast output that indicates the envy most of his colleagues felt but few were honest enough to express.)

"Damon was shy and the way he hid it, by assuming an aloof manner and making sardonic comments, was a piece of sham," Gene Fowler said. " 'Cold fish' was the word often used to describe him," H. Allen Smith wrote. "He was unsmiling and almost always looked churlish and irascible. Even people who didn't know him got out of his way when they saw him approaching." It was the view of Smith, and of many others who knew Damon in the newspaper world, that he was a remote and distrustful man whose bitterness was the byproduct of an unhappy life from childhood—his early loss of his mother, his lonely and half-starved youth, his own adolescent alcoholism and the later fatal alcoholism of his first wife. Certainly there is some reason for such a view, and in part it was shared by Damon's son.

> My father was left to his own devices as a small boy. His father, no family man, liked to debate with the town mouths at the bar. My father was a lonely, barefoot little boy about town.
> This background molded the man Runyon, as well as the writer. The loss of a mother, and the lack of a real father at so early an age, made him wary of forming close relationships for fear of losing them. The man grew up silent since there never was anyone in whom to confide his inner thoughts.

On the other hand, to his Broadway pals and associates of the nightclub and the gym and the track, Damon was a pleasant, dapper chap who knew his way around, had his head about him, and was a guy you could trust. He picked up tabs wherever he went and palmed dollar bills (sometimes fives or tens) to half the burnt-out cases on Broadway. In that world he was well known and loved; little distrust or suspicion were ever attached to him. His habits of aloofness and privacy were acknowledged and respected. After all, on the Big Street there was many a guy with a secret to keep. If Mr. Runyon was sometimes kind of standoffish, it was his business and it was okay with everybody. Besides, when he was feeling good he was always a very pleasant and courteous man, and that was most of the time. You never hear Runyon poorly spoken of among the survivors of the Broadway crowd. It is only among the writing set, with whom his livelihood alone allied him, that the backhanded remarks about his coolness and moodiness and cynicism arise. The boys in Jack's and Reuben's and Lindy's regarded Damon as a prince of a fellow and, what was rarer, a real gentleman to boot. What more could you ask of a guy?

> I can remember when it was quite the fashion for writers to put themselves away as former hoboes. I think it may have been in imitation of Jack London. Jack was the top writer of his time and he cast a long shadow of influence over that period and the years ahead.
> He was a flannel shirt fellow who was supposed to have "'boed it" all over the country in his youth and to have been an all-around rough-and-tumble gee, and a lot of anemic, hollow-chested pen pushers, journalists and story writers tried to pattern their lives after his, and sometimes went so far as to steal rides on street cars. —"A No. 1"

Damon was born in Manhattan, Kansas, on October 8, 1880, the son of a red-haired itinerant printer and publisher of small-time newspapers, lover of the classics, gambler, drunkard, and former Indian fighter named Alfred Lee Runyan. ("Runyan" was a corruption of Renoyan, the name the family had brought over from France in pre-Revolutionary War days.) The boy was named Alfred Damon Runyan; the Damon came from his mother, Elizabeth Damon, a descendant of the Massachusetts Bay Colony Whites.

Life for the Runyans was a struggle. The rigors of four home births, her husband's business failures, and spells of diphtheria and consumption combined by the mid-eighties to destroy the frontier housewife's health. Alfred Lee gave up his dream of becoming a great independent publisher and took a job as a printer on the Pueblo *Chieftain*. Although it was consideration of his wife's health that brought Alfred Lee to move his family to Colorado, the clear mountain air never got a chance to do its work. Shortly after their arrival in 1887, Elizabeth Runyan succumbed to tuberculosis. After her death, Alfred Damon Runyan's three sisters were returned to Kansas to be raised by in-laws, while the boy, scrawny and high-strung, was turned loose to run the dirt streets of Pueblo. The "little Pittsburgh" of the high plains was a wide open town in those days, with hundreds of bars and gambling houses and a thriving red-light district (where young Al was employed for a while as a messenger boy).

Trials of Transportation

School was not a place where Al was to be found with any regularity during the late eighties. Home life did not exist for the boy. Occasionally he was taken in as a nonpaying boarder by the mother of a friend or by some motherly widow, but none of these situations wore well either on the ragged, wild Al or on his benefactors, and none of them lasted. Left to his own devices, he recruited a gang for company and roamed, ran errands when there was a dime to be earned, or else stood at his father's side in the Arkansas Saloon and listened to tales of Custer's Last Stand (Alfred Lee had served briefly in Custer's 19th Kansas Volunteers), "Buffalo Bill" Cody, Billy the Kid, and Marshal Pat Dillon. Sometimes it was quotations from Shakespeare or Scripture, sayings of Confucius or Montaigne. It was an eclectic education, but young Al apparently preferred it to the confinement of Hinsdale School, from which he was formally expelled in either the fourth or the sixth grade, according to the stories.

His father had descended from the status of boarding-house dweller to resident of a ramshackle hilltop shed by this time, but at least young Al had a place to put his head at night—most nights. His old man slept mornings, drank afternoons and evenings, and set type in the wee hours. The boy was on his own to move as he pleased, and he did so, usually in search of the wherewithal to acquire his next meal. These were hungry times for the future star columnist, to whom the knowledge that he would one day be a regular diner at such spots as the Stork Club and the Colony would undoubtedly have come as a surprise.

The senior Al Runyan, himself a printer's son, had been the publisher or printer of papers in Manhattan, Clay Center, and Wellington, Kansas, before going on to Colorado. When young Al grabbed the bottom rung of the newspaper business at the Pueblo *Evening News* in his early teens, it was simply the extension of a family tradition. He was printer's devil, janitor, and gopher; he brandished a wet mop and hot type before touching pen or typewriter. Before long he was writing what would now be called human interest pieces (about kids and animals) and contributing verses. At fourteen he received his first news assignment, to cover a lynching in Pueblo. By fifteen he was a full-fledged news reporter, a chain smoker, and an accomplished barfly. Red Eye and oval Turkish cigarettes were the ice cream and soda pop of Al Runyan's childhood. He had his own boarding-house room, owned a decent suit of clothes, and diploma or no diploma, he was on his way. He ran everywhere for his stories, and after work he regaled fellow tipplers at the Home Café and Bucket of Blood with exaggerated versions of his exploits. He even toted a six-gun, not so much out of necessity as for the notoriety it gave him. He wanted to appear a veteran, a man despite his years. His childhood had not been particularly pleasant; he was impatient for it to be over.

By the age of seventeen he'd received his first byline—with the Pueblo *Evening Post*. A printer's error caused the name to come out "Runyon," which for some reason gave young Al a kick, and he decided to adopt it. (It was in another newspaper office—years later in New York—that the "Alfred" was pruned away, leaving our hero as simply Damon Runyon.) The following year, 1898, he took another long step toward manhood by talking his way into the 13th Minnesota Volunteers, an outfit heading for the Philippines to put down the Moro insurrection. (He had followed the Colorado volunteers to San Francisco, and been turned down because of his age, before being accepted for enlistment by the Minnesotans.) His ensuing Spanish American War experiences included none of the battle heroics Al had hoped for. Instead of a purple heart for a bullet or sword wound, he incurred nothing more serious than a skin eruption. The trip was fuel for plenty of story-telling and verse-writing activity upon his return, however—and for decades thereafter.

Young Al was discharged from the service at the Presidio in San Francisco late in 1899. After a tour de force of a two-week bender that exhausted his army savings, he headed East in the manner of any hardy and adventurous lad of those days—by hopping a train going in the right direction and hanging on for dear life to the nearest handhold.

"I just thought it was the thing to do to steal rides on freight and passenger trains and to go to places for no particular reason," he wrote years later, when his traveling had become strictly first class. "Wherever I went I had to work, so I might as well have remained in one place. My transportation thefts were limited and I never went real far, but I picked up much of the lore of the road through contacts with the real rovers and I accumulated considerable of their patter of that long-gone time . . ." Al picked up a Union Pacific east of Oakland, and for the next few nights, without the benefit of a ticket, rode the "rods," "blinds," and "decks" of eastbound U.P. trains. He was young, and eighteen months of three-squares at the expense of Uncle Sam had put enough flesh on his limbs to make the adventure no great physical hardship. One could crawl under the train and cling to the brake rods (a precarious, gritty spot, but out of sight) or else clamber onto the "blind baggage" or the top decks of cars and ride for free instead of five cents a mile. Travel *al fresco* had its pains—and its intellectual rewards. To young Al, who was fascinated by the outlaw life he'd heard of in his father's tales of the great days of the robbers and shooters, it was his first taste of the "real thing." More than a few of the 'boes with whom young Al "jungled up" were on the run from the law for various reasons. Al felt he was living among great semilegendary criminals, characters like those who'd populated his old man's conversation night after night back in the Arkansas Saloon. Their mythological notoriety (he heard the exploits of such famous hoboes as A No. 1, Cincy Skin, Peoria Shine, Cheyenne Red, and Reading Blackie), vivid private language ("bindle stiffs," "gay cats," "mooching"), and cheerfully dangerous behavior (in a "jungle" outside Provo a friendly rover named Kid Swift pointed out to Al a safecracker calmly skimming the nitro off liquid dynamite boiling in a tin can on a camp fire) were of great interest to the young man, who obviously considered the peripatetic life of the 'boes to be as ennobling as it was uncomfortable.

"Personally, I thought the manner of living of David Graham Phillips was to be preferred," Damon later wrote, referring to a great turn-of-the-century newspaperman. "He had a zillion suits of clothes and dined at Sherry's and Del's. And yet I have seen the day when I magnified a few little jaunts of my own into a regular hobo career, though of course I was no more of a real 'bo than one of the Rockefeller kids."

Al paid when he could afford the ticket, but some of the time he could not, and since he was constantly on the road it was not infrequently that he found himself traveling in the company of those who risked the brakeman's wrath. His early career as a newspaperman was an active but irregular one; his inquisitive disposition and explosive drinking kept him from holding any one job (or paycheck) very long, and in the years 1900–1906 Al Runyon apparently did a lot of open-air railroading.

He returned to Pueblo via the 'bo jungles of Provo in November 1899, soon moved on to Basalt Junction (near Aspen) and then to Glenwood Springs (where he worked for the *In-It Daily)* before doubling back to Pueblo and doing a short stint with his father's paper, the *Chieftain.* That was in 1900. 1901 found him in Colorado Springs, where he was well on his way to becoming the most famous elbow artist in town when his paper (the *Gazette)* was taken over by new owners who did not approve of bibulous reporters. In 1902 Al moved on to the St. Joseph (Missouri) *Gazette.* In 1903 it was back to Pueblo and the *Chieftain* again, then to the Trinidad (Colorado) *Advertiser* in 1904, and finally in 1905 to Denver, the twinkling-lights City of the Plain whose doors swung twenty-four hours a day. Al worked first at the Denver *Republican,* then at Bonfils and Tammen's *Post* in 1905. But the *Post*'s city editor, Joe Ward, pointed his famous long-billed copy-editing shears in the tipsy Runyon's eyes one day and gave him his walking papers. Al caught the U.P. to San Francisco (whether riding for free or not we don't know). In Frisco he worked for the *Post* for a few months before returning to Denver and catching on with the *Rocky Mountain News* in 1906. It was a six-year itinerary that would have done Kid Swift, or Damon's other hobo acquaintances, proud.

Al Runyon stayed with the *Rocky Mountain News* until 1910, achieving considerable success on that paper as a news and feature writer, particularly in a series of travel pieces that described his "chalk-talk and stunt" tour of the state in the company of a cartoonist named Doc Bird Finch. (The climax of their collaboration occurred at Union Station on Christmas Eve 1907, when a wobbly Runyon, in a Santa Claus suit, greeted the children of Denver with slurred good cheer and occasional kicks in the backside.) God only knows how Runyon and Finch, two fierce drinkers, made it from stop to stop; the records are scanty, though there are reports of certain special trains and private passenger cars hired by the *News* as part of the Runyon-Finch promotion—so we can assume that by this time Al was able to ride "legal" on at least some of his rail junkets. By now his verse (in the Kiplingesque mode) had appeared in such effete journals as *McClure's* and *Harper's Weekly;* it would not do to get busted on a ten-day "vag" charge (or over the noggin with a brakeman's stick). And Al was now attempting to make the delicate transition from noted hell-raiser to eligible swain in order to impress the assistant society editor of the *News,* Ellen Egan.

His romantic experiences up to the year 1907 had been casual and largely commercial in nature, since until then he had had neither the occasion nor the inclination to address his attentions to "respectable" members of the opposite sex. It was clearly in the latter class that the slim, pretty, well-spoken Ellen Egan was stationed, and thus it was that the rowdy, hard-drinking Al Runyon, when ordered by his city editor to accompany Miss Egan around and about on evening assignments, felt duty-bound to see her home afterward. Out of this grew their courtship, which cut only marginally into Al's all-night poker sessions at the Denver Press Club, since the front door always closed behind his petite, blond fellow reporter at precisely 11:15, a quarter hour after her newspaper chores ended. When Ellen had gone inside, Al stood for a moment on the porch, straw boater in hand, rail-thin in his tight trousers and high-button shoes, and bethought himself on the subject of his life and fortunes before stepping off toward the lights of the city to find himself a drink.

Like the far-off dream of New York newspapering, as epitomized by the elegant David Graham Phillips, Ellen represented to Al his ambitions to rise in the world. She was educated, charming, musical, the daughter of a well-to-do Irish Catholic railway super-

Trials of Transportation

Al Runyon in his Denver newspapering years.

intendent. She lived in a large home with a lawn full of trees in a fine neighborhood. Ellen saw in Al a young man with talent and ambition whose ragged habits she quickly took it upon herself to do something about. She made it clear to Al that she appreciated his poetry but not his drinking, an appeal to his self-respect that brought out rare displays of conscience in Al. On one occasion, when Ellen discovered him lying in a heap on the street in front of the *News* office after a binge, he refused to get up and walk down the street with her out of embarrassment. From his father Al had inherited old-fashioned ideas about comporting oneself around "ladies," and in deference to them he was always as polite as possible around Ellen, then and later. (Although capable of sharing—and creating—a bawdy joke or story in male company, Runyon all his life avoided the use of "low" language around women—and in his writing—and whenever he met one socially he bowed and elaborately doffed his hat.) Having been deprived of his mother in early childhood, Al had had little opportunity to experience the civilizing influence of the gentler sex. Whether this influence was now comfortably received by him from Ellen is an open question. At any rate she took a rain check on his affections, postponing any consideration of marriage until her suitor had succeeded in setting himself up in life.

Al in these later Denver years was composing the poems—mostly heroic ballads on military subjects drawn from his experiences in the Philippines—that were to fill two slim volumes, *Tents*

The World of Damon Runyon

of Trouble and *Rhymes of the Firing Line,* and writing the lively, personal newspaper stories which were to make up his passkey to the Hearst empire. Still, by the time he followed the natural evolution of every bright and ambitious young scribe of the hinterlands and left Denver for New York in 1910, his local fame as a newspaperman and versifier hadn't lined his pocket to any notable degree, and he was not able to afford the passenger fare for the cross-continental journey. The situation wasn't new, but Al was disturbed at the prospect of trying to cling to a brake beam or a roof deck with his best forty-dollar suit on his back and his worldly belongings slung over his shoulder. So he scouted the local undertakers, finding one who had a fresh corpse ripe for shipping to the East. In those days a corpse traveling by rail had to be accompanied by a breather. Al took the breather's ticket and, thanks to the convenient accident created by the traveling stiff (whose name was not passed down to history), rode free of charge to Penn Station in Manhattan. It was only ten cents to his former Denver friend Charles Van Loan's house in Brooklyn, Al's first New York home.

In later years Runyon wrote a number of short fiction pieces and daily columns that returned to his gratis railroading experiences at the turn of the century. The columns, like "Trials of Transportation" and "A No. 1," are rambling essays on the subject of hoboes and the hobo life. They mingle Runyon's own recollections of his early taste of life on the road with the considerable lore on the subject he had collected over the years. He recounts numerous anecdotes—submitted by amateur hobo historians from all over the country—about A No. 1, the well-educated, gentlemanly, high-strung little "King of the 'Boes" whose name was carved on the water tank of every railroad yard west of the Mississippi. ("The water tanks were the hobo registers in those days.")

> He was a neat man. He wore a small dark mustache, neatly trimmed. His clothes were always clean and neat. Over his street apparel when beating the trains he wore overalls, which he would remove and hide on arriving in a town. . .
> He applied the "A-1" to himself as meaning first class, or the best in the hobo line. . .
> He was not a complete bum. He would often pay his way for everything except railroad fare. The consummate ease with which he found rail transportation lends some color to the theory that he had some kind of an "in" with the roads. Yet had this been true there would have been no good reason for his being constantly on the go, as his method of travel was scarcely comfortable or convenient.

Take away the mustache, and the dandified A No. 1 Runyon describes resembles young Al Runyon himself more than, say, some of the motion picture portrayals of the character. (Lee Mar-

Trials of Transportation

vin plays a grizzled, roughneck A No. 1 in Robert Aldrich's *The Emperor of the North.*)

The Runyon fiction pieces on the 'bo life appeared as Sunday features in the Hearst *American Weekly* section in the twenties. They are interesting pieces, extended in length to around 5000 words and written to be broken down for serialization. The longest of them are "As Between Friends" and "The Informal Execution of Soupbone Pew." Of all Damon's pre-Broadway tales, the hobo stories best demonstrate his interest in the outlaw life as a subject—and in the "outlaw code" as a system of behavior, seen as preferable to the laws of society in general (as expressed by police, judges, etc.). Here the intention is considerably less precise than it is in the later Broadway pieces—the humor is broader, less ironic—but the characters are definitely familiar. Like the characters of the Broadway tales, the characters of the hobo tales are a criminal caste. Damon's 'bo repertory is a composite of men he'd actually met (the safecracker in Provo in 1900 returns to life, "boiling out soup," in "The Informal Execution of Soupbone Pew") and people he'd only heard about (A No. 1, Chicago Fat, 'Frisco Shine, etc.). One of Damon's main sources of information about life and types in the stolen-ride set was Jack Dempsey.

Runyon's portrait of the wicked "shack" ('bo talk for brakeman) who bounces a coupling pin on the end of a wire under a moving train "so that it would swing up underneath and knock a stiff off the rods" ("The Informal Execution of Soupbone Pew") is the key image in all his writings on the 'bo life. As a symbol of the wanton cruelty of authority, it fits Runyon's underworld ontology perfectly. In a universe where brakemen kill innocent poor boys with coupling-pin drops, or break their necks by knocking them off the decks of moving cars (as happens to Manchester Slim in "Soupbone Pew"), the "bad guys" suddenly become good guys.

The coupling-pin image first appears in Damon's version of Jack Dempsey's life story, "A Tale of Two Fists," for serialization in the Hearst papers in May and June 1919. The "biography" was in fact a string of Dempsey stories, some fact and some part of the young heavyweight's growing personal mythology. Damon was careful to bring in a good deal of romantic material on Jack's early free-ride days from 1911 to 1915 or 1916, when the fighter was beating his way around the bush league fight rings of the Rocky Mountain states. Jack himself presented Damon with the coupling-pin tale, and Damon inserted it in the Dempsey "life." He later had reservations about Jack's veracity on this point but claimed that the truth behind the image remained, insisting that the brakemen or "shacks" were capable of anything.

The World of Damon Runyon

I remember another legend of the "jungles" about a "shack" on the Santa Fe railroad running on freight trains between Dodge City, Kansas, and La Junta, Colorado, who was supposed to be the toughest brakie in the United States.

If he spotted a 'bo riding rods on his train, which is to say the brakebeams underneath a car, he waited until the train was at the peak of its motion, climbed on top of the car and dropped a coupling pin attached to a long wire down to the ground to trail alongside the car.

The motion of the train would bounce this pin underneath the car with terrific force and often dislodge the rod-rider with fatal consequences after giving him what must have been a terrifying preview of his finish in the bouncing coupling pin.

I never believed that yarn, either, though I put it in all seriousness in my story of Jack Dempsey's hobo days as having happened to Jack and in fact I think Jack imagined it did. But you see, long before I ever knew of Dempsey I heard the story as having happened on railroads other than the Santa Fe.

There is no doubt that some of those old time "shacks" were sadists. They would use brass knucks and blackjacks on 'boes with no compunctions of conscience and sometimes pistols, yet the coupling pin story always struck me as too premeditated. To me the topper was the tale of how a John Yegg or safeblower who had been knocked off his perch under a car by the coupling pin but escaped with his life, returned with a terrible revenge on the "shack."

It was said that he boiled himself up some "soup" or nitroglycerine which he carried in a bottle in his hip pocket, then climbed to the deck of the "shack's" train and deliberately baited the railroad into giving him a swift kick, the ensuing explosion devastating several surrounding counties and of course the "shack" and the Yegg. —"Trials of Transportation"

"Soupbone Pew" is another tale of a victim's revenge on one particularly cruel "shack." It is a strictly moral tale, à la early Damon Runyon, with the grisly execution of the brakeman probably coming as something of a shock to *American Weekly* readers of the period. Soupbone Pew, the wicked "shack," is variously shot, beaten, electrocuted, and strangled. The revenge motif evidently appealed to Runyon, but in "Soupbone Pew" he lays it on too thick, scuttling the humor of the tale in grotesque violence. A few years later, when he came to write the Broadway tales, he had his feelings under better control. By 1929 he had learned to mask emotion in a "half-boob air" that permitted him to say much more about the authority-outlaw question than he could in "Soupbone Pew"— and with considerably greater delicacy. The detached ironic voice of the later tales takes social injustice for granted. Their narrator does not get excited about it, does not worry about it. What good did that ever do?

In his own later recollections, Jack Dempsey was less effusive about his days of riding the rods than he'd been while talking to

Trials of Transportation

Damon in 1919. He remembered it strictly as hard times. The two narrow steel beams beneath a Pullman, he pointed out, didn't make much of a bed for a gentleman. "There's only a few inches between you and the tracks and roadbeds—and death," he said. "If you fall asleep you'll roll off your narrow steel bed and die. If you're so cold you can't hang on any longer, you die." Not too romantic, when you think of it. "If you had a few cents," Jack recalled, "you could ride upstairs, in the luxury of maybe a freezing freight car." He told of hopping a moving freight in Grand Junction, Colorado, and having his head beaten to a pulp by a brakeman with a broomstick while he held on for dear life. Finally Jack blacked out and crashed to the roadbed, the train roaring on at forty miles an hour.

Another time, Dempsey and his older brother, Bernie, were caught inside a boxcar full of sacked salt on its way to Colorado Springs. Railroad guards attacked the Dempsey boys with whips. The boys decked one of the guards and outran the others. Jack then had to make an even quicker exit from the scene than his famous run-with-the-money from the Shelby, Montana, prize ring to the Great Northern tracks on July 4, 1923.

During the early twenties, when Jack was taking potshots from the press for being a surly and ungrateful draft-dodging brute, he grew a little nervous about that part of his legend which Damon had glorified in the "coupling pin" and similar episodes of his biography. For a few years the champ made a point of disdaining his hobo experiences *in toto* whenever the scribes were present. A confusion thus arose. In a 1930 story in a New York paper, a sportswriter named Charley Murray charged that Damon's picture of Dempsey the free-rider was the result of a cosmetic job by Jack Kearns, who (Murray suggested) had "made up" the hobo story for Runyon's benefit. Not so, Damon said, responding to Murray in his column in the *American.*

> The truth of the matter is that I met Dempsey when he came to New York City for the first time in 1916, more than a year before Doc Kearns [Dempsey's manager from 1919 to 1926] ever heard of him. . .
>
> After the [New York fights] Dempsey . . . returned west. In that return, Jack rode the decks of passenger trains part of the way.
>
> I am not saying that riding the decks of a passenger train makes a man a hobo, but it surely doesn't make him a paying customer. Dempsey, on his own say-so, has given proof that he did a lot of traveling that way in his early days as a fighter. . .
>
> Well, after Dempsey won the world title, and following his defeat of Georges Carpentier, we were on our way to Europe. Jack turned to me and said:
>
> "Damon, let's forget that hobo business now, we want to be gentlemen after this."

Jack Dempsey

Meaning, of course, that he wanted to be so depicted.

If Murray has any more doubts about the hobo story, he may be surprised to know that I have witnesses who ate with Jack out of tin cans and rode with Dempsey on freight trains. Jack was mighty proud of his rough, rod-riding career at the time.

A Tale of Two Fists was written by me, and anyone who has traveled around the country with Dempsey as I have, and seen the weird characters that bob up on him in every town, mumbling of the old days and old experiences, knows Jack couldn't have met them in drawing rooms.

Trials of Transportation

The image of Dempsey the 'bo, dodging the bounces of hot coupling pins dangled by vicious "shacks" as he clung to the brake rods under a Pullman or KOing whip-toting railway guards with his budding right cross, had an obvious appeal for Damon, whose own knockabout youth, never so strenuous as Dempsey's, nevertheless blurred with and was summed up by that romantic image. He and Jack were outsiders, roamers. The roving life came natural to a poor boy from the east slopes of the Rockies, where the cold wind cut across the plains like a knife. Poor boys from that part of the world who were left to run loose early, often turned out to be traveling types, gunmen, or loners, Damon knew. But that was no crime.

2

The Demon of Denver

Alfred Lee Runyan, the red-bearded saloon orator, was a baseball devotee who mixed his opinions on that sport with the philosophical remarks and citations of the classics he delivered for the benefit of the patrons of the Arkansas Saloon in Pueblo, his son Al standing at his side and taking it all in.

The printer had been born and raised in the West, where boys played ball but knew of the major leagues only through sporting magazines and newspapers like *The Sporting News*. He made a point of keeping up with the top national clubs, and in 1888 he had a chance to see the real thing when Cap Anson's Chicago White Stockings, touring with a team of National League all stars, made two stops in Colorado. Alfred Lee Runyan attended both contests, or claimed he did, and later had plenty to say at the Arkansas Saloon about the great players he'd seen. Young Al now heard the names and exploits of famous diamond stars sprinkled among the Indian fighters, gunmen, bandits, poets, and sages whose deeds and words his old man constantly evoked. The ball stars quickly joined the boy's private catalog of saints, and years later he could still speak from memory of the speed of Arlie Latham and the power of Ed Delahanty—experienced only through his old man's conversation in Pueblo saloons of the eighties and nineties. Naturally, Alfred Lee Runyan was interested in the greatest team of that era, the Baltimore Orioles of Wilbert Robinson and Joe Kelley and John McGraw, and he spoke of them with reverence and enthusiasm. Certainly he had no reason to expect that these very men would one day be his son's compères in hunting resorts in Georgia, royal soirées in London and Paris, and the select sporting restaurants and clubs of New York.

As a boy Al Jr. played on vacant lots in Pueblo the ragged kind of baseball that poor kids played everywhere in the country, using a ball of tape or yarn and a broomstick. He was small and light, agile if not strong. As a player he never went beyond the backstreet rudiments of the game. When he grew older he began to follow developments in professional baseball from a distance. He had an opportunity to view at first hand the progress of the cruder brand of baseball played in the towns of the plains states where

The Demon of Denver

he worked as a young reporter. He saw in action all the amateur and semiprofessional clubs of Colorado Springs and St. Joe, Trinidad and Pueblo, and the barnstorming teams that passed through these places. He stored up a good deal of baseball knowledge and even tried his hand one time at managing a semipro club in one of the local fly-by-night leagues.

Around that dusty circuit of western towns to which Al's pursuit of a newspaper career took him, such leagues cropped up now and then, for a dusty summer or two, before lapsing into deserved oblivion. One such league—it never got so far as the first game of its season—owed its brief period of quasi-existence to the efforts of Al Runyon himself. That was in 1910, by which time Al was a successful sports and news reporter (and verse and features writer) for the Denver *News.* He had been contributing occasional stories on sports, usually boxing, football, and baseball, to all the papers he'd worked for since returning from the Philippines. In 1905, he'd worked in the sports department of the Denver *Post,* an exhilarating experience for an imaginative young man. Under Fred Bonfils and Harry Tammen, the *Post* encouraged immediacy and originality in its writers to an extent far beyond most papers of the time. Stunts, gimmicks, and angles were the *Post*'s stock in trade. (Bon and Tam's ideas of journalistic method had much in common with those of Runyon's later employer, W. R. Hearst.) Al learned the value of the "personal approach" on the *Post,* whose sports department was headed by the legendary editor Otto Floto.

Floto's name so appealed to one of his bosses that it became for no other reason part of the title of the famous Sells-Floto Circus. (Originally a Harry Tammen hobby, the Sells-Floto outfit grew to rival the Ringling Brothers and Barnum & Bailey productions.) A large and good-natured man, Floto wrote a daily column that was notable mainly for its verbosity and circumlocution, yet he was an acknowledged sporting expert, particularly in the area of pugilism, where the sovereignty of his opinions was disputed in the region only by Bat Masterson, the ex-sheriff of Dodge City who promoted sporting and gambling activities in Denver. (Bat went on to New York to become sports editor and boxing wizard of every horseplayer's required daily reading matter, the *Morning Telegraph.)*

Floto liked young Al Runyon's camp verses and chipper come-on and spent many an hour in the *Post* office filling him in on the lore of a lifetime in the sporting racket. Otto was a renowned raconteur, like Al's old man, and Al listened with interest to Floto's tales. Few other men west of the Mississippi could have provided Al Runyon with such a voluminous course in the basics of sportswriting. Charles E. Van Loan, a Floto protégé whom Al knew from the Denver Press Club, had gone on to great success as a sportswriter for Hearst and the Hearst syndicates in New York. Van Loan now earned four times what Al was making in Denver, and he was progressing not only in newspapering but in a lucrative career as a writer of sports fiction. The Van Loan story was a graphic example to Al Runyon of how far a knack for putting together a yarn about a prizefight or a ballgame might take a fellow.

Fred Bonfils was a boxing nut, so fistic promotions were a constant at the *Post*. Al Runyon arranged and refereed bouts that were held in a ring in front of the newspaper's office on Champa Street, among other places. Al also operated a World Series scoreboard, went up in a balloon, rode horses in races at a local track, and raced against a mythical record on a home bicycle trainer mounted on the boxing platform in front of *Post* headquarters. ("I did a hundred and one similar stunts and had a lot of fun doing them," he later wrote his son when Damon Jr. was starting a newspaper career of his own.) And now and then he wrote Otto Floto's daily sporting column.

Al Runyon's periodic binges, which lasted anywhere from three days to two weeks and often left him crumpled in some tavern or alley in a semicoma from which he awoke with an evil mouth and a blank memory, bothered Otto Floto less than they did Joe Ward, the paper's city editor. Al's confident use of the vernacular—which he perfected through such *Post* stunts as sleeping in hobo flophouses—struck Ward as pretentious, and when the brash young reporter added bad behavior to his grammatical sins, he and the city editor clashed. Al left the *Post* and went to the *Rocky Mountain News,* where he wrote not only sports but everything else—trials, business and labor news, political conventions, "city side" features, humor, verse. He became that paper's number one reporter and features writer, and the responsibilities this entailed left him considerably less time for sportswriting than he'd had at the *Post.*

Nevertheless his sports interests colored his other writing, even on such a divergent subject as religion. When the evangelist Billy Sunday visited Denver in 1909, Al's story recalled the preacher's career in baseball. Outfielder Sunday, in Al's old man's Arkansas Saloon tales, had wings of Mercury to do what normal men did with their feet. Now the same Billy Sunday, who as centerfielder of the White Stockings had once beaten Arlie Latham in a footrace to determine the fastest man in baseball, was beating his way around the gospel circuit like one of the Lord's own whirlwinds, picking up converts, publicity, and donations everywhere. Although Sunday's own ethics would later come into question, there was never any arguing his success in the revival racket or the extent of the moral whiplash his appearances caused, especially in rural towns. "He was credited with being the greatest single influence in the nation on the downfall of the saloon," a sober Damon Runyon noted thirty years later.

The evangelist's anti-saloon sermon fell on deaf ears in 1908. Al Runyon chain smoked Turkish oval cigarettes throughout Sunday's fire-and-brimstone attack on the evils of tobacco and booze, and once he'd stopped in at the *News* office to file his story, he stepped out on the town to touch as many as possible of the usual bases: the reporters' saloons, the Denver Press Club, the local pool hall and brothel, the various card and dice games. All were spots where a man could find a drink with no trouble when he needed it, and on the evening of Billy Sunday's visit, Al felt he needed it. He drank for relief; drinking relaxed him and made him self-confident. Sometimes, however, there were unfortunate consequences. On one occasion he made a fool of himself in a Denver saloon by taking an errant swing at a large stranger who in response lifted him into the air by the collar, laughed, and said, "Shut up, you little twerp!" (His exploits were earning Al a nickname that a later Denver newspaperman, Gene Fowler, would transport to New York and contribute to journalistic parlance as an important part of the Runyon *mythos;* the nickname was the Demon.)

Despite his irregular habits, Al was regarded by his employer, Senator Thomas Patterson (the millionaire owner of the *Rocky Mountain News),* as a valuable property. The popularity of Al's series of articles on his 1907 tour of the state with the bibulous cartoonist Doc Bird Finch convinced Patterson to give him a free hand when it came to picking his assignments. Al's interest in sporting subjects was then showing up in his other writing (surely in no other town on Billy Sunday's itinerary was the evangelist's appearance reported as an event of sporting significance by the local paper!). Even on the Doc Bird tour Damon had shown inklings of his future calling, managing, drunk or sober, to keep up with the various athletic schedules so that the Runyon-Finch entourage would conveniently arrive at a state fair grounds just before a baseball game, or at a campus on the eve of a particularly important college football game.

Since Runyon was then as always basically a "human interest" journalist, less concerned with the bare events in a story than with the qualities of drama, humor, and character to be conveyed therein, it was natural that he would gravitate to subjects that required of a writer not only "facts" but "color." He wrote many sports pieces for the *News* after 1907; he also continued to cover all the other "beats" in town and to write effectively on all subjects. (This quality of adaptability was an identifying characteristic of Runyon's newspaper work then and later. One day it would make it possible for him to turn spur-of-the-moment assignments into excellent pieces on subjects with which he was totally unfamiliar, such as yachting and polo, auto shows and political conventions.)

Runyon's first major personal involvement in the business of sports came during the early months of 1910, when he occupied himself with an ill-fated brainchild known as the Colorado State Baseball League. Like most of Damon's later promotional ventures in the sporting realm (his boxing and horse racing enterprises, for example), the CSBL flopped. In truth it was a project that was doomed from the start because the Rocky Mountain region was rodeo country that would not then or later support organized base-ball on the professional, money-making scale Al Runyon had in mind when he dreamed up the idea of his league. But the spirit of fearless promotional adventure was thick in the thin air of Denver newspapering in those days, and no doubt it was that spirit, mingling with his handed-down fascination with baseball, which propelled Al into his CSBL scheme.

In 1910 the top rodeos in Cheyenne and Denver could draw ten to fifteen thousand paying customers a day. But rodeo was indigenous to the area, as baseball, largely an Eastern, Midwest-ern, and Southern sport, was not; more important, rodeos didn't run every day for an entire summer. Furthermore, the intermoun-tain territory was so vast that travel expenses for a baseball league would be staggering. Finally, there were few suitable fields in the towns Al chose for his league. Despite all the drawbacks, however, Al Runyon was overcome by baseball fever. No doubt the great explosion of interest in the game in the Eastern cities had con-vinced him that baseball could be economically successful in the Rockies. Whatever arguments one advances on its behalf, as a business proposition Al's baseball league probably did not appear any sounder in 1910 than it does today. The idea may have been the product of a bacchanalian inspiration in the first place.

As the climax of an uproarious meeting in Pueblo on January 20, 1910, Al's fellow promoters—a mixed crowd of his sporting acquaintances from such towns as Denver, Pueblo, Cheyenne, and Santa Fe—voted unanimously to install him as president of the Colorado State Baseball League and then repaired to a tavern to celebrate the election and the earnest resolutions that had accom-panied it. Although many of the resolutions concerned the subject of finances, this area soon became the league's Achilles' heel. Al managed to hustle up a franchise commitment in Denver, where a local merchant offered sponsorship plus $135 a game for visiting teams, but his sporting acquaintances in Cheyenne, Santa Fe, Pueblo, and the other mountain towns all failed to establish them-selves on a dollar and cents basis.

When February came and went and his league continued to

The Demon of Denver

Young Al Runyon (1910)

limp along like some crippled prehistoric bird unable to take flight out of the conversational bog, Al started to panic. He made a trip to Cheyenne, where two different groups claimed to want franchises, and conferred with both, only to lose track of the results of the conference in the ensuing saloon action. Back in Denver he got a solid offer from a Grand Junction group, but by then it was March and there was still no league for Grand Junction to join. Al chewed the fat with some cowboy types who had eyes for franchises in Oklahoma, New Mexico, and Texas, but nothing came of it. Promoter Runyon was becoming the object of sporting men's ridicule throughout Colorado and even in his own *News,* where the regular sporting scribe commented briefly and acidly that the baseball league was "certainly a novel plan"—and then retreated into meaningful silence.

Al called a meeting in a saloon in Pueblo in the first week of April, and at the appointed time the delegates of the various towns came together to pour a solemn toast to the Colorado State Baseball League and to declare it defunct. After that they poured another toast. The secretary's minutes of the meeting show that a good time was had by all, particularly during the speeches, at the climax of which Al Runyon rose and spoke a touching word or two by way of elegy for his stillborn league. Those present and still conscious could not tell from Al's tone, which even though he was in his cups was as always slightly tongue in cheek, whether they should laugh or cry.

The failure of his baseball league to get off the ground was not the only blow Al suffered in the spring of 1910. One night a few months later, stinking drunk and in the company of two loud floozies, he ran into Ellen Egan, the girl he wanted to marry. The scene caused a major blowup between Ellen and Al. Their quarrel sent Al on another prolonged bender that eventually landed him in the office of a doctor who, as the story goes, warned the young reporter about the effects on his heart of further drinking bouts. At about this time Charley Van Loan, ex-sports scribe of the *Post,* passed through town on his way to the West Coast to cover the Jack Johnson-Jim Jeffries heavyweight title fight for the Hearst papers. He proposed that Runyon accompany him. Al didn't need a lot of talking into it. It was late June 1910, and the fight was scheduled for Decoration Day; Al cashed his last *News* paycheck and bought a ticket to San Francisco.

Life in that city was always wild and varied enough to distract Al Runyon from his immediate intentions, so when as a result of an imagined slight against the wife of Governor Hughes of California (who envied the reception Jack Johnson's arrival got in the streets of San Francisco) the fight was shifted to Reno, he stayed behind. Van Loan went on to Reno with fellow Hearst employees Tad Dorgan, *American* boxing writer and cartoonist, and W. O. "Bill" McGeehan, boxing scribe of the *Journal.* (Both would be close associates of Runyon in later years.) Al lingered in San Francisco for a few days, then returned to Colorado to gather his

The Demon of Denver

belongings. He'd agreed to meet Charley Van Loan in New York.

New York was a city he'd visited only once, for a few weeks in 1908 on assignment at a convention of electricians. Now Al, at the age of thirty, had no way of knowing if he'd find work in New York. There he would lack the experience and the ties he'd built up in Colorado and the West, and he would face the best competition in the way of writing that any city in the English-speaking world could provide. All that he had to recommend him was his work, his book of clippings of his stories, and a local reputation as a features writer. Against this was his notoriety as a drunk, which would inevitably follow him East and for all he knew cause him trouble there. Al vowed to live the bad rap down and began drinking coffee compulsively to take the place of booze. When he felt restless, he ordered hot java, cup after cup, gulping it as fast as it could be poured. Within a decade this surrogate addiction would reach the level of forty to fifty cups a day.

Al's way with a bottle had indeed gained him national celebrity among his fellows of the fifth estate. During his early years in New York—before it was evident that he was serious about his teetotaling—Al's new acquaintances regarded with cynicism his refusals of the traditional, convivial newspaperman's greeting, "Buy you a drink?" As his colleague and friend Bill Corum said some years later, "Damon had been a gutter drunk, an undependable lush in Denver. When he reached New York he was known as a fellow that you wouldn't see for three weeks if he had three drinks. But sometime, somehow, he had said to himself, 'I'll never take another drink.' And he never did. Runyon had annoying idiosyncrasies, yes, but he also had great character and the inner courage of a lion." The "idiosyncrasies" of which Corum hinted—Runyon's snappish moods, his occasional cruel remarks, his prolonged silences—were often attributed by friends to the tension caused by his avoidance of alcohol, always a constant struggle. Like most observations about Runyon's inner nature made by his friends and associates, this was pure speculation. "Nobody ever knew Damon," Bill Corum said on another occasion, echoing Gene Fowler's remark and those of others who were close to Runyon the man. "Anybody who thinks he did is kidding himself."

Fred Lieb, one of the first of the local sportswriters to make Runyon's acquaintance following the latter's arrival in New York, was also a nondrinker and was therefore pleased and surprised to find one dry companion among the thirsty scribes. By the time of their meeting in 1911, Runyon "drank no alcoholic beverages, not even beer," Lieb recalls. "He didn't feel virtuous about not drinking; he was in fact ashamed of it. 'I just can't drink, and now I'm smart enough to know it,' he once told me. 'I used to drink, hard. I frequently got stinking drunk. And when I was drinking I was real mean.'" Before long it was clear to Lieb and the others that Runyon was in earnest when it came to staying on the wagon. Two or three instances of his temporary falls from sobriety in the years 1910–1913 are documented, and others are rumored, most of them apocryphal—the product of his Denver reputation mixing with eager imaginations.

The reasons for Runyon's resolution to quit drinking were several: success, money, and marriage were three, and his memories of his father's futile brilliance comprised a powerful fourth that in Fred Lieb's view outweighed all the others. In his baseball autobiography, Lieb said Runyon "had a dread that he would follow in the footsteps of his father, whom he worshipped—a hard-drinking newspaperman, printer and proofreader, who was usually broke because of his drinking." It was a case not unlike that of the young Charles Dickens, who was inspired to the personal disciplines that made his work possible by the dereliction of his beloved and gifted wastrel of a father. Like the author of *David Copperfield,* to whom he often referred as a literary ancestor ("make 'em laugh, make 'em cry" he perceived to be their common goals as writers), Al Runyon did not wish to follow in his father's footsteps. He preferred, as he later put it, to "get the money."

Runyon wrote to his own alcoholic son in 1945, a year in which he himself no doubt thought often of how much he could use a drink.

> You ask me about my own experiences. I quit drinking thirty-five years ago in Denver and have not had a drink since. I quit because I realized that I got no fun out of drinking. Liquor only gave me delusions of grandeur that got me into trouble. It never made me happy and bright and sparkling as it does some people. It made me dull and stupid and quarrelsome. It made me dreadfully ill afterwards. I did not have the constitution to drink. It rendered me helpless. It destroyed my pride, my sense of decency.
>
> I quit because I saw that I was not going to get anywhere in the world if I didn't, and I wanted to go places. I was sorely tempted many times, usually in moments of elation over some small triumph or when I was feeling sorry for myself, a strong characteristic of the drinker, but I managed to stand it off.
>
> It was never taking that first drink that saved me.
>
> I had to endure loneliness and even derision as a result of my abstinence for some years but it eventually became a matter of such general knowledge that no one pressed me to take a drink any more and finally I became positively famous for hanging out with drunks and never touching a drop.

Conquering his drinking problem was a process of will that took all Runyon's concentration for at least three years—and more than a casual effort on many later occasions.

His drinking record aside, Al knew that surviving in the great Eastern newspaper jungle would not be easy. Along with the suc-

The Demon of Denver

cess stories of such up-and-coming New Yorkers as Van Loan of Denver and McGeehan and Dorgan of San Francisco, Al Runyon had heard hair-raising tales of journalistic failure and despair in the cruel and competitive print capitals of the East. Taking New York on cold was a real challenge; yet life for Al had already been one long series of challenges, and even without the beneficial helping hand of family or social connections, he had so far managed to negotiate most of the hard passages with aplomb. In the present case there was little he stood to lose. He left neither family nor close friends behind him. The exception was Ellen Egan, but she was a decent young lady who lived in a large house with a broad lawn—the kind of girl for whom Al could not qualify until he had improved himself in the world. His father, now suffering from tuberculosis (the same disease that had killed Al's mother), had left Colorado and was confined in a sanitarium in Arizona, where Al was to see him only once again, in the spring of 1911. (It was not a case of out of sight, out of mind; the son brooded constantly on the maxims and opinions of his father, whom he was eventually to make into a legend with a series of "My Old Man" newspaper sketches.)

In the summer of 1910 Al Jr. told Denver goodbye with no recorded sign of the kind of regret one shows when leaving one's natural home. Unable to remember having had one, he would have nothing in particular to miss.

3

Colorado Kid in the Press Box

In this era, the newspaperman was a very definite type. His work broadened his horizons far beyond those of the average man, who did not have such things as films, radio, or television to make him knowledgeable. Further, the reporter's contact with flamboyant figures in and out of Park Row usually added a flavor to his personality that was lacking in most other men of the day.

This was, in fact, the reporter's high point in history—a period when he was given a respect and importance he had never enjoyed before and would never enjoy again. According to Irvin S. Cobb, who arrived on Park Row from Paducah, Kentucky, in 1903, "The time of the Great Editor had waned and faded, the time of the Great Reporter succeeded it." Even if a Park Row newspaperman did not become a truly great reporter like Davis, Phillips, Julian Ralph, or James Creelman, he could at least bask in their reflected glory, and in his way live a life adventurous for the time. As a result, most Park Row newspapermen considered themselves a group set apart. They stuck together and drank together. At Andy Horn's, Perry's Hole in the Wall, Lipton's and other downtown watering places, they might grumble into drinks about the cruel peculiarities of James Gordon Bennett, the eccentricities of Joseph Pulitzer, and the less remote offenses of managing and city editors. But through it all ran the unstated belief that the newpaperman's life was withal a beautiful one.

—Allen Churchill, Park Row

There were thirteen morning and afternoon papers in New York at the time of Al Runyon's arrival in 1910, and while some were less great than others, together they made up a vivid entity known as Park Row, which to the young and aspiring reporters of the country must have beckoned like the end of the rainbow. The daydream of a great, distant city where brilliant and sophisticated reporters like Richard Harding Davis and David Graham Phillips strode in the glorious pursuit of truth was as common as it was unrealistic; it infected the copy room and city desk of every small paper across the nation. For the young reporters of the hinterlands, New York was the natural goal; in the decade after the turn of the century Park Row was for them, in Allen

Colorado Kid in the Press Box

Churchill's words, "the real newspaper world." On the beat in the boondocks they pined for scoops or wheedled introductions from some influential friend of a friend—anything that might bring them a summons from one of the great editors on Park Row. Lacking such a summons, many "took independent action." Al Runyon was in this class; he went to New York "on spec" because it was the only route available.

It took him six months to get inside an editor's door, but a few months later he had established himself for life in the New York newspaper business.

Al's Denver daydreams of dining in Delmonico's like David Graham Phillips did not last long upon his arrival in New York. Instead it was the poor man's fifteen-cent breakfast, dime beer with a free lunch (he gave his beer to the next guy down the bar), nickel cup of coffee, and dinner for two bits.

Al spent his first nine months in the city at Charley Van Loan's flat in Flatbush. Charley let Al have his spare room and minimal board in exchange for short story plots. It was an arrangement that suited Al perfectly; he was without capital yet considered himself a prolific fiction writer who could toss off a passable story plot without stopping long to think about it. In the fall and winter of 1910 he worked on his own fiction and on plots for Charley's sports stories, which were sold to Horace Lorimer of the *Saturday Evening Post* as fast as Al could dream them up and Charley could flesh them out in his lively style.

Van Loan had resigned from the sports staff of Hearst's *American* after covering the Jeffries-Johnson fight and was now writing fiction exclusively. This was a bold step on his part; in leaving Hearst he had walked out on a solid career that had included sports editorships in San Francisco, Los Angeles, and New York. But by early 1911 his story sales were bringing in $125 a week, twice what he'd been making for Hearst and a higher wage than that of anyone on the *American* staff except Hearst's top editor, Arthur Brisbane. The stories on which he and Al collaborated were published in Van Loan's name, of course. Charley had made a national name for himself; his colorful descriptive style was considered an innovation and in some places was even reproached as excessively daring. His most famous newspaper line, concerning Frank Schulte of the Cubs, was one that had enraged fundamentalists in the Bible Belt: "Schulte came home with the winning run like Balaam entering Jerusalem." His tales of athletic heroes (they had titles like "The Greatest Double Play of All Time: Sanguinette to Sweeney to Schultz") were essentially of the Frank Merriwell type, and as such they existed firmly in the mainstream of sports fiction of the time. For that matter, so did Al's attempts in the same line—"The Breed and the Ball" was purchased by

The World of Damon Runyon

Munsey's magazine for $65 early in 1911—but some of his other work, like the hobo tales he occasionally sold to a pulp called *Adventure,* showed a tougher view of life than anything Charley Van Loan had turned out. For just this reason, Al wasn't destined to become a *Post* star like his friend Charley. (When Runyon began his Broadway tales in 1929, his first effort, "Lillian," was rejected by the *Post* because Thomas Costain, who read it for Lorimer, did not like the hophead kitten in the story. Damon changed the cat to a lush and sold the story to *Collier's.*) All the same, Charley's obvious financial success with his (or their) fiction both galled and intrigued Runyon, and over the winter of 1910–11 he struggled on his own to produce stories of similar commerciality.

It did not work out, and by spring his mind was again on David Graham Phillips and Delmonico's. The reality of his situation was less pleasant than his reverie, however. The Van Loans were growing impatient with having Al, who was given to long sessions of brooding, as a permanent house guest. And Charley was beginning to feel he could make up his *own* plots. Al, too, was impatient with his own penury yet did little to relieve it. He wrote long letters to Ellen and prose sketches about the West, but when he sold the single story to *Munsey's* he spent the whole check on a yellow leather shoe trunk with brass fittings. Since Al did not own anywhere near a sufficient number of shoes to fill it, the Van Loans saw this as a senseless purchase, especially as they had been giving Al some strong hints in regard to an unpaid board bill. Runyon, who'd gone barefoot in summer well into his teens, saw the shoe trunk as a symbol of elegance and luxury that would inspire him to further production. (It was not long before he would own more than enough shoes to fill the trunk—so many pairs in fact that his sportswriting colleague Hype Igoe, who wore the same small size, 5½B, and served as a breaking-in horse for each new pair, claimed that he never had to buy a new pair of brogans of his own because Damon Runyon "kept him in shoes.")

In time Al paid all his bills at the Van Loans with the earnings from his verse and tales, but this was still not the kind of steady income Ellen Egan expected of a husband. She continued to respond to his eager long-distance proposals of marriage with delaying tactics. It was in the Runyon blood to repair to the newspaper trade when one's finances were in doubt, and Al now did so. He resolved to find a job on one of the New York papers.

A job fell into his lap within weeks of this decision. A future sportswriting protégé of Runyon's, Dan Parker, told the story like this. One day in February 1911, when the air seemed unusually springlike, a Hearst executive named Bill Curley invited Charley Van Loan out for a friendly round of golf. As they began playing, Charley got the feeling Bill Curley had something on his mind.

He kept talking about what a great writer Charley was and quoting lines from Charley's old stories.

Along about the sixth tee, Bill Curley's chat grew more specific. Before teeing off, he brought out two expensive cigars, carefully cut off the ends with tiny gold scissors he wore on a gold chain on his vest, lit one and handed Charley the other. Old Man Hearst wanted Charley Van Loan back and was willing to pay to get him, Curley said. Charley, who was happy with his fiction career, wanted no part of the offer.

"Sure, I'll come back," he told Curley. "If you pay me one twenty-five a week."

Bill Curley burst out laughing. "I'm not even making that much, Charley. You know that, don't you?"

"Well, I can make that off my short stories," Charley said.

"Be reasonable, Charley."

"How about a light?"

"How's that?" the Hearst man asked.

"You give me a fine stogie and then you won't even light it for me," Charley said. "Now I don't call that friendly, Bill."

"All right, Charley, have it your way. But I can tell you the Old Man wouldn't pay you a salary like that if you were Stanley on your way to find Livingstone."

"I know. Light my cigar."

Curley's day was spoiled. He knew Charley's outrageous salary request meant that he did not want to return. (Even Irvin S. Cobb, ace rewrite man and reporter of Pulitzer's *World,* made only $90 a week, and he'd been working on Park Row since 1903!)

Before they finished their conversation on the sixth tee, Charley did have one suggestion for Bill Curley: he advised him to look over some work by a friend of his from Denver who'd been staying at the house. "Al Runyon's the name, and he can write like hell. He knows sports, and he has a good mind for how a story works."

"Coming from you, Charley, that's praise indeed. Tell this Al of yours to send me some of his stuff."

That night Al went through his scrapbook of story clippings from the *Rocky Mountain News,* packed four or five of the best ones into a large envelope, and posted it off to Bill Curley. He had to wait only a day or two for his reply. Curley wanted to see him at the offices of the *Journal* and the *American* on William Street, just off Park Row. Here was Al's chance, the break he'd been shooting for.

Bill Curley was duly impressed by the bright, severe young man from Colorado whose clippings and credentials he'd approved, and Al was hired at a base salary of $40—which with Sunday work and occasional extra fees for longer stories could be parlayed into a grand sum of $60 to $65 weekly. Al liked playing the hard-boiled egg, but it was obvious to the Van Loans how excited he was. They were pleased, too; now there would be no problems about Al's room and board contributions. As it turned out, Al Runyon was not long for the Van Loan household.

The newcomer was assigned to the sports desk of the morning *American* under sports editor Harry Cashman. It was Cashman who in the interests of brevity amputated the "Alfred" from Runyon's writing name. Three-word reporters' monikers, Cashman told him, were a thing of the past; from now on it would be simply Damon Runyon. The subject of this surgery was less offended than flattered, for getting a byline at all was a triumph. In those days the New York morning papers never gave new sportswriters bylines, but Damon Runyon, the new man from Denver, was to have his name at the top of every story he wrote. At the time this made Runyon a minor sensation in New York sportswriting circles.

Damon, as he was henceforth known in the newspaper world, spent a few days learning his way around the *American* offices, doing the odd rewrite job like putting together baseball "dope" pieces out of the 200-word daily summaries that came over the wire from Sid Mercer of the *Globe,* the advance man in the New York Giants' camp in Marlin, Texas. (Normally the New York papers did not send a man to follow the baseball clubs first hand until the official opening of the camps in March.)

After a week on the job, Runyon was given his first outside assignment, an interview with the once great heavyweight John L. Sullivan, now fallen on difficult times. For Runyon, whose old man had demonstrated to him the Sullivan fighting stance many a time (as in future days Damon would demonstrate it to his own son), it was an awesome assignment, and Cashman's cautionary tone only enhanced his trepidation.

"He is pretty crusty nowadays," the sports editor told the young reporter, "but just mention Arthur Brisbane to him. That will soften him up."

For Damon this was terrifying advice; Arthur Brisbane was one of the last names he would be tempted to toss off lightly. The great editor, whom Runyon had not yet met, was a contemporary of Sullivan who had won fame as a reporter for his sentimental account of the Sullivan-Charley Mitchell fight in the eighties. Going back further, Brisbane owed his first promotion on the New York *Sun* to an account of another Sullivan fight that had caught the eye of *Sun* editor Charles A. Dana. Brisbane and Sullivan became great friends, and they stayed that way as long as John L. held the title. While Sullivan's career was now in decline—it was nearly twenty-two years since his last great bare-knuckle victory

Colorado Kid in the Press Box

in seventy-five rounds against Jake Kilrain—Brisbane's was definitely on the rise. Since 1896, when Hearst hired him away from Pulitzer's *World* to edit the *Journal,* Brisbane's salary, adjusted to a circulation clause shrewdly inserted by the editor himself, had risen from $200 a week in a series of quantum leaps that would eventually bring it to a quarter of a million dollars a year. (The ghost of his father, the Utopian Socialist Albert Brisbane, croaked hoarsely in its grave every time Brisbane boasted in public about his income—which he did constantly.) Arthur Brisbane, now editor of both the evening *Journal* and the morning *American* and widely respected and feared along Park Row, was one of the most somber and humorless of men. His employees did not throw his name around. (Damon, who eventually became Brisbane's right-hand man on the *American,* later nicknamed the editor—a bald man with a large cranium—Old Double Dome, but clearly that irreverent moniker was applied only behind Brisbane's back.)

Armed with Cashman's tip, Damon set out to get his interview, resolved to stoop to a little innocent deceit only if it became necessary. It became necessary about fifteen seconds into the interview, when it turned out that the ex-champion had an evil hangover.

> I found the then aging John L. in a Broadway hotel bundled up in bed and I was still trembling from his resounding roar "Come in" when I said mendaciously:
> "Mr. Sullivan, I was sent to see you by Mr. Brisbane."
> "Arthur?" queried Sullivan. "How is Arthur?"
> I said Arthur was all right, which was correct as far as I knew for to tell you the truth up to that moment I had never clapped eyes on the mighty journalist and I went away with my interview devoutly hoping that he and John L. would not meet again before the latter's memory of my visit had faded.   —"John L."

Runyon got two columns' worth of prizefighting reminiscences out of the old champ, ugly hangover or no. After turning in his story to Cashman, he went out on the town to celebrate his first byline, which would appear in the morning. He went with office mate Tad Dorgan to Jack Dunstan's, at Sixth Avenue and 43rd Street, fed himself on a fifty-cent porterhouse that must have weighed a pound, and then took the train home to Van Loan's in Brooklyn. It would have been a good night to get drunk, but Damon had to be at work early in the morning. Besides, there was the bothersome spectre of the as yet unseen but all-powerful Mr. Brisbane eating away at his mind. It took Damon a day or two to get over his anxiety. What if John L. suddenly dropped in to see his old pal Arthur? Damon shuddered at the thought. But John L. never dropped in, and Arthur didn't find out. Years later, when he and the great editor worked side by side for Hearst at political conventions, the World Series, and the Lindbergh trial,

The World of Damon Runyon

Damon's mind now and then drifted back to that February day in 1911 in a drafty hotel on Broadway.

> Long afterwards I confessed my perfidy to Mr. Brisbane and he merely gave out with a non-commital "Hah," like that. Then he regaled me with tales of Sullivan with whom he was rather closely associated as a newspaperman when "The Boston Strong Boy" was in his prime.　　　　　　　　　　　　　　　　　—"John L."

In the week following the Sullivan interview, Cashman kept Damon busy writing the daily sports page poem. One of these efforts, a baseball poem called "Ballad of the Oldest Player," made such a hit with Cashman that he had Damon follow it up with a series of Diamond Ditties. The prolific Runyon quickly turned out several small triumphs of doggerel on baseball subjects, and the general approval with which these were received convinced Cashman that in Damon Runyon he at last had an able successor to Charley Van Loan. (The *American*'s other baseball writer of the period, William F. Kirk, was a survivor of the old school of sportswriting, whose chief distinguishing features were its reliance on melodrama, euphemism, sentiment, and platitude.) Accordingly, in early March Cashman sent Damon to San Antonio to catch up with the Giants' spring entourage. Baseball, the sports editor had decided, would be Runyon's beat.

Damon was delighted to get out of the office. He packed a bag in Brooklyn—even in the early days the dudish Runyon never traveled without the appropriate wardrobe—and raced across town to catch his train. He rode alone through the South for two nights and on the third day arrived in San Antonio, where the Giants' barnstorming party was stopping. Damon registered at the Hotel Menger and spent an evening introducing himself to Sid Mercer and the other writers who'd already joined the club. The next morning and afternoon it rained steadily, so the ballplayers hung around the lobby. Damon got his first peek at the feisty little manager, ex-Oriole John McGraw (one of his old man's all-time favorites), and met and shook hands with one of his own baseball heroes—pitcher and "exalted man" Christy Mathewson, of whose three shutouts in the 1905 World Series Al Runyon had written one day while doing Otto Floto's column on the Denver *Post.*

On that rainy March day in San Antonio Damon made another new acquaintance, Arthur L. "Bugs" Raymond, a righthanded pitcher from Chicago with a spitball delivery and a screwball lifestyle who would shortly become the first legitimate "Damon Runyon character." As the other reporters told Damon, Raymond had been a pitching star for McGraw's Giants in 1909 and then fallen off to a 4–9 record in a season in which he made a habit of sneaking away from the ballpark during games and proceeding

Colorado Kid in the Press Box

Bugs Raymond

to the nearest bar, where he'd trade a hastily autographed baseball for two or three consecutive stiff shots. Bugs needed no chasers. Then he'd hightail it back to the park, hoping McGraw hadn't noticed his absence. After one such saloon visit the manager called him into a game in relief. Bugs had a hard time walking straight, but his spitter never worked better. He finished the game with ease under the evil eye of McGraw, who could see the condition his pitcher was in and was ready to jump on him for the slightest lapse. Episodes like this had perpetuated Raymond's nickname, which had nothing to do with insects. (It originated in fact with the owner of a minor league club in Georgia, to whom Raymond had boasted, "I shall pitch your club to a pennant." Although in the club owner's opinion this statement qualified the young pitcher for the bughouse, Raymond had gone on to prove his case by doing just what he had promised.)

Raymond's legend, which Runyon was to codify for the reading public, went back a few years. He'd been a minor league wonder, once winning thirty-five semisober games for the Charleston club, and with his renowned "three speed" spitball and his famous repertory of one-liners (most of them culled from the grape and the hop) he'd already staggered, pitched, and joked his way to a National League career of some note. In 1908 he'd won fifteen games for St. Louis, and after the season he was celebrating in a bar in that town with a reporter who asked his plans for the winter. "Either run a locomotive for the Great Northern or become a newspaperman," Bugs had mused with chin on palm and elbow on bar in a revision of the classic "thinker" pose. Just then a newsboy burst in with the morning edition, whose sports page headlined: RAYMOND TRADED TO GIANTS.

Meanwhile, in New York, John McGraw was telling reporters that "if I could handle Mike Donlin" (another player of the individualistic type) "I can do the same with Raymond." Taming recalcitrant players, particularly pitchers, was a self-professed McGraw specialty. Like a Frank Buck of the dugout, "Muggsy" put his head into many a lion's mouth—usually to check for alcohol on the breath. (Casey Stengel often recalled the story of McGraw's fining him $200 for a suspicious aroma on his person. In fact Stengel hadn't had a drop to drink in days but was wearing an expensive after-shave lotion mistaken by the manager for "cheap gin"!) The idea of a McGraw-Raymond relationship gave the scribes of the day premonitory shudders.

In the spring of 1909 McGraw treated Raymond with pig-iron gloves. Taking note of Bugs' proclivity for wine and ale, he imposed a fine for "undue liberties with liquids." The fine took the form of a nine-inning game, which McGraw forced Raymond to struggle through on his first spring outing. Bugs sweated it out, finished it, and went on to win eighteen games in 1909, not without hilarity. When hit on the head by a high inside pitch in a turn at bat, he provided inflatable copy for one scribe who related the news that "Bugs Raymond was downed today by one high ball. This unprecedented incident occurred while the Giants were playing the St. Louis Cardinals. The disgrace was deeply felt by Mr. Raymond, although he absorbed this particular high ball behind his left ear instead of through his usual channel. After he was resuscitated, Mr. Raymond described the effect as similar to the absorption of his usual high balls, but quicker."

The following year Raymond had a particularly raucous time in spring training and was briefly suspended by McGraw. Then, early in the season, when the manager discovered that Bugs had been throwing balls from the centerfield bullpen to fans in the stands who supplied him with beer in return, he placed guards on duty to circumvent such trafficking. Not so easily outsmarted, Bugs got hold of a bucket, some rope, and a willing confederate and devised a scheme whereby at prearranged times he could simply lower the bucket from the clubhouse window with money in it and haul it back up full of draft beer from the saloon across the street. Learning of this, McGraw cut off Raymond's salary and began sending the pitcher's paychecks to his wife. ("If she gets the money," Bugs complained, "let *her* pitch!") "Little Napoleon" also admonished the pitcher's teammates against loaning him money. After Raymond had requested a sizeable clothing allowance and then bought a cheap suit and spent the rest on booze, McGraw refused to give the pitcher so much as an unopened package of cigarettes for fear Bugs would resell it in a bar. The manager also hired a detective, named Fuller, to follow Raymond around—a development that delighted Bugs, who was now able to greet friends with a tipsy wink and the words, "This is my keeper—I'm full but he's Fuller."

Damon collected all the Bugs Raymond tales that were current, and there were plenty. One of the freshest was told by a New York writer who'd joined the club in Marlin a week earlier. At a fish fry celebrating the end of the Giants' training camp, Bugs had been horsing around with shortstop Al Bridwell and two or three other players. The "boys" would fling bottles and branches into the air for Bridwell to shoot. Suddenly Bugs Raymond called, "Hey, Bridey," and threw something into the air. Bridwell blasted it on his first shot. The "target" turned out to be an expensive watch that Bugs had received as an award for his pitching in the minor leagues several years before. The story had gained considerable currency in baseball cirles; Runyon now made it common knowledge in his dispatch to the *American.*

When the rain continued for two more days, Damon had a chance to get to know Bugs Raymond personally. One wet evening they kept dry in a saloon down the street from the hotel, where Bugs told Damon about his wife and two kids in Chicago and related a number of nonfamily stories. The pitcher spoke confidentially of the "cure" McGraw had made him take before coming to camp—which had consisted of two weeks of taking the baths and making the rounds at Dwight, Illinois. There had been, Bugs related, few baths but plenty of rounds.

As the weather cleared and the Giants' party began to move through Texas and Louisiana, playing games with minor league clubs in Dallas and Shreveport, Damon wired his daily stories to the *American.* He made the obligatory routine reports on the respective states of Christy Mathewson's pitching arm (sturdy as ever, though the great Matty, like Damon, had recently turned thirty) and John McGraw's disposition (delicate as ever; Little Napoleon handled his club flawlessly on the field and stepped on toes everywhere else). He also wrote several reports on Bugs Raymond's lore and legend that were much livelier than the McGraw or Mathewson pieces. While the brilliant manager and the great pitcher quickly won Damon's respect, Bugs had the stronger appeal: he stimulated the young reporter's sense of the bizarre. Damon's permanent affection for oddballs and off-the-wall types is first evident in the Raymond pieces.

They were an instant success in New York, where Giant rooters woke for the first time to the captivating personality of the pitcher they'd formerly regarded as a mere reprobate (as we'd say nowadays, a "flake"). As the club toured the South, Damon ignored the box scores and statistics and instead spent his time noting Bugs' antics with a feature writer's glee. At one barnstorming stop Bugs made his way to and from the mound on his hands and knees. In Baltimore Bugs saved up his meal checks for three days and then spent them all on one deluxe room service breakfast that (Damon delicately implied) he was too hung over to touch. The episodes reported by Runyon made Bugs a kind of antihero to the fans at home. The Bugs Raymond pieces also made Hearst money, for they precipitated a circulation increase at the *American* that in turn brought Runyon—already a popular success—a small raise in salary.

On night trains through the South, Damon played bridge and poker with Christy Mathewson in the smoking cars. The strapping, fine-featured Christy was as everyone said, a scholar and a gentleman. He was an advertisement for the game and its paragon—a graduate of Bucknell, a scientific pitcher with uncanny control and a computer's memory of the hitters' weaknesses ("You could catch him sitting in a rocking chair," said his former battery mate, Roger Bresnahan), an adept card player, golfer, and singer, and so good a checkers player that he could take on six players at once in concurrent games and beat all of them. He was also an educated man, with whom Damon found he could talk seriously on many topics.

John McGraw was another matter. The doughty ex-Oriole's intelligence was obvious to Damon, who marveled over the display of "inside" baseball the Giants—clearly mirroring their manager's intention—put on even in exhibition games. But McGraw always distrusted writers and lived in an uneasy peace with them at best. He forbade postgame interviews, discouraged all conversation between writers and players on or off the field (a proscription which, considering the players' and scribes' constant proximity in hotels and Pullmans, was unrealistic and largely ignored), and now and then took a sock at a reporter just out of spite. Even those scribes who were closest to the club weren't safe.

Runyon admired McGraw, but like all the other scribes he had to be careful with the explosive little man lest Mac get the wrong idea about Damon's "character" pieces on his players and come out swinging. So when John McGraw was the subject, Damon's typewriter keys wore kidgloves. His truest and probably most honest remarks about the Giants' manager did not appear in print until after McGraw's death in 1934. Damon brought up Little Napoleon in several late columns in the *Daily Mirror*, always as an example of the hotheaded "gladiatorial" type. And with good reason. McGraw's fights—most of them quick two-punch knockouts with McGraw on the losing end—were legend. Damon recalled how in the old days the writers had kept a box score to record McGraw's famous fights. The box was run in the papers next to the daily standings and averages.

The press box of the Polo Grounds was not an enclosed booth like modern press boxes but an area of reserved seats behind home plate from which the writers—only vaguely segregated from the general public—watched and reported the games.

In this section Damon Runyon sat on Wednesday, April 12, 1911, when the Giants opened the season against Philadelphia. It was the first regular-season major league baseball game Damon had ever *seen*, much less covered for a major newspaper in the greatest city on earth.

To the Polo Grounds at 157th Street, beneath Coogan's Bluff, came the cream of New York's sporting society on that bright Wednesday afternoon in April. John Brush, the clothing merchant who owned the club with McGraw, had created a spanking new stand of bleachers in the outer reaches of left field to allow for overflow crowds such as this one. On April 12 the grandstand seats shone, having been given a new coat of paint a few days before. Red, white, and blue bunting had been affixed to every support in the park. Before the game green Irish flags were planted by the groundskeepers at second base and in right field, where Erin's sons Larry Doyle and Red Murray played. The box seats adjacent to the press box were crowded with dignified and elegant citizens, among them bankers and Wall Street brokers (who'd had time to arrive by elevated train after the three o'clock market closing), police captains and politicians, businessmen and gamblers, big-name actors and vaudeville stars. The Lambs—John McGraw's own club—and the Friars, two great theatrical societies of the town, were always fully represented on Opening Day and at World Series games. There was much familiarity and fraternization among these fans, as if they'd all been chums for years, so that much of their attention was upon each other; the customers in the more remote grandstand areas and bleachers seemed more intent upon the various preparations occurring on the field.

At five minutes to four these differences dissolved when the band struck up "East Side, West Side" and the great metropolitan crowd stood and sang as one. Then Joe Humphreys, the familiar Madison Square Garden announcer, using only a cheerleader's megaphone for amplification, shot his brazen arrow of a voice up into the stands. Manager McGraw would now be presented with a small token of New York's esteem, Humphreys bellowed. There was a murmur of approval. And with that the groundskeepers trundled out an enormous good-luck horseshoe made entirely of fresh flowers, thousands of them. When Little Napoleon trotted jauntily out to home plate to accept the wreath with a smile and a bow, even the hard-boiled Runyon was moved. Clearly, he thought, this cocky bantam rooster of a man was New York from head to toe. Apparently there was no one in the park who didn't share Damon's thought, for the manager was applauded mightily as he strutted back to the Giants' bench.

At four o'clock sharp the band played again, patriotically this time, and the game began. It was an uneventful one, taken 2–0 by the Phillies, but to Damon the afternoon's most interesting aspect was its revelation of the press box cast. For the first time he got a chance to see all his fellow baseball writers assembled in one spot. Many of them had not been with the team in the South, but on this day all thirteen of the men who would cover the Giants regularly in 1911—as well as a number of irregular observers from the city beats of the big papers—were sitting close enough to touch one another. For Damon it was quite an impressive group, as indeed it seems to us today.

Next to Damon was a veteran writer in a floppy black hat whose good-humored Southern drawl and twinkling eye spoke of a pregame warmup or two among the spirits vendors beneath the grandstand. This was Bozeman Bulger, inventor of the term "fadeaway," which became the classic name for Christy Mathewson's chief pitch, the screwball. Some years earlier Bulger had come from the Birmingham *Age-Herald* to become one of New York's more noted sporting raconteurs as well as the popular baseball writer of Pulitzer's *Evening World.* Though Pulitzer's papers were perennially the chief competitors of Hearst's *Journal* and *American,* there was certainly no feeling of rivalry toward young Runyon in the heart of the good Boze, a man who was as congenial as a summer afternoon in Alabama is long. Seldom does a talker like Bulger happen onto so willing an audience as the new man from the *American.* Boze took Damon under his wing, told him endless stories, and became the rookie from Denver's unofficial press box guardian.

Irvin S. Cobb, the star reporter of the *Evening World,* had accompanied Bulger to the game, and Boze quickly conferred the great Kentuckian's acquaintance on Damon. The two Southerners huddled together for a moment, each tossing off a stiff one from the half-pint medicine bottle Bulger kept tucked in the lining of his broad-brim black hat. Then they commenced to exchange tales, continuing in nonstop alternation throughout the ball game. At appropriate moments they punctuated their anecdotes—which contained a raunchy blend of sporting gossip, "racial humor" (off-color jokes about darkies), and outright lying—with appreciative roars and bellows of laughter, mutual back-swats, and additional snorts from Boze's concealed happiness source.

Colorado Kid in the Press Box

Damon was flattered by the attentions this experienced pair paid him. Cobb, like Charley Van Loan, had stories in the *Saturday Evening Post,* and Charley had pointed him out to Damon as a "literary comer," but it was the Kentuckian's celebrity in the newspaper world—he was Pulitzer's top rewrite man—that impressed Damon most. After a number of such off-day press box visits by Cobb, he and Damon became close friends. In time they and Boze Bulger, Bill McGeehan, and a racing and baseball writer named Bill MacBeth would acquire a potbellied boat in which they adventured out into Long Island Sound to hunt for shore birds in the fall and ducks and geese in the winter. (In *Exit Laughing,* his autobiography, Cobb refers to his fellow sportsmen of these years as "The Four Horsemen.") Cobb, Damon said later, "enjoyed male companionships and the life of the camps. . . He was at his best in boots and canvas clothing before a roaring fire in the woods surrounded by hairy-chested guys who could eat and drink in quantity."

Damon and this crew of hunting pals eventually took longer voyages together, including one trip to Nova Scotia. They spent a number of winter hunting seasons after the war at Dover Hill, Yankee owner Cap Huston's shooting lodge in Georgia, where in the company of such sportsmen as Babe Ruth (who was to become Damon's good friend) and old Orioles Joe Kelley and Uncle Wilbert Robinson, the writers told stories and drank and did their best to observe the rule about keeping the right foot in the right boot and the left foot in the left boot at all times. A flagrant violation of the latter rule once caused Runyon, who carried only coffee in his thermos, to scold colleague Bill "Sheriff" McGeehan. "Only a dude would have noticed," McGeehan replied to Damon's criticism. "What difference does it make, right leg or left boot? I can still walk, can't I?" The Sheriff had been attempting to dress for a morning of shooting after consuming one of the explosive hot toddies laced with corn whiskey that Uncle Wilbert had sent around before daybreak to the rooms of all the hunters save Runyon.

The company of these hearties, and their conversation, was a boon to Damon at all times. Nevertheless, as early as that first day in the press box, he had to learn a certain caution. Just as on later hunting trips to Long Island or Georgia he would have to learn not to walk in front of his friends when they and their shotguns were loaded at the same time, now he had to learn to take in their press box conversation with his ears while keeping his eyes and at least fifty percent of his mind on the game. The writers who'd been regulars for years could afford to arrive at the park during the second inning and lose themselves in talk until the eighth, but Damon could not.

The World of Damon Runyon

Not all the press box worthies were as voluble as Bulger or Cobb. The typewriter contingent made up quite a cross section of human types, Damon saw. Among those who'd been covering the team in earlier seasons were the slim, dark-haired Sid Mercer of the *Globe,* who'd come to the big town from St. Louis in 1907 and was at this time the greatest admirer of McGraw and his Giants among the club's regular scribes; Sam Crane, the veteran from the *American's* sister paper, the evening *Journal,* another Giant loyalist in a white Civil War-style walrus mustache; Jack Wheeler of the *Herald,* a tall, quizzical-looking man in a bearskin coat whose wide, narrow mouth and side-angled cigar created the only horizontal lines in his long oval face; John Foster of the *Evening Telegram,* a dumpy little man in a porkpie hat not half so spiffy, Damon noted, as his own; thick, bluff Walter Trumbull of the *Evening Sun,* whose battered black hat belied his aristocratic origins; a couple of Harvard men, Harry Cross of the *Times,* a great joker, and Joe Vila of the *Morning Sun,* who despite his education was famous for his vacuous game stories that consisted of a final score followed by a play-by-play followed by excerpts from the rosters of the competing teams in the next day's game; and finally the elephantine George Tidden of the *Morning World,* who seemed to be Bozeman Bulger's pal since he rocked with hilarity every time the Alabamian reached the climax of some particularly ribald tale.

Damon had met a number of these men during the exhibition season, and those he hadn't met he'd read or heard about. But there was another group of writers whose names were as new to him as their faces. These were the other rookies—the young men who, like Damon, were matriculating in the Polo Grounds press corps in the spring of 1911. There were three of them, and together with Damon himself—whose carefully cultivated sardonic expression, jauntily tipped grey porkpie, high white collar, and elegant raglan sleeves must have made him seem impressive, enigmatic, and vaguely ridiculous to his peers that day—they made up a crew of newcomers that matched for talent any rookie crop of baseball writers anywhere, before or since.

Two of them were seven or eight years younger than Damon. Freddy Lieb of the *Press,* a boyish, frail fellow in a golf cap, Damon hadn't noticed until he came up to say hello. Like Damon, Freddy was no drinker, which set him apart from his colleagues; unlike Damon, however, Freddy never *had* been. Lieb came from Philadelphia, where in 1910 he'd been a fifty-cent-bleacher fan in Shibe Park at the Cubs-A's World Series. Although he'd written player biographies for magazines, Lieb was just breaking into newspaper work. This was his first experience of big league baseball New York style, as it was Damon's, but the look of awe on Fred Lieb's

Colorado Kid in the Press Box

New York baseball scribes at the Polo Grounds for the 1912 Giants–Red Sox World Series. Standing, left to right, John Wheeler *(Herald)*, John B. Foster *(Telegram)*. Seated, left to right, Sam Crane *(Journal)*, Fred Lieb *(Press)*, Damon Runyon *(American)*, Boze Bulger *(Evening World)*, Sid Mercer *(Globe)*, Grantland Rice *(Mail)*, Walter Trumbull *(Evening Sun)*. Front, Polo Grounds caterer Harry Stevens and grandson.

face made him appear even younger than his twenty-three years. Lieb's ambition then as later was to write honestly and accurately of the game he loved, and this became the trademark of his work—which continued for seven decades and eventually filled a dozen historical books on baseball and thousands of newspaper columns in the New York *Press* and *Post* and the St. Louis *Sporting News.*

One rookie was no stranger to New York: Heywood Broun of the *Morning Telegraph* had grown up in Brooklyn. He was the same age as Fred Lieb, but unlike Lieb, he had the advantages of the finest education then available in America. This huge, awkward young man was a barrel of contrasts. He came from a good family, had attended Harvard, was no athlete, had a great literary talent, and was conversant with politics and art and the things of the mind. But at Harvard he had cut classes to see the Red Sox play, and to his professors' disgust he preferred Christy Mathewson to Victor Hugo or Shakespeare. Accordingly, when he went into the newspaper racket, it was not to "intellectual" papers like the *Times* or *World* that he first applied but to the sports desk of the *Morning Telegraph,* a horseplayers' rag. The next year he would move to the *Tribune,* later to the *World,* and out of sportswriting, but from 1911 until the late twenties Heywood Broun's was a familiar face in the press boxes of the Polo Grounds and Yankee Stadium. Broun was a brilliant, emotionally uninhibited man who delighted in causes and crusades, fell in love with show girls, and gambled over his head. In time he became known as the worst dresser in the New York newspaper world; the preferred comparison for his unkempt appearance was "an unmade bed." But in writing of baseball he demonstrated the same loose genius he later applied to his columnist's and critic's and union organizer's roles, and on Opening Day 1911 he was thrilled from the top of his shaggy head to the worn soles of his oxfords just to be in the same ballpark as John McGraw and Christy Mathewson.

Damon and Freddy Lieb, of course, felt the same way, and so no doubt did the other new man in the press box that day. A pleasant, open-faced Tennessean with sandy hair and an intelligent smile who had just taken the baseball writing job at the *Mail,* this man shook Damon's hand, complimenting him warmly on his early reports from the Giants' camp, and then at last remembered to introduce himself—"I'm Grant Rice," he said. Grantland Rice was in truth no rookie. He was Damon's age, and he'd been working as a sportswriter for years, in such fair-sized towns as Nashville and Cleveland, before coming to New York; the $50 a week salary he had accepted from H. L. Stoddard of the *Mail* actually represented a cut in pay for Rice, but he had taken the job because in those days the only road to the top of the newspaper business ran through New York. Rice never had reason to regret

Colorado Kid in the Press Box

Heywood Broun

his choice. He went from the *Mail* to the *Tribune,* and after the war his sports column, promoted nationally by Jack Wheeler's Bell Syndicate, made him one of the most popular and successful sportswriters in the country.

On that April day at the Polo Grounds in 1911 neither Rice nor Runyon nor Lieb nor Broun had time to speculate on career futures; for the first time for each man there was a major league baseball story to write that would within twelve hours be available for judgment by the most knowing sports audience in the land. Whatever the distractions, that responsibility dominated the young men's minds during the game and kept them busy for a number of hours afterward.

And then the hours stretched into years.

In those days the writers did not flock to the players' dressing rooms after a game to discuss the action with the principals and to gather quotes, as they do today. A NO ADMITTANCE sign hung on the Giants' clubhouse door, and the McGraw-appointed bouncer who stood sentry duty was quick to inform nosy reporters that

The World of Damon Runyon

"This means *you,* pal!" If the scribes wanted to talk to the players, they could do so on the field before the game—*if* they got there that early (which many of the reporters found impossible to do, with their golf games and long lunches), *if* the players were in the mood, and *if* McGraw wasn't looking. This combination of conditionals made on-the-field interviews rare. It was more customary to obtain "inside dope" from the players *away* from the park—in the Pullman smokers, for those writers who went on the road with the teams, in the 155th Street saloons, or in Broadway restaurants like Jack's, where players and writers congregated when the club was in New York.

The writers for the evening papers had to dictate tentative leads and running play-by-play throughout the game, but the morning paper men, like Damon, could wait until the game was finished to compose their stories. Then, instead of dictating them to the teletypists, they could send the stories downtown by messenger or ride down on the elevated and deliver them personally. Damon came to prefer the latter method, as it gave him a chance to combine business with pleasure. He would turn in his story by hand and then spend the evening exploring the sporting haunts of Broadway.

Damon's daily baseball pieces in the *American* were unique from the start. Unlike most of his fellow scribes, he came early to the games and walked around the field and stands to pick up "color" or a human interest angle before the game began. Then, in the press box, he took copious notes on the game, often working in items snatched from the running conversation of Bulger, Cobb, and other talkative scribes. Somewhere in the afternoon—sometimes during warmups, sometimes when the game was done—he decided on an angle, a single line of attack that would yield the best story. Damon never settled for the slightly adorned play-by-play accounts that filled most of his colleagues' daily pieces. He always distilled the event into a single conception, often outlandish but usually inventive and interesting. He sought continuously for fresh viewpoints, gimmicks, tricks—anything to avoid the tedium of the standard "formula" baseball story of the day, which with its cliché-ridden slab of prose tacked onto a box score usually achieved a lifeless greyness like that of public monuments. Damon (who couldn't put together a box score to save his life and had to rely on Fred Lieb's boxes for the facts in his stories) might report an entire game from the viewpoint of a lady who had never seen baseball played, or that of a lizard or a group of yokels from Colorado. "I always made covering a standard story like a big race or a ballgame more or less of a stunt," he wrote to his son years later. "When the great Pittsburgh slugger Honus

Colorado Kid in the Press Box

Wagner came to town I covered the game, not from the press box, but from the bleachers and a rear view of Honus."

Damon was not the first to insert a humorous personal style and a storyteller's sense of form into sports prose. About the time he was breaking in at the *American,* a number of writers around the country were embarking on a similar course; Damon had known of some of them while he was working on the *Rocky Mountain News,* and he quickly heard of the others when he got to New York. With him in the press box were some of these men— Bulger, Mercer, Rice. On Damon's own paper, the *American,* and sharing the same sports room in which Damon typed his stories, was one of sportswriting's greats, the gifted and original Thomas Aloysius ("Tad") Dorgan, who wrote boxing and drew cartoons with captions that enticed Damon with their imaginative command of the vernacular. "The bum's rush," "the bunk," "23 skiddoo," "dumbbell," "nobody home," and "Yes, we have no bananas" were among the San Francisco-bred Dorgan's dozens of coinages. The slang phrases he popularized ("hard-boiled egg," "fall guy," "cheaters") numbered in the hundreds. "To all sportswriters, Tad's recorded speech was music," the *American*'s Bill Corum said. In 1911 Dorgan's verbal panache certainly came as music to the ears of new man Runyon. Already a serious student of the vernacular, under Tad's influence Damon became its champion, and, in his Broadway tales, its master—as a quick riff through the pages of Wentworth and Flexner's marvelous *Dictionary of American Slang* will show.

In Chicago, Ring Lardner had attracted Damon's attention with his arch, funny, free-style baseball coverage as early as 1908. Even before Lardner, there had been the *Tribune*'s "HEK," columnist Hugh E. Keogh, whose sharp satire Damon appreciated ("he could skin 'em alive in a paragraph," Runyon later testified). Charley Dryden of the Philadelphia *North American* (and later of the Chicago *Examiner)* had for several years been producing a prose that put "inside" knowledge of the game at the service of an artist's sense of form and a barroom comedian's sense of humor. Also in Philly, Bugs Baer was doing something similar but with wry twists which Gene Fowler later described as "philosophical overtones."

Damon also admired the swashbuckling Bat Masterson, whose anecdotes and exploits had been familiar to him since his Denver days. Now sports editor of the *Morning Telegraph,* Masterson made a second home of the Considine boy's Metropole bar, which soon became a regular nighttime stop of Damon's. The dauntless Bat, a short, balding man in a brown derby who still carried a pistol on his person at all times, held forth nightly for a sporting crowd

The World of Damon Runyon

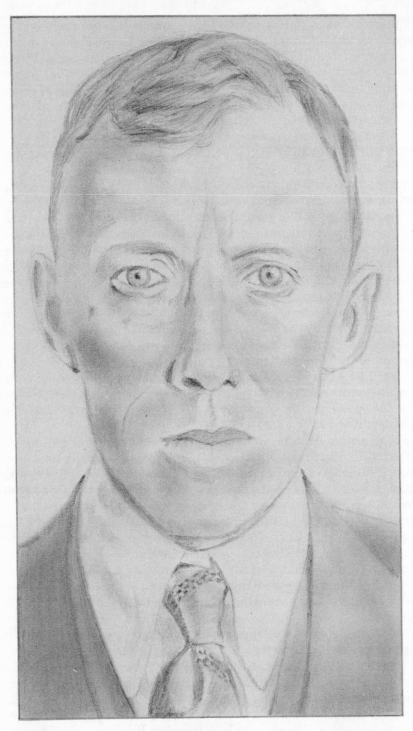

Tad Dorgan

Colorado Kid in the Press Box

that included Honest John Kelly, whose card and dice games Damon would often frequent over the years; "crooked" gambler Herman Rosenthal, whose demise the following summer would involve Damon in his first New York murder trial; Kid McCoy, née Norman Selby, ex-welterweight champ of the world, at whose murder trial Damon would later testify as, appropriately, a "character" witness (Selby's fight moniker inspired the expression "the real McCoy"); prizefight impresario Dan McKetrick; Western "dialect" writer Alfred Henry Lewis; and other personages interesting to young Runyon.

It was at the Metropole that Damon first met many of the touts, bookmakers, horse breeders, jockeys, promoters, and trainers whose speech was to become the special argot of the Broadway tales. And the nightly Masterson sermons fascinated him, for here was an obvious example of how a hard-bitten Western character—not unlike Damon's old man—could adjust without strain to the sporting milieu of the East. "Bat ¹ ad no literary style," Damon later wrote, "but he had plenty of moxie." The true grit displayed in Masterson's remarks was a quality Runyon aspired to incorporate into his own writing, even if with him it would never be more than a simulation of tone; Damon could never claim the personal fearlessness of Bat, who had in his day shot living men to back up his opinions. (Bat's legend was later immortalized—via Damon's tale "The Idyll of Miss Sarah Brown"—in the character Sky Masterson, played by Marlon Brando in the film version of *Guys and Dolls.)*

During the 1911 baseball season Damon also met the legendary "Wild Bill" Phelan, a Midwestern writer of great gifts and considerable eccentricity who was notorious for his animal collections. Phelan had once arrived in town accompanied by a poisonous South American snake, which he kept in a hatbox, and another time had stopped everybody's play-by-play accounts by pulling a large lizard out of his pocket. Phelan, when he finally came to town with the Cincinnati Reds (he was then working for the *Inquirer),* turned out to be even better than his legend as far as Damon was concerned. "When the great Bill Phelan came in with the Cincinnati Reds and a live squirrel in his pocket, I sat alongside him in the press box and wrote my whole story around the reactions of the squirrel," he reminisced in a letter to Damon Jr. thirty-five years later.

Bill Phelan was Runyon's idea of the stunt technique carried to perfection. During the "squirrel" game Phelan confided to Damon that in his apartment he kept a six-foot alligator, which he found a great inspiration to his writing. In the dog days of a later baseball season Damon would remember Bill Phelan's words and himself resort to traveling with and reporting the actions of a small alligator. (Anything to keep reader and writer awake!) Phelan not only wrote effectively on any subject but could do so while carrying on a conversation, a talent that once inspired Grantland Rice to compare him with Julius Caesar. As he sat and chatted with Damon in the press box, Wild Bill's fingers flew over his typewriter keys and the squirrel in his pocket nibbled peanuts out of Damon's hand. To Runyon the insane Phelan was a phenomenon, an example of journalistic individualism that was absolutely unprecedented.

All these writers, and others less prominent, were influences on Damon at a time when he was developing a personal sportswriting style. This style, hammered out during the 1911 baseball season, remained at Runyon's disposal for the next twenty-five years. And it was an important tributary in the mainstream of a new American sportswriting. That art reached its apogee in the second and third decades of this century, when the growing public interest in sports, particularly in baseball, created a need for—and wide acceptance of—a journalism as colorful, humorous, manly, and vital as the games and stars themselves. The result was two decades of the finest specialized news writing America has known. To a considerable extent the responsibility for this achievement was one all the great writers of that era shared. The traditional communalism of the sportswriting racket was never more apparent than in the generation of Baer and McGeehan and Runyon and Lardner and Rice and Broun.

It's now agreed that these men were placed on the sports desks of their respective papers largely because they were the best writers available at a time when the relationship between raw circulation figures and the quality of a sports department was acknowledged in every editorial office in every big city in the country. In the days before the tabloid explosion, a top bylined sports column could pull in readers like nothing else, and in the dog-eat-dog circulation battles that continuously afflicted the New York newspaper world, the slight edge a "name" sportswriter could provide was worth plenty to editors and publishers, as indicated by the high salaries men like Rice and Runyon eventually commanded. "The sportswriters were absolutely the best writers on the papers in those days," a survivor of the era, Marshall Hunt, tells us, "and baseball writing was the best of all the jobs on a newspaper."

In *The Tumult and the Shouting,* Grantland Rice talked with nostalgic authority about the great "change" that occurred in sportswriting after 1910. To Ford Frick, who arrived in New York a decade after Rice, the essence of the change was in the writers' adoption of "a more personal approach to the business of writing baseball." Frick attributed the change to improved press box conditions for writers, the growth of the byline system, and especially the individual genius of the group of writers who together pursued the new style and its large financial rewards. "During the decade from 1910 to 1920, the whole complexion of baseball writing changed for the better," Frick wrote in his memoirs. "Lardner, Baer, Runyon, Dryden, Van Loan and the others were largely responsible. They were the human catalysts who brought humor and fun into the baseball picture. The tongue in cheek style they developed in their writing established the fact that wrongs can be righted, phonies exposed, and evils corrected, without tearing down public faith in the game itself."

The part Damon would play in the birth of that style was evident from his first season on the Giants' beat. Within three years of Opening Day 1911 his paper would confidently bill him as "the greatest baseball writer in the country." Hearst promotions were famous for their superlatives, but this was one area where the *American* had reasonable claims to truth in advertising. Damon's use of stunts, bizarre conceits, and contrasting viewpoints to individualize and unify his pieces, and his emphasis on human interest angles and colorful characters, were his principal contributions to the evolution of the new common style. For the next two decades these would be familiar qualities in the work of the best sportswriters in the country. In exchange, Damon was bringing away from his involvement with such writers as McGeehan, Broun, Baer, and Lardner a lesson in backhanded humor that would prove invaluable to his own maturation as a writer. The precision of irony that he would eventually achieve in his series of Broadway stories, and which would be his work's greatest distinction, would owe more than a little to those gifted literary peers of his press box days—to whom in 1911 Damon Runyon was still only the Colorado Kid, a laconic high-plains wrangler with a touchy disposition and a nice gift for a turn of phrase.

4

Little Napoleon

I think we can win it—if my brains hold out.
          —John McGraw, during the 1921 pennant race

Damon's first year on the baseball beat was a triumph, and he owed his quick success in no small part to the team he was covering. The New York Giants provided much lively material in 1911.

The Giants of that era were a reflection and extension of the imperious personality of John J. McGraw, the greatest baseball mind of his time. The cocky little manager's newspaper nickname, Little Napoleon, was apt. He saw the sport as a field of battle on which mental and physical forces could be brought into play just as they are in actual warfare. He was a grand strategist who controlled the entire operation of the club, from the signing of players and the minor league operations to the management of the park and the groundskeeping, just as Bonaparte oversaw his great military empire. He dominated the National League as Napoleon had dominated Europe, and he was similarly loved and feared at home and despised "abroad." McGraw, indeed, loved thinking of himself as a field general. Contrary to the custom of the times, he managed not from the coaching lines but from the bench, where he could not only give signs but survey the action from a better vantage, talk to his men, personally select pinch hitters and relief pitchers, and in general inject most emphatically his strong force of character into his team. As his great pitcher Mathewson put it, "McGraw knew he could pull the team through from the bench—concentrate better, see more of what was going on. And he missed nothing."

McGraw's great managing strengths were his gift for strategy and his genius in handling men. Again they were military strengths. He thought variously like a mathematician, an engineer, and a psychologist—as a successful manager (or field general) must. He called pitches from the bench, signaled for bunts, stolen bases, hit-and-run plays, and changes of defensive position, and where no sign was given he insisted that his players think and anticipate on their own. This they did, to a remarkable extent; McGraw's clubs made notably few mental errors. Muggsy, or the Old Man, as his athletes called him, was merciless in his postgame

Little Napoleon

John McGraw and Damon Runyon

attacks on players whom he suspected of inattention on the field. He stressed the aggressive, intimidating game, which could only be played by intelligent, alert men. McGraw wanted no player who was not on his toes at all times. He imposed stringent training regulations, curfews, and behavioral rules. For every Bugs Raymond who chafed against the system, McGraw had a hundred players who obeyed it. He defended his men to the press and took their side in every dispute, no matter how he fumed against them in the privacy of the clubhouse, and for this he won the respect if not the affection of the great majority of his troops.

For all his strategic genius, it was in the area of human relations that McGraw's greatest talent lay. There were a few hard cases with whom he made no headway. Bugs Raymond, Damon's favorite player, went to a tragic end after a final blowout with the Giant manager; and it was a bizarre chain of circumstances initiated by McGraw that led to the expulsion from baseball in 1922 of pitcher "Shufflin' Phil" Douglas, another free-spirited indi-

The World of Damon Runyon

vidualist with whom Damon sympathized. There were other players McGraw "rode" too hard who left for greener pastures, like Rube Marquard. And no doubt there were brief times when his abrasive temperament caused even the most loyal of his men to hate his guts. But of those who played for him with the prewar Giants, few had anything but good to say of him when it came time to exchange the harsh glare of the present for the rosier light of nostalgia. Even Al Bridwell, a shortstop who once socked McGraw in the mouth in the Giants' dugout (and drew a two-week suspension for it) later called the manager "a wonderful man, a real fighter . . . he'd argue with the umpires, the opposing players, the people in the stands. Anybody wanted to argue, he was ready."

His players loved this bristling little man as long as his stings weren't landing on them. Rube Marquard, driven by the manager's harsh criticism to insist on a trade to Brooklyn during the disastrous season of 1915, in later years recalled only the good days with McGraw. "The finest and grandest man I ever met," Rube called him in *The Glory of Our Times.* "He loved his players and his players loved him." McGraw's California Mission Indian catcher, Chief Meyers, tells how the manager "fought for his players, and protected them . . . stood up for them at all times." "Oh, we held him in high esteem," the Chief told Lawrence Ritter in the sixties, "we respected him in every way." And Fred Snodgrass, a star outfielder for the Giants from 1910 to 1915, acknowledged McGraw's "vicious tongue" but remembered that "once he'd bawled you out good and proper, and I do mean proper, then he'd forget it. He wouldn't ever mention it again, and in public he always stood up for his players." Snodgrass' bottom-line comment on McGraw is one that recurs in practically every reminiscence from the Giant players of the early days: "He was a great man, really a wonderful fellow, and a great manager to play for."

In retrospect it's easy to see how McGraw won the admiration and respect of his players. His methods brought them convincing success. As with Napoleon or George Patton or Vince Lombardi, victory made allegiance easy to maintain. McGraw's clubs were usually at the top of the league or near it. He had won pennants with the Giants in 1904 and 1905, brought them home second in 1909 and 1910, and in 1911 he had a talented club that was as hungry for another championship as he was. It was a swift, heady young team with legs, brains, and great pitching. Bugs Raymond and one or two other grumblers aside, the players were behind McGraw all the way. So were the Giant rooters, who figured Little Napoleon was ready to lead another World Series march.

Damon had seen Mac rant and rave on the bench during spring games and had heard plenty of stories about him from the other scribes. The manager's colorful life story was well known to the

Little Napoleon

Wilbert Robinson, John McGraw, and Christy Mathewson

writing crowd, who regarded him as great material. Diphtheria, Damon was told, had killed McGraw's mother, step-sister, and three brothers when he was seventeen. Shortly thereafter he had been beaten badly by a drunken father for breaking windows and had run away from home to become a candy salesman on the railroads. Here and there he had played baseball. Despite his size (he had never grown taller than five foot six), he had scrapped his way up to the major leagues, become a star and manager with the Orioles, and taken over the Giants in 1902. Since then he had become a legend in baseball and on Broadway, where he was a well-known character by the time of Damon's arrival in New York in 1910.

McGraw was quite the man about town; he was an active member of the Lambs Club, the actors' and performers' society, and he socialized considerably with the Broadway theatre crowd. He would be seen of an evening at Jack's or Churchill's or the Metropole. In the little world between Sixth and Eighth Avenues his superstitiousness, his love for playing the ponies (the two went hand in hand), his taste for a drink, and especially his pugilistic proclivities were well known. It was said that McGraw carried into his personal life the same disposition he displayed on the ball field, where he baited umps, screamed at players, insulted opposing owners, and in general behaved like a man with his

The World of Damon Runyon

fist stuck out the window in hopes of having someone run into it. Given the fact that the manager had a notoriously short fuse at all times, and was long on confidence to the point of arrogance, it was no surprise that once you poured a couple of shots into him, he was liable to take a pop at anybody who happened to be around, be it foe or friend. This was a man who had once thrown a punch at Ty Cobb; was he to be afraid of someone in a bar? Apparently not, judging by the number of legendary mismatches Muggsy had taken on and the number of times (according to the scribes) he had ended up in the loss column. The two numbers, Runyon was told, were almost equal.

Over the next decade Damon had numerous opportunities on and off duty to catch the manager's main events (and some of the minor ones). Of those he did not witness he was informed in detail, within hours or sometimes minutes, for on the Broadway grapevine a new McGraw brawl was always a hot item. All the sports on the Big Street got a laugh out of John's bouts, which were never exactly in the league of Stanley Ketchel or Kid McCoy when it came to artistry.

Although the stories he'd heard concerning McGraw's pre-1911 scrapes, fights, feuds, fines, and suspensions would have filled a book, Damon always felt that it wasn't until the middle of the second decade of the century that the Giants' skipper came into his own in the field of gladiatorial absurdity. His surprise KO over southpaw pitcher Ad Brennan of the Phils in 1913 was observed firsthand by Runyon, as was his less successful clash the following spring with Houston Buffalo manager Pat Newnam, who followed McGraw under the stands after an on-the-field argument and beat hell out of him. That one dashed all Damon's hopes for McGraw as a boxer, but he was pleased to note that Giant shortstop Art Fletcher came to his manager's rescue and knocked Pat Newnam cold with one retaliatory blow. The spirit of Little Napoleon ran through his ball club like an angry virus.

In June 1917 Damon was in the Cincinnati ballpark when McGraw got into things with home plate ump Bill "Lord" Byron, a square-jawed man famous for his habit of humming snatches from popular songs while waiting for the pitches. McGraw, who'd been taking exception to Bryon's visual judgments all afternoon, finally came out to criticize the ump's musical offerings as well and was summarily ejected. Never safely humiliated, McGraw lay in wait under the grandstand; in the hotel that evening Damon heard that the manager had caught the unsuspecting arbiter under the chin with a running uppercut that left him spitting red and reeling. The next morning Damon and the other writers were sitting around the hotel lobby when the news came in over the wire that McGraw's attack on Bill Byron was going to cost him five

54

Little Napoleon

C's in fines and a sixteen-day suspension. Veteran scribe and McGraw loyalist Sid Mercer carried the news to the manager, who was in his room. McGraw read the telegram Sid showed him, rolled it up, threw it on the floor, stomped on it, and then exploded. He raved about the dishonesty of the president of the league, the president of the Phillies (the club he was battling for the pennant), the umpires, and anybody else he could think of, and then—when Mercer asked him if he could be quoted—insisted that he wanted "to see the quotes in every newspaper in New York."

Sid filed the story. McGraw repudiated it in print and in sworn statements. Mercer pressed the issue. The league president tacked another $1000 onto McGraw's fine. McGraw put the word out that Sid Mercer had been lying. Sid left the club and did not cover another Giant game—or speak to John McGraw—for several seasons. Damon and the other scribes learned a lesson from that one; nobody put words in McGraw's mouth for quite a while afterward, even words the manager had actually spoken. You never could tell what might set Mac off.

Damon's favorite tale of John McGraw's improvisations in the manly arts concerned events that took place during and following the evening and early morning of August 7–8, 1920. On that date the stout little sportsman celebrated at the Lambs Club, as was his wont, and in an unsteady manner was making ready to depart for home when he thought he spied actor Walter Knight, a particular enemy. Employing what Bill Fallon, McGraw's lawyer, later described to Damon as "third baseman's language," the manager approached his supposed foe at double-time. The personage thus rudely addressed rose, and he and McGraw fell to blows. It was not Knight, however, but William H. Boyd, another and sturdier actor who disposed of his attacker in a matter of moments by means of a water carafe across the baseballer's noggin.

McGraw was revived and accompanied to his home by a pair of peace-loving allies. However, at his residence on West 109th Street, McGraw became restless over the way one of his friends was attempting to help him up the front steps. Another scuffle ensued, in which the helpful friend—actor John Slavin—was thrown to the pavement. Slavin suffered a cut lip, two broken teeth, and a fractured skull and spent the next several days in a coma. It was only through the good agencies of attorney Fallon that McGraw escaped serious trouble this time. As it was, he slept off his hangover the next day while the district attorney's boys hung around outside the door. When reporters called, he slammed down the receiver without a word. One of the calls he treated in this fashion turned out to be from another Lambs Club pal, the dramatic star and noted conversationalist Wilton Lackaye. Lackaye then pursued his intention of bestowing get-well wishes in person.

The World of Damon Runyon

When he showed up at McGraw's door, the D.A.'s boys stepped aside. Mac opened the door a crack, and Lackaye stepped in; a moment later there was a racket inside, and the D.A.'s boys rushed in to find Lackaye on the floor with a bloody mouth and a broken leg. (The fracture he had presumably sustained in falling; no one ever suspected McGraw of deliberately breaking men's legs.)

Had not McGraw been an important personage and his lawyer the best in town, all of this might have cost him more than it did—which was a few months of lousy publicity (most of it in the form of talk behind his back) and expulsion from the Lambs Club for three years. Damon quickly picked up the whole story from his friend Fallon, but unless they were good at reading between the lines, the readers of his *American* column didn't. He'd written openly of some of McGraw's ball field fights, but his only references to the 1920 bouts were oblique. There was a criminal indictment involved (the manager was charged with—and later acquitted of—violation of the new Prohibition laws); there was also the fact that McGraw was a longtime associate whom Runyon felt compelled by loyalty to protect. Last but not least, who needed a punch in the nose from Little Napoleon? So Damon steered a wide berth past the Boyd-Slavin-Lackaye bouts, printwise, until McGraw passed away in 1934. After that he brought the matter up in a number of humorous columns that no doubt would have meant risking a fat lip if he'd written them in August 1920.

McGraw pops up, for instance, in a forties *Daily Mirror* column called "Forceful Remarks." Damon, addressing the subject of war and aggression in the anecdotal style typical of his late essays, begins with the question of whether Joseph Stalin "did or did not pat Marshal Semën Timoshenko on the pimple or head, with a vodka bottle," and proceeds through a variety of nostalgic remarks on bygone instances of violence to "John McGraw, the manager of the Giants [who] counted a day lost that [he] did not deliver or receive a punch-in-the-nose." McGraw, Damon says, "did not stand around complaining of wrongs or waste time calling up law books. [He] just punched somebody in the nose . . . or vice versa, and as reflecting the spirit of the times, the newspapers published far less about the matter than they do about a bit of shadow boxing in a nightclub in which nothing is exchanged but gestures . . ." (The dubious point of Damon's essay—conveyed with his characteristic "half-boob air"—is that in the days of McGraw "the good old punch-in-the-nose was a great sedative for violence.")

Another late Runyon column that evokes McGraw's fights is "Café Gladiators," also from the forties. This piece takes off from an unwise punch thrown by Damon's Hollywood restauranteur pal Prince Mike Romanoff at former racing driver Barney Oldfield and builds up to a reminiscence on the free-swinging days of Harry

Little Napoleon

Pollok (the hotheaded fight promoter, bike-racing entrepreneur, and sartorialist who fought and was licked by everybody) and John McGraw. McGraw, like Prince Mike and Pollok, is proposed by Damon as an example of the tactical unwisdom of "taking on an opponent without knowing who he is."

> A man can ad lib himself into a lot of K.O.'s by not picking spots, as John J. McGraw, the manager of the New York Giants, discovered years ago. McGraw was noted for getting himself flattened. He was a choleric and pugnacious little man and healthy and strong, too, but he couldn't fight a lick. Yet he was always fighting.
>
> Even when he was in his middle years and had a paunch, he was slugging it out with ball players, umpires, spectators and innocent bystanders. The New York newspapers made much of McGraw's fights, as they do of the battles of café society today, and with each account of a McGraw encounter they ran his record, which went something like this:
>
> Lost to Honest John Kelly.
> Lost to Ad Brennan.
> Lost to P. Sentell.
> And so on and so on.
>
> Comparatively late in his life, Mac discovered the Lambs Club and easier picking among the actors than on the ball fields and along Broadway. He is said to have given Wilton Lackaye a belting and polished Johnny Slavin, an old time musical performer, with a bottle. But he never licked any of the tougher competition elsewhere.   —"Café Gladiators"

From what we know about Runyon's own history as a café gladiator—two or three tales survive of his disastrous forays into saloon combat during the Denver years—he had ample cause to sympathize with McGraw in this respect. But in Damon's New York career there is no record of fisticuffs, so it's safe to assume he and John McGraw never came to blows. No, Damon got along with the Giant manager as well as any of the scribes.

A few writers disliked Muggsy intensely. Marshall Hunt, for one, recalls his contempt for the ornery little boss of the Giants, who once tried to pick a fight with him on a railway station platform because Hunt had written the truth about certain fines McGraw had imposed. Hunt considered the incident childish. And then there was the case of Sid Mercer.

Personalities apart, most of the writers who covered the Giants in the early years were later outspoken in their respect for McGraw's genius as a manager. Ring Lardner came to believe that the "inside" game advocated and perfected by McGraw was *the* classic style of baseball, a style that had been sacrificed to brute strength in what he called the "rabbit-ball" era after 1920. ("It ain't the old game," Ring complained in his vernacular mode. "Ball players which used to specialize in hump back liners to the pitcher is now among our leading sluggers.") In 1932, when ill health forced McGraw out of the game, Lardner sent him a touching note on this subject. "Baseball hasn't meant much to me since the TNT ball that robbed the game of the features I used to like best—features that gave you and the other really intelligent managers a deserved advantage. You were among the few men left who personified what I enjoyed in the national pastime." Bill McGeehan, who felt the opposite way about the arrival of Ruth and the rabbit ball (the Sheriff was convinced Babe's homers had saved the sport after the 1919 scandals), nonetheless agreed with Lardner in his assessment of McGraw's position in baseball history. "If I wanted to name anybody as the spirit of the American game incarnate," McGeehan wrote on the event of McGraw's death in 1934, "I would think of John J. McGraw."

Runyon thought likewise. Occasionally in the early years of their acquaintance Damon spent an evening on the road dining with the Giant manager, or a day at the track, or stopped at his table in a Manhattan nightspot to chat. Their common professional and recreational interests threw them together often, and eventually they became quite friendly.

When in February 1914 the Giants were nearing the end of their great world tour (they had barnstormed with the White Sox through the Pacific and across Asia and North Africa to Europe), Damon joined the party in Paris. It was his first trip to Europe and the Giant manager's, too. Damon's second day abroad was spent taking tea at the Parisian residence of Myron Herrick, the U.S. ambassador to France, with McGraw. Afterward Damon bought a *Guide to Paris,* commandeered a taxi, and instructed the driver in his best North Atlantic French, *"Au tombeau de Napoleon!"*

It was a cold, bleak day. The unfamiliar city streamed by the eyes of the rubber-necking writer and the baseball man at his side. The cab stopped at a large public monument, and Damon asked the driver to wait.

"What in Hades might this be, then?" McGraw asked, once he had his land legs.

"Something I want to show you. I figure it's that big stone gizmo over there."

McGraw gave the area a quick once-over, then looked at Damon. "Where are we, boyo?"

"It's his tomb, Mac," Damon said. "I figured you'd like to see it."

"Tomb?"

"Napoleon's," Damon said, his eyes twinkling.

"Ah!" The manager was pleased; he smiled broadly. He looked at the stone building again, then clapped Damon on the back.

Little Napoleon

They walked toward the stone building together.

Damon got a story out of the episode, with one nice quote from McGraw. As everyone knew, the Giants had been beaten in two of the last three World Series by Connie Mack's A's. So the McGraw tag line for Damon's story—authentic or not—was a natural.

"I too, met the Duke of Wellington," Damon's piece in the *American* has McGraw saying as he inspects the tomb of Napoleon, "only his name was Connie Mack."

5

The 1911 Season and a
Baseball Marriage

I suppose it was an important part of McGraw's great capacity for leadership that he would take kids out of the coal mines and out of the wheatfields and make them walk and talk and chatter and play ball with the look of eagles. —Heywood Broun

It's great to be young and a Giant.
—"Laughing Larry" Doyle

McGraw's 1911 Giants were the epitome of his kind of baseball. They had the league's best defense and pitching that consistently held opposing teams to less than three runs a game. At bat they pecked and scratched for runs, but they usually produced enough to win. Laughing Larry Doyle, the twenty-four-year-old second baseman whose glowering visage belied his nickname, led the club on offense with 25 triples, 38 stolen bases, and a .527 slugging average; after the season he was awarded the Chalmers automobile that went to the league's Most Valuable Player. Although the 1911 Giants hit only 41 home runs, they scored at a rate of better than four runs a game, mostly as a result of their great success on the basepaths. Disdaining the long ball, McGraw trained his men to capitalize on the "percentage" play, the bunt, the hit and run, the stolen base.

The style of ball the Giants played reflected his personal aggressiveness absolutely. "McGraw," Damon wrote, "starts his line of attack early. He is a great believer in speed. He always sends his fast men out to run on the opposing pitcher when they have the opportunity. McGraw argues that a man may as well be thrown out stealing as to have a put-out in some other fashion." Eight of his 1911 Giant players finished the year with 19 or more stolen bases. As a club they stole no less than 347—a major league record that stands to this day. It was tight, tense, demanding baseball, the way McGraw thought the game should be played. To the fans of that era it was also a delight to watch, and it usually got them home on time for dinner (unless there was a particularly big victory to celebrate.)

Damon rode the el to the Polo Grounds on Thursday, April 13 for the season's second game. One of McGraw's many "supersti-

The 1911 Season and a Baseball Marriage

tions" involved holding Christy Mathewson out of opening games, which meant Christy usually got to pitch against the opposition's number two man. 1911 was no exception, but McGraw's strategy didn't work. The Phils edged Matty, 2–1. Dode Paskert of the Phils made a great catch, one which Damon described enthusiastically, but Damon still hadn't seen the Giants win a big league game. The next day he wondered if he ever would.

Thursday night the Polo Grounds caught fire, apparently from a smoldering newspaper, and by morning the entire main stand had burned to the ground. It was one of the most explosive and expensive fires the city had seen. Only about 10,000 wooden outfield bleachers remained intact. On Friday the Giants were not scheduled to play, and for several nervous hours it seemed their season might be in jeopardy. But Frank Farrell, the owner of the Yankees (or Highlanders, as they were then nicknamed), came to the rescue, offering Giant owner John Brush the use of his Hilltop Park until the Polo Grounds could be rebuilt. (This piece of generosity was returned in kind by Brush two years later, when he let Farrell move his club into the new Polo Grounds, where they were to stay until the completion of Yankee Stadium in 1923.)

Brush, in an act that could not be duplicated today, waived competitive bidding and ordered an immediate start of work on the rebuilding of the Polo Grounds. The main structure of the new steel and concrete building, with 16,000 new seats in addition to the remaining bleachers, was erected in ten weeks and opened for play on June 28; the Giants had spent only three full home stands at Hilltop. By fall there were nearly 35,000 seats available for use. (Today such a rebuilding job would take several years.)

So it happened that Damon saw his first Giant victory in the old American League park at 165th Street and Broadway, one day after the fire. The following week the Giants left for Boston on their first road trip of the season. Damon traveled with the team on a Pullman.

When the club returned to New York, the Giants' owner threw a party for the writers to announce his plans for the new Polo Grounds. It was to be a fantasy palace, big enough to hold 50,000 fans, Giant executives declared (Brush, the owner, was then too ill to attend). Damon swilled coffee in the elegant Riverside Drive eatery and maintained his critical frown while his colleagues drank up the absent Mr. Brush's liquor and exchanged elbow nudges. My, didn't them blueprints look grand! During the speeches Damon heard Bat Masterson's snide comments from the rear of the room. "It's a veritable Eighth Wonder of the World!" Bat hissed at one point.

While the Giants were at home in early May Damon received an answer to a letter of proposal he'd written to Ellen Egan shortly after Opening Day. She wrote to say yes, and a few days later Damon met her at a railway station in Manhattan and took her to the Van Loan house, where they stayed briefly after being married in a Roman Catholic ceremony at a local rectory. The newlyweds soon took two rooms in a boarding house in Flushing. Damon barely had time to move his bags into their new home before he had to catch a train; the Giants were heading for Philadelphia.

In May Damon wrote of the trials of Bugs Raymond, who was drinking and pitching to beat the band and getting himself deeper in McGraw's doghouse with every ballgame. Bugs kept disappearing mysteriously in the middle innings of games. Another "problem" pitcher, lefty Rube Marquard (Damon referred to him as "our distinguished scion of Marseilles and Cleveland, Richard de Reuben de Marquis Marquard"), was experiencing sudden success. Marquard, for whom the Giants had paid an enormous eleven G's in 1908, had been so ineffective with New York that he had become known as "the $11,000 lemon." By May 1911 he appeared to be washed up at the age of twenty-one and destined for the minor leagues. His "last chance" came against the Cardinals shortly after Damon's wedding; McGraw pulled Christy Mathewson in the second inning of a game in which the Giants had scored nine or ten runs in their first at bat, and brought in Marquard. Rube, permitted to work with the luxury of a big lead, relaxed and threw his best game as a Giant, striking out 14 and winning with ease. As Damon soon noted, that was the game that put the sensitive young Marquard in the proper state of mind for pitching; he went on to win 24 ball games and strike out 237 batters in 1911. Beginning in the second month of the season, Rube gave McGraw the extra boost he felt he needed to beat his chief competitors, the Pirates, the Phils, and the Cubs. Coincidentally, the "arrival" of Marquard as an effective starter made the always unreliable Bugs Raymond expendable. For Bugs, Marquard's great game against the Cards in May was the first tolling of the bell.

In mid-June the club made a long Western trip during the first hot spell of the year. It was a sweltering major league baptism for Damon. The long overnight train ride from Philadelphia to St. Louis left him hot and dusty and caked with sweat in his Pullman bunk. Even the normally equable Matty was cranky during the poker games on this trip, scowling at Damon and the other scribes and swearing under his breath when his cards were running bad. There was no air conditioning then on the Pullmans; the players drank beer, strummed ukuleles, and sang for hours, but they always wound up grousing about the heat. *This* was what a baseball season was all about, reporter Runyon realized: cramped berths, sweaty underwear, smoke and grit, sleepless nights, bitter coffee, and stale sandwiches, all in an endlessly repeated round that, however much they griped, the veterans took for granted and the rookies, like Damon, had to learn the hard way. The road was its own Dark Continent.

The one member of the Giants' party who did not survive the June trip was Bugs Raymond, who got drunk and tangled with McGraw on board the night train to St. Louis. McGraw, in a fit of rage, leaped on the big pitcher and knocked him down with several surprise punches, then got up and walked away. Bugs assumed that McGraw, a much smaller man, had merely been rough-housing in fun. When teammates told him otherwise, Bugs blew his top. "Why, if I'd known the little bastard was serious, I would have killed him," he said.

The following morning Bugs disappeared from the station. The players were supposed to be at Sportsman's Park at noon for the three o'clock game. Along about two-thirty the Giants were completing their pregame warmups when Bugs, still in street clothes, made his way out of the stands and across the field toward the visiting clubhouse (which was located beyond the outfield fence). He walked with a pronounced list but with great determination, and he had almost made it to the clubhouse door when McGraw saw and intercepted him. The manager gave the pitcher his walking papers, suspending him on the spot. "Take your uniform and go," Little Napoleon said. "I am sorry about this, Raymond, but I am not running a rest home here on this club."

Bugs, briefly crestfallen, repaired to the clubhouse to claim his baseball togs. (In those days the players owned their own equipment.) The next day Bugs and his uniform were on their way back to New York.

Despite the enervating weather and Bugs Raymond's departure, the June road trip was a great success for the Giants. McGraw bitched at the players and they at him, but the ball club kept winning, and by the time the team returned to New York at the end of the month McGraw was looking back at the other contenders and airing such statements as "We have them all beaten to a frazzle."

On June 28 the grand opening of the still incomplete "new" Polo Grounds took place. Bands played, the bunting was brought out, the new concrete grandstand was full; the atmosphere was that of a second opening day. This time Matty pitched and knocked the Braves off with his usual effortless mastery, 3–0. The festive crowd went home happy, and no doubt extravagant tales of the grand new stadium were told to those at home—except in Flushing, where Damon's new wife was not interested in games of ball or the places where they were played.

Pretty Ellen Egan felt stranded and alone in New York; Damon was never at home. She pined for a life in society such as she had possessed in Denver, or for the vivid life of Manhattan, which she imagined but had not yet experienced. Damon was sympathetic but too busy to worry. He figured Ellen would soon adjust. Before long he would be earning enough money to move them both to a new home in Manhattan; there, he hoped, Ellen would find the active life she craved.

A few days after the opening of the home stand Damon noticed a new window display in the 155th Street and Eighth Avenue saloon where the ballplayers congregated. There was a white flannel Giants' uniform pinned to a black velvet backdrop and a large placard reading BUGS RAYMOND TENDS BAR HERE. Damon went in and interviewed the shaky Bugs, who claimed to have found a new life as a bartender.

Damon covered the July visit of the Pirates to New York from the centerfield bleachers, from which vantage he could view the pitches through the bowlegs of Honus Wagner, the great shortstop who at the age of thirty-seven was on his way to his eighth National League batting title. After each game Damon rode down to the *American* office with his story, then dined on the town before returning to Flushing. It was often the small hours when he got home. And Ellen often waited up for him; the young couple had to make the most of what brief time they had together. After Decoration Day Damon was off on another road trip.

On July 10 the Phils, one of the Giants' principal antagonists in the pennant race, suffered a severe blow when their leftfielder and defending batting champ, Sherry Magee, was suspended indefinitely for knocking out some of an umpire's teeth in displeasure over a close call. The loss of Magee was a handicap that dropped the Phils from the race despite the heroic work of their young pitching workhorse "Pete" Alexander, who won 28 games before the season was out. That left McGraw with only two clubs to beat, and he hoped to finish them off by September 1.

In July the Giants appeared capable of that and more: they were growing hotter with the weather and were beating everyone in sight. On their long Western trip in July McGraw had picked up a good-luck token in the form of one Charles Victor Faust (later known as "Victory"), a strange but friendly would-be pitcher who'd shown up during a Giants' workout in St. Louis with a tale about how a fortuneteller had told him he would lead the New York club to the pennant this very year. At the mention of the word "fortuneteller" McGraw's ears pricked up. His superstitious nature made him listen to Faust's story and give the loony fellow a tryout—which eventually extended into a ticket to ride with the club all season as mascot and "bull-pen pitcher." The Giants had won their game the day of Faust's tryout. They also won the next day, and the next. Naturally McGraw took Charley along to Chicago,

The 1911 Season and a Baseball Marriage

Charley Faust

and when his men swept three there over Frank Chance's club, Victory Faust's place with the Giants was cinched. Charley was John McGraw's personal rabbit's foot. Thereafter he traveled with the club and warmed up (with a motion like a windmill, Fred Snodgrass said) before every game the Giants played.

Faust stayed with the team through two pennant-winning seasons, during which he served as a sort of psychological punching bag for the ball club, submitting with naive glee to every practical joke in the book. The players loaded his suitcase with bricks, advised him to sleep with his pitching arm nestled in a hammock, and sent him out to buy left-handed monkey wrenches and striped paint. Only Christy Mathewson ("a gentleman among hooligans," one writer said) refused to take part in Faust's humiliation and even defended him at times. (When in 1913 the club went into a losing streak and McGraw decided Victory had worn out his value as a good-luck charm and sent him packing, the well-meaning oddball went completely round the bend, dying within a year in a state insane asylum in Washington.)

Even without Bugs Raymond, by mid-July 1911 the Giants had quite an interesting pitching staff, with the brilliant young Rube Marquard and the still masterful Matty laying victories back to back with the efficiency of a couple of Swiss clocks and Charley Faust doing his daily windmill imitation in the bullpen. There were Hooks Wiltse and Red Ames, too, and a burly young curve-baller from Indiana, Otis Crandall, described by Runyon as "the piano-legged proprietor of the largest fish-hook farm in the Hoosier state." McGraw was calling the strapping Otis into more and more games to bail his second-line starters out of difficult situations, a procedure which nowadays seems basic, but which before 1911 had been employed regularly by no other manager. Most of Crandall's 41 game appearances for McGraw in 1911 were in relief. When by the end of the season he'd nailed down 7 of his 15 wins and 5 saves in this role, a number of cynics—who'd laughed up their sleeves at McGraw for removing perfectly good starting pitchers before the ends of games—were forced to change their minds. Damon, at least, had approved of Crandall's "emergency" role as early as June. In July he began calling Otis "the doctor of sick ball games." The phrase was picked up all around, "doctor" was shortened to "Doc," and Crandall had a baseball moniker that stayed with him the rest of his career.

During the Giants' hot streak in June and July Damon's writing grew more confident and singular with every story. By this time it was often necessary for the readers of the *American* sports pages to consult a play-by-play account (one usually accompanied Damon's story) in order to learn the details of the game. From Damon they got high humor, low gags, ironic twists, flights of burlesque wit, satiric mini-epics—anything to keep things interesting. If nothing else, Runyon's game stories were always highly entertaining.

About as straightforward as Damon ever got in his July pieces was this lead for a July 16 account of a Mathewson victory over the Reds, who hadn't beaten Matty in three seasons:

> Mathewson pitched against Cincinnati yesterday.
> Another way of putting it is that Cincinnati lost a game of baseball.
> The first statement means the same as the second.

The next day the Reds beat the Giants. But you'd have figured the score wasn't of much importance if you'd read only Damon's

The 1911 Season and a Baseball Marriage

piece, which plays up a meaningless home run by a thirty-three-year-old substitute outfielder, Mike Donlin, who got into only two other games for the Giants all year. The point of the story—for Damon and his readers—was not the home run but the fact that Mike had hit it. The dapper "Turkey" Mike Donlin was a rough, tough veteran and one of John McGraw's (and New York's) favorite players, a former Oriole who'd led the Giants to a pennant in 1905, become a vaudeville star, married actress Mabel Hite (his stage partner), and in time become known—in the words of *Vanity Fair*—as "Broadway Mike Donlin, the Beau Brummel of Baseball." He was traded to the Braves two weeks after this piece, which is 1911 Runyon at his most flamboyant:

> Viva la Mique Donlin, anyway!
> Mique pecked a home run into the rightfield bleachers yesterday afternoon after Griffith's Cuban Stouts had built up the foundation and superstructure of an 8 to 2 score, the said home run keeping it from being 8 to 1. [Clark Griffith, manager of the Reds, employed a Cuban pinch hitter named Armando Marsans.]

The Runyon *bizarro* phase was at its most intense three days later, when the Cardinals came to the Polo Grounds. Damon's lead was an absolute non sequitur: "Toledo is in Ohio, a statement which may be immediately verified by reference to any well-ordered map, railway guide, or automobile prospectus."

Later in his story Damon precariously connects the Toledo background of St. Louis catcher-manager Roger Bresnahan with the politics of that city, the local electric light system, and, incidentally, the results of the baseball game. (The game itself is summarily disposed of in Damon's *second* sentence: "The score yesterday afternoon was 4 to 2 in favor of the Giants." Then: "It is a large and thriving mid-western city . . .") The "Toledo" piece would certainly have pleased Hans Arp, the founder of Dada. The fact that to the sports readers of the *American* such stories were not only intelligible but delightful speaks well for the sophistication of the baseball audience of that time.

The following afternoon Damon stayed on the case of former Giant Bresnahan. The Giants had won again, on a Marquard shutout, but only far down in the body of the story did Runyon reveal that fact. His lead paragraph is a cartoonlike assault on the Cardinal catcher-manager: "As for you, Roger Bresnahan, with your oily voice and city ways—take that! Zam! Pow! (Noise of villain falling off the front stoop, bleeding from the nose.)" In such pieces Runyon was clearly capitalizing on the familiarity of his audience with his subject. Roger Bresnahan's "oily voice," as Damon's readers were well aware, had been the subject of censure by league president Lynch, who shortly after opening day had warned the St. Louis backstop to "stop abusing batsmen . . . with the constant

The World of Damon Runyon

use of profane and indecent language on the field." Runyon's "inside" humor captured these baseball fanatics in the first line, though undoubtedly it would have eluded an Oxford don completely.

Damon grew more and more daring, took greater and greater leaps, and his readers somehow hung on. The *American*'s circulation grew with each Giant victory and Runyon "stunt." On his hands and knees on the floor of his suite in the Clarendon on Riverside Drive, Old Man Hearst drew large black circles around Damon's pieces with his blunt copy pencil and instructed his subeditors to inspect them with care. "This young man, whoever he is, seems to be making us money," he scribbled on the margin of the page. "Read what he writes!" (Damon was to remain a Hearst favorite throughout his career, and in later years as a columnist he would display with pride a memorandum from San Simeon instructing all editors to "Run Runyon Daily No Cuts No Matter What Serious Pieces You Have To Omit.")

By the end of July Damon was pulling out all the stops, writing daily baseball pieces as colorful and individualistic as anything that had been done in the medium. He (and his editors) found that *American* readers were willing to go along on his experimental prose excursions no matter how bizarre, obscure, or dilatory they became—information that was the source of some shock for the editors and no doubt considerable pleasure for Damon. It was now conceded by those in the know that the reason for Runyon's instant success was his ability to play on his readers' expertise; instead of feeding them the statistical pap they could (and did) get elsewhere, he teased their minds, tested their knowledge, challenged their curiosity. He wrote "up" to the baseball audience, and it worked.

His method, of course, required considerable homework, since he had to keep up with the players and teams as closely as possible in order to attain the confident and nonchalant command of the sport his stories displayed. When the Giants went on a long tour of the Midwest at the end of July, Damon stayed behind a few days to cover Yankee games at Hilltop Park, and it was apparent immediately that he was a great deal less familiar with the Yankees and the American League than with the National and the Giants. He poked fun at his own ignorance in his story of July 28. Here his "angle" was the visit to Hilltop Park of "J. Krum," a citizen of Golden, Colorado, and a party of friends. The Westerners, self-assured "boobs" bewildered by the big city (as Al Runyon himself had been until an embarrassingly recent date), attend a two o'clock pregame exhibition between two playground teams in the belief that it is the Yankees and the Browns they are watching. The joke of the piece is in the Colorado tourists' ignorance

The 1911 Season and a Baseball Marriage

of the four o'clock New York starting time for ballgames. Damon's gentle self-mockery appears between the lines of this satire of provincialism, as Ring Lardner's was doing in similar vernacular pieces for Hearst's Boston *American* this same season.

Damon got a small raise on the first of August. He bought a new black suit, elegant and somber to match his self-conception, and caught a New York Central train going West. He had to catch up with the Giants.

No sooner had Damon rejoined the club in Pittsburgh than they dropped three straight to Fred Clarke's Pirates. The Smoke City club had a hot hitter in Owen Wilson, a big outfielder who that year tied Chicago's Frank Schulte for the league RBI championship. Wilson and Honus Wagner hit Mathewson and Rube Marquard hard, and after the third loss McGraw's boys were happy just to climb into their Pullman and get out of town. McGraw, though, was not so happy. With the club on the skids he was in an ornery mood, and the writers gave him a wide passage on the way through Pennsylvania.

Damon and the other scribes sat grimly with the players in the smoking car, trying to keep interested in their card games and adventure magazines while the sweat dripped from their noses. Minor arguments erupted every few minutes. Nobody was in a joking mood, and when one player ribbed another over a misplayed poker hand, cards were thrown down and threats exchanged. Big-shouldered Chief Meyers got between the combatants before a blow was struck, but that ended the card games for the night.

Even Mathewson looked tense that night in the smoker. He confided to Damon and one or two other writers that he feared some of the younger boys might be "choking." Larry Doyle, who was sitting nearby reading a magazine, overheard the great pitcher's words.

"Matty," the second baseman said, "that is just a load of what dropped out of the other end of Farmer Brown's bull, and you know it." Laughing Larry, the team captain and no young man to be called a choker, glared at the pitcher.

"I wasn't speaking of you, Larry," Christy said. "What I said wasn't meant for you."

"I think," Damon said, "it would be a good idea to get a bridge game going."

"Good idea," Sid Mercer said.

"I was just going to turn in," Matty said. He got up and walked down the swaying corridor.

Laughing Larry grumbled something inaudible and went back to his adventure magazine, leaving the writers to their windows.

The World of Damon Runyon

Outside the invisible cornfields of Indiana flew past like a river of oblivion. Damon lit a cigarette and stared out into the great Midwestern night, wishing he had a cup of coffee.

The next afternoon in Chicago the Giants took gas again. Wild-fire Schulte of the Cubs busted a long double off Doc Crandall in the last of the eighth, but that blow was only the rude finishing touch to a messy contest that had been marred for McGraw by several Giants' misplays. The area around the visiting clubhouse at the West Side Grounds on Polk Street was a dour place after-ward. The writers were not told what Mac had said, but from the ears-pinned-back looks the players carried out of the clubhouse it was evident a tongue-lashing had taken place. None of the ath-letes wanted to talk or play cards that evening. They ate alone or in small groups and told the reporters to go soak their heads. It was what would now be called an uptight ball club.

At the hotel Mac spoke to the writers who were hanging around the lobby. He was in a subdued mood, having talked himself out after the game. The conversation naturally got around to remedies for the club's current nosedive. One veteran writer said something about how Wilbert Robinson ("Uncle Robby," McGraw's old Oriole teammate) used to be a great man to have around a club when it was going bad. McGraw laughed. He and Robby had been pals for twenty years, and even in retirement Robinson often visited the Giants' training camps.

"*There* was a fellow who knew how to relax a bunch of boys, all right," the manager said.

The old writer laughed too and told several stories about the mornings he'd been awakened in hotel rooms by the sight of Uncle Robby in a nightshirt, standing in the doorway with a shaker of homemade rum toddies . . .

"Yes," McGraw said, interrupting the veteran with a smile, "al-though I am not so sure that is the kind of relaxing I meant."

"Robby could pick a club up," the writer mused, no doubt con-tinuing to review the old days in his mind.

"Aye," McGraw said thoughtfully. Then he spoke more softly. "The fellow we need right now is old Robby, all right." He looked around at the rest of the writers, who were listening with interest. "Say, why don't you boys fix up a telegram to Robby? Tell him we could use him."

McGraw's impulsive decision to hire his old Oriole teammate as a coach was typical of his genius, Damon later felt. Such flashes of instinct, or whatever they were, dictated most of Little Napole-on's managerial moves. Runyon cheerfully pitched in with the other scribes, and within minutes a telegram to Wilbert Robinson had been composed and sent.

The 1911 Season and a Baseball Marriage

COME ON FIRST TRAIN AND BE IN FOR THE BIG FINISH. TEAM IS ABOUT TO
GO TO PIECES THROUGH WORRY. COME ALONG AND HELP STRAIGHTEN OUT
THEIR NERVES. THEY WON'T EVEN PLAY POKER. MC GRAW.

The Giants were belted around again by Frank Chance's
club on the following day, making it five losses in a row for the
road trip, but that evening Wilbert Robinson hit town on a train
from the East. The portly Uncle Robby had a brief conference
with McGraw and then went to work. The manager had told him
that Chief Meyers, the sturdy young Indian, had been having his
problems behind the plate and at bat. Robinson located the Chief
in the lobby, bought him a brandy, and had a long talk with him
about catching, hitting, and life. Then he looked up Rube Marquard, who was scheduled to pitch the next day against the Cubs.
Robby took the twenty-one-year-old southpaw out to a North Side
beer bar, then to a vaudeville show.

In the morning Robinson got together with first baseman Fred
Merkle and centerfielder Fred Snodgrass, two slumping regulars,
and organized a pool tournament at a billiards academy near the
hotel. Then he and Merkle and Snodgrass went out shopping for
some fashionable new duds on Michigan Avenue.

That afternoon Merkle, Snodgrass, and Meyers had RBIs, and
so did seven or eight other Giants. Marquard toyed with the Cubs.
New York won the game by a dozen runs, and the Giants were
back on the track. Mac's inspired decision to call for Uncle Robby
had saved the season. (McGraw's memory of the occasion, however, was insufficient to prevent him from firing Robby in a snit
after a petty dispute during a World Series two years later.)

The Giants went on to St. Louis, where they pounded lumps
on oily-voiced Roger Bresnahan and his Cardinals for three days
running. It was clear to Damon and everybody else that Wilbert
Robinson's arrival had loosened up the ball club and put the players again within reach of a pennant.

Playing great ball throughout August and September, the Giants coasted in, a country mile in front of the Cubs and Pirates.
On the last day of the season McGraw let Charley Faust loose
on the pitching mound for an inning or two in a "laugher" being
won by the Brooklyn club. Crazy Charley, in his first chance to
pitch in a game, did handsomely as the Brooklyn players joined
in the fun and enacted dramatic intentional outs. When Victory
came to bat, they pitched him a slow ball that nicked his jersey.
Awarded first, Faust "stole" his way around the bases and home,
as the Brooklyns deliberately muffed throws, missed catches, and
tripped over their own feet in exaggerated pratfalls. It was all
in the spirit of fun, and Brooklyn won the game easily; in those
days there was room for this kind of humor in the sport, at least

when a particular contest didn't count in the standings. Naturally Damon got a story out of it. Victory Faust, like Bugs Raymond, was an interesting character even if he was no ballplayer.

The unfortunate Bugs had pitched his last inning for the Giants or anybody else. At the age of twenty-nine he was involuntarily "retired" from baseball. Who wanted a drunken spitball pitcher who couldn't be trusted to show up at the ballpark? In 1911 Bugs had appeared in 17 games, starting 9 and completing 4. He won 6, lost 4, had an ERA of 3.30. Altogether he had won 44 big league ballgames. Those were to be his last statistics, except for the date September 7, 1912, on which Raymond died in a cheap hotel room in Chicago, the city of his birth. His two children had preceded him to the cemetery by a few months. The whereabouts of his wife wasn't publicized at the time.

The incident that caused Bugs' death occurred, ironically, on the same sandlot ball field where he had pitched as a youngster. Despondent over the recent deaths in his family, Bugs had taken a drop or two at a neighborhood bar and on his way home stopped to watch a ballgame. In a dispute with a fellow bystander he was badly beaten, receiving a fractured skull. He died six days later of a cerebral hemorrhage.

Damon had ridden a sick horse in Bugs Raymond, who'd given him material for a dozen fine and funny stories. No doubt beneath the humor he sensed an affinity of spirit with the alcoholic pitcher. Even though Damon was now officially on the wagon, he couldn't help recognizing in Bugs' antics the self-destructive alcoholism with which he himself continued to struggle. But observations at this level, if he made them, were kept out of Damon's writing at this stage of his career. If he perceived Bugs' personal tragedy, the perception did not make its way into the rough and funny Bugs Raymond legend the Runyon stories had created. Damon's aim then and later was to entertain. It would take him years of work as a writer before he would also be able to contain within the hard, ironic frame of his "humorous" prose something of the more painful side of his vision of life.

The first of the two dozen or so World Series Damon would cover for Hearst opened in the Polo Grounds on October 14, 1911, with space in the press box at a premium (fifty telegraphers were on the job, relaying the play-by-play to papers in cities as remote as Los Angeles and Havana). Christy Mathewson, on the mound for the Giants against the Philadelphia A's, was, like his teammates, dressed all in black. The superstitious McGraw had ordered the same black broadcloth uniforms his team had worn in their 1905 World Series victory over Connie Mack's A's. And in the opener at least this seemed an inspired stroke, as Matty, pitching

The 1911 Season and a Baseball Marriage

great "pressure" baseball, stopped the A's, 2–1. His battery mate Chief Meyers raced home with the winning run after doubling in the seventh. This was the typical, close-to-the-vest, "inside" ball McGraw loved. It appeared to Damon and the nearly 40,000 Giants fans who left the park smiling that only a week of ballgames now stood between their club and a world championship.

Two days later at Shibe Park in Philadelphia, and again the following day at the Polo Grounds, it was still "inside" ball, but of a kind preferred by Connie Mack. Frank Baker, Mack's third baseman, broke up pitching duels in both games with late-inning homers, one off Marquard and one off Matty, that won him the nickname "Home Run" Baker and put Philadelphia ahead to stay in the Series. Damon's reports, appearing on the front page of the *American*, were painful postscripts on sad happenings as far as Giant rooters were concerned. They were in no mood for humor, and Damon wisely did not try to give it to them. His funereal game accounts, considerably more conventional and straightforward than his lighthearted midseason pieces, were punctuated at intervals by drawings of cartoon characters representing the A's and Giants' team logos. The small white Philadelphia "Joys" and black New York "Glooms," drawn by the *American*'s gifted cartoonist Thomas Powers, pursued each other in, around, and through the newsprint columns of Damon's stories, the "Joys" getting the best of it.

Game Four of the Series was scheduled for October 19 in Philadelphia, but it began raining on the 18th as the Giants' traveling party rode south on the Pennsy. While the train "splashed juicily over the Jersey paddyfields" Damon took notes on his fellow scribes' activities. One stout writer proposed that he could invariably tell a stranger's home town from his looks, and another bet him a satchel of wine that this was but an idle boast.

> The wager was laid. Together they started on a tour of the train to make the test of the stout man's observational powers.
> They came upon a man in the chair car who was slumped far down in his seat; a pallid, dejected-looking man, whose eyes were expressive of deep woe.
> "Ah," said the stout man triumphantly. "Ah. Here is a New Yorker."
> The dejected looking man sat upright, indignant.
> "No sir," he denied, "not me. I'm from Dadeville, Alabama. I've been sick."

The rain in Philly lasted six days. During the downpour Damon drank coffee, smoked cigarettes, and paced hotel lobbies, combing the crowds of beached baseballers for a new angle on a story; after the first few days they were harder to come by. Once he'd worked over the lobby of the Majestic, the hotel where he and the Giants were staying, Damon splashed over to the press

The World of Damon Runyon

hangout at the Bellevue-Stratford, where he discovered fresh news items to be a scarcer commodity than four-leaf clovers. One day the Runyon dispatch to the *American* told how a hotel-bound scribe had opened the window of his room and sent out a dove of inquiry; the dove, Damon said, had come back in galoshes, carrying an umbrella.

Some of the other writers were less conscientious than Damon in pursuing story angles and enjoyed themselves more. Wild Bill Phelan, the heroic Ohioan, and Chicago's fun-loving Hughey Fullerton conspired to establish a "modeling agency" in a hotel room they rented. They put an ad in the *Inquirer* along about the second day of rain, and a day later their "office" was stormed with hopeful applicants. The elated scribes, hard put to believe the instant success of their venture, were kept busy for several days "measuring" the applicants and promising further interviews. By the time the commissioner of baseball finally declared the Series would go on, rain or no, and Bill and Hughey had to dissolve their corporation and return to work, they had "processed" dozens of comely applicants.

On October 24, the last drizzle conveniently ceased, Shibe Park was jammed to the rafters. The only modeling done that day was performed by the Giants and Mathewson, who were required to spend much of the pregame warmup period posing for pictures for the newspapers. ("Who am I working for, the Giants or the photographers?" Mathewson was heard to bark at one point.) For Lloyd Lewis, then a collegian in the Philadelphia area, it was a day to cut classes and worship the lords of ball. Newspaperman Lewis in a later memoir described his awe at first sight of the visiting heroes.

> I knew them from their pictures as, clad in dangerous black, they came strutting across toward their dugout . . . Muggsy was first—stocky, hard-eyed. Behind him came slim, handsome Snodgrass, striding as became a genius at getting hit by pitched balls and in scaring infielders with his flashing spikes. Then came swart, ominous Larry Doyle; lantern-jawed Art Fletcher; Buck Herzog, whose nose curved like a scimitar; lithe little Josh Devore; burly Otis Crandall; flat-faced, mahogany-colored Chief Meyers, the full-blooded Indian; Fred Merkle, all muscles even in his jaws, a lion-heart living down the most aweful bonehead blunder ever made in baseball . . . Then came Marquard, 6 feet 3, his sharp face and slitlike eyes smiling—his head tilting to the left at the top of a long wry neck . . . and then suddenly, there [Mathewson] was, warming up . . . He held his head high, and his eye with slow, lordly contempt swept the Athletics as they warmed up across the field. He was 31, all bone and muscle and princely poise . . .

Baker and the A's banged Matty around as rudely as the cartoon Joys were banging the Glooms, taking a 3–1 lead in games. A day later, when the teams returned to New York, the Giants

The 1911 Season and a Baseball Marriage

retained a precarious life in the Series with a dramatic come-from-behind ninth-inning victory that induced a ten-minute demonstration by the frustrated Polo Grounds crowd. Silenced since the first game, the Giant rooters now erupted in a sustained show of feeling that, Fred Lieb said, "could be heard all over upper Harlem and the lower Bronx." Damon and the others in the press box were showered with straw hats, peanuts, sausages, scorecards, beer, and even money as the fans behind them threw into the air whatever was in their hands and applauded wildly.

But this noisy throb of emotion by the Polo Grounds crowd proved to be New York's last gasp. Within twenty-four hours the A's had given Marquard another rough going-over at Shibe Park and taken the world title in a 13–2 rout. Damon's story of the humiliation was removed by his editors from the front page to the inside of the *American* (civic pride, after all, was touchy). In it he declared that words to describe the final game of the Series were not to be found "in all the bright lexicon of Noah Webster."

What was the point of trying to soft-soap an embarrassing loss? None, as far as our reporter could see. "A searching finger slides past 'massacre' and 'slaughter' as too sedate and conservative to fill the case," Damon wrote that final afternoon in the press box at Shibe Park. He tapped out the rest of his piece, chain smoking as he worked, and when he had finished he yanked the last piece of soft copy paper out of his typewriter and handed it to his teletypist; then he stood, stretched, and left the park to find a taxi to take him to the station.

His first baseball season was over, and he found as he rode through the Philadelphia traffic that he had no particular feelings about the outcome. The loss of the Series had been the Giants' and McGraw's, not Damon Runyon's. He had done *his* job, from spring training to the end, and looking back he could say he had done just fine. There was no 1911 World Series defeat for Damon. Later, perhaps, when he had experienced more of life's peaks and valleys himself, the emotional ups and downs of the athletes he wrote about would affect him more. Now he felt that he was alone, apart from the joys and sorrows of the teams, as a writer should be. One had to maintain a distance or the McGraws and Mattys and Bugs Raymonds would become too large to be seen in perspective.

"To be a great sportswriter," Runyon wrote in a "Postscript on Sports Writing" over thirty years later, "a man must hold himself pretty much aloof from the characters of the games." Chances are it was just such an injunction Damon used on himself during that long train ride home from Philly.

* * *

The World of Damon Runyon

In 1912 and in later seasons, Damon was allowed to pick his baseball assignments from among the home games of the Giants, Yankees, and Dodgers, traveling with the teams only for key series. Similarly, he picked his own football assignments in the fall. Baseball continued to be Damon's main beat through the early twenties, but as the years went by his reportorial skills made him more and more valuable to Hearst and Brisbane as a house "policy man" on such assignments as the 1916 U.S. Army pursuit of Pancho Villa in Northern Mexico, the battle of the Argonne and the Occupation in 1918–1919, and political conventions and major trials (like the 1912 Becker-Rosenthal murder trial, which introduced him to the vocabulary and mores of the New York underworld). Even so he went to spring training and the World Series every year and covered five or six dozen ballgames every summer, all the way into the early thirties.

Both of Damon's children—Mary on August 24, 1914, and Damon Jr. on June 17, 1918—were born at home while their father was reporting baseball games at the Polo Grounds. Baseball was indeed responsible to a large degree for Runyon's absence from the family home during the early years of his marriage, and as time went by and he ceased to travel the baseball beat exclusively, the absences grew more prolonged. Either he was overseas, or at a football game or political convention in the Midwest, or off in Long Island, Maryland, or Pennsylvania on one of his frequent hunting trips. (The aftermath of the latter especially annoyed Ellen Egan Runyon, who was not at all interested in *looking* at a kitchen full of bloody dead birds, much less cleaning and serving them for her husband.) The male company of the press box and the hunting lodge obviously appealed to Damon more than did domestic life, increasingly during the period following World War I (in which he served briefly as a correspondent), and indefinitely thereafter.

At home, of course, was the gentle Ellen, who was turning out to have a surprising personality of her own. In the long hours left to her by her husband's constant absences she began seeing fortunetellers, swamis, card readers, crystal ball gazers, and palmists; she wanted to know how long it was going to take the Runyons to become millionaires, and she was growing impatient with the replies she was getting. With her rich friends from Denver, some of whom were now in New York, she could at least act out the role of the aristocratic lady in which she cast herself in her mind. With Alfred (as she continued to call her husband, and Mr. Hearst be damned!) this was much more difficult, for Alfred was ever the realist.

In her son's words, Ellen Egan Runyon was a natural but frustrated actress who "compensated by being on stage in everyday

The 1911 Season and a Baseball Marriage

Runyon in the Polo Grounds' press box at the 1924 Giants–Senators World Series.

life." In Ellen's play the Runyons were swells. She had definite ideas about elevating her life with Alfred to the social status she desired, which was that of the Astors and Vanderbilts. To this end she was, again in her son's term, forever trying to "polish" her husband by such means as grand pianos, tuxedos, table manners, and dancing lessons. For Damon, who was developing ideas of his own on the subject of manners, Ellen's affectations (as he considered them to be) were sheer torture. He was equally fond of her extravagance. The young Mrs. Runyon's daily shopping trips to Fifth Avenue usually included covert peeks into the windows of elegant brownstones (to glimpse, if she could, a style of life she envied) as well as lavish, impulsive purchases of perfumes, shoes, and gloves.

Between the births of Mary and Damon Jr. the family breadwinner grew less and less comfortable with the life at home (which in those years meant a series of modest Upper West Side flats) and began to spend more and more time in the company of his Broadway and newspaper cronies—who, after all, did not expect a man to be something he was not. Damon's feelings for Ellen were summed up in a remark to Bugs Baer: "Give a woman a couple of kids and she'll let you alone."

At the office, with his *American* mates like Baer and Tad Dorgan and Gene Fowler, Damon was known for his straightfaced sense of humor; to his son, who saw him only at home, he usually just looked "angry." The strict regimen of the Runyon household

The World of Damon Runyon

Sports columnists Bugs Baer and Damon Runyon in the William Street offices of the New York *American.*

revolved around Damon's unusual habits. He seldom arrived home much before dawn and did not rise before noon, as a result of which mornings were a time of cautious silence in the Runyon home. When Damon awoke he began his day with his children, conversing or dispensing lectures, after which he consumed an hour over breakfast, coffee, and the newspapers, another in the bathroom, and a third in selecting and donning his outfit for the day. And then he was gone—to a ballgame, a horse race, a gymnasium, anywhere!

"The kids are your job," Damon told Ellen. Despite his angry looks and sullen moods, he was a softhearted parent. He left all discipline to Ellen, who swung a mean hairbrush. When Mary was an infant, Damon wheeled her along Riverside Drive in a fancy baby carriage, and as she grew older he treated her with exaggerated deference—"in the grand manner reserved for ladies," Damon Jr. said. Damon Jr. himself was treated to endless fascinating stories, as his father before him had been by *his* old man. (So fantastic were many of Damon's tales, particularly those of soldiering and the Wild West, that his son simply didn't believe them. "I thought he was telling a lot of stretchers to be amusing," Damon Jr. said later.) Although he did not have much time for them, and did not take Damon Jr. along on his hunting trips or interfere in Ellen's harsh punishments of Mary (who was frequently "bad"), Damon loved his children, and when he could

The 1911 Season and a Baseball Marriage

afford it he attempted to make up for his deficiencies as a father with abundant gifts. Among his Christmas presents to his son during the early twenties, for example, were two huge electric trains, scale model motorboats and sailboats big enough to carry human cargo, and an electric 16mm. movie projector; but such fabulous gifts only left the boy silent, stunned by their "immensity," and Damon in turn took that for disappointment.

These were delicate straits, the Runyon family holidays, for they only increased the growing distance that children and parents mutually felt. Damon's expensive Christmas gifts were a poor surrogate for feelings that went unexpressed. "Many a rich kid has no doubt had the same experience," Damon Jr. wrote years later; "[a] poor kid may be better off, even if he doesn't realize it, with his ten-penny toy, provided he has parents with a wealth of good feeling." This the boy did not have, at any time in his life. After Mary's infancy, Damon's heart had for complex reasons turned away from his wife and family. A man as emotionally guarded as any who ever lived, he did not leave us evidence on the subject beyond the fact of his turning away.

6

Of Baseball Graft, Napkin Technique, Shoeless Joe Jackson, and The Brain: Damon Runyon at the 1919 World Series

The napkin in the lap has its staunch adherents. They are mostly skinny persons. However, we think that even they will concede the superiority of the napkin in the collar when they are advised of the origin of the napkin in the lap as explained by William Moffit. Mr. Moffit states that the napkin in the lap was born of skullduggery. He says it goes back to a most corrupt era in England in the 18th century, when Walpole was Prime Minister.

It seems that Walpole used to like to pass a little money around among his deserving political followers, especially those in the social set. He would give big dinners and the guests would find theirs in the folded napkins. It was much more genteel than just taking them into the powder room or up an alleyway and handing it to them in an envelope.

Before Walpole introduced this classy method of taking care of the boys, the napkin in the collar was the vogue. But naturally a guest at a Walpole dinner soon got leery of shaking out his napkin preparatory to unfurling it 'neath his second chin, lest he inadvertently strike a lady across the table in the eye with a flying pound sterling.

That would have caused gossip. The guests soon learned to drop the napkins unfolded in their laps and to transfer the packet to the pocket from there. As they were the hot men of society in those days the rabble got the idea that this was the proper place to wear the napkin, and thus the napkin in the lap became a custom which endures to this day in many circles.

—"Napkin Technique"

Runyon, writing from a distance of twenty-one years, was warming up to reminisce upon the infamous Black Sox Scandal of 1919.

To understand what happened in the 1919 Series one has to go back and look at the economics of baseball in the days immediately following World War I, particularly as applied to the Chicago White Sox.

In our day Joe Morgan's paycheck is comparable to that of the chairman of the board of du Pont, Steve Garvey's to that of the chairman of the Bank of America; the earnings of the Yankee starting lineup rival those of the nine highest paid officers at, say, Xerox. But in 1919 ballplayers' salaries resembled railway brakemen's or shipping clerks' earnings more closely than those of executives or tycoons. Even top stars were paid relatively little, considering the large crowds that were already attending games in the many new stadiums. And the lightest payroll of all belonged to the Old Roman, Charles Comiskey, whose Chicago White Sox just happened to be the best team in baseball.

The labors of a top Hearst reporter were certainly better rewarded than those of any of the Old Roman's players. Only second baseman Eddie Collins—a veteran whose $14,000 was a carryover from his days in Philadelphia, where he'd been the kingpin of Connie Mack's "Million Dollar Infield" before Connie peddled him to Comiskey—was making over $6500. Shoeless Joe Jackson, the illiterate cotton mill hand from whom Babe Ruth had copied his swing ("His is the perfectest," the Babe explained), made that. Dandy little Eddie Cicotte, a 29-game winner in 1919, made $6000. Buck Weaver, the finest third baseman in the league (and at least the equal of Pittsburgh's Traynor), 23-game-winner Claude Williams, centerfielder Oscar "Happy" Felsch, and first baseman "Chick" Gandil each made $4500 or less. Shortstop Swede Risberg and utility man Fred McMullin were in the $2500 range, as were most of the rest of the Old Roman's worthies.

In baseball Comiskey's parsimony—not unlike that exhibited in a later era by Charles O. Finley—was legend; the tight purse tactics of Comiskey led to the 1919 scandal as directly as Finley's led to the great free agent scramble of the seventies. (In the present labor-management situation, a Shoeless Joe could have squawked for his freedom, asked for five million bucks, and watched the Autreys and Steinbrenners fight to be first in line.) And with Comiskey, as later with Finley, the habit of pennypinching survived even the loss of his top-dollar stars. After the 1919 affair—over which the Old Roman expressed great grief and shock—he remained the stingiest boss in the major leagues. A case in point is the story of Dickey Kerr, the most noteworthy of the "honest" members of the Black Sox. Dickey won two of the three games the Sox *didn't* blow in that waltz they called a Series and forty more American League contests over the next two seasons—and even then he couldn't coax a raise out of Comiskey. The Old Roman refused to pay Dickey one cent more than the $4500 he'd paid him in 1919. Kerr left the big leagues to play semipro ball for

"The Old Roman," Charles Comiskey.

$5000 a season, was suspended by Comiskey, and ended a too-brief career in the big leagues at the age of twenty-eight. Dickey was no Catfish Hunter, but he deserved a better shake.

During the 1919 season a group of unhappy White Sox players appealed to manager Kid Gleason to intercede with Comiskey about their salary requests. The sympathetic Gleason put in his two cents, and Commy roared no! The Sox grumbled and made long faces in their humble clubhouse but continued to win; they clinched the pennant with ease. On their last Eastern swing, Ed Cicotte and Chick Gandil went looking for a gambler. They had a plan in mind. Hal Chase, a ballplayer pal, put them in touch with a betting man from Boston named Sport Sullivan. Cicotte laid his plan on the line for Sullivan. The pitcher explained that he wanted $100,000 in cash to pay off ten ballplayers to blow the Series. Sullivan told them he'd try the idea out on Arnold Rothstein, the big money man of New York City.

Gandil and Cicotte figured the deal was set and enlisted their teammates. But when the players were ready, Sullivan didn't call and Cicotte couldn't reach him by phone. In New York Cicotte talked again to Hal Chase ("Prince Hal" was the nifty-fielding and shady-dealing first baseman who'd been playing with the Giants in 1919). Chase, a man with connections, put the Sox in touch with another gambler, Bill Burns. "Sleepy Bill" was a rangy Texan who'd pitched for the Senators, Phils, Reds, Cubs, White Sox, and Tigers (1908–1912), later made a bundle in oil speculation, and became a noted plunger. Like Sullivan, Burns claimed he couldn't raise the hundred himself and brought up Rothstein's name. See what you can do, Cicotte said.

"With me, it's brains—that's all," Arnold Rothstein liked to say. His pal Damon Runyon called him The Brain, a nickname Rothstein loved. He was the highest roller of his time, crowned "King of the Gamblers" by the tabloids. He employed "boys" like Legs Diamond and Dutch Schultz and had at least a small piece of any type of action you could name.

Burns, who didn't know Rothstein personally, sent an ex-pug, journeyman ballplayer, and small roller named Billy Maharg (out of Philly) to talk things over with the big man. Maharg consulted gamblers in Philly who referred him to Rothstein. At an appointment in the Astor the New York bankroller listened to Maharg's message with interest, expressed doubts, and declined to contribute the required capital. (Some say Sleepy Bill Burns also approached Rothstein personally, the same day, at Jamaica racetrack. If so, Burns undoubtedly got the same answer his messenger had.)

Rothstein had already heard of the proposition from the ballplayers' first emissary, Sport Sullivan. With Sullivan Rothstein had also been skeptical. "I don't want any part of it, it's too raw," he had said. "Besides, you can't get away with it. You might be able to fix a game, but not the Series. You'd get lynched if it ever came out."

Even though he'd turned it down, The Brain had been fascinated by Sullivan's proposal. The extravagant and fantastic appealed to him, especially extravagant and fantastic amounts of money, such as he sensed could be made off a "fixed" Series. Therefore, after his encounter with Maharg and Burns, he made up his mind to keep an eye on the deal. No doubt it occurred to him that by simply stringing these minor operators along, he could look on in safety while they set up an arrangement that might in the long run benefit him greatly without costing him a shilling (or no more than a few at worst). He got in touch with a sporting friend, Abe Attell.

Attell already knew the deal was in the works. He'd heard about it from Hal Chase; in fact he'd helped Chase put the players in touch with Sport Sullivan in the first place. Abe got around.

Abe Attell was an ex-fighter (world featherweight champ from 1908 to 1912) who could always be found around and about in the betting world. At Rothstein's request Abe agreed to establish connections with Burns and Maharg for the gambling king. Attell would be Rothstein's link for reconnaissance—plus whatever else might come up.

The dapper Abe approached Burns, who knew him well enough and was perfectly happy to talk turkey with a man he recognized as Rothstein's representative. Burns ran through the deal again for Attell, adding that he was sure the whole thing only needed about $10,000 worth of cement in the form of advances to the ballplayers.

Attell reported the news to Rothstein, who in turn spoke with his casino partner, Nat Evans—a man he could trust. Evans agreed the matter was risky but worth keeping track of. To men like Rothstein and Evans, a green paper portrait of James Madison was no more than a subway token might have been to an ordinary fellow. Attell was summoned and informed that the down payment would be taken care of.

Attell contacted Burns, and Burns wired Billy Maharg, the Philly puncher, who was by now back home: ARNOLD R. HAS GONE THROUGH WITH EVERYTHING. GOT EIGHT IN. LEAVING FOR CINCINNATI.

The "eight" were White Sox players, notables all, Comiskey's nonpareils of the West, the glories of their times.

Burns, Maharg, and Attell were in Cincinnati the next day, the Series only a couple of days off. Attell had holed up at the Hotel Sinton with a crowd of some two dozen of Rothstein's "boys." The boys stood in the lobby with cash in their fists and tried to buy as much action (at 5–3 on the Reds) as they could. Grantland Rice's Alabama pal "Champ" Pickens listened to the gamblers' pitch, then went upstairs and flung his tickets for the first game on the bed, exclaiming angrily, "This Series is fixed—I'm going to the race track!" Damon Runyon, who was staying at the Metropolis, had to plow his way through a mob of swarthy fellows with foliage in their hands every time he passed between the stairs and the cab stand. It was the same at the Gibson and at the other

Damon Runyon at the 1919 World Series

Abe Attell

big hotels in town. Very little of the lobby traffic was local.

On the eve of the Series, Rothstein's partner Nat Evans went to Cincinnati, met with Burns and some of the Chicago players, and was convinced the fix was on. He phoned Rothstein and said as much, predicting the Series would be thrown whether further payments were made or not. "They're in so deep, they've got to go along now even if it doesn't make them a dime," Nat told Rothstein.

But Rothstein waited until a few hours before the first game to make his plunge, and even then he bet only a moderate sum on the Reds while picking up a few side wagers on Chicago that would serve as insurance in case of a double cross. He bet lightly (for him) and hedged his bets. His ultimate decision was to play the Reds on a game-to-game basis. In the end, using this method, he won three or four hundred thousand—nothing like the millions he could have won with a large plunge on the entire Series. His caution cost him plenty, but later he could cite his bets as proof of "innocence."

A year later, Arnold Rothstein told a grand jury that Abe Attell did the fixing, using his (Rothstein's) name. "I wasn't in on it," Rothstein told the jury. The jury indicted Attell, Sullivan, a book-keeper of Rothstein's, and eight players. The Brain escaped indictment.

As Jay Gatsby said of Arnold Rothstein ("Meyer Wolf-sheim") in *The Great Gatsby,* "They can't get him, old sport. He's a smart man."

> The Brain's right name is Armand Rosenthal, and he is called The Brain because he is so smart. He is well known to one and all in this town as a very large operator in gambling, and one thing and another, and nobody knows how much dough The Brain has, except that he must have plenty, because no matter how much dough is around, The Brain sooner or later gets hold of all of it.
> —"A Very Honorable Guy"

On the morning of the first game of the Series Billy Maharg and Sleepy Bill Burns approached Abe Attell and asked for the hundred G's to turn over to the players. It was not forthcoming. The boys needed all the cash on hand to place bets, Attell said. Instead, he told Maharg and Burns, the Chicago players would be handed $20,000 after each game they managed to lose. (It was to be a best-of-nine game series.) Maharg and Burns relayed this arrangement to the players, who agreed.

Everybody in Attell's crew bet heavily on the Reds the first day and won a bundle. The following morning the Ohio Valley air was like the inside of a boiler, but it did not match the betting action around town for heat. Maharg and Burns arrived at Attell's hotel suite early. The floor, beds, tables, chairs, and dressers were covered with stacks of cash. Attell and his boys had been up all night counting. A plug-in fan with slow, fat little blades pushed hot air at Abe, whose open collar lacked its usual look of freshness. The former champ was perspiring heavily under the weight of the lapful of bills he was counting. His rolled sleeves revealed the powerful forearms that had made him (in Damon Runyon's oft-quoted opinion) "one of the five great fighters of all time." He had been out of the ring only four years and had the looks of a man who hadn't slowed down at all. He gave the visitors a nonde-script glance of greeting while his fingers went on riffling the bills.

Sleepy Bill Burns asked him politely for the players' share.

"Don't bother me now," Abe said. "I need all the dough I can lay my hands on. We got to make a cleanup tomorrow. It takes capital, partner." He looked back down at his counting.

Burns and Maharg exchanged doubtful looks. Burns cleared his throat. Billy Maharg shuffled his feet. The players, Burns said, were getting kind of worried.

"What *they* got to worry about?" Abe asked without looking up.

"They was promised twenty grand at the end of each game."

"You go on," the chunky little Attell shot back, "and tell 'em not to burn."

"Then when does the ghost walk?" Burns pressed. His neck was wet.

"Tomorrow," Abe said absently. "Now beat it. I got money to count."

Abe's boys, who'd been listening, looked up and grinned at Burns and Maharg, then went on counting in low whispers. It sounded like church, Burns thought.

When they got out into the street Sleepy Bill mopped his face with a big red railwayman's handkerchief. He lit a cigarette and smoked it, glaring at the heat waves rising from the sizzling pavement. He was in over his head. "Billy," he said to Maharg, "I want you to go to New York. Talk to Rothstein."

Maharg caught the next train. What Rothstein told him when he got to New York, no one ever found out. The judge later told Billy Maharg he didn't have to talk about it.

After dropping the second game the White Sox players began to find money in odd places. Ed "Knuckles" Cicotte, the losing pitcher, found $10,000 in small bills under his pillow. Other sums turned up here and there—first sacker Chick Gandil found twenty grand in cash, money he later insisted he distributed among four of his teammates—but the total sum received by the players was probably no more than forty or fifty thousand dollars, a small fraction of the fortune that was won as a result of their actions. The players, as Arnold Rothstein's biographer put it, were "a flock of lambs who appealed to a wolf to protect them." The wolf was Rothstein.

> We do not recall any notable discoveries in napkins in our time, but we remember when some big league baseball players got to finding money under their pillows. It was wrong money, as it turned out. Twenty-one years ago, come next World Series, it was. The Cincinnati Reds had won the National League championship and were opposed to the Chicago Sox of the American League and the Sox were as good a ball club as ever was mobilized and figured to massacre the Reds. Then gamblers made a deal with important members of the Sox to throw the Series. The ball players put it over, too. They were paid various amounts, the sum total a mere pittance compared to what the gamblers won, and when the exposé came and the players had to explain where they got the money, some of them said they found it under their pillows. The explanation was deemed implausible. In those days practically nobody was going around placing anything under anybody's pillow.
> —"Napkin Technique"

* * *

The World of Damon Runyon

Damon Runyon's was a familiar face in most of the sporting haunts along the Great White Way. He was well known, for instance, at Jack Doyle's billiard parlor at Broadway and 42nd Street, where his tragic plunge on a first-round Dempsey KO in the Willard fight in July 1919 was as familiar a tale as the Charge of the Light Brigade. (One who loved telling it was Sam Harris, the theatrical producer, who was holding Damon's large bundle of 100–1 that day in Toledo.) Runyon was no stranger to most of the gambling world characters named above; he'd met or heard of all of them, and one, Abe Attell, he knew quite well, having been a public admirer of Abe's ring form as far back as his salad days in Denver. But friends or no, the gambling boys weren't spreading any of their World Series sure thing around to the Demon and his writing pals. This one was too big.

As a man about town Runyon had enjoyed Arnold Rothstein's acquaintance since before the war. The two sports had patronized many of the same social and dining spots, such as Churchill's restaurant, at Broadway and 48th, and Reuben's delicatessen, on upper Broadway, where Rothstein held court in the pre-Lindy's days. However, in early October 1919, Damon received no tipoff on the gambling king's interest in a big Series play. If he'd known what was going on, he would have reported the games between the White Sox and the Reds far differently than he did.

Runyon's first reports from Cincinnati hint of no tinge in the Sox other than that of purest lamb's wool. It took him and his press box cohorts a few games to catch on to the fact that they were being made fools of along with everybody else. It is hard to blame their ingenuousness without first recalling that before 1919 no American symbol (except perhaps the flag) inspired a blinder reverence among Americans than the World Series. Like a major religious holiday, it brought millions to worship—not in cathedrals but before the great magnetic "play-by-play" boards put up by newspapers in every city, such as the one in Times Square. (It was the popularity of the Series, and the fame of the great White Sox club, that caused the Series to be temporarily expanded from a best-of-seven to a best-of-nine game format in 1919.) The experienced and intelligent gentlemen of the press box—the Runyons, Lardners, Brouns, and Rices—went along with the man on the street's opinion that the World Series was something too big to tamper with. If even Arnold Rothstein had shown doubts about the power of money to buy baseball players' hearts, cannot the writers be forgiven for at first refusing to believe their eyes?

The day before the Series, Runyon reported in the *American* that the odds on Chicago were down to 7–5 but that the action was still slow. Runyon himself liked the Reds, but only as any guy who is neutral will root for a hopeless underdog. He was as shocked as everybody else when the Reds raced to an easy victory in the first game. White Sox starter Ed Cicotte (as he later confessed) was supposed to plunk the first man up as a sign that the fix was on. No doubt Abe Attell and the boys—assuming they were present—were relieved to see the slim little "shine ball" artist place his first pitch squarely between the shoulders of Morrie Rath, the Reds' leadoff man. It was a green light to any doubtful plungers left in the stands. The Sox were going to tank it!

This was a big day for Cincinnati. Runyon told in his *American* story of the morning's difficulty of getting through the lobby crush ("a slow march," he called it) at the Hotel Sinton and of the "coagulation" of the huge crowd of 30,000 outside Redland Field. "Soft hats predominate," Damon noted, "it is a Middle Western and Eastern crowd. The hard boiled derby of the Easterner appears only on the head of Abe Attell, the former featherweight champion, and the sporting writers from New York . . ."

Runyon's notation technique delivered the look and feel of the day at the ballpark: the heat of the afternoon, the shirtsleeved crowd ("the right field bleachers look like a bank of snow"), the smoke from factories across the valley, the walnut trees on the hills beyond. Nothing in his pregame color story suggests that he expected to see anything other than honest baseball.

Perhaps he and his colleagues began to raise their eyebrows after the smooth-sailing Cicotte suddenly lost his stuff and was knocked out of the game in the fourth inning. The press box party supplied by Reds' president Garry Herrmann (beer and knockwurst) got the writers through the dismal events of the fourth, but when the Sox continued to stumble in the late innings, Fred Lieb noted that Ring Lardner was making with the Owl Eyes, as if something were not quite right. When the game ended Hughey Fullerton of the Chicago *Tribune,* who'd never seen his Sox so listless, announced that he detected an odor of rodent other than mouse. He carried his suspicions to Ban Johnson, president of the American League. "Ban, all this betting going on," Hughey said, "I don't like the looks of it." "You are imagining things, sir," quoth the well-oiled Johnson in reply. "Have another drink."

Writing of Game Two in the New York *American* of Friday, October 3, Damon reported that the betting activity had increased noticeably overnight. The odds were sliding rapidly, he noted, with those favoring the Reds "taking even money where a few hours ago they were asking odds." You didn't need a microscope to read the writing between those lines. There was something in the air, the Demon and his colleagues were beginning to agree.

In Game Two they saw Claude Williams, the ace Sox lefty,

demonstrate his usual prowess—until the fourth inning, at which point he deteriorated inexplicably and awarded the Reds three free passes, three runs, and the game. "I'm forever blowing ballgames," Ring Lardner crooned in the press box—to the tune of the famous ditty about bubbles—while Williams fiddled on the mound. Later, when Happy Felsch elected to lay down a bunt with his team trailing and placed the bunt directly into the hands of the Redleg pitcher, Damon wrote, "it struck some that a sacrifice play was peculiar, as Felsch is a good hitter." The Runyon irony, heretofore held in reserve, would henceforth lace Damon's reports of the games. No doubt quite a few things were now beginning to strike some as peculiar.

One who was being struck hardest by the peculiar decline of the Sox was the Old Roman, Comiskey. By now he couldn't help knowing something was wrong. On the train back to Chicago he expressed his fears to National League president John Heydler. Heydler conveyed Comiskey's statement to the Old Roman's archenemy Ban Johnson, who was aboard the train. "That's the yelp of a beaten cur," the league president snorted, furious at being interrupted in the midst of a private drinking party.

Dickey Kerr, pitching his heart out to overcome the dead weight created by the bunch of stiffs behind him, let only six balls get past the infield and shut the Reds out, 3–0, at Comiskey Park in the third game. Nevertheless doubts remained, and they increased the following day when Cicotte too pitched shutout ball—except in the fifth inning, when he threw one ball away on an easy play and knocked a relay throw off course on another, bringing about two "unearned" runs, the only runs scored all day. The formerly noisy White Sox bats kept a curious silence behind Cicotte. The one Chicagoan to reach third, Chick Gandil, did so standing up— and was thrown out for his failure to slide. The writers agreed this was strange. Gandil had been playing the game all his life— had run away from home at seventeen to play it, as a matter of fact. Had the memory of how to slide suddenly escaped him?

The stories carried strong hints, no more. CICOTTE CRABS HIS OWN ACT, ran a Baltimore *Sun* headline; GANDIL FAILS IN A PINCH. The *Sun* writer, C. Starr Matthews, told how Cicotte's own "meddling . . . brought about his second defeat" and how for the third time in the Series "Gandil failed miserably when only a decent fly ball was needed." In the *American* Damon Runyon noted that "lots of guys who always thought the Reds would win the series are now coming up for air. There were about eight of them in the whole country before the series started and there are now about eight million."

Damon Runyon at the 1919 World Series

After a rainy day off the Sox did a little more swimming of their own in Game Five, paddling their way through a 5–0 shutout loss. Once again Claude Williams "blew," this time in the fifth, immediately after Happy Felsch and Joe Jackson (who a year later was to confess he deliberately took his time chasing the ball) let a pop fly drop between them. That was the game. The 1920 *Reach Baseball Guide,* written before the official admission of the fix, commented with a straight face that "Jackson, whose mind appeared to be puzzled by the jinx that had settled on his lucky hairpins, was slow in getting under the ball, and Felsch was too far away." That was the whitewash version.

Abe Attell and his boys were happy with the goings on so far. The Sox, performing like trained seals, trailed the Reds four games to one. Now the Series returned to Cincinnati, where the "kill" would be applied, the inside boys supposed. But at Redland Field the Sox suddenly awoke from a 26-inning scoreless slump, came back from four runs down, and took the sixth game behind brave little Dickey Kerr. When Eddie Cicotte returned to pitch beautifully and win the seventh game, it appeared to some of the "boys" that a double cross might be underway; others on the inside simply figured orders had gone out not to make things look too easy.

The Series moved to Chicago once more. No one knew what to expect. Hugh Fullerton told Fred Lieb before Game Eight, "Keep your eyes peeled."

"I still don't like it," Hughey whispered, "just look around." After talking with Hughey, Lieb went to the men's room, where he overheard a guy at the next stall say, "It'll be all over in the first . . . watch for that big Red first."

It came off like clockwork. Claude Williams blew in the first, getting only one man out, and the Reds pushed four runs across before poor Kid Gleason could get another pitcher warmed up. It was all over for Comiskey's Sox. The South Side of Chicago would not see another World Series game for fifty years.

A summer later the small boys of the city congregated outside the White Sox clubhouse and begged Shoeless Joe Jackson to deny the rising charges that the players had thrown the 1919 Series. "Say it ain't true, Joe," the boys pleaded. "Say it ain't true." Joe walked past them without a word, never looked back, and never set foot in a major league ballpark again.

> The guilty ball players were given the hoovus-groovus from baseball for the rest of their lives. Among them were some of the greatest players that ever laced on cleated shoes—Buck Weaver, a third baseman, for one, and "Shoeless Joe" Jackson for another. "Shoeless Joe," as he was then, would now be worth $300,000 of any ball club's money. He was the greatest natural hitter we ever saw, not barring Babe Ruth or the mighty Ty Cobb.

The World of Damon Runyon

Shoeless Joe Jackson

Against the lively ball of today, "Shoeless Joe" would be hitting 'em across townships. He could hit .350 when he was just clowning and better .400 when he was serious. You talk about hitters—why that old "Shoeless Joe" could drive the ball farther with the breeze on his missed strikes than most ball players can send it off their bats. Ask anybody that ever saw him in action, or look up the book on him.   —"Napkin Technique"

Damon's story of the final game was brief and noncommital, and the *American* editors, sensing his nervousness, removed it from its reserved place on the front page to the interior of the paper. This Series was being treated with kid gloves in high places; everybody knew by now that something was fishy, but no one in authority was willing to say just what. There were too many unconfirmed rumors, too many conflicting tales. Damon conferred with his colleagues in the Hearst camp. Charges began to appear. On October 30, 1919, the *American*'s sports editor wrote of Rothstein's apparent involvement and that of Abe Attell. But the story did not move beyond the perimeters of hearsay and gossip for a full year.

When it did, near the end of the 1920 season, it cost the White Sox a possible pennant; they were a game out of first with three left to play when seven players (and Chick Gandil, now retired after a salary fight with Comiskey) were indicted. The Old Roman, with trembling voice, announced the suspension of Cicotte, Jackson, Williams, Weaver, Felsch, Risberg, and McMullin. That was that for the White Sox in 1920—and for half a century thereafter.

Ed Cicotte, in tears, told the grand jury of pillows stuffed with greenbacks. Joe Jackson, who'd hit .375 in the 1919 Series, told how he'd loafed on fly balls, made weak throws, and chosen on certain at-bats to merely tap the ball. Witnesses told how Claude Williams had received $10,000 as payment for his three "blown" starts. Chick Gandil's twenty-grand windfall was described. Buck Weaver, a lone voice of dissent, refused to admit any part in the scandal. "I hit .333," he told the press. "That should be a good enough alibi."

It was, sadly, not good enough. Anticipating a criminal conviction (which never came), Commissioner Landis—famed as a federal district judge for handing down stiff sentences—included Weaver among the eight players he declared ineligible for life. Landis' blanket expulsion implied equal participation and equal guilt among the eight, even though one, Weaver, had only "guilty knowledge" of the fix; another, Jackson, never met with gamblers; and a third, McMullin, appeared in the Series only as a pinch hitter and in the end was dropped from the state's list of indicted players. Landis' summary proscription of all eight Chicago players would stand, he said, "regardless of the verdict of juries," and none of them would ever again play professional baseball. It was clear that Landis (whom a later historian described as "never one to permit judicial impartiality to interfere with his personal biases and leanings") was less concerned with the question of degree of guilt than with making a grandstand play, a sweeping gesture that would impress the disenchanted baseball audience and give them a feeling the game had been "purged." (Such gestures were characteristic of the judge, whose career, Heywood Broun said at the time, "typifies the heights to which dramatic talent may carry a man in America if only he has the foresight not to go on the stage.")

Buck Weaver's fans—10,000 of them—later addressed to Landis

The World of Damon Runyon

Judge Kenesaw M. Landis

a petition urging their hero's reinstatement. The flinty commissioner ruled that even if Weaver didn't profit by the "fix," he knew about it and didn't tell. Weaver, who never played another inning of organized ball, became a pari-mutuel clerk in Chicago, protesting his innocence of wrongdoing in the 1919 Series to his dying day.

At the time of the 1920 grand jury inquiry, Runyon reminded his readers that the *American* had indicated details of the "fix" only a few days after the Series.

"What did Heydler, and Johnson, and all the rest do?" Damon asked in his impromptu "Sport Editorial" on September 27, 1920.

> They did nothing. They kept quiet. We believe in the integrity of baseball. We believe that it will be all the better for the cleansing it is now undergoing.
>
> But we believe the "shush" policy of the league officials has been very damaging to the best interests of the game.

While nobody connected with the dark chain of events ever spent a day in jail as a result of the 1919 Series, the game itself barely survived the moral backlash that swept the nation in the wake of the grand jury exposures. Conveniently for them, none of the prime movers of the fix—including Attell and Rothstein—were forced to stand trial. (Ironically, Rothstein's woman book-keeper was indicted, but thanks to the twin weapons of his vast bankroll and his resourceful mouthpiece William Fallon—who cunningly advised him to stage an indignant appearance before the grand jury—The Brain got off easy, suffering nothing worse than a little bad publicity. Similarly shielded by lawyer Fallon was Abe Attell, who when arrested at the Canadian border claimed he was not the "real" Abe Attell, a claim surprisingly corroborated by the original complainant against him.)

The players took all the heat. Acquitted in the courts, they remained blacklisted from the sport and paid for their reputed "crimes" with their careers. Beyond the individuals, the game itself suffered. Many a fan, Runyon among them, swore in their hearts never to forgive baseball the 1919 affair. Had it not been for a fellow named Ruth, the national pastime might have died a slow death after the revelations of 1920. It was the Babe, with his great sincerity and his great swing (and with the help of the new rabbit ball), who drew Runyon and the rest back to the fellowship of the game. Among the scribes only Ring Lardner, to whom the fall of the team he'd covered for a decade was too much to take, remained permanently embittered by the Black Sox scandal.

When Arnold Rothstein went down with a gangster's fatal bullet in the groin in 1928, Broadway columnist Runyon (who in a later story noted that The Brain "always sits facing the door so nobody can pop in on him without him seeing them first, because there are many people in this town that The Brain likes to see first if they are coming in where he is") had very little to say— for newspaper consumption.

By 1940 Damon could look back with no more than a trace of irony lining his fondness when he wrote again of Joe Jackson, who'd thrown a Series of which he could have been the star. Here is the final paragraph of "Napkin Technique":

> We felt sorrier for Joe than any of the others. He was not a smart fellow except up at the plate. There he was the wisest man in the world. We do not remember now where he said he found his bit of wrong money. Maybe he was one of the pillow men. It is a cinch he did not find it in his napkin because "Shoeless Joe" was strictly a devotee of the napkin in the collar, a fact that causes us to doubt that the napkin there, protective and democratic though it may be, is always the badge of complete integrity.

7

A Diamond Scrapbook: Four Final Notes on Runyon and Baseball

"These old sports pages—so many columns and words on baseball!"

"Oh yes, baseball was big *then!"*

"But the stories—they're all so full of great jokes and poems and metaphors and descriptions—what was it, George? Were the readers all such fans that they knew all the background already, so these guys like Runyon and the rest could just go out on a limb and write?*"*

"Yes! Oh yes! They were real *writers then. There's nothing like that now."*

"It seems like there was more written because the fans were more interested. They cared more about it."

"You have to understand—in those days baseball was the big thing. You didn't have professional hockey and ice skating and professional football and basketball and tennis and all that, that takes up the sportin' page now. Baseball used to be it. *That was the main topic."*

—From an interview by the author with George "High Pockets" Kelly, Hall of Fame first baseman and a New York Giant from 1915 to 1926

My God, major league baseball was such a big thing then, occupying a third of the front page of the final editions of the New York, Boston, Philadelphia and Chicago papers. Politics, everything else was pushed aside.

—Marshall Hunt, reminiscing on sportswriting in the 1920s

[1] Casey Stengel's home run,
October 10, 1923

Damon Runyon's most famous baseball story is his *American* piece of October 10, 1923, in which he describes Casey Stengel's game-winning home run in the first game of that year's World Series. Damon's account of the game, which runs to several thousand words, is representative in its thoroughness and lively style of the seventy or eighty such pieces he had composed during his dozen press box autumns, but the short "prose poetry" passage on Casey's homer is a singular gem that several anthologists have chosen to typify the Runyon mode of sportswriting.

The 1923 Series was the first ever played in Yankee Stadium, which had opened in April. It was quite a year for the Yankees. Their great hitting star Babe Ruth, who batted .393 and led the league in just about every offensive category, had paced the club to a third straight American League pennant. Now, playing in their new superpalace in the Bronx, the suddenly respectable Yanks were expected (and favored by the bettors at Jack Doyle's Billiard Academy) to win their first World Championship by knocking off the Giants in the Series.

McGraw's club had also won three pennants in a row, and they had beaten the Yanks in two consecutive Subway Series, but the glamor of the Babe's home runs that season was already beginning to swing the bright beam of newspaper publicity across the Harlem River from the Polo Grounds to the shiny new "House that Ruth Built." Top writers like Runyon and McGeehan now covered even the Babe's late-winter trips to Hot Springs to "take the tubs"— not to mention the goings on at the Yanks' camp in New Orleans and the team's home games in their new 70,000-seat stadium in the Bronx. (Damon, growing more and more famous among the scribes for his laconic demeanor and long silences, was reputed to have ridden all the way from New York to the Yankee camp in New Orleans with Bill McGeehan in March 1923 without speaking a *single word* except for a dry "Okay" in response to McGeehan's "Nice trip" as the train pulled into the station.)

The 1923 Series opened at the Stadium, but there was an equal division of Giant and Yankee rooters among the 55,000 who turned out on Wednesday afternoon. It was a contest so important to New Yorkers that the *Times* had to close down its switchboard in the second inning after an unprecedented flood of phone calls inquiring about the score. Attendance at schools and places of business dropped off sharply as young and old fans pursued the course of the game in person or by various other methods. Bill McGeehan, who was covering the game for the *Herald Tribune,* assisted Graham MacNamee in the first live World Series radio broadcast. It was heard up and down the Eastern seaboard by fans able to afford or to get close to radios. For those less fortunate there were the World Series scoreboards and magnetic "play-by-play" boards; in Times Square tens of thousands gathered to "watch" the action on a New York *Times* display board.

The game itself was later described in the *Times* as "the greatest ever played between championship teams." It contained a series of brilliant defensive plays that had the big crowd in a state

Casey Stengel

of high excitement by the ninth inning, which began with the score knotted at four all. The Giants' first two batters in the ninth went down without incident, but then up to the plate stepped Casey Stengel, a thirty-three-year-old outfielder and funnyman who had played in 75 games on unsteady legs that season, his twelfth in the majors. Casey, a lefthanded hitter, took pitcher Joe Bush to 3 and 2, then lined one into the gap in left center. While Bob Meusel and Whitey Witt chased the ball down in the deepest part of the big park, Casey moved around the bases in a painful hobbling gallop. He was wearing a rubber pad over his heel, which had been badly bruised earlier in the season. Later he explained that as he was making the turn at second base he "had the feeling that this shoe with the heel pad was going to come off, so I commenced dragging the shoe, and everybody said afterward that I looked like an old man out there."

The "everybody" to whom Casey referred was Damon, whose syndicated account of the play made it one of the memorable incidents in Series history even for those who did not attend the game.

> This is the way old Casey Stengel ran yesterday afternoon running his home run home.
> This is the way old Casey Stengel ran running his home run home to a Giant victory by a score of 5 to 4 in the first game of the World Series of 1923.
> This is the way old Casey Stengel ran running his home run home when two were out in the ninth inning and the score was tied, and the ball still bounding inside the Yankee yard.
> This is the way—
> His mouth wide open.
> His warped old legs bending beneath him at every stride.
> His arms flying back and forth like those of a man swimming with a crawl stroke.
> His flanks heaving, his breath whistling, his head far back. Yankee infielders, passed by Old Casey Stengel as he was running his home run home, say Casey was muttering to himself, adjuring himself to greater speed as a jockey mutters to his horse in a race, saying "go on, Casey, go on."
> The warped old legs, twisted and bent by many a year of baseball campaigning, just barely held out under Casey until he reached the plate, running his home run home.
> Then they collapsed.

Stengel's inside-the-park home run won the game for the Giants, who were to bow eventually in the Series to the Yanks' superior (and less comical) power—but not without this moment of glory, which Damon's prose captured for all time. In his autobiography Ford Frick cited this passage as exemplary of the maturation of American baseball writing in the 1910s and 1920s—and as evidence of Damon's "lyrical" gifts. "Runyon often hit that chord in his daily writing," Frick wrote after quoting the Stengel home-run piece. "To me, that's poetry."

The World of Damon Runyon

[2] Phil Douglas and "Baseball Hattie"

As a baseball writer with Broadway credentials, Damon had a chance to view the sport he covered as a reporter through the eyes of the gambling crowd with which he socialized in his off-duty hours. And he was not the only man with contacts in both worlds. The grey area between organized sport and organized crime was populated, he learned, by a number of individuals whose daytime identities as sporting heroes were shadowed—and sometimes compromised—by their activities in the behind-closed-doors, nighttime life of the underworld. Sometimes the distinctions were hard to keep track of. Ballplayers and boxers were commonly seen in the saloons (later the speakeasies) where gamblers and gangsters circulated, and gamblers and gangsters were seen in the boxes and ringside seats at ballgames and fights. Men like Abe Attell, Hal Chase, Sport Sullivan, and Sleepy Bill Burns, all principals in the Black Sox scandal, were active "sportsmen" in both senses of that term—first as athletes, later as speculators on and engineers of athletic contests. The penumbra of big-time sports contained many such dubious characters; their names and faces were well known to Damon once he'd been in the business a few years.

The infiltration of criminal elements into sports had become so common by Damon's time that a "clean" athlete such as Christy Mathewson was regarded in some circles as a freak. To editorial writers who cared for the public image of sport, Mathewson's life was a text to be held up as a line-and-verse testimonial. Damon's colleague Bill McGeehan opined in print that if the magnates had not ignored the warnings of Mathewson—who had denounced Hal Chase as a gamblers' tool in 1918—there might have been no Black Sox scandal. "In this sporting game more than in any other walk of life they raise false idols. They make heroes of brutes, they make demigods of inconsequential young men without character or true courage, they make saintly characters out of the vicious. But when they made a national idol of Christy Mathewson of Bucknell College, they made one out of true metal . . ."

Damon, with his involvements in both worlds, often found himself caught between loyalties. On the one hand he went along with McGeehan and the other more conscientious scribes in deploring the influence of gambling interests in sports, but on the other hand he had, shall we say, interests in common with those interests. He had sympathies on both sides of the fence—and often it seemed as though there was no fence. He could condemn the criminal influence in the 1919 World Series in a righteous editorial on the *American*'s sporting page, but on the day the paper came out he could be seen chewing the fat with Arnold Rothstein. In his column he could point the finger at some blatantly scripted "tank" bout, but when the paper hit the streets he could be seen kibitzing with the fixers and the touts on "Jacobs Beach," the strip of sidewalk outside Mike Jacobs' Garden office. It was a complicated issue. Later Damon claimed it was this dilemma, not the tedium of the games, that drove him out of sportswriting by the late thirties. He wrote about it in a forties "Postscript on Sports Writing."

> I had softened up too much long before I quit it. I had become too relenting and too friendly and had too many personal contacts. Instead of the district attorney which I hold should be the role of the sports writer and especially the columnist or editorial commentator, I found myself too often playing the part of the counsel for the defense.
>
> To be a great sports writer a man must hold himself pretty much aloof from the characters of the games with which he deals before his sympathy for them commences to distort his own viewpoint. There is nothing more engaging than an engaging rogue and there are many engaging rogues in professional sports. I fear I knew most of them, and that is not good for a sports writer.
>
> The very nature of nearly all professional sports and some amateur sports, too, makes them subject to influences and practices that are harmful to public morals and, inasmuch as the newspapers recognize the reader interest in sports to the extent of giving great space to them and hiring many sports writers, it is the duty of these writers to severely police their field.

Damon's "policing of the field" came largely in the form of occasional lip-service editorials, often inspired no doubt by Hearst or Brisbane. Apart from that, he kept his comments on sports morality to a sardonic hint here or there in his columns, an oblique remark in the middle of a story. By the early twenties he was regarded by his colleagues as an expert and scholar of underworld lore, and questions on that area of life were brought to him as a matter of course. But few of his answers appeared in his sports columns.

In his years of commuting between the ball fields and Broadway, Damon had seen a lot and heard about even more. There was the Black Sox episode. There was the strange career of Prince Hal Chase, the nimble first baseman of the Yankees and the Giants, whose clever way of making errors that helped his teams lose games had become familiar stuff to Damon and the other writers long before Chase was blacklisted. There was Lee Magee, a Cub outfielder discovered to have been a playmate of Chase and thrown out of the game with Prince Hal in 1919. There was Heinie Zimmerman, third baseman of the Giants, who in that same dark season connived with gamblers and was caught in the act by McGraw (to whom Heinie's teammates had turned after the infielder offered to cut them in on his "fix" deal). Heinie too was expelled from baseball. Over the next few seasons, so were several other variously guilty players: Gene Paulette, Benny Kauff, Joe Gedeon, Claude Hendrix, Phil Douglas, Jimmy O'Connell. Those who were punished for their crimes or underworld associations may have represented only the tip of the iceberg. Accusations, innuendo, and rumor implicated many other players, some of them very well known. Strong "hearsay" cases were brought against such stars as Ty Cobb, Tris Speaker, Carl Mays, and Bullet Joe Bush. Dutch Leonard, a pitcher for the Tigers in 1919, charged that Cobb and Speaker conspired to throw a game to the Indians on September 25 that year; Mays and Bush, Yankee pitchers, were suspected (by persons including Colonel Huston, the owner of the club) of throwing World Series games in 1921 and 1922.

The amateur district attorneys who prosecuted these cases in saloons across the land were convinced that the national pastime was rife with foul play. Many of their arguments were based on weak evidence, but one who spoke with authority on such matters, attorney William Fallon, told Damon that the public had no idea how deep the gambling connection with baseball went. Fallon, dubbed the Great Mouthpiece by biographer Gene Fowler, had represented Attell and Rothstein in the 1919 World Series case and appeared for Giant coach Patrick "Cozy" Dolan in a 1924 trial ensuing from the blacklisting of Dolan by Commissioner Landis. It was suggested in the latter case that Cozy, a colorful character and gifted raconteur, was in collusion with gambling interests when he persuaded a young Giant player named Jimmy O'Connell to make a cash offer to an opponent in return for a "thrown" game. At the behest and expense of John McGraw, Fallon went to court (unsuccessfully) to recover a World Series check Dolan felt he had coming. Damon was a friend of both Fallon and Cozy. The lawyer confirmed Damon's belief in Dolan's innocence but informed him that there were dozens of other baseball men who were into gambling up to their necks. This was in the mid-twenties, by which time the game had supposedly "cleaned up its act" after the 1919 debacle.

Had the game cleaned up? The thought made Damon laugh. In 1919, while the first rumors of conniving were being aired, the owners had allowed the sale of the New York National League franchise to Charles Stoneham, John J. McGraw, and Judge Francis Y. McQuade. Damon knew more about these three men than he needed to. Stoneham? Damon found out some years later from Nat Ferber of the *American* (as he had already suspected) that Stoneham was one of the biggest "bucket shop" boys on Wall Street. His stock transactions were made with funny money, and half the town knew it. His other business interests included rum running and, according to Bill Veeck, ticket scalping and bookmaking.

Charles Stoneham

Stoneham was quite a high roller on the ponies too, as was McGraw, whom one writer termed "an inveterate gambler." (In 1904 Muggsy had been briefly jailed at Hot Springs for gambling and resisting arrest.) In 1919 Stoneham and McGraw became the principal owers of a Havana racetrack complex that included the Oriental Park track, Jockey Club, and Casino Nacional. There were a lot of gringo dollars going into Cuban gambling at the time, and for at least the next two winters the New York baseball men cut themselves a healthy slice of the pie. (It was at the Stoneham-McGraw track that Babe Ruth dropped a good part of the $40,000 he'd earned in his barnstorming tour of Cuba with McGraw's Giants in the winter of 1920.)

Judge McQuade's sporting connections were notorious. He had once been bribed by no less a sportsman than Arnold Rothstein, whose gambling house, the Partridge Club, was the scene of a shooting that came to trial in McQuade's court. (Three policemen had been shot, but McQuade obligingly dismissed the charges against 20 of the 21 persons arrested.) For that matter, Rothstein was no stranger to McQuade's partners either. The gambling king bankrolled Stoneham's bucket shops and rum-running operations, backed the Stoneham-McGraw racetrack enterprise, and even put money into a pool hall venture of McGraw's. (The poolroom, next door to the old *Herald* building, had become a favorite hangout of The Brain, who in those days liked to shoot nine-ball for $50 and $100 a game.) Naturally, Rothstein brokered the McQuade-Stoneham-McGraw purchase of the Giants in 1919—and was thereafter a frequent box-seat guest at the Polo Grounds.

In 1921 Judge Landis ordered McGraw and Stoneham to divest themselves of their Havana racetrack and discouraged further use of the owners' box by Rothstein. But the McGraw-Stoneham-McQuade triumvirate remained in command. (McQuade was to resign in the wake of the Seabury inquiries in the early thirties, and McGraw would die in 1934, leaving Stoneham in control.) Damon couldn't help feeling there was something hypocritical in a "sport" that could admit such doubtful parties in the role of corporate statesmen and then throw some poor underpaid ballplayer out on his ear for grabbing at a buck when a gambler waved it in his face.

Damon rarely incorporated such antiestablishment sentiments in his columns. More often he reserved them for private conversation, either with fellow scribes like Sid Mercer and Boze Bulger or (when he felt there had been a particular miscarriage of justice) with the authorities. Aboard a World Series-bound train in the late twenties, he addressed Landis in the judge's Pullman drawing room with a prolonged and unsuccessful plea for the reinstatement of Jimmy O'Connell, a blacklisted player he'd run into a few weeks before on the San Francisco docks. He also approached the question of baseball's peculiar punishments from the oblique angle of his fiction (as always, using "indirection" and a "half-boob air") in one of the Broadway tales, "Baseball Hattie," first published in *Cosmopolitan* in May 1936. "Baseball Hattie" states the Runyon case for the game-throwing ballplayer, whom he depicts as the innocent victim of circumstances. (Among the circumstances, however, as Damon is careful to show, are the ballplayer's own ignorance and weakness of character.) His portrait of Haystack Duggeler, a talented but softheaded young Giants' pitcher duped into a "fix" agreement by a gambler named Armand Fibleman, is based on the real-life stories of Bugs Raymond and "Shufflin' Phil" Douglas.

Phil Douglas was a player Damon knew well, a character cut from the same crazy quilt as Raymond, his predecessor by about a decade on the Giants. A gifted pitcher but a difficult "type" like Bugs, Phil got in the end what Damon always figured was a raw deal from the Giants, much as Bugs had. With Douglas, as with

A Diamond Scrapbook

Phil Douglas

Raymond, there was a personality mismatch between player and club. The Giants of 1902–1932 had no room for a player who rubbed John McGraw the wrong way, and Raymond and Douglas were such players. (Ironically, both were talented baseball "untouchables" whom McGraw brought to his club as personal reclamation projects.)

Damon's Haystack Duggeler and the real-life Phil Douglas had more in common than the similarity of their surnames. Both were gifted pitchers, country boys, and noted sowers of wild oats around the towns of the National League. Both were trusted by John McGraw—as far as he could throw them. Both pitched splendidly for the Giants at times, and both lost their careers for reasons other than the losing of games. Although Runyon inserted in his portrait of Haystack details from the stories of Bugs Raymond and the Black Sox stars, it was the life of Phil Douglas, whose personal tragedy Damon believed to be as much a loss to baseball as to the man himself, that formed the real-life template for the parabolic tale of Haystack Duggeler.

Like many a ballplayer, Shufflin' Phil got his nickname from Damon, who was amused by the pitcher's trudging ballfield gait, and later incorporated several of Douglas' physical and behavioral traits into the central character of "Baseball Hattie." Like Haystack, Phil Douglas in 1920 was a tall, lanky fellow who took a drink now and then and had no particular genius except when it came to knowing how to get batters out. At that, however, he excelled (at least when in condition), a fact that had tantalized

105

his various managers. But none of them had been able to make a star pitcher of this diamond in the rough. The strapping, six-foot-five Douglas, a colorful product of the rural South, possessed a powerful fast ball, a sweeping curve, and a much-envied "spitter" (called the best in baseball by his teammate, Frank Frisch, and actually prepared with the juice of slippery elm twigs from the top of the tallest tree in Pikeville, Tennessee). He could control all these pitches better than he could control himself, which was why his major league jobs were usually of short duration. Wilbert Robinson, manager of the Dodgers, picked Douglas up from the Reds in 1916 and announced that "if I ever can get this fellow sober, I've got the best pitcher in the league." Two months later Robinson, confessing failure, released the big hurler to the Cubs. In Chicago he lasted two seasons, showing flashes of brilliance and, in one four-game series, defeating the great Grover Cleveland Alexander *twice.* "There was no harm in that fellow," his manager with the Cubs (Fred Mitchell) later said. "He didn't fight with the boys or bust down houses. It's just that I never knew where the hell he was, or if he was fit to work."

John McGraw, who could always use a pitcher of Douglas' gifts, and who prided himself on his ability to handle "hard cases," took a gamble and made a trade for the Shuffler in 1918. (The "gamble" was of the penny-ante variety, for Douglas came to the Giants with an annual salary of around $2000, approximately one-fourth of what the club's other starting pitchers earned.) "I know I am getting myself in for something when I take on Douglas, but I am sure I can handle him," McGraw told Damon and the other scribes. Within a few seasons big Phil made him look good, too. In 1921 Douglas won 15 games (including two over Pittsburgh in one crucial September series), and then, having pitched McGraw's club to a pennant, he subdued Babe Ruth's Yankees twice in October to ice the world championship. (Phil, riding high, struck out Ruth twice in one game of that World Series; after the second strikeout, Ruth in returning to the outfield muttered to Douglas that he had a sore throat—to which Phil replied, "Hell, Babe, you ain't battin' with your throat!")

By that time McGraw had already struck on a plan for "handling" Douglas: he paid a series of detectives to shadow the big pitcher day and night to make sure he showed up sober for all his starts. The manager's bird dogs hounded Douglas' every move outside his front door or hotel room. Although the subject of all this attention did not enjoy it much, it proved to be a successful managerial strategy at least for the season of 1921 and the first half of 1922. "That man could win as many games for me as Christy Mathewson if he behaved himself and concentrated on his pitching," McGraw had often said, and by early 1922 it looked as if the manager's claim might be more than a wild exaggeration.

Shufflin' Phil got off to his best start ever that season. Despite a spell of early-season arm trouble and the advent of the lively ball (which was driving batting averages and scores sky high), Douglas allowed less than 2.5 runs per game through the middle of July. That figure led the league, as did his 11–3 record. Opposing batsmen complained quietly of being overmatched: "There should be a law against a fellow as big and smart as that having all that stuff," Walter "Rabbit" Maranville of the Pirates moaned after Douglas had buffaloed his club with speed and spitballs one midsummer afternoon. By that time Phil's arm and his other problems seemed only a memory. In fact it looked to columnist Runyon (and to most people) as though McGraw's boys would ride the strong right wing of the Shuffler to another pennant; only the Cardinals, with Rogers Hornsby's smoking bat, looked capable of making a race of it. As July wound down, Hornsby was hitting well over .400 and St. Louis clung to the Giants' heels in a virtual first-place tie. Then trouble broke out on the New York club in the form of Phil Douglas—but it was John McGraw himself who was the trigger.

A detective named O'Brien had been chosen by McGraw as Phil's shadow for the 1922 season. At first it seemed a fortunate selection, for Douglas and the detective got along "like two pigs in a poke," as the rustic pitcher phrased it. Not only did the Shuffler enjoy his shadow's company, he soon learned O'Brien subscribed to the "where's the harm in it?" philosophy when it came to an occasional highball. Happily and many a time did the athlete and his shadow violate the laws of Prohibition, in New York speakeasies and Philadelphia hotels and Pullman sleepers, and all was well. While Phil's physical condition normally suffered when he drank, his pitching now mysteriously resisted such natural deterioration, and he won start after start. "I took a lot of vacations this year, but I won a hell of a lot of games, too," he remarked to Damon one day. It was the truth. But, as it turned out, the games Phil had won were not good enough for John McGraw.

When the rumor reached the manager that his private eye was tippling with his pitcher on the club expense account (this was only partially true; Phil was picking up his own tabs), there was a clubhouse explosion. It happened late in June. McGraw, renowned for his vicious tongue ("the worst in baseball," his players agreed), took a bite out of Douglas' hide, fired O'Brien, and posted Giant scout Jesse Burkett (an old-time ballplayer who possessed all the personal charm of a boa constrictor) as Douglas' "keeper" for the rest of the season. The grim and abstemious Burkett, whose company his convivial ward found oppressive, was assisted by private detectives at various times. "Daddy couldn't make a move but what there was somebody watchin' him," Douglas' daughter (a young girl at the time) later recalled.

McGraw had been riding him about his pitching, too. No sweetheart at the best of times, the Giant manager had grown increasingly critical and caustic as the 1922 pennant race moved into the tense dog days of late summer. After one game against the Cardinals in the last week of July, McGraw reproved Douglas viciously for throwing five straight strikes to Rogers Hornsby (Hornsby had fouled off two of the pitches). The basis of McGraw's infuriated critique, that Douglas had thrown too many good pitches to a dangerous hitter, was of doubtful logical quality, but this fact tempered the manager's criticism not at all. Douglas, normally an easygoing man, often grew wayward under pressure. McGraw's spying and ridicule had for some time humiliated and angered him. The day after this particular upbraiding Douglas confided to Hornsby and another friend on the Cardinals, Les Mann, that he wished he were a member of their club instead of his.

In those days there was no recourse for an unhappy player like Douglas other than to grin and bear it, which Shufflin' Phil did—until July 30, when, after another McGraw tongue-lashing in the wake of a 7–0 loss to the Pirates at the Polo Grounds, the pitcher eluded Jesse Burkett near Times Square and took off on one of his little "vacations." This one was to be his last. New York police detectives rounded him up in an apartment near the Polo Grounds (where they found him passed out cold on a bed) and turned him over to the ball club. The ball club promptly committed the stupefied hurler to a sanitarium on Central Park West, where for the better part of a week he was confined against his will, by means of force and involuntary sedation. Upon his release he returned to the club and was greeted with a bill for $214.30 to cover his sanitarium and taxi expenses—and by another brutal lecture from McGraw, who further informed him that he would be fined $100 and a week's salary.

This combination of punishments put the hung over, confused, and despondent pitcher in a $500 financial hole and a nasty state of mind. Boiling with vindictive feeling against McGraw, he sat down in the Polo Grounds clubhouse and wrote a letter to his friend Les Mann of the Cardinals, offering to abandon the Giants for the rest of the season ("go to fishing camp," as he put it) if the Cardinal players would "send the goods" to his home address. ("I don't want this guy to win it," Douglas wrote, referring to McGraw, whom in his befuddled state he now perceived to be the cause of all his torments.) Mann, a YMCA enthusiast and a well-known boy-scout type, promptly turned the note over to his manager, Branch Rickey, who in turn ordered him to forward it to Commissioner Landis.

Though the pitcher himself didn't know it at the time, for a week Douglas' fate hung in the balance. Sporting a new diamond ring and a chipper attitude, he rejoined the Giants in Pittsburgh on August 15 at the beginning of a Western road trip, apparently hopeful that his letter to Les Mann (which he now regretted sending) and the police and sanitarium episodes had been forgotten as quickly as the details of his earlier "vacations." None of the other players or writers with the club—Douglas was well liked among both groups—so much as hinted to him that the truth might be otherwise. But when, on the morning of August 16, Douglas was summoned to the manager's suite in the Hotel Schenley and found there the snowy-haired, craggy, and frowning Judge Landis seated in a chair next to the little banty rooster McGraw, he knew something was wrong. Before Landis and McGraw there was a table and across from it an empty chair meant for Shufflin' Phil. Just like in Russia.

The judge, who possessed the wizened look of a Biblical patriarch and a sense of his own juridical function that would have better suited Solomon's courts than those of twentieth-century America (he considered himself a "giver" of laws rather than an interpreter of them), confronted Phil with the letter to Les Mann on Giant stationery and in his own handwriting.

"Did you write this?" Landis asked ominously.

Douglas, turning red to the roots of his hair, replied in his high Cumberland Mountain tenor that he had indeed.

Landis passed the "guilty" note to the Giants' manager to peruse. McGraw, who'd probably read it already, glanced again for form's sake and shook his head mournfully; no doubt in his mind he was already sifting prospective candidates for the Shuffler's replacement in the New York pitching rotation.

Abruptly Landis looked Douglas in the eye and pointed a bony index finger at him. "Phil, you are out of baseball for good," he said, giving the sentence his gravest inflections. (The tones were indeed suitable, for the judge's verdict permanently deprived a thirty-two-year-old father of two of his chosen livelihood.)

Landis saw the Douglas case (as he saw everything else) in terms of absolute black and white, and proceeded to punish Shufflin' Phil's "crime" (Douglas had never offered to throw a game) like a man swatting a fly with a baseball bat. The penalty he imposed was totally disproportionate to the offensiveness of its object. The facts that the Shuffler's "guilty" letter was the product of a man momentarily deranged by a distressing set of circumstances, that it was quite harmless, and that it was quickly regretted by its author, never entered into the judge's consideration of the matter.

That evening McGraw, obviously unwilling to face the unhappy pitcher in person, slipped Douglas a hundred bucks via the club's shortstop, Dave Bancroft, and sent him back to New York. Then the manager and the commissioner met with the press in the former's suite at the Hotel Schenley. In a prepared spiel McGraw dwelt at length on his ex-pitcher's moral failings, leaving nary a stone (or "vacation") unturned as background for his revelation of the Les Mann letter and the consequent sentence. "Douglas will never play another game in organized baseball, and not a league will knowingly admit him to its parks," the manager told the scribes. As he spoke he glanced toward the corner of the room in which Landis sat silent and frowning in an armchair, his head sunk on his chest; it was clear to the writers that Phil Douglas could expect no mercy from *that* quarter.

There was a short silence in the room after McGraw completed his recital of Douglas' perfidy. Landis, who had a train to catch, looked more agitated in his grim silence with each passing moment. No questions were asked. McGraw looked around, cleared his throat, and with his best cock-of-the-walk air added the finishing touches to his character assassination of Phil Douglas. "Personally," he said, "I'm glad to be rid of him. Without exception, he is the dirtiest ballplayer I have ever seen." The scribes tried to keep straight faces at that one. Was the Old Man kidding? Phil Douglas, as everyone knew, had had his problems, but he was popular with his teammates and was a basically honest man—two things that could not have been said of quite a few others on the Giant payroll.

That night the commissioner caught his train to Chicago. The Giants went on to the West. McGraw picked up a couple of pitchers to replace Phil Douglas and with his usual junkman's luck went on to win the pennant with them. Phil Douglas returned to New York and took to his bed, tearful and bitter and confused. "McGraw had it in for me," he told a reporter who went to see him. "I knew all along he was going to throw me out. I'm as innocent as a child . . . They ain't seen my side of it!"

Later that month Damon Runyon was at Saratoga Springs, covering the annual racing meeting and staying at the United States Hotel. Saratoga in those days was a melting-pot resort where Broadway sporting types were commonly found mixing with the hoi polloi, so it was no shock to Damon that he ran into Phil Douglas under the elms in front of the Grand Union Hotel one day toward the end of August. Phil had been drinking and looked somewhat down on his luck, having (he told Damon) spent the past two days and nights in unsuccessful assaults on the gaming tables.

He'd come out of it broke—a situation Runyon could well understand, since he'd been cleaned out once or twice himself. While Phil told his story Damon reached in his pocket and pulled out all the bills that were there. When the conversation ended, he palmed them into Shufflin' Phil's big paw by way of a friendly handshake. The unfortunate Douglas—formerly a positive, exuberant man—smiled his thanks shyly from behind eyes made wary by his recent experiences. "This here will get me back to New York, Mr. Runyon," he drawled, half turning away in his embarrassment. "I'm mighty indebted."

Damon shook his head and said nothing, so Phil wheeled and flat-footed it away. The last Damon saw of him he was shuffling back down the path under the elms toward the hotel casino. It was the last glimpse any of the New York scribes ever had of this talented athlete and troubled being whose pitching skills his tormentor, John McGraw, had once compared to Christy Mathewson's.

In "Baseball Hattie" Runyon grafts the most colorful features of Bugs Raymond, Shoeless Joe Jackson, and several other of baseball's wilder characters on to the story of Phil Douglas and comes up with Haystack Duggeler.

> Haystack Duggeler is maybe twenty-five at this time, and he comes to the big league with more bad habits than anybody in the history of the world is able to acquire in such a short time. He is especially a great rumpot, and after he gets going good in the league, he is just as apt to appear for a game all mulled up as not. He is fond of all forms of gambling, such as playing cards and shooting craps, but after they catch him with a deck of readers in a poker game and a pair of tops in a crap game, none of the Giants will play with him any more, except of course when there is nobody else to play with. He is ignorant about many little things, such as reading and writing and geography and mathematics, as Haystack Duggeler himself admits he never goes to school any more than he can help, but he is so wise when it comes to larceny that I always figure they must have great tutors back in Haystack's old home town of Booneville, Mo.
>
> And no smarter jobbie ever breathes than Haystack when he is out there pitching. He has so much speed that he just naturally throws the ball past a batter before he can get the old musket off his shoulder, and along with his hard one, Haystack has a curve like the letter Q. With two ounces of brains, Haystack Duggeler will be the greatest pitcher that ever lives. . .
>
> A month before the close of his first season in the big league, Haystack Duggeler gets so ornery that Manager Mac suspends him, hoping maybe it will cause Haystack to do a little thinking, but naturally Haystack is unable to do this, because he has nothing to think with. About a week later, Manager Mac gets to noticing how he can use a few ball games, so he starts looking for Haystack Duggeler, and he finds him tending a bar on Eighth Avenue with

his uniform hung up back of the bar as an advertisement. The baseball writers speak of Haystack as eccentric, which is a polite way of saying he is a screwball, but they consider him a most unique character and are always writing humorous stories about him, though any one of them will lay you plenty of nine to five that Haystack winds up in umbay. The chances are they will raise their price a little, as the season closes and Haystack is again under suspension with cold weather coming on and not a dime in his pants pockets.

In Damon's tale Haystack Duggeler married Baseball Hattie, a Giants' loyalist. (Hattie is actually drawn after a legendary lady roughneck and Ebbets Field rooter of the twenties named Apple Annie, whom Damon observed in action.)

The baseball writers are wondering what Manager Mac will say when he hears these tidings, but all Mac says is that Haystack cannot possibly be any worse married than he is single-o, and then Mac has the club office send the happy couple a little paper money to carry them over the winter. Well, what happens but a great change comes over Haystack Duggeler. He stops bending his elbow and helps Hattie cook and wash the dishes, and holds her hand when they are in the movies, and speaks of his love for her several times a week, and Hattie is as happy as nine dollars' worth of lettuce. Manager Mac is so delighted at the change in Haystack that he has the club office send over more paper money, because Mac knows that with Haystack in shape he is sure of twenty-five games, and maybe the pennant.

Haystack does indeed "reform" long enough to pitch the Giants into the midst of a pennant race, but then he begins to backslide. He takes to betting on the nags and meets Armand Fibleman, a Broadway gambler who invests heavily in baseball games. In late August, with an important series against Brooklyn coming up and Haystack scheduled to work the first game, he is visited at home by Fibleman.

Hattie can hear every word they say, as the kitchen is next door to the dining room where they are sitting, and at first she thinks they are joking, because at this time nobody even as much as thinks of skulduggery in baseball, or anyway, not much. It seems that at first Haystack is not in favor of the idea, but Armand Fibleman keeps mentioning money that Haystack owes him for bets on the horse races, and he asks Haystack how he expects to continue betting on the races without fresh money, and Armand also speaks of the great injustice that is being done Haystack by the Giants in not paying him twice the salary he is getting, and how the loss of one or two games is by no means such a great calamity.

When Haystack insists that he will accept the "fix" money despite Hattie's opposition, that good lady (she "once works for three years in a shooting gallery at Coney Island") pulls out a .38 and opens fire. Armand Fibleman escapes, but Hattie wounds Haystack in the shoulder, ending his pitching life.

The ironic "twist" ending of Damon's plot involves the reincarnation of Haystack Duggeler's talent in his and Hattie's son, Derrill Duggeler, a promising Giant pitcher of the next generation. But it's clear that the dismal fate of Haystack himself, who loses his career, reflects in parabolic form Damon's view of the plight of the uneducated, loose-living young athlete who has his livelihood pulled out from under him as the result of an impulsive decision. There were all too many "real" Haystack Duggelers and very few instances on record of disciplinary action against a dishonest baseball owner, manager, or gambler.

Haystack Duggeler, in Damon's tale, left baseball and became a grocer in Los Angeles. Phil Douglas returned to the South, where after losing his baseball savings in unwise real estate investments he worked on the roads and played ball with any kind of team that would have him. When he was too old to play, he coached and managed youngsters' teams up and down the length of the valley where he lived. He sang hymns in his wheelchair in his last days and went to his deathbed protesting his innocence of intent in the 1922 affair, insisting he had been "framed" by his own club, which had been looking for an excuse to "get rid of him." When he died in 1952 there was an unpaid mortgage on his hillside cabin in Tennessee—and a wreath from nearly every family in the Sequatchie Valley at his grave. Although in his native area Shufflin' Phil remains a hero—a sort of Robin Hood to the mountain folk he sprang from—in sports history his name, like that of Bugs Raymond, is now no more than a cluster of fine black print on the white pages of the *Baseball Encyclopedia.*

To Damon Runyon and most of the others who watched Phil Douglas pitch from the Polo Grounds press box in 1919–1922, his tragedy symbolized the general tragedy of the dozen or so young athletes whose careers were sacrificed to the "purification" of the national sport in the years when Judge Landis dispensed his bitter "baseball justice." But even Damon's Haystack Duggeler, who took a bullet in his pitching shoulder, fared better than Phil Douglas, who lost his honor as a man. At least Haystack's son returned to become a star in the baseball world. Phil Douglas' offspring, who loved their daddy with loyalty and pride, have waited to this day to have his name "cleared"—and are still waiting.

[3] The passing of Matty

Christy Mathewson, the handsome and gifted pitcher called by Bill McGeehan "the incarnation of all those virtues with which they endow the ideal American," went to war for his country a few months before the Great Armistice. He sailed for France the same week as foreign correspondent Damon Runyon, in October

The World of Damon Runyon

1918. Runyon went to the Argonne forest, where from the front he reported the death of Sergeant Eddie Grant, former Giant third baseman and the only major leaguer killed in battle. (On the front lines Runyon also ran into infantryman Grover Cleveland Alexander and artillery lieutenant Grantland Rice before moving on to Coblenz with the American Occupation Forces.) Shortly after the signing of the peace treaty, Matty was assigned to inspector's duties in the trenches surrendered by the Germans, and in one of these trenches he ran into a lingering pocket of poison gas. The gas affected his lungs. Within six months of his repatriation the former athletic paragon was in a tuberculosis sanitarium at Lake Placid, a seriously ill man.

A Polo Grounds benefit engineered by Fred Lieb in 1921 raised $45,000 to finance Matty's recuperation, which continued for several years. Then in 1923 the strain that came with a part-time job as president of the Boston Braves exacerbated Matty's illness and caused a relapse. Although his condition had been for some time a worry to his old sporting pals, it came as a shock to most of them when on October 7, 1925, he passed away at Saranac Lake, New York.

The first game of the 1925 World Series was played that day at Pittsburgh. Damon sat in the press box that wet, gloomy afternoon and watched an exciting ballgame won by the Pirates on Kiki Cuyler's bases-loaded double off Walter Johnson in the eighth. After the game Damon wrote his syndicated column in the press box—the Hearst services had a younger man on hand to prepare the mundane game account—and next to him Ring Lardner, who hadn't been seen at a World Series since 1922, did the same.

Back at the hotel that night the writers learned that Mathewson was dead. The great, stalwart man—gone! Damon, Ring, all the older scribes were stunned. Bill McGeehan went to his room with a bottle of whiskey and composed "The Passing of Matty," his tearjerking obit for the *Herald Tribune.* "While the Captains and the Kings of baseball were gathered here last night after the first game of a World Series there died at Saranac the best loved of all the baseball players and the most popular of all American athletes of all time—Christy Mathewson. . ."

Damon, who was to turn forty-five the following day, was only a few weeks younger than Mathewson. The closeness of their birth dates was a coincidence that had attracted the great pitcher to Damon in 1911, when the writer was a rookie. Mathewson seldom fraternized with the younger scribes in those days, but he and Damon had hit it off from the first. It was those cardplaying nights on the Pullmans that flashed first into Damon's mind when he heard the news from Saranac. He went alone to his room to consider Matty's memory. His colleagues, he knew, would be drinking heavily in honor of the dead hero, and he did not want to be tempted; he was feeling too low to keep up a tough front.

Ring, on the other hand, did not like the prospect of thinking about death by himself. He too felt awful low, suddenly regretful that he'd accepted this World Series assignment at all. His room was full of drinking pals he hadn't seen in years, and now he had no choice (and no wish) but to get stiff with them to commemorate Matty's passing. (As he wrote Scott Fitzgerald when the Series was over, he stayed drunk the rest of the Series and wrote "seven terrible stories out of a possible nine, including the rainy days.")

John McGraw led a delegation of baseball men that included the National League president and the owner of the Boston Braves to Matty's funeral the following day. Damon and the other writers had to stay in Pittsburgh for the ballgame. The players, Walter Johnson and Goose Goslin and Kiki Cuyler and the rest, donned black armbands. Before Vic Aldridge's first pitch to Sam Rice of the Senators, there was a minute of silence for Matty. In the press box and even in the dugouts of the two clubs, handkerchiefs were seen fluttering in and out of pockets well into the first inning.

[4] Damon and Ring

Damon Runyon and Ring Lardner, acknowledged by their peers to be the greatest of a great age of sportswriting humorists, were at best distant friends whose mutual admiration and respect was tempered on both sides by competitive feelings and differences of life style, personality, and opinion. Ring lived and played with the Great Neck set in his later years, while Damon strayed toward Broadway. Ring drank and Damon did not. Ring had great success as a fiction writer while Damon was still only a newspaperman, and by the early twenties he was socially conversant with a "literary" crowd that was never to accept Runyon—and vice versa. Ring distrusted the "criminal" element that Damon embraced (and was embraced by) and never did much more than dip a toe in the whirling night life of the Avenues. Edmund Wilson and Scott and Zelda Fitzgerald and Dorothy Parker—bright, exportable moderns all—were Lardner's friends, while Runyon moved with and among such indigenous figures of town and track as Jimmy Walker, Lou Clayton, and Abba Dabba Berman, and numbered Al Capone and Arnold Rothstein among those he could count on for a favor. The contrasting milieus were instinctive choices that reflected the opposing characters and upbringings of the two men, between whom there was in fact seldom any love lost. Once in the early twenties, when a junior executive on the Sunday *American* (for which both men wrote at the time) placed a syndicated Lardner feature above one of Damon's own on the

Ring Lardner

same page, there was hell to pay with Runyon. Damon, the top Hearst feature star then and always, complained "upstairs," and the "mistake" was never repeated.

Nevertheless Runyon and Lardner could drop their differences when they were alone together on an assignment, side by side in a press box or at ringside. Between them they had seen enough seasons and Series go by and shared enough of the life of the sporting writer to give them a kind of permanent understanding that, since the two men seldom spoke, must have literally gone beyond words. What records we have of their public contact are of polite encounters and occasional friendly words. Since Ring died first, he never got a chance to make a final comment on Damon's work, which he appeared to enjoy when he saw it. Damon spoke highly of the Lardner style after Ring's death in 1933. That summer, when Paul Gallico (who'd quit the racket) came out with a critical attack on the sportswriters, calling them "innocent" and "wide-eyed," Damon rallied to his colleagues' defense, using Ring as his standard. "If ever a more hard-boiled or cynical sports writer than Ring Lardner lived I must have missed him," Runyon said in what for him were words of high praise.

To a later generation of sportswriters, Ring and Damon loomed as twin masters of the sharp, cunning, tongue-in-cheek style. "Damon was a cynical humorist," Jimmy Cannon told an interviewer in 1972. "He was like Ring Lardner. I didn't think he thought very much of the human race." The same was frequently said of Ring.

Like Damon, Ring in his later years and without much public show kept up with the coming and going of the baseball seasons. In the spring of 1933, dying like Matty of tuberculosis, Ring wrote to his son from Palm Springs that he'd been sent the preseason baseball odds by Jack Doyle (Damon's friend, the billiard academy manager) and had placed several parlay bets on the pennant race. Around the same time he wrote to a friend that he had "a yard and a half on the Yankees."

The Senators beat the Yankees out that season and faced the Giants in a World Series Damon covered from the press box for his column. But Ring didn't have to pay off on any of his losing bets; he died in his East Hampton home on September 25, 1933.

A few weeks before that Damon had visited Ring for the last time in a New York hospital. The two great ironists were noted for their long silences, so one may imagine that this last interview did not differ much from their other meetings over the twenty-five years they'd been acquainted.

Ring was propped up on his back in bed, reading a magazine, and didn't hear his guest come in.

Damon removed his hat, dropped his cigarette to the floor and ground it out, and cleared his throat.

Ring's eyes rolled up from the magazine and performed their act of recognition. "Hello, Damon," he said quietly. The magazine fell on the covers in front of him.

"Hello, Ring," Damon said. He sat down on the edge of the sick man's bed.

Silence fell over the room. Half an hour went by; a nurse took Ring's temperature and pulse and left again; still nothing was said. Ring lay back and glared at the ceiling. Damon sat on the edge of the bed, frowning and staring down at his new shoes, which were too tight and hurt his feet. (Ring's last published piece, an O. O. McIntyre parody that would appear in the *New Yorker* a few weeks after his death, would have a line about "Damon Runyon's tight shoes.")

Finally Ring made a small, impatient noise and said, "Damon, who was the greatest pitcher in the world?"

"Matty," Damon said.

Ring, Damon knew, was a Walter Johnson man—he'd always favored the "Big Train," even over Matty. Hearing Damon's reply to his question, Ring rolled his eyes again, away from Damon this time, and turned over on his side.

"Goodbye, Damon," he said.

"Goodbye," Damon said.

8

Shelby, Montana, Stages a Fight

Damon Runyon wrote not only baseball but boxing for Hearst's morning *American*. The boxing writer of the afternoon *Journal* was his distinguished colleague Hype Igoe; they worked in the same set of William Street offices but at different hours. Runyon wrote his stuff at night, Igoe his in the daytime. Hype's off-duty hours were often spent with Tad Dorgan, who created his *American* cartoons and stories at a desk next to Damon's. It was through Tad's auspices that Runyon and Igoe met.

Runyon looked up to the older writer who had once managed the great middleweight Stanley Ketchel before Ketchel threw two six-guns on the table and told Hype he wanted Wilson Mizner for a manager instead. (The six-foot-four, 250-pound Mizner, a great friend of Damon's, was the first legendary promoter-publicist of the century; he made millions on schemes and deals that took him from Guatemalan jungles to Klondike goldfields, lost his shirt in 1924 when the Florida land boom went bust, and started over as a Hollywood scriptwriter—an experience he compared to "taking a ride through a sewer in a glass-bottom boat.") Mizner managed Ketchel until a jealous husband shot the tough-as-nails fighter to death in Conway, Missouri. "Start counting to ten over him," Bill Mizner said when he heard the news of the shooting. "Stanley will get up at nine!" Ketchel, Hype Igoe's fighting ideal, had ruled the world from 1908 to 1910, when the disconsolate Walter Dipley shot him down at the age of twenty-four. Igoe always claimed Stanley might have been the best of them all had he lived.

"He finally came to write the most interesting and colorful tales since Pierce Egan, the Irishman who was the historian of the London Prize Ring over 200 years ago but whose furbishment of fistic fact has never been surpassed," Squire Runyon wrote of Hype Igoe in the Days of Retrospect. Damon had become Hearst's top New York columnist by the time Hype passed away; his obit on his old crony is an elegiac essay that reads beautifully today, a softly graceful pugilistic *Lycidas*.

When Hype walked into Jack's restaurant to play his ukulele, Damon recalled, Jack Dunstan took great anguish because Hype's playing caused the customers to sing along, and this slowed down trade. (Jack's place was the busiest in town, packed door to door twenty-four hours a day.) "So they took to frisking Hype when he entered and confiscating the uke and putting it in the ice box which caused the strings to shrink and ruin the tone," Runyon lamented. "The only time Jack would stand for the uke was when he himself was in a mellow mood. Then he would demand that Hype accompany him to a secluded table in the back room and play Irish lullabies for him." Those were the days of butting between the eyes and Spanish John O'Brien, Frank Ward O'Malley and Jack's "flying wedge" of waiters. There were always a number of sporting and theatrical parties present in Jack's (at Sixth Avenue and 43rd Street), as later in Billy LaHiff's Tavern, or after that in Lindy's and Toots Shor's. "And Hype was not infrequently the life of not one but all parties," Damon reminisced in the affectionate "Young Igoe." "The legends about him would fill a book."

Hype Igoe was sitting behind a typewriter in Dempsey's camp at Saratoga Springs before the Firpo fight. It was August 1923 and the champion was back in training after getting over the embarrassment of a world title bout in Shelby, Montana, that had turned into a historic fiasco. He was making ready for the Wild Bull of the Pampas, the Fat Angel Firpo, by taking apart one sparring partner after another. Jack took every sparring partner seriously. "Dempsey simply cannot continue to be either good-natured or loquacious once he has the gloves on," Heywood Broun had once remarked. The cruelties Jack rained upon his spar boys daily shocked even the veterans at their Coronas and Remingtons. "When they went in to spar against Dempsey they expected no mercy and got none. When his trainer called 'Time,' he set out to beat them into insensibility, and generally did," Paul Gallico later wrote. "They have even trained Joe Louis to hold back a little when he gets a spar boy going, but Dempsey never eased up in all his life." Jack had not yet met the beautiful Estelle Taylor and begun to taper off—not that he eased up even then, though he learned to smile more.

Hype Igoe sat at his machine and watched the champion destroy his spar boys one by one. It was a Sunday, and three thousand people were in the audience at a buck apiece even though it was only part of Dempsey's regular training. His first three partners on this particular Sunday were speed types, giving Jack a chance to pratice ducking and to perfect his moves and defense. Then he had two bigger boys on deck for heavy hitting. On this particular day one of the bigger boys was young Gallico, at twenty-four a six-foot-three, 192-pound husky in his first year on the sports beat. Though no fighter, Gallico had put in four sweaty years on the crew team at Columbia. He thought himself a stalwart fellow and had argued persuasively enough on this point to convince the champion's handlers to allow him to don headgear, trunks, and a rowing shirt and to spar a round or two with Dempsey just for fun. Jack Kearns, Dempsey's perfumed manager, had been away at Atlantic City. Kearns would never have allowed such a stunt had he been given due warning of it, but now the tall young scribe stood before him, and Kearns as referee had no choice but to smile his way through the event, even if it proved to be fatal. He gave Dempsey hell for it later, though.

Before Gallico stepped into the ring, Hype Igoe stopped typing for a minute, looked up at Paul, and inquired if it was really true that he was intending to spar with the champ. Gallico, looking more bashful by the minute in his Columbia rowing shirt, managed a nervous affirmative reply and added that it was his understanding Dempsey was only going through the motions to play along with the gag.

"He's going to take it easy on me," the tall lad from the *Daily News* announced hopefully.

Hype peered back over his spectacles. "Son, don't you know that man *can't* take it easy?"

Kearns called out the champ's name and the paying customers roared. The contender in the opposite corner, being an unknown, was greeted as his own name fell upon the Sabbath gathering by a kind of hush more familiar at funerals than training camps. Gallico got his instructions from Kearns and advanced knock-kneed, his left arm out in a simulation of classic style. Dempsey walked into it face first, winced with surprise, then began to pursue like a large cat on the trail of prey. A left hook made an arc over the retreating reporter's head, but a second was more accurate and dropped him into Lethe for an eight count. The ringside scribes bowed their heads. But up popped Gallico, for no reason at all. Dempsey clung to the wobbly lad in a clinch and, fatherly, instructed him to hang on. Following this he launched six rabbit punches to the apex of the scribe's spine, and Gallico fell for good, like a building falling. After half an hour he had a cut lip, a headache, and his senses back and he was writing his story—a lucky man, everyone agreed, to be living at all. He had survived a knockout in the mismatch of the ages.

That's how Gallico always told it. The laconic Runyon saw it differently and later expressed his reservations about the legend that grew out of this day, referring disparagingly to the tale of Paul's knockout as a "tradition" rather than a fact. A great follower of the heavyweights all his life, and a particular chum of the charmingly ruthless champ Dempsey, Damon wondered in print (tongue as usual surrounded by cheek) when recalling the champ's supposed KO over the young reporter. "Personally," he told the readers of his column years later, "I was always of the opinion

The World of Damon Runyon

Dempsey . . . was too smart to slug an influential tub thumper like Gallico was in those days and that what really happened was Jack burped as Paul put up his hands and the scribe swooned."

Runyon probably felt closer to Dempsey than he did to any other athlete except the great Christy Mathewson. But if Matty was the epitome of manhood (to writers like Broun and Runyon and McGeehan), Dempsey was the opposite, the perfection of something animal. Dempsey in the ring evoked from the scribes images of brutal feline power: in the prose of the Rices and the Gallicos, the evangelists of the time, he always "stalked" his opponent, never simply pursued him. He was a jungle cat who possessed "smoldering truculence." Clearly no mere human, perhaps he was a god or, as Gallico suggested, a "son of Mars." Certainly this picture-book fighter's dark eyes, blue-black hair, and constant five o'clock shadow imaged dark power beyond mortal reach. He was seen as being "utterly without mercy or pity, asking no quarter, giving none."

This charming brute approved sufficiently of Runyon to cause envious discontent among the boxing writers. Jack Kearns' habit of passing Dempsey exclusives to Runyon alone infuriated the *Herald Tribune*'s redoubtable McGeehan, who so hated to see all the champ's scoops landing in the Hearst camp that he never forgave Dempsey for it and regarded him permanently with a malign distrust. Such were the velleities of an exciting business. Even McGeehan would have had to admit the existence of facts that explained Runyon's success in penetrating the Dempsey entourage. Fifteen years older than the champ, Damon came from the same background; each had scuffled his way out of dead-end streets in Colorado mining towns and created a star of such heat as to burn its way from the Rockies all the way to Gotham. Runyon had arrived at the sports desk of the *American* a mere five years before Dempsey hit town and found his way to Graupp's Gym on 116th Street. Each was preceded by a minor legend and a budding reputation, but—as Dempsey put it—nobody threw ticker tape at either one of them. For both it was strictly a case of work your way to the top because there's no other way to get there.

In 1916 Runyon was learning the speech of the uptown characters who filled the streets and corners near his flat at 111th Street and Broadway. Jack Price, who'd signed Dempsey to fight Joe Bond in Ely, Nevada, and accompanied him East, finally found the hungry young fighter an opponent after three weeks of "stalking" the alien gyms and parks; the opponent was André Anderson, and the match was made by Billy Gibson, who acceded to Price's pleas and designed an affair for the newcomer at his Fairmont Club. (Ironically, Gibson would later go on to manage the handsome reader of the *Rubaiyat,* Gene Tunney, eventual thief of Dempsey's crown.) Anderson hunkered in at a stolid 215; the Colorado lad, who ran the parks all afternoon, came into the bout a 162-pound stripling. All that held body and soul together for him were the free lunches he stuffed into his mouth in bars.

Anderson knocked Dempsey down numerous times in the early rounds, then fell victim to fatigue in the fifth. Jack had run him to death, as he would do many better men later. He decorated the Swede's skin with leather for the final five rounds. In those days, before the passage of Saint James Walker's Holy Boxing Law, no decisions were given. Bets were won and lost, believe it or not, on the strength of boxing writers' opinions ("newspaper decisions," they were dubbed). Ned Brown of the *World* favored Dempsey; so did Runyon of the *American.* Bets on Dempsey were paid. Jack and his braintrust, Price, split the twenty-dollar take, two bucks going to the towel artist in Dempsey's corner. The future champ had a full stomach when he went to sleep the next couple of nights, and for the first time since he'd hit New York his bed was not a park bench.

It didn't take Dempsey long to start moving up in the world. Within three years he was slicing the giant Jess Willard to ribbons before 19,000 blood-crazed, sun-drenched partisans on the Fourth of July 1919 in Toledo, Ohio. This widely ballyhooed fight was the first dawn of the Golden Era; newspapers throughout the country sent their scribes to Toledo for a three-week party that sorely tested the brand new Ohio prohibition laws (the state had gone dry one year ahead of the rest of the nation) as well as the iron constitutions of the reporters, exposed for the first time to the cheap bathtub gin of the new age of outlaw drinking.

Eyes made bleary by dawn visions of glory (and by all-day, gorilla-sized hangovers) were the credentials of the sportswriting crowd at Toledo. Damon Runyon, sipping coffee in the restaurant of the Hotel Secor, watched his colleagues' behavior with a wry grin; whether he was tempted to join in the fun, no one could say. Damon was in the audience of Herman Saxon's theatre one night a week or so before the fight when Ring Lardner, the new star correspondent of John Wheeler's Bell Syndicate, played and sang his "Toledo Blues" ("I guess I've got those there Toledo Blues,/ About this fight I simply can't enthuse") with a choral accompaniment provided by sportswriter-cartoonists Tad Dorgan and Rube Goldberg, among others. A few days later Runyon escorted his wobbly colleagues to the local links and wired the *American:* "Rube Goldberg snatched Ring Lardner in a golf contest this morning with Grantland Rice seconding Goldberg, and Bob Edgren behind Lardner. They took advantage of Lardner in getting him up early, however."

The World of Damon Runyon

Perhaps the synthetic hilarity had a therapeutic value in that most of the scribes were too anesthetized to perceive the true dimensions of the fight itself. It was a carnival of violence, all Dempsey's. "I couldn't miss, wherever I swung he was there," the new champ said later, when asked why the fight had resembled target practice. The gigantic Jess had jaw and ribs shattered, yards of tissue turned into a lacy refuse. Ironically, in a (probably ghostwritten) piece in the New York *American,* Willard had claimed to be afraid of "killing" the much smaller challenger. Certainly there were those in the crowd at Toledo who expected as much. Willard brought to Toledo the role of favorite he had carried with him from his days as the principal sporting attraction of the Sells-Floto Circus, where perhaps his size had tempted Fred Bonfils to match him against large animals rather than men.

In his Denver *Post* days Runyon had refereed Sells-Floto bouts, and what he didn't already know of Willard's might he'd learned in watching the huge Kansan conquer Jack Johnson in their marathon battle in Havana in 1915. The fresher memory on the eve of the Toledo battle, however, was the way the blue-black panther of a contender had disposed of Fred Fulton a summer earlier. Fulton, the favorite in his encounter with Dempsey, had spent exactly eighteen seconds on his feet. Even though Damon had been draping his coat over his chair at the time of Dempsey's first blows in the Fulton fight (and thus missed all the action), he'd recognized in Dempsey's victorious scowl an awesome ferocity and therefore dubbed the kid the Manassa Mauler, a nickname which struck even those who didn't know Manassa from Minnesota as just right. In the months preceding the Willard bout, he'd been ghostwriting the Colorado puncher's life story—"A Tale of Two Fists"—for the *American,* relying heavily on "color" material from Dempsey's ragtag youth on the east slopes of the Rockies. (Jack had once picked fruit for a living in Montrose, Colorado, a fact that permitted Damon to call him "the only peach-snatching heavyweight pugilistic prospect the ring has ever seen.")

In Toledo Damon put his money on Dempsey, but most of the other scribes favored the champ, who stepped into the ring at 260 pounds. Dempsey, a head shorter, had stuffed himself with bananas to get his weight up into the 180s for a public scales ceremony conducted by the master promoter, the lanky, thin-lipped son of the Lone Star State and former faro dealer of Nome, George "Tex" Rickard.

Lardner, Broun, Rice, Rube Goldberg, Irvin S. Cobb, and Runyon had all attended a big party on the outskirts of Toledo the night before the fight, but the teetotaling Demon had apparently preserved a clear head and was touched only by the 110° heat when he tapped out his story. Dempsey's violent assault on

Jack Dempsey and Tex Rickard

Willard lasted only three rounds, but it opened a permanent vein in Runyon's imagination. He was clearly in awe of the most potent and singleminded specimen of his favorite beast, the heavyweight, that his experience had yet produced. Other writers hated and feared Dempsey; Runyon enthroned him in prose that was on this and similar occasions hideously sanguine.

> At the feet of the gargantuan pugilist was a dark spot which was slowly widening on the brown canvas as it was replaced by the drip-drip-drip-drip of blood from the man's wounds. He was flecked with red from head to foot. The flesh on his enormous limbs shook

like custard. He was like a man who had just been pulled from the wreck of an automobile, or railroad train. He blinked one eye through which he could still see daylight at the glaring sun, looking out over the head of the crowd that had gathered to see something like this. . . . In the corner opposite him, tugging at the ring ropes like a pit terrier tugging at a leash, and scratching his feet on the resined canvas with sinister impatience was the saddle-colored demon who had ripped and pounded and slashed this tremendous fellow into this distressing state.

It was the beginning of an epoch: Jack had a date with destiny, Damon was effusive. Bill McGeehan was more concise. He saw Willard "flounder on a stool with his right eye closed and a torrent of blood gushing from his gaping mouth. . . . a signal that a new heavyweight champion had arrived." But then The *Herald Tribune* men were expected to maintain some restraint; at the Hearst offices there were no such compunctions. Even Arthur Brisbane, the most respected editor in New York, preferred output to accuracy if the two were in competition.

Jack had shed his first wife, taken in Hollywood, had his first taste of champagne (it reminded him of milk of magnesia), been befriended by stars ("I got along with Charley Chaplin, and Douglas Fairbanks was my pal"), and was "free as a bird" after the obliteration of Willard. Two years later, after he had battered the fair-haired Frenchman Georges Carpentier on a muggy afternoon (Don Marquis, Broun said, poured $1 worth of beer and $3.50 worth of charged water over his own head just to cool off) at Boyle's Thirty Acres, New Jersey, in the first Million Dollar Fight, he was freer still, being one of the nation's several hundred budding millionaires.

Tex Rickard had cleverly engineered public sentiment in favor of the frail Parisian, who was pictured as a war hero while Dempsey photos given to the press showed the champ safely working the war away in a shipyards. This only served to hype the gate, as the shrewd Tex had planned. The gross was $1,626,580 from 91,000 fans, most of them rooting for the "valiant" pale Frog. (Additional thousands across the country experienced the fight imaginatively through radio in the first national sports broadcast.) Before the fight Rickard reminded the champ that there was quality in the crowd—"Jack, you never seed anything like it; high-class society folks, and *dames!* I mean *classy* dames. *Thousands* of 'em!"— and begged Jack not to kill the Frog. "If you kill him, you'll kill boxing," Rickard pleaded. To give Tex his show, Jack carried the Frog four rounds before he put him away. Everybody was happy. After Carpentier's vacant eyes had regained their lights, he came across the ring and gave the scowling victor a smile. Jack was

Shelby, Montana, Stages a Fight

Water Babies of 1921: Damon at Atlantic City with Jack Dempsey, Joe Bannon, and Joe Benjamin before the Dempsey–Carpentier fight.

happy too; he took $300,000 home, not to mention what he picked up off the movie rights.

Dempsey returned to New York in triumph and was fawned over, lionized, and adored by Lillian Lorraine, Sylvia Sidney, Mabel Normand, and Claudette Colbert, Jimmy Walker and Herb Swope, Rube Goldberg and Bugs Baer, Grantland Rice and Damon Runyon. *Let* the Brouns and McGeehans and Gallicos think of him as half animal; they too had to worship at Jack's shrine, for he was the champ. He was enjoying himself now.

The champ relaxed among bootleggers and swells, writers and Follies girls, at Billy Seeman's parties, at Billy LaHiff's Tavern, the Cotton Club, and the Silver Slipper, mixed with the best and worst and most exciting of worlds, and in 1922 took off on a tour of Europe that left half the beautiful women in New York with a piece of their heart missing. For Jack it was strictly a pleasure trip; he took along only his manager and a few friends, one of them Damon Runyon. Still innocent of grammar, and in need of a shave every four hours, Dempsey was the toast of several capitals. Newspaper baron Lord Northcliffe entertained him in London. When Runyon came to the door, Northcliffe gave him the cold shoulder; the champion was his guest, and no reporters were required. Damon, Jack said, never recovered from the insult to his dignity. "He had known me when I was a bum," the champ laughed.

In Paris the crowd found more girls and better action, and Damon was turned away at no doors. In Berlin Dempsey took him to see some lady boxers. (Both watched popeyed as Steffa Bernart of Silesia scored a seventh-round KO.) The trip cost Jack plenty; Hearst paid Damon's way, but Dempsey picked up the tab for the rest of the group of six or seven (or fifteen or twenty, depending on which night you were counting). On his return to the States he was forced to pick up a few tame matches in out of the way places like Michigan City and Boston to pay the bills from the tour. One night in Montreal he knocked out three separate men. Meanwhile Kearns was looking around for a better buck to be made. That, in the early days of 1923, was the origin of the Shelby fiasco.

The time was ripe for heavyweight bonanzas. Hero or villain, Dempsey had the appeal to fill any arena or stadium with any opponent you could name. Money was loose, and it meant something to be seen at a heavyweight championship bout, as any Dempsey bout in the early days of the Golden Era was bound to be. Tex Rickard knew how to put on a good show, and his shows went off like clockwork. Harking back to the days in Nome when money was gold, he printed his fifty-dollar tickets on gold-backed card stock that gave his promotions a subtle aristocratic touch not unnoticed by those who drove high-priced cars, owned beautiful country homes, had fat bank accounts, and dressed like millionaires. These were the people who bought Tex's top-priced ducats; they were also the people who fought the bouts for him, because Tex paid his boys nicely—and he paid no one as nicely as he paid Jack Dempsey.

In those days the business paid pretty well for everybody. Damon Runyon, elevated to the prominence of a sports columnist, was drawing $25,000 a year and had moved his young family (Mary was nine, Damon Jr. four) from a somewhat cramped 95th Street and Broadway flat into a lavish seven-room apartment on Riverside Drive overlooking the greenery of Riverside Park at 102nd Street. For the present he was at the top of his game, widely read and highly respected in the writing racket and throughout the sporting trade where he traveled. He was regarded as highly quotable in baseball and boxing, in college football ("What a football player, this man Red Grange: he is melody and symphony, he is crashing sound, he is brute force"), and in the equine sport—perhaps particularly in the latter, for it was only a few months before the trip to Europe with Dempsey that Damon had sprung his Corona Muse for the famous poetic lead he was to use and vary half a dozen times in describing victories of the classic rider, Earl Sande: "Gimme a handy/Guy like Sande,/Bootin' them babies in!" (No sports poetry ever achieved wider fame in America than the verses about Sande, which the canny Runyon trotted out with minor revisions every time he wrote a Sande story over the next eight seasons.)

The Shelby spectacular, which Dempsey would later call "the most fouled-up promotion of my boxing life," was scheduled for the Fourth of July, like the Willard bloodbath four years earlier. It was a fight that twenty-six years later Dempsey said "couldn't come off today." It very nearly didn't come off *then*, either, for the Shelby promotion was almost too ridiculous even for the Era of Wonderful Nonsense (Westbrook Pegler's coinage). The Shelby battle took place only because the times permitted (and even encouraged) schemes that in other epochs would have seemed sheer folly. Who knows; if Tex Rickard had promoted it, the thing might have made a million bucks.

Shelby was and is not much of a place. It lies twenty-five miles from the Canadian border, on the east slopes of the Rockies where the plains begin. In 1923 a brief strike at oilfields near Shelby caused the town's population to expand from two to ten thousand and convinced those who were buying up local real estate that a whopping land boom was on the horizon. The boys wanted to get that boom going any old way they could think of. Not that any of them hadn't been able to think of a way; it was just that land in the area of Shelby didn't have a very attractive look, and oil or no oil, nobody back East wanted any whatever the price.

A fight manager out of Minneapolis-St. Paul, Mike Collins, was barnstorming his way across the state of Montana with a nondescript string of battlers, putting on boxing shows in any town wealthy enough to pay a couple hundred bucks. Collins, like many a guy in the fight racket by this time, was an old crony of Damon's. Runyon and he had first crossed paths some years before, when Collins was promoting Fred Fulton, a fighter who had the only left-hand uppercut Damon had ever seen—and, Collins confessed, a heart no bigger than a pea. Collins had not been in Montana long when he ran into a fellow with what Damon called "the improbable name of Foy Molumby." Molumby, the head of Montana's American Legion (Damon later thought him "a very nice chap . . . whose only idea was to put Shelby on the map"), had never before encountered anyone connected with the fight game. One drink led to another, and soon Foy Molumby had Mike Collins up in what according to Grantland Rice was a very flimsy airplane, "cruising all over the state . . . shooting off horse pistols and calling for wine." On the ground again, the two pals met Jim Johnson, the Mayor of Shelby and the president of the Shelby bank. Collins, Molumby, and Johnson talked business and boxing, and then Mike Collins made for the phone.

The World of Damon Runyon

Tom Gibbons

He called his friend Eddie Kane in Minnesota. Eddie handled Tom Gibbons, a thirty-four-year-old journeyman boxer out of St. Paul who'd been on the heavyweight circuit for as long as anybody cared to remember and done himself occasional credit here and there over the years. Mike Collins proposed a Dempsey fight. "Listen, Mike," Eddie Kane hollered into the receiver, "you get Dempsey out there anywhere, and Gibbons will fight him for nothing. All you gotta do is pay Dempsey. How do you like that?" Collins and Johnson and Molumby liked it fine.

When Johnson and Molumby had done some business, Collins got on the blower to Jack Kearns in Chicago. Damon Runyon happened to be hanging out with Kearns at the time. Kearns took the call in a phone booth and came out with a big grin on his face. "That was Mike Collins," he told Damon. "He has got his kiddin' clothes on. He says some guy has wired him offering me $200,000 to fight Tom Gibbons in some place in Montana called Shelby."

"I never heard of Shelby," Runyon said.

"Neither did I," Kearns said, "and I've been around Montana quite a bit. I don't think Mike ever heard of it himself. He is just putting on a rib."

"What did you tell him?"

Shelby, Montana, Stages a Fight

"I told him I would take $300,000 of which $100,000 had to be paid me when I signed for the fight and the balance put in escrow for me."

Kearns, Damon explains, was "strictly of the 'I' school of managers"; his usage of the first person indicated that he was speaking for the heavyweight champion of the world.

A couple of days later Mike called again to say Kearns' counterproposition had been accepted. Then Kearns told the champ about the fight he had just lined up for him on the Fourth of July.

"Where's this Shelby?" Dempsey asked. "I never heard of it."

"It ain't a big place," Kearns said. "The money's there, though. Mike Collins tells me some oil fellows out there want to put the town on the map, sell some oil stocks."

"I don't want to fight in no place called Shelby, Doc. It's crazy."

"They're going to give us two-fifty and fifty percent."

"Well, okay," the champ said. "But I'm going to hold you responsible for the money."

Dempsey claims Kearns never talked about the fight with Tex Rickard. Promoters like Rickard did not retain exclusive rights to fighters, and Kearns wanted to put the show on himself and thereby avoid cash splits. For that matter, Kearns did not even have a contract with Dempsey; things were less formal in those days.

The first $100,000 was delivered the day Dempsey signed a contract for the fight. The contract called for a second payment of $100,000 thirty days before the fight, but rather than wait for that time, Dempsey and Kearns decided to go West and set up a training site. In May they found a headquarters in Great Falls, 86 miles south of Shelby.

Eddie Kane and Tom Gibbons went direct to Shelby. Kane set up a camp and rented a house on top of a bare hill for Gibbons and his wife and two kids. Dempsey had not liked the looks of Shelby ("a crossroad in the middle of a desert," Grantland Rice called it) and had fled to the comparative urbanity of Great Falls. Indeed the burg of Shelby had only a handful of permanent dwellings, one or two of which passed for travelers' hotels; Tom Gibbons' rented cottage was not much inferior to them.

The hoopla began. Plans for special trains from New York, Chicago, and San Francisco were being laid by the exuberant promoters. As always with a championship bout, the boxing writers descended in force and well in advance. Late in June Runyon boarded a Great Northern Line Pullman in Chicago with a crowd of writers that included Broun, Rice, and the celebrated Hugh Fullerton, then of the New York *Evening Mail.* Arriving in Montana, they made a temporary mecca of Dempsey's camp in Great Falls before traveling on to the more prosaic Shelby.

The champion had his headquarters in a grove of cottonwoods. His training proceeded as it did before all his fights: up in the morning for roadwork, then a rest, lunch, play a little cards, then a workout, rubdown, dinner, play cards again. For his workouts he had the best opposition available—ten, maybe fifteen different sparring partners. A boy might last an hour or ten days; as soon as one was too beaten-down to give the champ a good workout, Kearns discharged him and a new mate was selected from the large corps of nervous but hungry volunteers.

Runyon and the other writers arrived in Dempsey's camp on June 24, the champ's twenty-eighth birthday. They learned that he was in good spirits. His dad, a "Jack" Mormon (a nonabstemious strain) from Logan County, West Virginia, was hanging around the camp. So was his cousin, a big fellow who was a legitimate member of the Hatfield clan. Dempsey was working hard; it had been two years since his last defense of the title, and the living had been easy in the interim. He rubbed bear grease on his face to toughen his skin, and it made the skin thicken and darken and grow shiny in the sunlight. Grantland Rice said the facials made the champ's face take on the general texture of a boar's hide.

The imagery was always animalian. "Even walking, he seemed to slither along, snakelike, his muscles glinting in the sun," Rice wrote. The mascot of Dempsey's camp was an even better talisman: a timber wolf cub. The pat-pat-pat of leather on skin filled the air of the camp as Dempsey "stalked" and "savaged" his spar boys among the flowering cottonwoods. Small boys from Sweetgrass and Sunburst and Oilmont snuck into the camp and mingled with the writers and other hangers on, their mouths open and their eyes wide with wonder at the violence the champ performed with such a casual air upon his various partners of an afternoon.

Damon Runyon sent off daily reports on the champ's training progress, most of them fairly desultory in the early going—except for the day a small black and white kitten rubbed against his cuff and convinced him to take it back to his hotel. There the hard-boiled scribe provided emergency dishes of milk. The Runyon dispatch that day contained a description of his new traveling companion; his readers were invited to suspect that there was no news of earthshaking import from the camp of the champion.

As Dempsey's training proceeded, however, a note of anxiety was sensed. Damon heard from Kearns that the Shelby interests were having a hard time coming up with the second $100,000 installment. Mayor Jim Johnson had done everything but mortgage the Shelby bank. Foy Molumby had run out of funding ideas and, Runyon said, "was eventually eased out of the pugilistic picture when the situation became highly complicated because of difficulties attendant upon raising the money." Kearns himself gradually took over more and more of the promotion.

The thirty-day deadline had come and gone, and Dempsey was getting nasty about the second payment. "Where's the money?" he asked Kearns.

"Now, don't worry kid," the manager began.

"Hold it, Doc," the champ interrupted him. "No money, no fight."

"I'll get it," Doc Kearns promised. "Count on me."

Dempsey still had his doubts. He called Tex Rickard at Madison Square Garden and filled him in. Tex, whom Dempsey regarded as "a big league fellow," made an immediate and gentlemanly offer to buy out the whole show and move it to New York, where it could be put on in a proper way. The champ liked that idea and was ready to pack on short notice, but the people of Shelby did not like the idea at all. The land boom people still figured the world would beat a path to their real estate if only they could fork over the second payment, so they bellowed to the champ about the contract while behind their backs they did a little fast shuffling. The local American Legion treasury was sprung open, and a number of local shopkeepers' tills were tapped, all in the interest of civic promotion. It was broadly, if not desperately suggested that certain interests would resort to force if the Dempsey group attempted to leave town while the money was being anted up. Finally the ante was achieved, and the champ was paid.

Another payment of $50,000 was scheduled for ten days before the fight. That was ridiculous; as Dempsey said later, "There wasn't that much money left in the town." Kearns and Dempsey, regarding discretion as the better part of valor, decided not to tempt the patience of certain loud and dangerous-looking local cowboys and waived the ten-day limit. Kearns smiled at everybody and said he'd take the champ's last payment out of the gate. By then that idea was strictly a joke; the fight had been canceled and uncanceled about half a dozen times, leaving the promoters of special trains and prospective ticket buyers on both coasts in a state of perplexity.

On July 1, three days before the fight, Dempsey took on his top sparring partner, George Godfrey, a powerful black man who outweighed the champ by more than forty pounds. A Godfrey right drew blood on Jack's chin, but a moment later Godfrey was moaning on the canvas with two broken ribs while Jack danced over him, pounding his gloves together and looking around to see who else was on hand. The next man to be served up could not meet his gaze. (Two weeks earlier Dempsey had smashed to pieces the jaw of a seven-foot-two cowboy named "Big Ben" Wray. Doctors had had to encase Wray's head in a chunk of plaster with small openings for seeing, breathing, and feeding.) After his long layoff, the champ had obviously gotten himself back into shape and was physically "ready."

Back in Shelby, Tom Gibbons (who was fighting for nothing) trained hard and pretty much by himself at his little place on the hillside. No cottonwoods, no shade trees, not so much as a stalk of long grass shielded Gibbons' place from the boiling Shelby sun. He had his own spar boys; Eddie Kane was bringing Gibbons along the best he could. It was to be the fight of Gibbons' life, and there was no distraction in his preparations.

For everyone else concerned with the fight, however, the preparations were one long distraction. The festivity was only slightly lessened by Shelby's lack of suitable housing for visitors. Those who hit town on wagons slept in them, those who came on muleback, horseback, or on foot slept in tents and lean-tos of various types, many of them constructed with planks and old feed bags. The few rooms to be had in Shelby's modest Rainbow Hotel were snatched up quickly by the early arrivals, the Western Union supervisors and telegraphers (who set up their offices in Shelby's City Hall) and the representatives of the larger New York papers, who'd sent advance scouts. Bill Corum, then a cub reporter with the *American,* got in three weeks before the fight and secured the only room in the Rainbow that had running water. When McGeehan and Runyon pulled into Shelby from Great Falls, Runyon escorting the kitten he'd adopted at Dempsey's camp, they were accompanied by an aide-de-camp recruited from Damon's Broadway circle, Little Solly Harris. Little Solly ran errands and confiscated Bill Corum's bathtub for use as "Sheriff" McGeehan's beer cooler. (For Damon, who drank neither beer nor red-eye and liked fine dining, Shelby was a total culinary loss; he could not even find a decent cup of coffee.)

Private railway cars and soft drink stands filled the Shelby sidings. (When arriving passengers complained that the Shelby railway station was inadequate, the local promoters hired a gang of workers to saw the building in half, move the ends apart, and construct a new center segment, thereby making it the largest station in the state!) Writers unable to find other accommodations lived in parked Pullmans. Mrs. Baker, the Bromo Seltzer heiress, had her private car, the Palm Beach, parked nearby. Mae Murray, the Ziegfeld beauty, was living out of her private Pullman on a Great Northern siding in Shelby.

There was great revelry, blaring bands, snake dancing in the night. If Prohibition existed at all in the minds of the celebrants, it was only a memory. Mrs. Alfred Gwynne Vanderbilt was placed hip-to-jowl with One-Eyed Connolly, the era's most notorious gate-

Shelby, Montana, Stages a Fight

Mae Murray

crasher. At the height of the fun, the *World*'s star columnist, Heywood Broun, cabled Florenz Ziegfeld in New York that he had discovered a raving beauty named Patricia Salmon, the fairest lass in all Montana and a natural for Flo's Follies. The Great Ziegfeld cabled back, SEND COWGIRL AT ONCE. Ziegfeld's private car was dispatched to Shelby to fetch this vaunted lovely, who turned out to be short, fat, and possessed of a mustache that would rival that of a New York policeman. (Refusing to lose face for his error, Ziegfeld signed the girl and designed a Montana Cowgirl number for her in the Follies!)

Hugh Fullerton, hanging around Tom Gibbons' camp a day or two before the fight, saw a couple of Blackfoot braves in full war regalia looking on at the proceedings. Sensing a story, he asked them in a combination of sign language and baby talk what they thought of the fight. They turned out to be Carlisle Indian School graduates who gave him a ten-minute discourse on the subject of how they liked Dempsey, "since power usually prevails over skill." Hughey reeled away with an excellent story.

The Shelbyites were whooping it up as best they could considering the empty state of their pockets and purses. Anti-Dempsey feeling, inspired by what was regarded to be the champ's ungenerous and greedy grumblings and threats of pulling out of the bout, expressed itself in the form of random shouts and yells, plus a series of extemporaneous parades of protest. "You've got to pay Dempsey every cent, or you won't see Dempsey at all," was the chant.

Runyon's job at Shelby was no bowl of cherries. On July 3 Jack Kearns "officially" canceled the fight no less than seven times before deciding to go along with the cowboys' request and gamble on the take at the gate. Every time the fight was called off or on, Runyon, Broun, Rice, and the others had to rush fresh teletype bulletins to New York. On the eve of the fight, exasperated, they finally decided to cease cabling any news at all until it could be determined exactly what was happening. It was well into the night before it was clear that the morrow's fight would actually take place. By that time Shelby was a virtual madhouse. From impromptu saloons the wail of saxophones and tinkle of pianos issued into the dirt streets. Drunken cowboys and society dames danced in the gutter and bought each other drinks. Indian braves and Hollywood stars Charlestoned. Mae Murray peeked from the curtained windows of her private car at the snake dancing and the bonfires, then pulled the curtain back. Nobody knew who was in there with Mae—or cared.

Tom Gibbons looked down on the wild scene from his hillside shack and stoked his dream.

* * *

Shelby, Montana, Stages a Fight

The fight was to be held in a huge wooden bowl built for the event and intended to hold fifty thousand. Only seven or eight thousand spectators showed up on the morning of the fight, and of these only a few hundred held the fifty-dollar ringside tickets the promoters had printed. There were several thousand cowboys and hard riders on hand, and they were carrying guns, whiskey bottles, and lariats. Some of them bought twenty-dollar tickets, but most chose a cheaper route of entry. Impervious to the warning shots of Internal Revenue agents, they pushed the gates down, lassoed the fences, and poured through in large groups. Thousands got in for free. They booed Dempsey and screamed for blood when he was introduced. "For the first and only time," Jack admitted later, "I was more worried about getting hurt by the crowd than by the guy I was fighting."

For all the hell the crowd raised, no one laid a finger on Dempsey—and that was probably more a matter of the champ's good luck than anything. If the angry crowd had charged him, he would have had very little defense. His bodyguard, a character named Wild Bill Lyons whom Jack had brought along from New York for the extra protection in just such a spot, was carrying a pair of pearl-handled pistols, but when the champ looked around for him, Lyons was nowhere to be found. It turned out he had been hiding under the ring since the preliminaries.

Gibbons put up the fight of his life, which was all he had come to do. He took Dempsey the distance. The champ later called Tommy "a good boxer and a very clever man," but this day he was almost more than that. For fifteen rounds the two men fenced and danced like featherweights. And this time Gibbons won the animalian comparisons. He was "a wildcat that steaming afternoon," wrote Grantland Rice, who also said he'd never witnessed as much sheer speed in a heavyweight bout. Damon Runyon's kitten clung to his shoulder, terrified by the whoops of cowboys urging Tom Gibbons on. Damon's fingers flew over the typewriter; he was the only writer in the fight crowd who could type a running account so that the teletyper could move his story right off the paper and onto the wire—which meant his stories always beat everybody else's into print.

Gibbons was a better fighter than most people expected, Runyon and Dempsey included. Jack later claimed that he was not in good enough shape for the bout. That was not the case. Gibbons stuck to a single plan: stab and run. Dempsey hurt him in the first with a straight right to the thick part of his skull above the forehead, and Tommy was dazed for four rounds. But he kept moving out of range all that time, and Dempsey never hit him squarely again; at the end the champ held him and tried to beat him in close. After the seventh round the crowd woke to the fact that it was an excellent fight. The cowboys rooting for Gibbons and the New Yorkers rooting for Dempsey made enough noise for a crowd five or ten times as big.

Shocked as Damon and the other scribes at ringside were by Gibbons' staying power, there was little doubt in their minds as to who would be declared the victor. For the referee and only judge, James Daugherty, was a pal of Dempsey's and the manager of the champ's chief sparring partner, George Godfrey. (Daugherty owned a roadhouse and gym in southeastern Pennsylvania as well as kennels in which he kept hunting dogs for his close friend Damon Runyon—to the readers of whose sporting column he became well known as the Baron.)

The decision was a tough moment; Dempsey knew that he and Kearns were going to be heading out of town with $200,000 and that there were bound to be more than a few broke and disappointed cowboys who knew it too. Daugherty clutched the champ's arm, both to indicate him the winner and (as Bill Corum half-jokingly suggested) for moral support. Then both men bolted through the ropes and away from the ring at top speed, followed by Kearns, the champ's handlers, and a shower of cushions and bottles flung by unhappy customers. According to one story, Kearns hid out in the basement of the Shelby barbershop with a bag containing eight thousand silver dollars and lammed out of town before dawn on the caboose of an eastbound freight. A more dependable version (Corum's) has the entire Dempsey party, the Baron included, sprinting a quarter mile to a rail siding where a two-car train waited (at Kearns' behest and Dempsey's expense) to carry them to Great Falls. The engine had a full head of steam up, and its wheels were turning the instant the fleeing champion's entourage was aboard.

Shelby went bust that July 4. Three of the fight's biggest backers had gone broke; the town's three banks had closed their doors; mortgages were quickly foreclosed; and most of the substantial property in town, from business establishments to the very planks used to construct the boxing arena, were seized by creditors. What profits the event had generated disappeared overnight aboard the champ's special train to Great Falls. Nor did Dempsey and Kearns tarry long in *that* frontier metropolis, catching the first train back to Chicago. "I don't know what would have happened if we had hung around until the promoters started remembering that we were the only ones who made money off the fight," Dempsey chuckled years later. "Poor Tommy didn't get a quarter."

Tom Gibbons got seven or eight weeks on the Pantages circuit and a shot at Gene Tunney two years later out of the deal. Tunney knocked him out in twelve, and Tom retired and became the sheriff of St. Paul. Whenever anybody in later years asked him about

Shelby, Montana, Stages a Fight

the Dempsey bout, Gibbons always said, "I'd like to fight him again, for money."

Although he and Kearns took out at least their expenses, and probably a good bit more, Dempsey then and later regarded Shelby as a disaster. Undoubtedly he did not care much for the image of thief that it had earned him. Still, Tom Gibbons had toughened him up to a point where later in the summer he would be able to put away a much more menacing opponent, the Wild Bull of the Pampas. Literally belted out of the ring in the first round, he nevertheless survived to KO Luis Angel Firpo in Tex Rickard's second Million Dollar Fight, at the Polo Grounds in September 1923, two months after the battle at Shelby.

Runyon and Broun and Rice and the other writers boarded their Great Northern Pullman on July 5 and headed back to the civilized end of the continent, where the Giants and the Yankees were busy winning pennants to set up a World Series that everybody figured would show that New York owned the baseball world outright—if not everything else.

Runyon reminisced about the Shelby affair two decades later, when except for attending an occasional big fight he had left the sports beat for good and was writing a syndicated feature column Hearst insisted he call "The Brighter Side."

> It was at Shelby that Heywood found pretty Patricia Salmon singing in a tent and waxed so enthusiastic about her at the expense of pugilistic publicity that Flo Ziegfeld signed her and put her in the Follies. She yodeled, as I remember. She afterwards came out on the stage at the Hippodrome yodeling on a white horse when Bugs Baer was master of ceremonies.
>
> "Ladies and Gentlemen," said Bugs, "lest there be any misapprehension in your minds, that was not the horse doing the yodeling."

Them were the days, as one of Damon's sporting pals might have commented.

9

A Dumbbell Murder and Other Trials

Between 1913, when Damon rented the Runyon's first Manhattan apartment (at 111th Street and Broadway), and 1928, when
he "officially" moved out of the family home (then at 113th Street
and Riverside Drive), there were some half dozen different Runyon
households. All were within a single mile-square area on the Upper West Side, but in terms of luxury the early apartments—that
on 111th Street where Mary was born in 1914 and the one two
blocks north where Damon Jr. was born four years later—and
the later Riverside Drive places were light years apart. Damon's
accelerating income was responsible for the variation. Every few
years he could afford something a little closer to his wife's idea
of proper residential elegance, which was a complicated proposition involving numerous large and well-furnished rooms in a fashionable area with lots of trees—something on Fifth Avenue near
Central Park, say. The life Ellen Runyon wanted always seemed
slightly out of Damon's reach, no matter how high on Mr. Hearst's
gold ladder he climbed.

One middle-years Runyon household, at 251 West 95th Street,
was on the top floor of an old building overlooking the busy corner
of 96th Street and Broadway. That corner was reputed by Damon
to be "one of the haunts of the bootleggers and gangsters of the
period." He befriended these dignitaries of the neighborhood, paying tribute in the form of respect (and handouts where appropriate) and pumping them for their stories. They were talkative mugs,
so this was not too difficult. It was the beginning of Prohibition;
the "corner sharps in jazzbo getups who stood around making
gimlet eyes in front of a corner cigar store" were, as Damon Jr.
later pointed out, the prototypes of many of the two-bit mobsters,
hustlers, and petty crooks of his father's Broadway tales.

Shortly after 1920, when Damon signed a new contract with
the Hearst organization that elevated him to the $25,000-a-year
range as a sports columnist, the family moved into the grand
seven-room apartment at 320 West 102nd Street at Riverside Drive.
With the place came a new Steinway piano for Ellen and a view
overlooking the Hudson River. The Runyons, as Damon Jr. later

put it, had "arrived." But by the time of their arrival, Damon himself was gradually fading from the family picture. On Riverside Drive, and later in the even more elaborate apartments the family would occupy, the Runyon paterfamilias kept a room of his own where he slept when—less and less frequently over the years— he stayed at night. Ellen, of course, had *her* private bedroom. Damon Jr., recalling the marital difficulties of his parents, epitomized their differences by describing their respective rooms.

> Thinking back to try to understand what happened to my parents I remember best their rooms at the Riverside apartment and their different ways. I think of my father as leather, real leather with a good creak to it. His room was a small boy's delight. Mexican spurs with large star-pointed prickles that spun around. Whips my father could make lash out and snap. Shotguns of all calibers, some kept broken down and fitted into real leather cases. A curved knife which spoke of the Philippines. A Colt .45 six-gun, the McCoy, long and too heavy for me to handle. His World War I uniform, covered with campaign ribbons dating back to the Spanish-American War. The green arm band with the white C of the war correspondent. A Sam Browne belt. Army compass. Binoculars. Saddle soap. Footballs and baseballs. All the McCoy.
>
> Dominating my mother's room was a gigantic chandelier of cut crystals that jingled with a passing breeze and were a maid's nightmare. The bed was an oversized affair fit for a movie queen. It was painted with Colonial garden scenes and the headboard was tufted. My mother went in for dainty frilled clothes and I remembered most a black taffeta evening gown with huge red roses. The dress went swish-swish-swish which always was a comforting sound to a sleepy child when she would tip-toe in our bedroom to check us while a party was in progress over the rest of the house. Her room was a girl's paradise for my sister and her friends to dress up in playing grown-up. *—Father's Footsteps*

In the company they kept the Runyons were as remote from each other as they were in their feelings. During the early years of their marriage, Damon and Ellen had many common friends among Damon's sportswriting colleagues and their wives: Grantland and Kitty Rice, Rube and Irma Goldberg, Westbrook and Julie Pegler, Gene and Agnes Fowler. This changed after the birth of Damon Jr. in 1918, when Damon—who due to the requirements of employment with a morning paper had always spent much of his time away from home—began to prowl for purposes of recreation as well as duty and to cultivate new friends whom Ellen found disagreeable and who were therefore unwelcome in the Runyon home.

"Alfred has the damnedest assortment of friends," Ellen once told Agnes Fowler when her husband—who was away in Europe— asked her to purchase some Christmas presents for his pals. "How can I know what to choose for some bum with tin ears? Or for that waiter at Haan's who used to be a lookout man for Canfield?

The World of Damon Runyon

If Alfred should die—God forbid!—I wouldn't know a soul at his funeral." Nor would she have wanted to. After one or two unpleasant attempts, Damon never brought his more flagrant "Broadway" friends home. This meant he now began to spend not only his days and his evenings but also his nights "on the town."

With the advent of Prohibition in 1920 there had begun to flourish an attractive new kind of Broadway nightlife that offered cabarets where an astute reporter might sit and gather news while he viewed the merchandise—which usually included leggy young ladies in brief costumes, the chorines or "chorus Judys" by whom the scribes of Damon's tales (like Ambrose Hammer and Waldo Winchester) are so often charmed. Damon himself was far from impervious to the temptations of the flesh that turned up constantly on his nightclub rounds. For the Broadway reporters who were proximate to the female performers on a regular basis, liaisons were neither avoidable nor difficult to arrange. Perhaps for rubbernecks and tourists "night club quail" was "hard to make up to," as Jack Lait and Lee Mortimer wrote in *New York Confidential,* but for the gangsters and musicians and scribes who were always on hand, "propinquity . . . was Cupid's net." For some of the writing crowd, in fact, the nightclub coils of Cupid turned out to be binding. Scribes who fell for and later married show girls included Mark Hellinger, Heywood Broun, and—in the early thirties—Damon Runyon.

In the twenties Damon carried one torch after another for the song and dance dolls who called themselves "actresses" and were sometimes as glamorous as Paulette Goddard, Joan Crawford, or Barbara Stanwyck—all graduates of the chorine ranks—and sometimes much less lovely. The lighting in the nightclubs tended to equalize the differences, though some claimed it was less the lighting than the bootleg hooch provided by the club owners or the customers themselves. And Damon wasn't drinking anything but coffee.

Ellen heard rumors from the other sportswriters' wives about Damon's late-night interviews with chorus girls, and she interrogated him sharply. He swore he had simply been collecting atmosphere for his work. "It is my observation," he wrote in his column one day, "that much of the lying in this world is done as a result of dames asking questions. Of course it is very wrong in anybody not to tell the truth at all times and I am against a liar, but if dames are not around asking questions the chances are the lying in this world will be cut down fifty per cent and maybe more."

The answers she got did not satisfy his wife. Loneliness had already taken its toll of the pretty, respectable Mrs. Runyon. Ellen's capacities for life had not been tapped, and now her frustration got the best of her. This trim, inquisitive, extravagant, superstitious, impulsive woman, who still had (as she said) "the form of a sixteen year old girl," was no longer the innocent maid Damon had married. Damon's prolonged absences had given birth in her first to bitterness, then to a defiant independence. In 1918, after reading aloud what her friend and confidante Agnes Fowler later called "a nice letter" sent her from overseas by her war-correspondent husband, Ellen commented sadly that "he's only being polite—he's further off than France from me. He might as well be in Siberia, even when he's here in New York."

In her estrangement, real and imagined, Ellen began to develop new habits. Once the scourge of the alcoholic Al Runyon of Denver, around 1919 she had secretly taken to the bottle herself. By the early and middle twenties it was no longer much of a secret. Her poorly camouflaged trips to the closet and cupboard for reinforcing "nips" from hidden liquor caches worried old friends like Agnes Fowler and infuriated Damon. Turning from the concern and disapproval of those who cared for her, she found among the Long Island and the summer resort set of the Catskills and Connecticut new friends who shared her taste for illegal pleasures and her disenchantment with domestic life. She developed an avid interest in the new musical and movie productions, often commandeering the family chauffeur to drive her and Damon Jr. to the shows and the big studios, where they could rub shoulders with stars like Adolphe Menjou and Norma Talmadge. She made a point of appearing with her son at the scenes of famous crimes like the Rothstein and Snyder murders (both of which Damon was covering for his paper).

When Damon found bottles in the cupboards at home, there were wild arguments late in the night that mystified and terrified Damon Jr. The Runyons' daughter, who in these difficult circumstances had developed personality problems, had been packed off by Ellen (over Damon's mild objections) to a convent in Riverdale on the Hudson River, where she became an unwilling boarding student. Damon and Ellen's marriage was a shambles by 1924, and all their friends knew it.

Damon began to spend all his nights out. He slept sometimes at the Friars clubhouse at 110th West 48th Street, sometimes a few blocks west, above Billy LaHiff's Tavern, where he shared a rooftop apartment with Bugs Baer and nightclub singer Harry Richman. Restauranteur LaHiff was a close friend, and he and Damon often breakfasted together. Sometimes Damon adjourned to the apartment above LaHiff's in the early morning after leaving Lindy's, which was just around the corner, and did his daily writing chores. The crowd at LaHiff's was one Damon found especially congenial. A large and varied group, it represented all levels of the sporting and sportswriting rackets; on a given evening in

The World of Damon Runyon

LaHiff's one might bump into the likes of Jack Dempsey, Tex Rickard, John McGraw, Herbert Bayard Swope, Jimmy Walker, George M. Cohan, Jack Kearns, or Georgie Jessel and writers like Hellinger, Winchell, Broun, Rice, Goldberg, Pegler, McGeehan, Corum, Dorgan, Igoe, Mercer.

One of Damon's affairs of the heart grew so intense early in 1924 that, when it proved unrequited, Runyon literally shipped out in frustration. He was sitting in the grill room of the Friars Club one early spring day when the general manager of the Hearst newspapers dropped in to ask him if he'd be willing to take an assignment on a Navy vessel that was venturing into the North Atlantic to chaperone some around-the-world Army flyers. Damon, in a funk over the latest in a series of rejections by a young lady he particularly favored, said yes without asking the duration of the mission. He boarded the U.S.S. *Richmond* the next day carrying only an overnight bag, and he didn't find out until the *Richmond* was under a full head of steam, heading into the steely grey of the February ocean, that he was bound for Reykjavik and the Danish Straits and would be at sea an entire month!

A few years later another temporary amour of Damon's, this one slightly more successful, precipitated the final collapse of his and Ellen's marriage. Ellen Runyon had again been hearing rumors, and when Damon spent some weeks at home that summer recuperating from bouts of appendicitis and pneumonia, there were several savage arguments. Stung by his wife's accusations (they were quite accurate), Damon confronted Gene Fowler, whom he suspected of spilling the beans to Ellen about his nighttime activities. The charge was undeserved, but when Fowler tried to explain this, Damon refused to listen and announced he was going to "go out and get good and drunk." Fowler stopped him. "Damon, you can't do that—it would be the worst thing you could do and wouldn't solve anything." Runyon choked back his rage for the time being, but a few weeks later there was a final blowup at home on 113th Street.

Ellen had been drinking and no doubt berating him about his latest romantic alliance. Damon in turn had gone into her closet and discovered the cache of liquor she kept there. Damon Jr., in the house at the time, later recalled hearing a long, door-slamming row followed by his father's departure from the house. Damon had gone to his "other woman."

Ellen went off the deep end. Her alcoholism, now chronic, began to destroy her. She left the apartment and moved to Bronxville with Damon Jr., then ten. There, three lears later, she would die.

For a few weeks after Ellen left town Damon was in obvious emotional turmoil, as an episode recounted by Bill Corum attests. Visiting Corum's suite at the Chase Hotel in St. Louis, where both

A Dumbbell Murder and Other Trials

men were covering the 1928 World Series for the *American,* Damon noticed that the mantelpiece was full of small bottles of booze. He eyed the bottles and asked where "that stuff" came from. Corum explained that he had a lot of Missouri friends.

> He walked over to the mantelpiece and surveyed the assortment—scotch, gin and what I've always called "red" whiskey, a rye-bourbon mix. He took down a bottle of red, pulled out the cork, smelled it, studied it, and shook it. I've never seen a man want a drink more than Damon did then. It wasn't my place to say, "Won't you have a drink?" On the other hand, I didn't think it was my right to suggest, "Why don't you put that bottle back?"
>
> I said nothing. Damon took another sniff. With a sigh he replaced the cork, replaced the bottle and said, "If I started drinking that, it would be no good."
>
> "What do you mean, Damon, it would be no good?"
>
> "That wouldn't even warm me up. Unless I had a case under the bed, I wouldn't dare take a drink of that."

Damon didn't give in and take that first drink, not in the period of tension and doubt that followed his final breakup with Ellen, and not in later years when he was experiencing difficulties much more extreme.

Instead Damon kept to the routine his work provided. He moved into bachelor quarters in the Hotel Forrest, a "theatrical" hotel at 224 West 49th Street, between Broadway and Eighth Avenue. The hotel was located between two theatres, the Coronet and the Forrest; at the corner, to the west, was the new Madison Square Garden; across 49th Street was the Brill Building, Broadway's songwriting factory; a block south was Billy LaHiff's; and kitty-corner across Broadway was Lindy's, Damon's permanent Mecca. Leo Lindeman's all-night delicatessen, opened in 1921, would soon be made famous by a certain side-table regular named Runyon, first during the 1929 Rothstein murder trial, when Damon would take great pains in his *American* trial stories to dispel the popular notion that the delicatessen was owned by its most famous patron, the late Gambling King, then in ensuing years in the Broadway tales that would turn "Mindy's" into a Manhattan monument. (To accommodate all the business Damon's plugs brought him, Lindeman found it necessary first to expand his place, then in the thirties to open a new Lindy's at 52nd Street and Broadway.)

Lindy's was a favorite of Damon's not only because he enjoyed the food and coffee and company but because it was at the geographical heart of his favorite neighborhood. From whatever spot he was calling home at any particular time in the middle and late twenties, it was never more than a convenient stroll.

The block between 49th and 50th Streets in front of Lindy's was called "Jacobs Beach" by Damon in honor of Mike Jacobs, his ticket speculating pal (later the man behind Joe Louis), who had an office in that block. There on the Beach any fair afternoon the Broadway sporting crowd—scalpers, horseplayers, touts, bookies, fight promoters, and managers from the Garden—mingled to take the sun and gossip of the latest odds and oddities in their respective trades. On Jacobs Beach a guy could always pick up the latest betting line on that day's action—at the tracks (Belmont, Jamaica, Aqueduct), the ballparks, the fights at the Garden or St. Nicholas Arena, or almost anywhere. Damon, who liked to take his news fresh off the street, always stopped to "chew the fat" (as he called it) with the boys on the Beach as he crossed Broadway back and forth between Lindy's and LaHiff's or the Forrest.

Damon lived at the Forrest off and on until he remarried in 1932. It was the favored Runyon residence in those years, partly because of the cast of Broadway scholars that congregated in the lobby and in Damon's suite to discuss the finer points of life. In regular attendance at these semilearned symposiums were such luminaries as attorney Bill Fallon, scribe Boze Bulger, boxer Joe Benjamin, actor and betting commissioner Butch Tower, jeweler Chuck Green, clothier Mendel Yudelowitz, and fight managers Jack Kearns and Eddie Walker. Often Damon would step out of a room full of conversive friends, sit down at his typewriter and work for a while, then emerge to rejoin the discussion without missing a beat. For a while the Runyon bachelor ménage included two pets, a cricket that lived in a flowerpot, and a large white cat; but when the cricket—to which Damon and his circle of friends had grown quite attached—disappeared one day, circumstantial evidence pointed to the cat, who was summarily disposed of.

At 5 A.M. in the Forrest lobby Damon often met the hotel's crew of professional dice players on their way back from their night's activities. They kept him informed of developments on the betting line that had occurred since his last visit to Jacobs Beach. The Forrest was also adjacent to the nightclub district and several of Runyon's favorite gambling spots, like Honest John Kelly's Manister Club. No abode could have provided Damon better access to Broadway life. (It was from his penthouse suite at the Forrest that he would make his first big splash into fiction in 1929 with the initial Broadway tales.)

The life he found at the Forrest was congenial enough to keep Damon from thinking too much about the disaster that had befallen his marriage. It was quite a few years before he even hinted in print at the details of that disagreeable period in his life, and then it was only a comment or two in his column that indicated something of how he'd felt during the difficult days of 1928. Clearly he felt that the responsibility for their troubles had lain on Ellen's side. In his view, her drinking and scolding, though both had been consequent to his infidelities, had been intolerable. At the time, he felt, even his work had suffered. (There was some truth to this. The daily Runyon column, usually glittering with intelligence and humor, was relatively dull in the last years of his marriage. Sports topics were discussed soberly, without much feeling—as if the author's mind were elsewhere.)

> I think it would be a good thing if all men with nasty wives would talk them over with their friends or even with strangers if they can get any to listen, because it would let out a lot of bile that husbands are inclined to secret in their souls and would make them feel better afterwards.
>
> Personally, I find such disclosures interesting and entertaining. Just as you think you know all the cussedness of which a dame can be capable, up bobs some fellow whose wife has a new twist of meanness. Of course each and every one of my lady readers will understand that she is not the kind of woman I am talking about, though I will bet that they know some that fit the blueprint perfectly.
>
> Many men with sour wives are too proud or have that mistaken sense of the proprieties that prevents them from bringing up their marital curses at the round table, yet if they just had a leg shot off they would think nothing of discussing that lesser misfortune. They ought to speak up and unburden themselves on their wives because keeping their woe buried inside is nothing less than fermenting spiritual acid.
>
> Many a man is misunderstood by his friends through failing to explain to them that what ails his disposition and what may be hampering his work is a wife who is a rumpot, who nags, who is an emotional mess, who is foolish in the head, or otherwise a washout, and many a wife trades on a husband's gallantry in this respect by making it appear that he is the floppo of the combination.
>
> I think another reason why a man should give his marital mistake a complete airing is the protection of his fellow man. You see, if he eventually steps out of the picture still holding his tongue about her, other men will have no line on her and she may be able to corral another poor mugg and thus further spread human misery.   —"Out with Her"

He seems to have been speaking from experience.

It was perhaps an ironic coincidence (or perhaps a symptom of the much-advertised New Morality) that in the very years when Damon's own marriage was coming apart, his professional attention was focused on the flawed institution of American wedlock in the two biggest murder trials of the age. The New Jersey shooting and carving of Edward Hall, a minister, and his paramour, by Mrs. Frances Hall and several members of her family, and the Long Island bludgeoning of Albert Snyder by Mrs. Ruth Snyder and her paramour, Judd Gray, were particularly lurid crimes that

The World of Damon Runyon

in an earlier epoch might have inspired only public revulsion. In 1926–1927, however, a growing and general fascination with adultery and its aftermath made these spectacles of blood and sex the subject of front page editorializing. That two such sordid cases appealed so strongly to the public, who were buying "sensation" in any vicarious form the tabloids could provide (this was the season of the Fatty Arbuckle and "Peaches and Daddy" scandals), was itself a sign that Damon's wasn't the only household in which the old and new moralities were doing battle.

The husbands of Mrs. Hall and Mrs. Snyder—the one a cuckolder, the other a cuckold—had suffered far greater indignities at the hands of their wives than anything Damon had put up with from Ellen. Still, Damon was quite familiar with the basic themes of love and jealousy that were involved. No doubt the relevance of the issues of the courtroom to his own private "trials" lent intensity to his reporting. His column in 1926–1927 may have lacked the customary Runyon sparkle, but his coverage of the Hall-Mills and Snyder-Gray murder trials in those years definitely did not. Possibly, like his courtroom colleague Alexander Woollcott— and like many other husbands, dallying or not, across the land— Damon was haunted by the realization that these diffident killers he saw on the witness stand "also bore an embarrassing resemblance to the woman across the dinner table."

Clearly it wasn't Runyon's personal experience of the issues at hand that moved Mr. Hearst to assign him to the great domestic murder trials. In the days before television Damon's talent for providing a verbal "picture" of an event made him the most valuable piece of reporting property in America, and he was permanently on call to cover major news stories on direct assignment from his editor Arthur Brisbane. (Hearst *American* house stars Runyon, Bugs Baer, and cartoonist Winsor McKay all held special contracts that elevated them to the rank of "private staff" for Brisbane on certain news assignments.) When in June 1927 Charles A. Lindbergh, just back from Paris after his trans-Atlantic flight, was formally welcomed by the American people in Washington, Brisbane dispatched Runyon to write the story. The result was a triumph of élan and verve, a snapshot in prose of one of the republic's most buoyant moments. Damon's lines in the *American* caught the national elation with a portrait photographer's accuracy.

> A bashful looking long-legged gangling boy with cheeks of pink and with a cowlick in his hair that won't let the blond locks stay slicked down, came back to his home folks today one of the biggest men in all the world.
> LINDY
> My heart, how young he seemed!

A Dumbbell Murder and Other Trials

Charles A. Lindbergh

The World of Damon Runyon

A Dudley Nichols could capture accuracy and pathos in a story, but not even that star reporter of the New York *World* could write with the imagistic immediacy of Runyon, who made small physical details his cornerstones just as a poet might.

Damon's gifts and his style as a reporter were ideally suited to trial work. Thanks to his experience in covering boxing and baseball, he was able to dictate to his teletypist a running account of courtroom events of sufficient quality to go directly into print. Only a lead paragraph was left to do, and that Damon added when he had finished dictating the body of his story. It was a method that had the advantage of speed, but it put great pressure on the reporter's powers of attention and observation. Not only was Runyon able to bring it off; the prose he turned out under these conditions was admirably thorough, vivid, and exact. It was read from coast to coast in November 1926 and in April 1927 in two courtroom series that won Mr. Hearst a large new circulation and Damon a reputation as the ace trial writer of the land.

The 1922 murder in New Brunswick, New Jersey, of Reverend Edward Hall, a forty-one-year-old Episcopal rector, and his pretty, thirty-four-year-old choir director and principal soloist, Mrs. James Mills, had been the subject of a four-year "campaign for justice" in the Hearst papers. Clearly Hearst understood the potential news value of the case, which involved sex, killing, religion, and the moneyed classes. All the evidence pointed to Mr. Hall's wife, the wealthy and well-connected Mrs. Frances Stevens Hall, and her two brothers (one a gentleman hunter, the other a moron who rode fire engines for fun) and cousin (a member of the New York Stock Exchange). It was said that this clan of pharmaceutical millionaires ruled the New Brunswick area like feudal overlords. (The state prosecutor would later refer to them as "the reigning family of the Johnson and Johnson aristocracy of New Brunswick, whose crest is a mustard plaster.") It was also claimed—by Hearst's *Daily Mirror*—that this baby-powder barony had conspired to bribe witnesses and cajole and threaten law enforcement officials in order to obtain freedom from prosecution at the time of the crime.

Lest it appear that the *Mirror* was simply trying to stimulate interest in the case in order to sell papers, its managing editor, Phil Payne, issued a "challenge" to Mrs. Hall on July 17, 1926, daring her to sue him for libel if his accusations against her were proved to be incorrect. This may have sounded to some like mere circulation hype, but Phil Payne, who'd been investigating the case for years, was sincere in his charges. He firmly believed that Mrs. Hall and Co. were guilty (as, in the end, did most of the other newspapermen who covered the trial). Payne, however, had stuck his neck out, and when six months later the jury of her neighbors girded themselves in what Damon called "Jersey Justice," squatted, wheezed, and rose together as one to throw the overpowering case against her out of court, Mrs. Hall sued. Phil Payne's invitation to libel action had backfired, and the *Mirror* was stuck on the paying end of a hefty out of court settlement.

In classic example of the fashion in which newspapers create news, Phil Payne's zeal (and that of a few other inquisitive editors) was a big factor in bringing Mrs. Hall and two of her brothers to trial in 1926. The *Mirror's* competitors were soon gulping black ink from the vein Phil Payne's inquiry had opened. Every big paper in the country had a man in the Somerville, New Jersey, courtroom when the trial opened on November 3, 1926. Runyon of the *American* was not the only well-known name among the 300 reporters on hand; all the "regulars" were there, and Peggy Hopkins Joyce, Mary Roberts Rinehart, and Billy Sunday were among those filing reports as "special correspondents." The New York *Times* delegation included four stenographers, an unparalleled example of journalistic overkill (Runyon alone did a stenographer's job of transcribing quotes *and wrote his story at the same time).* Before the trial ended it would hold the front pages of the New York papers for twenty-four days and inspire enough printed comment to fill a fair-sized novel on each of those days (some fifteen million words in all).

Damon, who found "the same interest in a murder trial that I find in any city on the eve of a big football game, or pugilistic encounter, or baseball series," reported on his first day at Somerville that things had already "taken on some of the aspect of a big sports event. In fact, the telegraph switch board used for the Dempsey-Tunney fight has been installed in the courthouse and forty-seven telegraph instruments have been hooked up. An enterprising radio outfit will unofficially broadcast the proceedings play by play, so to speak." The resemblance to a World Series or heavyweight title fight atmosphere amused Runyon throughout the trial. That first day he described the "big crowd of visitors" that jammed the courthouse in search of "morbid entertainment." (Six months later he would see many of the same faces at the Snyder trial.) These, clearly, were a new breed of sports fanatics, people who wanted to get close to spouse killers the way baseball devotees wanted to approach Babe Ruth. They were murder fans. To them the big trials were, in Damon's sardonic phrase, "the Main Event."

On the trial's opening day Damon set the external scene (across the street from the courthouse a theatre advertised Gene Tunney in *The Fighting Marine)* and then entered the courthouse to intro-

The World of Damon Runyon

Mrs. Hall

duce the principals in thumbnail sketches that are small marvels of characterization. The sharp-eyed description of the state prosecutor demonstrates Runyon's talent for capsulized portraiture.

> He is chief of the prosecution, a small jockey-sized, fox terrier-like, little man with a wheedling voice with his fellow man. You can call it personality.
>
> He dresses like a small town sport, fancy colored shirt, black leather spats, and a dark suit with a pin stripe. His hair is gray and curly and oiled.
>
> He stepped up to the jury and in quiet, almost confidential manner, as if telling them something on the strict Q.T., and using little, short words, he explained how Mrs. Frances Noel Stevens Hall and her two brothers, Henry Stevens and William Stevens, were there charged with the murder of Mrs. Eleanor Mills four years back.

Jockey-size, fox terrier-like, small town sport, the strict Q.T.—these inspired descriptive touches were Runyon's stock in trade, the kind of "punchy," immediate prose that had made his reporting style famous.

Later that day, when the defendants entered the courtroom for the first time, he turned his guns on bigger game. It was Mrs. Hall, not her brothers, whom Runyon cast in the starring role in his narrative. His first description is painstaking, deliberately neutral, as though he were bending over backward to avoid an implication of guilt—and wanted his readers to know it.

> My mental picture of Mrs. Hall based on what I had read of her, was as a proud, cold, emotionless woman, of immense hauteur,

and hard exterior. With that sort of picture in mind, I was scarcely prepared for the entrance of the real Mrs. Hall.

There was nothing dramatic in her appearance. She slipped in through the rear door with her brothers, a solid looking woman in a black hat and black cloth coat with a collar of gray squirrel. Under it she wore a black silk dress with a low collar edged with white. Her shoes were black. In her hat she had a bright silver ornament. She suggested what she is—a wealthy widow.

She carried a large flat black pocketbook, and wore gray silk gloves. Her garb is probably expensive. It displayed what I would say is excellent taste. She has a motherly appearance, no less. She is one of the last persons in the world you would pick out as a potential criminal of any kind.

Her face is large, her expression set, almost graven in its seriousness. Her complexion is white to pastiness. Her skin is fairly smooth but there are folds under her chin. Her hair, such as showed around her temples, is sprinkled with gray. She looks more than the fifty-one years she admits. Willie is around fifty-two, Henry is fifty-eight.

Mrs. Hall looks older than the others. Her experiences have told heavily on her.

During the early testimony the husband of the dead choir singer was asked to take the stand. This man had sold his wife's love letters from the Reverend Hall to the tabloids for $500 and was even now picking up a "reporter's" fee from one paper, facts that did not particularly endear him to the regular members of the press—as Damon's sketch indicates.

"Jimmy" Mills, husband of the murdered Mrs. Eleanor Mills, and a veritable little mouse of a man, who might have been the cartoonist Opper's original for the harassed Mr. Dubb of his cartoons, was the chief witness for the State today.

A shoemaker by trade, a church sexton and school janitor by occupation, he is middle-aged and has a peaked face, and sad eyes, and stooped shoulders. His voice is low—an apologetic voice. His manner is self-effacing.

He is such a man as you might imagine to be a hen-pecked husband at home, a man bullied by his children and by all the world, a man anybody would push out of their way without protest from him, a harmless, dull little fellow.

As the trial proceeded Damon reflected the continuing testimony in the reactions of Mrs. Hall, of whose turpitude it was hard for his readers to have much doubt. When the prosecution brought out a medical dummy to demonstrate the wounds of the petite Mrs. Mills, who'd had her "singing organs" excised by her murderers, Runyon noted the stolid widow's response in elaborate detail. The arrival of the dummy, he reported, gave her a "slight start."

You couldn't blame her. She would be all that has been said of her, and more, if she had been able to pass the incident over without some sign. The black hat on her head shook as if she had taken a swift breath, then dropped forward again, and she began fumbling with her black pocketbook. She seemed to have difficulty opening it. She produced from it some sort of document and fumbled it with nervous fingers.

She kept her head down during the early stages of a sort of lecture by Dr. Schultze, then looked up at the ceiling. Not once did her eyes turn to the dummy, as her ears heard the doctor tell how the singing voice of the woman who stole her husband's love had been literally carved from her throat, tongue, windpipe, and larynx, that black night in DeRussey's bloody lane when the State says Mrs. Hall was present.

Perhaps Mrs. Hall thought at first that the grisly figure was a likeness of the murdered choir singer. It was a likeness of no one in particular, just a medical dummy used for demonstrations of that part of the human anatomy.

It looked for a moment as if Mrs. Hall would collapse. You couldn't say if she turned color because there is no color in her face anyway. She would scarcely appeal as a sympathetic figure, but today I think everyone felt a little sorry for her.

The case of prosecuting attorney Alexander Simpson hinged on the testimony of a fifty-six-year-old former circus bareback rider who kept a pig farm near the scene of the killing. Jane Gibson, known as "the Pig Woman," supposedly dying of cancer at the time of the trial (she lived four more years), was wheeled into the courtroom on a hospital gurney and a wave of formaldehyde to tell the judge how she'd seen and heard the murder. This, Damon made clear, was the trial's critical point of evidence.

"I heard a woman's voice say after the first shot, 'Oh Henry,' easy, very easy, and the other began to scream, scream, scream so loud, 'Oh my, oh, my, oh, my,' so terrible loud. That woman was screaming, screaming, screaming, trying to get away or something, screaming, screaming, screaming, and I just about got my foot in the stirrup when 'Bang, bang, bang,' three quick shots."

One of the faces she saw, "the pig woman" said, was the face of Mrs. Hall as she knelt down, fixing something on the ground. Mrs. Hall wore no hat, she said.

The nurse and doctor raised "the pig woman" up in her bed so that she faced Mrs. Hall sitting with her relatives.

"Do you mind removing your hat, madam," asked Senator Simpson.

With a disdainful gesture, Mrs. Hall lifted her black hat from her head, disclosing a wealth of iron-gray hair very careully groomed, as if she might have been expecting such a request. Mrs. Hall's eyes did not meet the eyes of the staring "pig woman."

"Is that the woman?" asked Senator Simpson.

"Yes," said "the pig woman," and her attendants lowered her down in the bed again.

Mrs. Hall's hopes, and those of her brothers, were based on the friendly jury. Prosecutor Simpson, in his summation, challenged the jurors to let conscience overcome local ties—a tack Damon considered risky. "No man ever faced a jury with less regard for what it thought," he wrote. Simpson's challenge failed.

A Dumbbell Murder and Other Trials

After five hours of "deliberation," a verdict of not guilty was brought in on December 3, 1926. Mrs. Hall celebrated briefly and then returned to her round of tea parties and church socials, and her brothers went back to their shotguns and fire trucks. Damon and the other byline writers scoffed among themselves at the verdict, exchanged I-told-you-sos, and then folded their typewriters and headed home. For nearly a month they'd kept murder fans supplied with all the gruesome play-by-play they wanted, and as in the press box after a big game, there would now be no cheering or weeping among the scribes over the final score.

The fans were out in force the following April when Ruth Snyder and Judd Gray went on trial for treating Mr. Snyder's head like something they throw you in batting practice. Albert Snyder of Queens was a $115-a-week magazine art editor of whom Damon said after the trial, "I never got a right good picture . . . except that he was a fellow who liked to putter around with motorboats." Mr. Snyder was of no consequence to anyone, particularly Mrs. Snyder and Mr. Gray; he had just happened to be in the way. Damon's "star" this time was Snyder's wife Ruth, a thirty-two-year-old peroxide blonde and the mother of a nine-year-old daughter.

Ruth Snyder had met Judd Gray, a foundation garment salesman from East Orange, New Jersey, in a Manhattan speakeasy in 1925. As she had been shopping for a corset at the time, it was only natural that Judd invited her to a hotel room to try on one of his. Once she'd removed her dress, Ruth had complained of a sunburn. "I offered to get some lotion to fix her shoulders and . . ." Judd's testimony trailed off into the unspoken thought of his downfall. He was no genius. The charming Ruth had quickly enlisted him in her plan—an old one she'd already tried out on several other traveling salesmen—to remove Mr. Snyder from the scene in order to collect a $50,000 double indemnity policy she would talk him into buying. (James M. Cain, then a young trial reporter, turned this aspect of the case into a famous novel.)

When push came to shove, Judd Gray proved to be not much of a murderer, Ruth not much of a mastermind. They barely managed the deed itself, taking the better part of a half hour to assassinate Mr. Snyder in his sleep, and Ruth badly botched her subsequent attempt to divert suspicion to a mysterious "burglar." She quickly cracked under police interrogation and spilled her story, implicating Judd, who was arrested in a Syracuse hotel.

Since the story contained the basic elements all twenties murder fans and newspaper editors loved most—illicit sex among "respectable" married people, violent crime, and the near-certainty of awful punishment—it was to be expected that the same large crowds of reporters and onlookers would descend on the Queens County courthouse in Long Island City as had appeared in Somerville for the Hall-Mills show. If anything, this time the circumambient hubbub was greater. "Experts" on the "moral question" delegated by the newspapers included such ethical philosophers as Aimee Semple McPherson (who used the example of Albert Snyder to warn young male readers of the *Evening Graphic* against marrying any woman who was not "just like mother"), the Reverend John Roach Straton (who said Ruth and Judd had broken "all Ten Commandments"), and the inevitable Peggy Hopkins Joyce (whose many marriages evidently qualified her as a scholar of the subject).

Damon, who had no moral tubs to thump, went to Long Island City on the eve of the trial, watched the fans line up early for the few available spots in the courtroom, and wrote a sardonic account of the murder-trial virus, numbering himself among the afflicted.

> Perhaps you did not know there are murder-trial fans. They are mainly persons who have no direct interest in the affair. They are drawn by their curiosity.
>
> Some come from long distances, but do not marvel over this. Persons have been known to travel halfway across the continent to see a basketball game.
>
> I am not one of those who criticize the curiosity of the gals who storm the doors of the court room, as we say in the newspaper stories of a trial. If I did not have a pass that entitled me to a chair at the press table, I would probably try an end run myself.
>
> If I had not seen them, I know I would have been consumed with curiosity to peer at Mrs. Snyder and Judd Gray just to see what manner of mortals could carry out such a crime. It is only a slight variation of the same curiosity that makes me eager to see a new fistic sensation, or a great baseball player.

Whatever "bug" had bitten the murder fans of the mid-1920s, it attacked Damon too. "A slight case of murder"—as Damon later called his play—was, after all, a solution to an unsatisfactory marriage that could not be rivaled in terms of finality. In Damon's opinion Ruth and Judd simply had not been smart players of the assassination game. (They had performed like bumbling beginners, in fact.) He obviously found their lack of expertise and their sheer mechanical incompetence (in making their crime unnecessarily cruel) more appalling than the ethical transgression involved. His phrase for the slaying—"The Dumbbell Murder"—became a common tag wherever the case was discussed. It was perfectly apt.

Damon's first lead from Long Island City, on April 19, was a classic piece of punch-in-the-eye journalism that told just where he stood on the Snyder murder and put the protagonists into a

A Dumbbell Murder and Other Trials

sharp but overblown clarity whose finer details would be filled in later.

> A chilly looking blonde with frosty eyes and one of those marble, you-bet-you-will chins, and an inert, scare-drunk fellow that you couldn't miss among any hundred men as a dead set-up for a blonde, or the shell game, or maybe a gold brick.
>
> Mrs. Ruth Snyder and Henry Judd Gray are on trial in the huge weatherbeaten old courthouse of Queens County in Long Island City, just across the river from the roar of New York, for what might be called for want of a better name, The Dumbbell Murder. It was so dumb.
>
> They are charged with the slaughter four weeks ago of Albert Snyder, art editor of the magazine, *Motor Boating,* the blonde's husband and father of her nine-year-old daughter, under circumstances that for sheer stupidity and brutality have seldom been equalled in the history of crime.
>
> It was stupid beyond imagination, and so brutal that the thought of it probably makes many a peaceful, home-loving Long Islander of the Albert Snyder type shiver in his pajamas as he prepares for bed.
>
> They killed Snyder as he slumbered, so they both admitted in confessions—Mrs. Snyder has since repudiated hers—first whacking him on the head with a sash weight, then giving him a few whiffs of chloroform, and finally tightening a strand of picture wire around his throat so he wouldn't revive.
>
> This matter disposed of, they went into an adjoining room and had a few drinks of whiskey used by some Long Islanders, which is very bad, and talked things over. They thought they had committed "the perfect crime," whatever that may be. It was probably the most imperfect crime on record. It was cruel, atrocious and unspeakably dumb.

When Damon introduces Ruth Snyder close up, it is as a sort of icy Long Island Circe, a *femme fatale* whose every glance refrigerates.

> Her eyes are blue-green, and as chilly looking as an ice cream cone. If all that Henry Judd Gray says of her actions the night of the murder is true, her veins carry ice water. Gray says he dropped the sash weight after slugging the sleeping Snyder with it once and that Mrs. Snyder picked it up and finished the job.

This description, no doubt intended to send shivers down husbands' spines, contains the best evidence of Damon's personal reactions to Mrs. Snyder. It also suggests that either the inspiration of the moment or the unwillingness to disillusion his reading audience (perhaps a little of both) was guiding Damon's hand, for in the photographs that survive, the murderess appears to be somewhat less of a bombshell than Runyon's "frosty-eyed" blonde. Her eyes *do* appear large and bright, however; maybe it was into these pools that Judd had tumbled and Damon was dipping his toe.

When Judd Gray took the stand he made his former lover into a "modern Borgia," reciting her various murder ideas in a hideous

Ruth Snyder

litany: "gas . . . sleeping powders . . . poison . . . knockout pills in the prune whip." ("I thought she was crazy," Judd said of that last one.) Damon apparently felt that Judd was being a little un-chivalrous and something of a cry baby. After all, wasn't he old enough to have known better?

> Right back to old Father Adam, the original, and perhaps the loudest "squawker" among mankind against women, went Henry Judd Gray in telling how and why he lent his hand to the butchery of Albert Snyder.
> She-she-she-she-she-she-she-she. That was the burden of the bloody song of the little corset salesman as read out in the packed court room in Long Island City yesterday.
> She-she-she-she-she-she-she-she. 'Twas an echo from across the ages and an old familiar echo, at that. It was the same old "squawk" of Brother Man whenever and wherever he is in a jam, that was first framed in the words:
> "She gave me of the tree, and I did eat."
> It has been put in various forms since then, as Henry Judd Gray, for one notable instance close at hand, put it in the form of eleven

long typewritten pages that were read yesterday, but in any form and in any language it remains a "squawk."

"She played me pretty hard". . . "She said, 'You're going to do it, aren't you?' ". . . "She kissed me". . . She did this . . . She did that . . . Always she-she-she-she-she ran the confession of Henry Judd.

When Judd Gray was requested by the prosecutor to demonstrate his form with the murder weapon, Runyon resorted for his simile to knowledge gained on the Polo Grounds beat.

Henry Judd has a sash-weight stance much like the batting form of Waner, of the Pittsburgh Pirates. He first removed his big horn-rimmed glasses at Wallace's request.

"Show us how you struck."

"I used both hands, like this."

So explained the corset salesman, lifting the sash weight, which weighs five pounds, and looks like an old-fashioned coupling pin over his right shoulder. He "cocked it," as the ball players would say, pretty well back of his right ear. He is a right-hand hitter.

It took the jury only 98 minutes to bring in a verdict of guilty. Ruth and Judd both went to the chair. Damon went home to Ellen.

10

From the Links:
Lou Clayton and Broadway Golf
in the Nightclub Era

I remember the time Frankie Chester, with two Mickey Finns in him (one is enough to cripple a gorilla) peeled off a 67 to beat Lou Clayton in the bettingest golf match Broadway has ever seen . . . —"From the Links"

Damon Runyon never cared much for golf, except for the African kind played along Broadway by the bone specialists and connoisseurs of the freckled cubes whose lives he pinned to paper in his short stories. His fellow scribes, especially the Great Neck crew, cultivated the Scottish game, but when Damon heard Lardner or Rice boasting of their scores, he had to grin. Golf was a joke to him, a hobby for boobs in plus fours, not a man's sport like boxing or baseball or playing the horses. "The use of the word courage in connection with golf playing is puerile," he wrote, "because golf doesn't require any courage, except the pants." He once covered the National Open and filled his story with anecdotes of his car trip to Skokie, ignoring Gene Sarazen's close win over Bobby Jones. Another time he put together a column of snickers at the expense of Bugs Baer and other members of the 48th Street One-Club Golf Association. (Bugs, it seems, favored the mashie.) The only positive golf reports to emanate from the eminent Doctor Runyon were those pertaining to his good friend Lou Clayton. Lou, who was Jimmy Durante's senior partner, business brains, tap dancer, and bodyguard, was a competent man in all respects and just happened to be known up and down the Big Street as the nightclub world's number one golfer. He was also quite a gambling man, on and off the links.

Lou Clayton was a tough and talented fellow who had come up the hard way. Born Lou Finkelstein in Brooklyn in 1887, as a kid he'd been run over by a streetcar and nearly lost both legs, yet he went on to become one of the greatest soft shoe dancers since minstrel days. He earned a fortune in his theatrical career and blew most of it on gambling. Slim and lanky, he knew how to use his dukes: he was famed for an early barefisted battle with a fighter named Kid Piper over a charge of loaded dice. When roused, the deadpan Clayton became an adversary who made the likes of Mad Dog Coll and Arnold Rothstein back down.

One day in the fall of 1923 Lou was out of pocket after a bad betting season. He borrowed his wife's wedding ring, raised two C's on it from a floating crap game Shylock (interested onlooker acting as short-term loan agent), expanded it to a pot of 98 G's in two nights, and then blew the wad on the third night. Wandering down Broadway shortly afterward in search of a suitable place to drown his woes, Clayton happened into the Club Durant on 58th Street. Jimmy Durante stopped in the middle of a song and looked up from his keyboard. Clayton asked the large-nosed entertainer if by chance he knew "Willie the Weeper" (the title of one of Lou's own musical compositions). Durante said he did not have the pleasure of knowing the gentleman. Persevering, Lou hummed a few bars. Jimmy played and sang along. Time went by; several bottles of wine were opened.

If ever a man could think on his feet (or, for that matter, when in his cups) it was Lou Clayton. He saw in the rough Durante style a potential gold mine—and he saw that Jimmy himself didn't have the "push" required to exploit it. Within a few hours of his down-at-the-mouth entry to the Club Durant, Lou had conceived a whole new nightclub act, one that in only a few nights he would make a reality. He took Jimmy away from the piano and brought in singer-comedian Eddie Jackson. The new act would be called Clayton, Jackson, and Durante. He gave Durante the nickname Schnozzola, which turned out to be a linguistic stroke worth several million bucks. And he assumed charge of the trio's relations with the racketeer overlords of the town—an area in which Jimmy had proven himself less then proficient. With Clayton taking care of the booze and the hoods and the rest of the "hard" end of business, Durante had time to develop as a comic. His raucous genius bloomed under Lou's sheltering wing, and the Club Durant thrived until it was padlocked by dry agents late in 1925.

In its heyday the Club Durant was one of the busiest and most popular of the town's thousands of "wet" nightspots. The Club opened at 11 P.M. and stayed open until eight the next morning. The capacity of the room was only 110, but it was always full for the Clayton, Jackson, and Durante shows. Damon Runyon discovered the act, and his fellow journalists flocked to the Durant and agreed loudly in print with Damon's opinion: "I doubt if a greater combination ever lived." Perelman, Benchley, Dan Parker, and Charles MacArthur were regulars at the Durant. So were Walter Winchell, Ed Sullivan, Louis Sobol, and Bill Corum. Runyon brought Bugs Baer along one night (as two years before he'd brought Bugs to the *American* sports page, across which their col-

Eddie Jackson, Jimmy Durante, and Lou Clayton performing in the Club Durant.

umns now faced one another every morning), and Bugs in turn brought George M. Cohan, who rarely went to clubs but hung around the Durant for several hours and decorated the cash register with a couple of portraits of Ben Franklin on his way out. The new Durante trio, Lou Clayton's brainchild, was a smash hit on the Big Street.

Damon soon got to know Lou Clayton well. He'd come in at two or three in the morning and watch the show, drink a dozen cups of coffee, and chat with chums. After the show Clayton would join the columnist at his table to chew the fat; Lou favored the ponies, and his store of racetrack yarns went into Damon's accumulating file of future fiction material. The lore and lingo of Lou

Clayton were to come to life a few years later in the High-C Homers, Nathan Detroits, and Hot Horse Herbies of the Broadway tales.

If Clayton didn't feel like talking, and the two men were in an active mood, he took Damon on his rounds of the fixed and floating games of the town. Lou was welcome wherever serious gambling took place. Damon could play or look on, as he chose. At the dice games he remained a spectator, taking mental notes on the dialogue of the players. He talked little but knew how to behave and was a great listener, talents which made him well liked or at least tolerated in circles where louder observers would have drawn curious glances or worse.

Shortly after dawn, bankers and brokers on their way to another day of profits on Wall Street stopped in and mixed with the racketeers and writers at the Durant. Some of the big money boys were fanciers of golf, and they transmitted the bug to Lou Clayton. Lou was a perfectionist; whatever he took up, he had to master. A natural athlete anyway, he soon became an expert golfer by applying himself to a rigid training schedule. He would go out to a Long Island course instead of going home after closing the club in the morning. Once he had achieved a level of play at which he was able to wipe out most comers, he began to place wagers on his games and even on individual holes. Unlike his other gambling interests, Lou's golf had a positive effect on his finances. He estimated he made over sixty thousand dollars on the links in his career.

Lou was quite a busy man at the club during these years. In addition to performing, he had to keep an eye on things. It was his job to arrange liquor deliveries, to frisk and disarm mob guests (their rods were kept in a special storage box), and to administer Mickey Finns. Lou Clayton was the acknowledged master of the art of slipping the "little Michael" to uncooperative guests. To avoid fights or other unpleasant scenes, Lou would invite the offensive party to have a drink and would spoon the Mickey Finn (a horse laxative) into the client's glass along with the crushed ice. So deft was Lou that the customer, often aware of Lou's skill, was never able to detect him in the act. "And when you got that into your glass," Lou said—"brother! You could be a lion singing bass, but a few minutes later I made a tenor singer out of you. You were a baby in my hands, because when Mickey worked you belonged to me . . . ."

The trio prospered. Their years at the Club Durant made them famous; by 1925 the place had "caught fire." Nightclub hostess

Texas Guinan

From the Links

Texas Guinan stopped in, looking for laughs on her way home to the Village following her own act at Larry Fay's club. Jack Kearns, Dempsey's elegant manager, stepped in and spread C-notes around with ostentation; his favorite request was Clayton's rough-voiced medley of torch songs, on performance of which he would drop five hundred bucks in the till. George Raft, then a starving Charleston dancer, did his stuff on the dance floor whenever he needed a meal badly. The customers covered his dancing feet with foliage in the form of hundred-dollar bills.

A man without facial emotion, Lou Clayton gave the scene his radar stare from the bandstand. In his pocket a dozen little Michaels rattled. As soon as Lou saw something unruly, he was into the crowd like a shot, ready to buy the guy a drink. One night George McManus, later to be accused of the slaying of Arnold Rothstein, took a drunken hankering to shoot a jockey named Tiny Cal. Lou disarmed the unruly McManus with friendly words and gave him a little Michael which left George wanting to fight nobody. Lou was firm and subtle at the same time; his was one of only a handful of nightspots that entertained gangsters without paying the price of frequent shoot-em-up activity. The Club Durant was one of the few nightclub floors that remained free of customers' blood through its entire tenure.

Shortly after Prohibition agents closed the Durant, Lou Clayton picked up a fistful of thousand-dollar notes, ten in number, thrown down in a crap game by the well-known professor of African golf, Nick the Greek. The new Clayton capital went into the Dover Club at 51st Street and Sixth Avenue. Lou bought sixty percent of the club from a man called the Quaker (when frightened he shook like Jell-O). Along with the deal came a halfwit house bouncer named Zimp who shot holes in the rose hangings by way of target practice.

Clayton, Jackson, and Durante made a quarter of a million dollars in 1926 at the Dover Club. Not that they didn't have to work for their money; Vincent Coll, the "frozen stare" killer whose tender years and youthful appearance were belied by his pathological behavior behind a trigger, tried to put the snatch on Durante on a residential street in Brooklyn. Jimmy eluded the snatch attempt, and Clayton went to see the Mad Dog killer.

"What's on your mind?" Coll inquired with a smile.

"Here's what's on my mind," Clayton said. "Anybody that touches Jimmy Durante will be beaten to death by these." He showed his fists to the boy murderer.

Coll backed down and turned charming. Later, humiliated, he tried to snatch Clayton but was foiled by Lou's ability to think quickly in a pinch. Not long afterward one of Dutch Schultz' boys contributed fifty slugs to Coll's anatomy, all between the shoulders and the knees, in a drugstore phone booth.

Another noted receptacle of lead with whom Clayton had had a serious encounter was Jack "Legs" Diamond. On New Year's Eve 1926 the virtual destruction of the Dover Club was brought about by a misunderstanding between a mountainous character named the Great Pete and the frowning Diamond (whose constant pained look could be traced variously to attacks of conscience over his dozens of murders, pain from his stomach ulcers, and the numerous bullets in his system—some thirty-two at the time of his death, provoking Gene Fowler to quip that "he had as much lead in him as the east window of Westminster Abbey").

The trouble erupted from a verbal dispute which was missed by Clayton, who was on the floor performing before a packed house at the time. Arnold Rothstein, who had a chance to stop the argument at an early stage, characteristically preferred discretion and was seen slipping out of the club just as Legs' wife was crowning the Great Pete with a wine bottle. Diamond's henchmen pitched into the fray. Durante and Eddie Jackson fled, but Lou Clayton saw to it that the hoods' guns stayed on ice—and looked on helplessly as the brawl destroyed every piece of glass and china in the place. Lou later claimed the fight cost him twenty thousand dollars worth of business because all the clients took fright of a gang battle and headed elsewhere in a hurry without bothering to pay their bills.

The Diamond-Pete battle was the beginning of the end for the Dover Club. A few months later Clayton, Jackson, and Durante moved over to the Parody Club on East 48th Street. To say the owners of the Parody were gangland characters would be like saying water is moist; the same was true of all the nightclubs. The Parody was run by Johnny Hodge and a notorious fellow named Big Jim Redmond, whom Damon charitably called "no better than he should have been." Redmond and Bill Duffy, who ran the Silver Slipper, a larger club located kitty-corner from the Parody at the corner of 48th Street and Broadway, were golf nuts. Duffy, for that matter, was quite a sporting character all around; he had in his time done a good deal of fight managing and even some high jumping, if you include the second-story work which won him a scholarship to Dannemora early in his career. But Duffy's partners in the Silver Slipper, men like Owney Madden and Larry Fay and Arnold Rothstein, had even less engaging public reputations, so it was Duffy who greeted the guests out front.

The Silver Slipper was one of the most popular of the top-dollar gangland dives. The liquor might have been no better than what you'd find next door, but the company had color and flash, and

From the Links

Harry Richman and his wife, ex-show girl Hazel Forbes.

the chorines were not unpleasant to behold. In the middle and late twenties it was a favorite Runyon spot. His office in the King Features Syndicate building at Columbus Circle was only a few blocks away. He would end an evening on the town at the Silver Slipper or the Parody, take in a show and sip coffee and have breakfast before strolling to his office at ten in the morning to write his daily column. Separated from wife and family, Damon was a bachelor in these years, but he never lacked for female company. The chorus "ponies" on Broadway—the dolls and Judys and beautifuls of his tales—were a form of fauna he knew as well as he knew the horseplayers or gunmen or prizefighters. In fact he knew them quite a bit better. One such young lady Damon had an eye on was a Silver Slipper chorine named Patrice Amati Del Grande Gidier. She was a glamorous blond dancer with Spanish blood (Damon later evoked her family history in the hilarious "Madame La Gimp") and several names inherited from previous alliances.

Patrice Amati was a young veteran of the Broadway nightclub stage. She had performed for such entrepreneurs as the noted Mary Cecelia Louis "Texas" Guinan—the Miss Missouri Martin of Damon's tales, at whose clubs (he wrote in "Bloodhounds of Broadway") "there are many young dolls who dance around with no more clothes on them than will make a pad for a crutch"—and Harry Richman. Richman, a former honky-tonk piano player who went on to great heights as a Jolson-style vocalist and swain of such starlets as Clara Bow, had shared rooms above Billy LaHiff's tavern with Runyon for several years in the mid-twenties and naturally invited Damon to his own club when it opened. The Club Richman quickly became a watering hole renowned for the personality of its owner and master of ceremonies. (It was hotly argued whether Richman or Texas Guinan—the two most flamboyant of the nightclub stars—had coined such famous trade phrases as "butter-and-egg man," "Hello, sucker!" and "Give the little girl a great big hand.") The Club Richman was also noted by sharp-eyed nightclub historian (and *Herald Tribune* city editor) Stanley Walker for its "practically naked dancing." It was through Harry that Damon was introduced to the lovely Spanish dancer at the Club Richman. In 1932 she would become Damon's second wife. Waiting for Patrice one evening outside the Silver Slipper, Runyon bumped into Eddie Chester. Damon recalled the occasion, and the story that went with it, in "From the Links," a column composed some fifteen years later.

> In the days of the gold rush on Broadway, in the mid 20's, Frankie Chester was a good-looking, dapper, blond kid who seemed to have plenty of potatoes, which he showered on café owners, the prize broads of the period, auto salesmen and other vendors of luxuries. He was a high-rollin' fool and also a crack amateur golfer.
>
> In those days he hung around the Silver Slipper Café in the basement at 48th and Broadway, owned by Bill Duffy and his combination, and kater-cornered across Broadway, also in a basement, was the Parody Club, where the greatest unit of café entertainers of all time were working, I mean Jimmy Durante, Lou Clayton and Eddie Jackson.
>
> The Parody was owned by Big Jim Redmond, and he and Duffy were golf bugs. Lou Clayton then as now was a superb golfer. He has practically lived on a golf course since I have known him, and that is many years. Redmond was bragging about Lou's skill one night when Duffy said he had a guy who could beat him and that developed the match for a big side bet. Money was just something you played with in those days.
>
> The match was the talk of the big street. It came off one dawning after Clayton was through work and Chester through play. The Clayton contingent courteously bought the drinks before the contest and that is when they gave Chester Mickey Finn No 1.

According to bystanders, Lou Clayton had invited Frankie Chester and his backers to stop by the Parody for a drink before the match. Though all eyes were on him, and despite potential complications involving the New York manslaughter laws (the horse laxatives were a potent dosage for a man), Clayton managed to slip Finns not only into the round he fed Chester at the Parody but into a shaker of fresh spirits he packed for the trip to the course and which was consumed there by the unsuspecting playboy.

The boys were ready to tee off when a Claytonian, not satisfied with Chester's calm demeanor, suggested another round of drinks. They gave Frankie his Michael No. 2, a practically diabolical proceeding as anyone familiar with the reaction of the treacherous little finnola will tell you.

But as I say, Frankie stepped out and uncorked 67. I was on the verge of saying he shot a 67, but it would be just like a printer to fumble at this particular point and come up with a typographical error. Our hero was heard to say once on his journey around the course that the dame he was out with the night before must have been a member of the Borgia family, otherwise he never complained.

I have always thought it was a good thing for Frankie he had such a stout constitution. Another man might have thought of dying and Frankie's backers were not citizens who would have tolerated demise with their money at stake.

The Clayton, Jackson, and Durante act moved across the street from the Parody to the Silver Slipper, opened in the autumn of 1928, and closed ten days later when the place was padlocked. Then the trio went to work for a different crew of gangsters, the Frankie Marlow-Frankie Yale combine, at a lavish new club called Les Ambassadeurs, which quickly became the Rendezvous; from there it was back again to the Silver Slipper in 1930 for a stint that continued several years until Durante's departure for Hollywood in mid-decade.

Damon continued to follow the trio's act and remained friendly with Lou Clayton. He called Durante "the funniest guy in America" in his column, picked the Schnozz's "My Street" (from Ziegfeld's *Show Girl*) as "the greatest song I ever heard," and wrote a hilarious nostalgic column about the diet prescribed by Durante's doctor during a gall bladder attack. For all his fondness for the singer, Damon's true pal in the trio was always Clayton. When he wasn't doing the town with Patrice, Damon was often out with Lou. They went to the Garden on Damon's fight beat and to the card and dice and faro games on Lou's. There was also another notable round of golf.

In 1930 miniature golf was a national craze. Among enthusiasts there were competitions to build the most bizarre and hazardous course. Damon had seen the brightly illuminated Lilliputian fairways spread out along the Jersey shore on the road from Atlantic City, and one night on Broadway he got a chance to attend his first match. It pitted Lou Clayton against restauranteur Billy LaHiff, grocery magnate Billy Seaman, and man about town Lou Davis, and it took place in the Manhattan apartment of Jack Kearns. Drinking glasses took the place of holes. Kearns had a lot of sunlamps around, and these were used to maintain something like visibility, although what with the state of some of the players, even floodlights might not have been sufficient. Damon, the only scribe on hand, chose not to disclose the score of this match, but there is little doubt that the low score belonged to Lou Clayton. Considering the competition, Lou probably did not need to resort to the Mickey Finn route to win this one. He could have handled it with his club tied to his crooked leg.

Bets were taken on the occasion, and Kearns held the cash. There is no record of how much was bet, but action against Lou Clayton was reportedly light.

11

Regret, the Horseplayer

*. . . by the time Sorrowful gets through explaining how things
are with him, Regret feels so sorry for him that he goes out and
puts the bite on somebody else for the raw and gives it to Sorrowful . . .*   —"Little Miss Marker"

On the pages of Damon Runyon's Broadway stories we meet
many interesting characters. We run into, for example, Educated
Edmund, a Brooklyn colleague of that well-known party Harry
the Horse. Edmund once goes to Erasmus High School and is considered a very fine scholar; lately he makes a fair living playing
klob with Little Isadore. Educated Edmund is a handy guy to have
around in case any reading becomes necessary, for he is able to
read even small print, unlike many a guy you will run into around
and about.

And we run into such guys as Dave the Dude, a very fast man
with a dollar, who is an importer of Scotch and champagne from
the Bahamas; Dave the Dude's doll, Miss Billy Perry, who is once
a tap dancer at Miss Missouri Martin's Sixteen Hundred Club;
and Waldo Winchester, a scribe who writes pieces about Broadway
in the *Morning Item* and for a brief time takes a liking to Miss
Billy Perry (and if it is not for one thing and another, might even
marry her).

We encounter The Louse Kid, who is a wonderful hand with
a burlap bag when anybody wishes to put somebody in such a
bag, which is considered a great practical joke in Brooklyn; Rusty
Charley, a hard guy indeed and a big wide guy, with two large
hands and a great deal of very bad disposition; Jack the Beefer,
who is a runner for Nathan Detroit's floating crap game; Solid
John, who is Nathan Detroit's doorman; and Ikey the Pig, a short,
fat-necked guy who runs a gambling joint and employs such noted
dishonest dealers as Dopey Goldberg, the famous card cheater.

We meet Israel Ib, ugly as a mud fence but a coming guy in
the banking dodge on the Lower East Side, where he runs a jug
known as The Bank of the Bridges, and we meet Silk, a chorus
doll from Johnny Oakley's joint on 53rd Street, who takes Israel
Ib for three million one hundred bobs.

We run into such high-class riders of the tubs—transatlantic cardplayers—as Little Manuel and the Lacework Kid and also Doc Daro, who is once one of the top guys at bridge and poker until the rheumatism cripples his hands and ruins his shuffle.

And we are treated to the acquaintance of Professor D, an old pappy guy who reads a lot of books when he is not busy doping the horses; of Miss Dawn Astra, a very beautiful young Judy who is playing the part of a strip dancer in a musical show; and of Joe the Goat, a guy who has a bum lamp taken out in Bellevue one time.

We also meet Joe Gloze, owner of the Canary Club; Philly the Weeper, a little dark-complected guy who's always weeping about something, no matter what; and the Seldom Seen Kid, a young guy of maybe twenty-five who always chucks a good front but is seldom seen after anything comes off that anybody may wish to see him about. And we are fortunate enough to greet Cleo, a brown-haired pretty who has a dancing background and now works for Buddy de Sylva in a show by the name of *Panama Hattie*.

We run into Joe the Joker, who gives the best hot foots in Broadway; and Frankie Ferocious, to whom Joe the Joker gives a hot foot even though Frankie is a very solemn guy from Brooklyn who has no sense of humor at all; and Ropes McGonnigle, who puts people in sacks for Frankie Ferocious.

Not only that, but we run into Joey Perhaps, a well-dressed guy and a handy guy with the dolls—but with a reputation for being a wrong gee ever since he plugs a guy with another shakedown artist named Jack Ortega in Rochester, New York, and Jack Ortega goes to the chair in Ossining for it while Joey Perhaps definitely does not. And we meet Ollie Ortega, Jack's brother, who stabs Joey Perhaps in the throat at the Harvard-Yale game.

We meet Hymie Banjo Eyes, a horse trainer whose eyes bulge out as big and round as a certain five-string musical instrument; the Humming Bird, a good-looking, able young guy who represents certain brewery interests in Cleveland, Ohio; and Big False Face, an operator of breweries on the Atlantic seaboard and a native of the East Side of New York.

We bump into Doc Beerfeldt, the great pneumonia specialist, and we come across Milk Ear Willie, an ex-prizefighter from the West Side who is known to carry a John Roscoe and has knocked off several guys. Blondie Swanson, a big guy from Harlem, is known in his day as the largest puller on the Eastern seaboard due to the fact that for upwards of ten years he brings wet goods into New York from Canada; Blondie Swanson's good friend Miss Clarabelle Cobb, once the most beautiful doll in New York, is now a performer in shows such as Georgie White's *Scandals*.

We meet Last Card Louie, a former rider of the tubs who always gets much strength from the last card in a game of stud poker; Joe the Blow Fly, a fink in every respect; and Heine Schmitz, a very influential citizen of Harlem, where he has large interests in beer.

We meet Short Boy, and Ooky, and Okay Okun, and Black Emanuel, and the Lemon Drop Kid; Gloomy Gus Smallwood, One-Eyed Solly Abrahams, Saul the Soldier, Jack O'Hearts, and Jo-Jo out of Chicago; and Daffy Jack, the shiv artist who stabs The Brain at the request of Homer Swing.

We encounter Feets Samuels, a big, heavy guy with several chins and extra-large feet, who is generally broke, and Doc Bo-deeker, a Park Avenue croaker who buys Feets' body for four C's.

We run into Ike Clonsky, the fight promoter, and Ike Jacobs, the ticket speculator. We run into Ears Acosta. And we stop and chat with Asleep, a former high-priced character in the business of taking care of people, who is away at college in Dannemora from 1931 to 1936.

And last but not least we run into Regret, a horseplayer who once wins a very large bet the year the Whitney filly Regret wins the Kentucky Derby—and can never forget it.

In the introduction to Runyon's first collection of stories, *Guys and Dolls* (1931), Heywood Broun wrote that the happenings in Runyon's tales moved and excited him "because I recognize the various characters concerned as actual people who are at this moment living and loving, fighting and scuttling no more than a quarter of a mile from the place in which I live."

Broun's view of the Broadway tales as social documentary thinly veiled as fiction is one that many readers—especially "local" ones—shared. Walter Winchell and Gene Fowler and others close to Runyon insisted the characters of the stories were drawn from real people. "He has caught with a high degree of insight the actual tone and phrase of the gangsters and racketeers of the town," Broun claimed.

Of the hundreds of fictional characters in the Broadway tales (many of whom appear and reappear, sometimes as principals, sometimes as "extras"), there are several dozen who bear obvious resemblance to public or semipublic figures of the time. In many cases the resemblances are generic or superficial; in others the similarities show an interest in relating actual character from life to fiction in a semidocumentary manner. The portrait of The Brain (in "The Brain Goes Home" and "A Very Honorable Guy"), for instance, contains some interesting evidence about the person-ality of the real-life gambler Arnold Rothstein, who was Runyon's model; whereas the resemblances between, say, such mobster types as Dave the Dude or Joe the Joker and their actual correlatives (Frank Costello, Legs Diamond?) are broad and without much point.

In many cases Runyon deliberately created a sense of recognition and familiarity in a character by this "documentary" identification method. To a reader of the period it was obvious that Runyon's Detective Johnny Brannigan "was" New York's famed strong-arm plainclothesman, John Broderick; Good Time Charley Bernstein, the barman, "was" Walter Friedman, bar owner and prize fight entrepreneur; Ike Jacobs, the ticket speculator, "was" Mike Jacobs, Garden ticket agent and later a fight promoter; Bookie Bob, the affluent turf accountant snatched by Harry the Horse and friends, "was" Billy Warren, a well-to-do Broadway bookmaker kidnapped in 1931 by Vincent "Mad Dog" Coll; Ike Clonsky, the fight promoter, "was" Tex Rickard; Waldo Winchester, the scribe, "was" Walter Winchell; Miss Missouri Martin, hostess of the Sixteen Hundred Club, "was" Texas Guinan, and so on. These associations were simple and direct.

With the underworld figures, Runyon was forced to use a far more cautious method; it might not pay to be too specific about the real life styles of the Diamonds and the Schultzes, the Capones and the Costellos in print. Here and there, however, he gives inside tips and hints that allow any "educated" reader to track down the sources of his characters. Angie the Ox, an importer of liquor with a side interest in artichokes and extortion, had a real-life prototype in Ciro Terranova, a gangster famed for his success in cornering the New Jersey artichoke market (it was impossible to buy them from anybody else). Ignaz the Wolf, the predatory Sicilian in "Too Much Pep," could be no one but Ignazio Saietta, a professional killer who bossed the infamous Unione Siciliana; Saietta was known as Ignazio Lupo and Lupo the Wolf. To the same readers, John the Boss, an importer of liquors, was recognizable as Joe (The Boss) Masseria, Saietta's successor as head of the Unione Siciliana, who reorganized that multifaceted body into a bootlegging concern in 1920.

Take the case of Daffy Jack, the shiv artist who stabs The Brain at the request of Homer Swing. The character might not mean much to a reader in Nebraska, but inside the Broadway world it was well known that George McManus, a large, good-natured man who was a prime suspect in the Arnold Rothstein murder case, was very likely Runyon's model for Daffy Jack.

And there is the similar and more interesting case of Regret, the horseplayer. More interesting because, unlike Daffy Jack, Regret is a substantial and recurring character in the tales—and because Abba Dabba Berman, the real-life character on whom Regret is based, was of considerably greater interest to Runyon than was a mere thug like George McManus. The actual person along whose lines Runyon drew Regret was a man Damon knew well. His fondness shows through in the writing: Regret is a portrait composed with something like love, or at least very strong liking.

Damon introduces Regret in the second line of the first story in his first collection. The book is, of course *Guys and Dolls,* and the story is "The Bloodhounds of Broadway."

> One morning along about four bells, I am standing in front of Mindy's restaurant on Broadway with a guy by the name of Regret, who has this name because it seems he wins a very large bet the year the Whitney filly, Regret, grabs the Kentucky Derby, and can never forget it, which is maybe because it is the only very large bet he ever wins in his life.
>
> What this guy's real name is I never hear, and anyway names make no difference to me, especially on Broadway, because the chances are that no matter what name a guy has, it is not his square name. So, as far as I am concerned, Regret is as good a name as any other for this guy I am talking about, who is a fat guy, and very gabby, though generally he is talking about nothing but horses, and how he gets beat three dirty noses the day before at Belmont, or wherever the horses are running.
>
> In all the years I know Regret he must get beat ten thousand noses, and always they are dirty noses, to hear him tell it. In fact, I never once hear him say he is beat a clean nose, but of course this is only the way horse racing guys talk. What Regret does for a living besides betting on horses I do not know, but he seems to do pretty well at it, because he is always around and about, and generally well dressed, and with a lot of big cigars sticking up out of his vest pocket.

To informed citizens of Broadway, the identity of this personage was clear. He was Otto Berman (née Biederman), a roly-poly follower of the nags and a minor mathematical genius who had been nicknamed "Avisack" by Arnold Rothstein in memory of a horse by that name on whose nose Berman had won a couple of large bundles. (Regret, the thoroughbred whose moniker Runyon gives Berman in his fiction, had been a sensational longshot victor at Churchill Downs in 1915.)

Like the fictional Regret, Berman was a fat and gabby character who talked about very little besides horses. Unlike Regret, who is always losing by a nose, Berman won his share. Some of his handicapping streaks were legendary. For a while his skill with numbers earned him a tax-free $10,000 a week on the payroll of bootlegger and racketeer Dutch Schultz. But when he went down with Dutch in the bloodbath at the Palace Chop House in Newark in 1935, he had only $87.22 in his pocket, which suggested that Runyon was right about Regret after all—and about racetrack speculators in general. "All Horse Players Die Broke," the Demon titled a late story, a tale patterned after the life of a Saratoga veteran Runyon called Unser Fritz—one of hundreds of minor gamblers on whom for years he had been laying an endless series of two-dollar loans as "advances" on their life stories—but it might as well have been the story of Otto Berman, who ended a top career in the racing racket with change in his pocket, six slugs in his left side, and no one to mourn him except Damon Runyon.

> It is along about two o'clock of a nippy Tuesday morning, and I am sitting in Mindy's Restaurant on Broadway with Regret, the horse player, speaking of this and that, when who comes in but Ambrose Hammer, the newspaper scribe . . .
> —"So You Won't Talk"

After his introduction in "The Bloodhounds of Broadway," Regret returns to the Broadway tales six times. Usually he and the narrator are standing around speaking of this and that, and one thing and another, as though they are pals from the winter meeting at Tropical Park or the predawn seminar at Mindy's or around and about. Both Runyon's nameless narrator—like the author, a nonintrusive, listening sort—and Regret are bit players; they are onlookers or helpers in the larger drama going on around them.

Regret is always a helpful fellow, ready to lend a hand to a friend in need (such as the tightwad Sorrowful in "Little Miss Marker") or even a stranger in need, if she happens to be a doll. In "Princess O'Hara" Regret's Robin Hood instincts lead him to commit a horse theft at the rodeo at Madison Square Garden—strictly on the Princess' behalf, of course. And in "Broadway Financier" Regret takes a thoroughly paternal interest in the education of the young doll, Silk, explaining to her how to build up a sucker to betting on a hot horse, and other such matters of importance.

On other occasions Regret's assistance takes the form of advice, particularly on subjects relating to horses and tracks and odds and things speculative in general—as when, in "Sense of Humor," he states that although Joe the Joker is about the best hand in town at giving hot foots, Joe can have twenty to one any time that he will not give any hot foots to Mussolini and get away with it.

On the first page of "Little Miss Marker" it is Regret who is standing around chewing the fat with the narrator in front of Mindy's one evening toward seven o'clock when who comes up the street with a little doll hanging onto his right thumb but a guy by the name of Sorrowful. In Hollywood a few years later the doll becomes Shirley Temple, and it is the film version of Damon's story that pushes her to the top of the box office charts, even over such beautifuls as Greta Garbo. In the Hollywood version there is a kindly horseplayer who is Otto Berman's spitting image. Damon inserted the enlarged role in the screenplay, which he was working on in Hollywood in 1934, during the period of Berman's apogee as a Schultz aide in the Harlem policy rackets.

Berman's associates sometimes called him Dutch Otto; Rothstein called him Avisack; Berman himself preferred the name Abba Dabba, which he selected because it had a spooky ring. The 220-pound Berman was a funnyman, a great joker, and was regarded as very good company. When, in the post-Prohibition era, Schultz' profits as a beer supplier dropped off, he called on Abba Dabba to implement a scheme the fat horseplayer had dreamed up years before. It was a complicated piece of business which gave Schultz' profits in the Harlem numbers racket a fantastic boost and caused the normally stingy "Dutchman" to lavish ten G's a week on Otto Berman. It was also a scheme that demonstrated Abba Dabba's mathematical mind better than anything else he ever did—although some sporting critics argued that his famed streak of twenty-eight handicapped firsts in twenty-nine races was an even greater exhibition of braininess.

Berman's numbers plan went like this. In the numbers rackets of those days, winners were indicated by the third digit in the pari-mutuel totals for the first, third, and seventh races. For example, if the pari-mutuel totals for races one, three, and seven were $212.90, $435.86, and $682.50, the winning number would be 252. Abba Dabba's plan was to go to the specific track whose totals were being used—in Cincinnati, say, or New Orleans—and call in the figures he obtained before the seventh race every day. A Schultz representative in New York read back to him the numbers that had been most popular in the day's policy sales on the streets of Harlem. As the story goes, Abba Dabba then went to his forms and charts and in a few moments calculated and placed a number of bets on the seventh race that were designed to prevent the final digit of the pari-mutuel total from corresponding to the final digit of the day's favorite policy number.

By his successful implementation of this improbable procedure, Abba Dabba Berman rigged numbers payoffs in such a way that Schultz' Harlem policy earnings *doubled* between 1933 and 1935. But by that time the former beer baron of the Bronx had other problems that were even more serious than his budgets, and so did Abba Dabba. The Dutchman had been getting on people's nerves. State Prosecutor Tom Dewey had been after Dutch's Harlem policy game, and in retaliation Schultz had made crude threats against Dewey. Such stirring up of legal hornets' nests did not appeal to the major gang bosses of the time—Lepke, Luciano, Siegel, Lansky, and the rest—who were afraid the rash

The World of Damon Runyon

Dutch Schultz

Dutchman might actually attempt an assassination of the special prosecutor. Dutch had put his foot in his mouth, and this placed him in a type of double jeopardy that also affected his henchmen whenever they were around him.

After the mass execution at the Palace Chop House (four dead; second biggest in gangland history) the newspapers made Abba

Regret, the Horseplayer

Dabba out to be a Schultz bodyguard. This was hardly true, for despite his size Berman was never a strong-arm type.

Runyon, clearly affected by his friend's demise, spoke out pointedly on the subject in his *American* column shortly after the killings. In reaction to the papers' description of Berman as a thug, columnist Runyon said that Abba Dabba "would have been about as efficient a bodyguard as a five-year-old child." As the owner of a string of mild-mannered, cream-puff-punching heavyweights, Damon knew full well that a rough exterior did not necessarily—in his friend Abba Dabba's case, even approximately—denote an evil heart. He would just as soon take Shirley Temple down Broadway with him as Abba Dabba, if it was bodyguarding he required, Damon said.

In the morgue the police had looked through Berman's pockets and found some papers containing mysterious figures that the investigating officers interpreted as relating to the numbers racket in Harlem. Damon told them they were wrong. Abba Dabba had simply been a "system player," Damon wrote; those were Abba Dabba's charts on the races, nothing more.

Both sides were right. The cryptic figures in Berman's pockets *were* merely his calculations on the races, but those calculations were the key to the Schultz gang's dishonest earnings in the policy game—earnings that kept the pockets of numbers players in Harlem empty. The police were right in that regard. Not that the ethics of it mattered then to Abba Dabba; a gaming man, he had lost in the end, even on his sure thing. But then, as a veteran sport, Abba Dabba Berman (like Runyon) would have known that there were no sure things. That was the lesson Sky Masterson (in "The Idyll of Miss Sarah Brown") said his father had taught him. It was a lesson Runyon received from his old man, and one he repeated frequently in his columns and "fictions."

His father's point was reinforced for Damon many times by the object lessons of the gamblers' and gangsters' lives—many of which he saw come to a bad end. All were sure thing players; he had seen the biggest of them, the Rothsteins and the Capones, come and go. And as he watched them die one by one—not always with the fondness and the *true* regret he had felt at Otto Berman's passing—the same lesson kept coming back to him: no matter how nice the price, no matter how good the system, no one stays ahead of the game for keeps in this dodge called life.

12

An Evening in Lindy's
with The Brain

From 1911 to 1928 Arnold Rothstein and Damon Runyon—
The Brain and the Demon—were constant and complementary
figures on the Broadway scene. Rarely a night went by in those
years that they did not bump into each other in Churchill's or
Jack's, in Reuben's, or later in Lindy's. Both were teetotalers who
spent long hours in all-night cafés and eateries, sitting and talking
and keeping up with the action. Runyon gulped coffee, Rothstein
sipped orange juice. Damon's nocturnal occupation consisted
mostly of watching and listening, putting in an occasional word
while the machinery in his head made notes on the conversation
and scenery; out of this his writing came. Rothstein did another
kind of business. At the height of his power in the mid-twenties,
he conducted a nighttime bourse in Lindy's that would have made
an Antwerp merchant envious. Each evening he would arrive,
pick up his messages, make whatever phone calls the messages
required, and then hold court at his table for hours, speaking in
whispers to his bodyguards, dealing in hushed tones with his petitioners one by one.

This was how you did business with The Brain. The table was
his office, the waiters his secretaries; those who wanted to speak
with him often had to wait in line. When one's turn came, he or
she was motioned to sit down and invited by the arachnoid gambler to "tell me the story." The conversation, like a gentle suspira-
tion, would be inaudible to those nearby. "The way he talks, you
could stand right beside him and not hear anything," the night
cashier of Lindy's told the officers who were investigating the
Rothstein murder. "Besides, who listens?"

The night cashier's name was Abe Scher. His statement to the
police is of some interest, since it exhibits the constant use of
the historical present tense which prevailed both in the Broadway
world of the period and in the fiction of Damon Runyon. Not that
Scher was alone in this; all the other witnesses at the Rothstein
inquiry testified in an identical syntactical patois; it was the neighborhood dialect of the Big Street. Damon himself spoke it much
of the time.

An Evening in Lindy's with The Brain

Arnold Rothstein

It has been claimed variously that Runyon adopted the historical present from the "Dick and Jane" editorial style of his *American* boss, Arthur Brisbane, that he got it from the rough dialects of the Old West, and that he made it up. It takes only one look at the police transcripts—or at those of *any* "Broadway" trial or government crime committee hearing—to demonstrate the actual source of his inspiration. The historical present is a gimmick Runyon picked up on his chosen beat; he copied it faithfully, purified it to remove inconsistencies, and made a jargon-within-

The World of Damon Runyon

a-jargon of it, which he then placed in the mouths of his narrator and the characters the narrator meets in his goings around and about.

Abe Scher, talking in the historical present, recalls the evening of November 4, 1928.

> Mr. Rothstein comes in. Every night he comes here. Regular as clockwork, he comes here. Sunday night, Monday night, any night. Everybody knows that. Like always, there are some people waiting for him. They are waiting near his table, the same one where he is always sitting . . . You got to understand. This place, it is like an office for him. People come in and they are leaving messages for him. All day and night, they are telephoning for him here. It ain't that Mr. Lindy likes the idea, but what can he do? An important man like Mr. Rothstein, you do not offend. So, like I am saying, he comes in and he goes to his table. He is saying "hello" to people and they are saying "hello" to him. Some fellows, they go to his table and they are talking confidential to him. You know, they are talking into his ear . . . Did he give anyone money? . . . Who knows? Mr. Rothstein you see, but you do not watch . . . Does he have his little black book? Is there a time when he is not having his little black book?

The little black book was the repository of Rothstein's phone messages and business notes. It contained a cryptic record of his many loans—how much he was owed, by whom, when payable, at what terms of interest. He consulted it frequently, licking the tip of his pencil and scribbling fresh notations even as he conducted his interviews. When the person to whom he was listening had completed his or her request he either shook his head, signifying no and terminating the interview, or brought out a sheaf of large coarse notes, stripped some off, and handed them across the table. He would then murmur a few final remarks about repayment, which usually contained a veiled warning. (One had only to look to the next table to see Rothstein's bodyguards, and the ominous lumps in their coats, to know that the warning was to be taken seriously.) Rothstein licked his pencil, jotted some figures, and looked up to see who was next.

Over the years, professional observer Runyon had been witness to thousands of such interviews and had himself often stopped at Rothstein's table for a talk—though it was stories the D-Man was after, not cash. These The Brain gave for free when he was not too busy. He shared with his favorite typewriter artist his occasional insights on life, business, and human nature. He liked to expound on how his casinos, gambling clubs, high-priced floating card and dice games, and expensive nightclubs all catered to the average boob's snob instincts. "People like to think they're better than other people," A. R. told Damon one night. "As long as they're willing to pay to prove it, I'm willing to let them."

An Evening in Lindy's with The Brain

On an average evening, those who filed to and from Rothstein's table might include judges, politicians, gangsters, horseplayers, show girls, drug smugglers, fight managers, lawyers, reporters small businessmen, killers. On an ordinary night the cast of supplicants might include a guy like Ciro Terranova, who used a strong-arm squad to charge tribute on vegetables shipped into the metropolitan area—and to provide muscle and protection for his lucrative liquor-importing business. Ciro appears in the Runyon Broadway saga as Angie the Ox in "The Old Doll's House," where he is "an importer himself . . . besides enjoying a splendid trade in other lines, including artichokes and extortion." This particular night it is a personal favor Ciro wishes to ask of The Brain. He needs a suite of rooms for a few days. Can do, Rothstein says, and he makes a note in his black book. A suite of rooms will be waiting for Mr. Terranova at the Fairfield Hotel (which Rothstein owns) in the morning. Ciro mutters his thanks and reminds the Big Bankroller that if there is ever a favor he can do in return, don't hesitate to ask. With a grey smile Rothstein assures him he would not hesitate.

And the party approaching Rothstein's table now—isn't that Walter "Good Time Charley" Friedman? Walter, the well-known inspector of tin ears, had the dubious distinction of being the discoverer of Primo Carnera, the large Cinderella out of Italy whose big feet the mob stuffed into the glass sneakers of the heavyweight champion of the world. Before the Carnera cash-in Friedman had driven cab, played the horses, and performed small favors for The Brain. He was a favorite character of Damon's; the Broadway chronicler turned him into Good Time Charley Bernstein, the friendly proprietor of a little speak on West 47th Street, the Gingham Shoppe, and formerly of a livelier spot on 48th Street known as the Crystal Room and of several other speakeasies in that neighborhood. The nameless narrator drops by Good Time Charley's place of an early evening when there is nothing much doing anywhere else in "Dream Street Rose"; in "The Lily of St. Pierre" the narrator is sitting around Charley's place with three friends at about four o'clock on a Tuesday morning, doing a little quartet singing. In "Dancing Dan's Christmas" the same personage drops by the evening before Christmas to wish Charley a merry Christmas and have a few hot Tom and Jerrys with him. Charley and the Runyon narrator are convivial souls; when they get together they always tip a few and talk over old times.

On that evening before Christmas ("Dancing Dan's Christmas" was written on assignment for the holiday issue of *Collier's* in 1932), Good Time Charley and the narrator have worked through enough Tom and Jerrys to get them into quite a sentimental mood, when all of a sudden there is a big knock at the door, and who comes in but a guy by the name of Dancing Dan, with a large package under his arm.

> This Dancing Dan is a good-looking young guy, who always seems well-dressed, and he is called by the name of Dancing Dan because he is a great hand for dancing around and about with dolls in night clubs, and other spots where there is any dancing. In fact, Dan never seems to be doing anything else, although I hear rumors that when he is not dancing he is carrying on in a most illegal manner at one thing and another. But of course you can always hear rumors in this town about anybody, and personally I am rather fond of Dancing Dan as he always seems to be getting a great belt out of life.

Now this Dancing Dan has been seen dancing with Miss Muriel O'Neill in the Half Moon nightclub of late, which is a cause of concern for the narrator, who knows that Miss Muriel O'Neill is a doll who is well thought of by Heine Schmitz, a guy who has very large interests in beer and will just as soon blow your brains out as look at you. (Heine Schmitz is a Dutch Schultz caricature.) But the matter of Heine Schmitz is soon forgotten in the ensuing events—which include Dancing Dan's recital of the sad tale of Miss Muriel O'Neill's grandmother, who is about to drop dead without finding out whether there is really a Santa Claus, and the convenient arrival and collapse of Ooky, a derelict in a Santa Claus suit.

After a few rounds of song (the narrator does a first-rate job on Jimmy Walker's "Will You Love Me in December As You Do In May?" but personally he thinks Good Time Charley Bernstein is a little out of line in trying to sing a hymn in Jewish on such an occasion) Dancing Dan slips into Ooky's Santa suit and the three celebrants take off to slip Dancing Dan's package (which naturally turns out to be freshly heisted diamonds to the tune of 500 G's) into Gammer O'Neill's stocking. The old lady wakes the next morning, satisfied to learn of the existence of Santa Claus, then kicks the bucket in a good mood. The cops reclaim the diamonds, and the agile Dan heads for San Francisco to become a dancing teacher so that he can come back and marry Miss Muriel O'Neill in style. We learn at the end that by leaving Good Time Charley's speak dressed in a red suit and whiskers Dan has escaped assassination by Shotgun Sam, Mockie Max, and Gunner Jack, three of Heine Schmitz' hired thugs. Who could blame them if they didn't recognize Dancing Dan dressed as Saint Nick?

The "real" Dancing Dan, one of Damon's favorite characters, was a charming, quick-witted, thoroughly dishonest fellow named Dapper Don Collins, whom Runyon met through everybody's favorite connection, Arnold Rothstein. Rothstein had financed a number of Dapper Don's ventures, which included daring exploits

An Evening in Lindy's with The Brain

William Fallon, "The Great Mouthpiece."

in the fields of liquor and drug smuggling and various shakedown and confidence rackets. Dapper Don was one of the clever men in town, and Rothstein made constant use of him. Through The Brain, Runyon knew Don Collins' story well. Collins' real name was Robert Arthur Tourbillon (he was sometimes called "Ratsy" due to his initials). He was a Southerner who had come to New York at the turn of the century as a circus performer—he rode a bicycle into a lion's den—and stayed on to become a dandy, a womanizer, a philosopher, and a chameleon criminal who could change his racket on the spot to match any demand.

Collins picked up his nickname and his fancy dressing habits shortly after he hit the Big Town; he went to work for a Fifth Avenue tailor, paid attention to the clients who came in and out, copied their manners, and in a few months had turned from Ratsy into Dapper Don. By that time he was also helping out around the Broadway pool hall of Curly Bennett, a gambler and Rothstein protégé. Curly saw Dapper Don as a comer and informed The Brain. Rothstein made a note of it. Meanwhile Dapper Don organized a ring of coinbox robbers on the Upper West Side, a sideline that was turning in a steady cash flow at the time of Don's arrest in 1916. The feds, who wanted him on a Mann Act charge, took him away from the state authorities and sent him to Atlanta.

When he got out of the pen, Dapper Don forayed into upstate New York with a partner. Impersonating federal officers, they talked their way into the home of an old German who was reputed to have 20 G's locked up in a trunk. The trunk turned out to be empty. The old German called the federal cops, and Dapper Don was back in jail. In court he was defended by William Fallon, the Great Mouthpiece and Broadway's most famous lawyer. In Fallon's first case in federal court, he won Don Collins an acquittal. Damon Runyon got the story of Collins' upstate escapade from

The World of Damon Runyon

George White

Fallon and used it as the basis of his Christmas tale for *Collier's* in 1933, "The Three Wise Guys."

Fallon befriended Collins, whom he found fascinating. "He is a philosopher as well as the Chesterfield of crime," the fast-talking mouthpiece told his friends. Fallon was in the habit of quoting Collins' opinion that between the ages of sixteen and sixty no man is completely sane except for the ten minutes immediately following orgasm. It was a theory Dapper Don put to the test repeatedly and with ardor. Many of his best confidence scores came at the expense of women who had fallen for his easy charm. He left behind a trail of disappointed lasses that ran from Broadway halfway across Europe.

Rothstein's profits from the Wall Street "bucket shop" rackets, which he bankrolled, were turned over to European drug salesmen as down payment on shipments of opium, morphine, and heroin. Dapper Don went to Europe and did most of the leg work for The Brain. He was also valuable to Rothstein in the rumrunning sphere, having once toted 1200 cases of The Brain's booze from the Bahamas on a speedy yacht. On the same run Don had hauled 150 cases of his own but was tricked out of them by the hijacking Diamond brothers, Legs and Eddie. The etiquette of thieves was doubtful in the dark. Dapper Don was able to laugh it off; he was a good-humored fellow who enjoyed life to the hilt. The first judge ever to sentence him (on a robbery charge in 1911) called him "as smooth a rascal as ever came before me. He is a real Raffles.

An Evening in Lindy's with The Brain

I consider this man a very dangerous character, for he is such a smooth talker and fine dresser . . . " *(And he will go far,* the judge forgot to add.)

Dapper Don liked Rothstein. He admired intelligence and wit and particularly enjoyed Rothstein's ability to mimic voices. Once Rothstein had imitated Lillian Lorraine's voice on the telephone and ordered six dozen club sandwiches, caviar, pickles, and twelve quarts of milk from Reuben's—a joke that caused an angry misunderstanding between the delicatessen owner and the Ziegfeld starlet, whose usual order was *one* chicken sandwich and a glass of milk. For Rothstein's part, he appreciated Collins' skills but trusted him about as far as he could throw him. Since Rothstein was no physical culturist, this was not very far. But then The Brain never trusted anybody in his life; there was no percentage in it.

Back at Lindy's on this ordinary evening in the twenties, we might next see Rothstein's table approached by Georgie White, the producer of the *Scandals,* whose half-dressed beautifuls (like Miss Clarabelle Cobb in Damon's "The Three Wise Guys" and Miss Hortense Hathaway in "A Very Honorable Guy") are often the apple of the eye of a Runyon guy. Georgie comes to see The Brain about a small matter of his recent losses at Belmont. The Brain peels off a large coarse bill, makes a notation, and sends Georgie off smiling.

Now we see nightclub owners, racketeers, and mobsters approach. Here is Larry Fay, the gaunt, horsefaced gangster and kingpin of the New York cab rackets, whose grey taxis with black swastikas on the side are often seen by night on the back roads of New England, carrying liquor in from Canada. Fay approaches Rothstein's table deferentially, takes a seat, and begins filling in The Brain on the latest fiscal reports of the nightclubs they own in common, such as the Rendezvous and the Silver Slipper. (The latter is a favorite dawn-hours haunt of both Rothstein and Runyon, whose current most-desired doll is a dancer there and who before long fictionalizes the place as the Golden Slipper.) The Brain nods, licks his stubby pencil, and makes notes as Fay speaks. Larry goes away looking relieved.

Fay's sometime partner, Frankie Marlow, appears. Marlow is also a nightclub man and has pieces of the Fay and Rothstein clubs. His "real" name is Gandolfo Civito, though he is sometimes called Frankie Curto, and for that matter a number of other things, some of them not so friendly. A few years hence Frankie is to be "put on the spot" by Little Augie Carfano, a.k.a. Little Augie Pisano, a good friend of Damon's and in the thirties a frequent guest at the Runyon villa on Hibiscus Island, near Miami. At that

The World of Damon Runyon

Little Augie Pisano

future date Little Augie allegedly disposes of Marlow with one neatly placed .38 slug, at point blank range, and dumps his body under a bayberry bush near a rural graveyard.

This particular night there is no talk of .38s or bayberry bushes, since Frankie and Arnold are not interested in crystal ball type stuff. They are only interested in sure things. And Frankie has one: the upcoming Mickey Walker-Dave Shade welterweight championship bout in the Garden. The ref and the two judges are on Walker's side, Frankie whispers hoarsely. A. R. nods; this is useful information. He scribbles a note, flashes Frankie a thin smile of thanks, and orders that a phone be brought to his table. (Three nights later he wins $80,000 on the fight, which is a controversial decision won by Walker and contested by all present except the ref and the two judges. This is Arnold Rothstein's kind of bet.) From several tables away Damon observes the action at the Rothstein table, recalls that Marlow has an interest in Mickey Walker, and makes a mental note to check the odds on the fight. He is never sure what is going on in The Brain's mind, but sometimes he thinks he has a fair idea.

There is further business on the prizefight front. Rothstein is now giving audience to Billy Gibson, the manager of Gene Tunney, who fears that his fighter will be up against more than just Jack Dempsey when the two boxers meet in the City of Brotherly Love in a few weeks. What precisely are you afraid of? Rothstein asks softly. Dempsey has a lot of tough mugs on his side, Billy Gibson says. He has a lot of muscle behind him. I want to get a fair shake for my boy. And if I get you a fair shake? Rothstein asks, his eyebrows drawing the question. With a fair shake, my boy wins, Gibson says. Rothstein nods and scrawls a note in his book.

The next day he phones Maximilian "Boo-Boo" Hoff, mob overlord of Philly, and makes a few arrangements; then he buys a big piece of Tunney at four to one. A couple of weeks later Tunney pounds Dempsey for ten rounds in the rain and makes off with the championship on a decision. It is a decision which wins Arnold Rothstein $150,000. There is speculation about a fix; Ring Lardner, who loses $500 on the bout, privately accuses Dempsey of tanking it. Damon, contemptuous of the aspirations to civilization and literacy of the Greenwich Village Irishman, Tunney, is badly shaken; can the guy he once calls the Manassa Mauler come out on the losing end to a reader of the *Rubaiyat*, a would-be poet who uses words like "ineffectual" and "cosmeticize"? Can Lardner be right? And what about the recent occasion on which Billy Gibson turns up at Lindy's? Was Jack battling against a stacked deck? The Philadelphia fight leaves many questions in Damon's mind.

But we are back at Lindy's on an ordinary evening, and lo, the next person to approach Arnold Rothstein's table is a figure of no significance at all, compared with those who have gone before him. In fact he is not even a real person. He is a fictional character by the name of Feet Samuels, a big, heavy guy with several extra chins and very large feet who is generally broke and who turns up one night at The Brain's table in Mindy's. This happens in the 1929 Runyon story "A Very Honorable Guy."

Feet Samuels is a lot like many of the small-time petitioners who fill The Brain's time between matters of larger import. Feet is only dealing with The Brain because he has nowhere else to go. It is his last resort. And it is also not the first time. Feet is a hustler around the racetracks and crap games and prizefights who picks up a few bobs here and there as a runner for the bookmakers, or scalping bets, or steering suckers, but he is never really in the money in his whole life. He is always owing and always paying off, and Damon's narrator never sees him but what he is troubled with the shorts as regards dough. Feet's one saving grace is he is known as a very honorable guy, who makes good on all his debts.

> It is because Feet's word is considered good at all times that he is nearly able to raise a little dough, even off The Brain, and The Brain is not an easy guy for anybody to raise money off of. In fact, The Brain is very tough about letting people raise dough off of him.
>
> If anybody gets any dough off of The Brain he wishes to know right away what time they are going to pay it back, with certain interest, and if they say at five-thirty Tuesday morning, they better not make it five-thirty-one Tuesday morning, or The Brain will

consider them very unreliable and never let them have any money again. And when a guy loses his credit with The Brain he is in a very tough spot indeed in this town, for The Brain is the only man who always has dough.

Furthermore, some very unusual things happen to guys who get money off of The Brain and fail to kick it back just when they promise, such as broken noses and ankles and other injuries, for The Brain has people around him who seem to resent guys getting dough off him and not kicking it back.

On this particular evening, Feet raises a C-note from The Brain. When the time comes to pay it back, he is caught in a tough spot until he gets the idea of selling his body to Doc Bodeeker, a Park Avenue croaker who is willing to advance four C's against possession of Feet's earthly form—payable on thirty days' delivery. This creates a whole new problem for Feet, who pays The Brain back his C-note with a sawbuck interest but now has Doc Bodeeker on his trail. The Brain steps in at the end to resolve the situation and assumes the terrified Feet's obligation to the Doc—but only at the cost of Feet's credit rating on Broadway, which is destroyed forever. Not that Feet minds much, for he is by this time off in New Jersey with Hortense Hathaway, the tall doll with feet like a first baseman's who formerly works in Georgie White's show. They are a perfect couple.

Feet Samuel's repayment problems with The Brain were only a slight exaggeration of the difficulties experienced by actual small-time borrowers known to Damon Runyon. He could recite dozens of such tales. One in which he was personally involved was the result of a loan made by Rothstein to a friend of Bugs Baer, Damon's colleague at the *American*. The friend of Baer had gone to Rothstein with a story that contained Bugs' name. That name was a trusted one on Broadway, so The Brain handed over large, coarse notes to the total of $1,000, made a notation in his black book, and sent Bugs' friend on his way.

The friend did not repay the loan on time. Rothstein let the newspaperman know he considered him responsible for the debt, since Bugs' name had been given as guarantor of the loan by his friend. Bugs grew exceedingly nervous; broken noses and sprained ankles did not appeal to him, and he had heard of people who had welched on Rothstein and suffered consequences even more severe. Like fatal. So he went to Runyon with his tale.

Bugs explained to Damon that his friend had dropped the money on a chorine, a situation Runyon could be expected to understand, since he did the same thing himself on a regular basis. Bugs begged his fellow columnist to intercede, and Damon went to Rothstein and explained the entire tale. Coming from Runyon, whose word he knew to be good, the story did not sound quite so

An Evening in Lindy's with The Brain

bad to The Brain. He agreed Bugs was not guilty in this case and told Damon to tell Bugs not to worry about the money. Baer did not hear from Rothstein about it again.

Gene Fowler was working at the Garden as publicity man for Tex Rickard in the early autumn of 1928. One day Rickard told him he expected Rothstein would be shot before the year was out. "He's been askin' for it," the promoter explained. "They tell me he's been mighty slow makin' good on some big losses in the floatin' card games."

Fowler thought about Rickard's remark several times over the next month or two. There was also an incident involving Lou Clayton. Lou had been rattling the bones in a Park Avenue crap game funded by Rothstein, won nearly eleven thousand, and had a hard time collecting cash for his chips at the end of the evening. Clayton cankered over the matter for a week or so, then confronted Rothstein. "All I came here for was to get my money, A. R.," the song-and-dance man told The Brain. "If I don't get it, I'm not going to any D.A., but I'm gonna disgrace you. Everybody on Broadway will know you're a god damned welcher." Lou Clayton was a man of his word; Rothstein would have to either pay him or kill him. He paid him.

Lou Clayton was nothing to Rothstein as enemies go. Yet the Clayton case was a sign. Something was in the air. The Brain was getting slower and slower about covering his gambling losses. Word was around that some big people were getting burned up.

In late October Fowler went to work at the *Morning Telegraph* as managing editor. Another newsman, Johnny O'Connor, tipped him that Rothstein would be shot coming out of Lindy's. Gene called Walter Howey, editor of Hearst's *Mirror*, passed along the tip, and asked Howey's opinion of its newsworthiness. Howey, a close friend of Damon's, rang off and phoned back a few minutes later.

"You're barking up the wrong shotgun," Howey said.

"What do you mean?"

"Well," Howey said, "I decided to call Damon Runyon about it, and Damon said that you and O'Connor should change your bootleggers, or better still quit drinking."

The police had also received the tip. They cased Lindy's for a few nights, but Rothstein came and went in his usual shadowy fashion, and there was no trouble. Things calmed somewhat.

On November 4 the bankroller came into Lindy's about nine o'clock, as per his usual according to Abe Scher, and ran through his regular routine of calls and messages. He spoke briefly to several people and at length to one man, Damon Runyon. He summoned Damon to his table and spoke softly for about an hour.

The World of Damon Runyon

Now and then Runyon asked questions, but Rothstein did most of the talking. What they talked about Damon never said.

Later that night Rothstein took a phone call at his table and in response went to the Park Central Hotel. According to one version of the story, the call had been an invitation to a card game, in the course of which a drunken gambler (probably George McManus) reproached Rothstein for welching on a personal debt, pulled a Roscoe, and shot him in the lower belly. Another (probably more accurate) version has Rothstein appearing at the hotel in response to a call from McManus, to whom he owed $250,000, and being "executed" summarily without the cardplaying preliminaries. However it was dealt, this was The Brain's last hand. He died in the hospital two days later, a couple of hours too early to learn that Hoover had defeated Al Smith. Rothstein had placed a number of large bets on the election, and the results would have brought him nearly a million dollars in winnings had he lived. Even so, he left an estate of $3.2 million.

His murder was never solved. Rothstein had too many high political connections in New York City to allow the state to get very far in its case against George McManus. Hands were slapped from on top. Rothstein's records disappeared. Jimmy Walker and his Tammany Hall allies breathed a sigh of relief. The can of worms an inquiry into A. R.'s business life would have opened remained permanently shut. But keeping the lid on took effort, and the strain was felt at weak points in Walker's administration, such as the crooked magistrates' courts. Reports of old Rothstein bribes to the magistrates began to circulate after A. R.'s death; these led to the Seabury investigations, which proved fatal to the Walker regime.

Damon, who steered clear of the details of the murder trial in his columns (he knew far more than he could say in print), nonetheless credited Rothstein with a final noble gesture in refusing to name his assailant to the police. The Brain, who'd once boasted that "if anyone gets me, they'll burn for it," had nonetheless foregone his opportunity to put McManus (or whoever it was) in the electric chair. This shocked more than a few of The Brain's acquaintances, obviously including Runyon, who wrote at the time of the trial that the fact that Rothstein had "died game" showed "how little you really know of a man."

On October 26, a year after Rothstein's death, Dapper Don Collins was sentenced by Judge William B. Haley to a three-year term in the New Jersey State prison at Trenton. Dapper Don had been convicted of conspiring to defraud an Egg Harbor, New Jersey, apple farmer to the tune of $30,000 (thirty units, in the language of the Avenues). Word got around that Don had taken a hard fall.

An Evening in Lindy's with The Brain

"The boys tell me," Damon wrote in his column a few weeks later, "that R.A.T. Tourbillon, otherwise Ratsy, otherwise Don Collins, or Dapper Don who is in stir in New Jersey with plenty of time wrapped around his neck, is there on a dead wrong rap, as they say." Damon didn't discuss the merits of Dapper Don's case; it was just his way of putting out a word to the wise about the popular Don's whereabouts and extending a sympathetic note to the charming confidence man along the jungle telegraph of the underground grapevine. Damon could be sure that Collins would hear of the mention and appreciate the gesture. It was all the Demon could do for a fellow in trouble.

Dapper Don spent the time in stir reading books and magazines to improve his mind, telling everyone that the minute he got out he was heading for Paris.

13

Two High Shots: Nick the Greek and Ray Ryan—Damon Runyon and the Gambler's Dream

Nick the Greek continues in brisk action right along . . .
—a Runyon column from the late thirties

. . . when I see such guys as Harry the Horse, from Brooklyn, and Sleepout Sam Levinsky, and Lone Louie, from Harlem, I know this is a bad place for my blood pressure, for these are very tough guys indeed, and known as such to one and all in this town.

But there they are wedged up against the table with Nick the Greek, Big Nig, Gray John, Okay Okun, and many other high shots, and they all have big coarse G notes in their hands which they are tossing around back and forth as if these G notes are nothing but pieces of waste paper . . .

—"Blood Pressure" (1930)

Nicholas Dandalos, or Nick the Greek, was the symbol and paragon of the "high shot" in his era. The Golden Age began for Nick in Canada shortly after World War I. "Every generation seems to produce its own fabulous figure in lofty gambling," Runyon wrote in one of his several columns concerning Dandalos. " 'Nick the Greek' has been the name used to connote high rolling for years."

Dandalos had made a quarter of a million dollars in a series of large plunges on the ponies north of the border, and when he decided it was time to come south to pursue the big money, it was only natural the man to whom his path should lead him was Arnold Rothstein. This was around 1920, by which time the sallow Rothstein was already the number one gambling entrepreneur and bankroller in the East.

The Greek regarded gambling as a sport. He played big, according to his gut instincts as well as his head, and was willing to challenge the percentages anytime, unlike Rothstein, who was all business and really no sportsman. The Brain was strictly a sure thing player who owed his success to "inside" information and arrangements—and to the size of his bankroll. Only the thickness of Rothstein's wad enabled him to ride out the challenge of the

194

young Greek when the two finally met in a series of card and dice games in New York.

Nick selected poker as his game, and Rothstein wiped him out at table stakes. The two shook hands and the Greek vowed he would be back. The Brain nodded and smiled thinly and whispered something the Greek didn't catch. They met again at a floating crap game not long afterward. Nick pressed the New Yorker hard and bent but could not break him. He won time after time, but Rothstein had the cash to outlast him. And the Greek was no piker. Let Runyon tell it.

> He was then admittedly the highest and fastest gambler of the day. He made the mighty Arnold Rothstein, then the great potentate of Eastern gambling, take back one night when, as Rothstein told me the story, $98,000 in cash lay in the middle of a bed and Nick, holding the dice, said:
> "You can have all or any part of it."
> "I took just a part of it," Rothstein said to me.
> —"Two Gamblers"

Rothstein soon separated the youthful native of Crete from a small fortune the latter had just acquired in a successful tour of Chicago and the Coast. Runyon speculated that the Greek might have lost a million dollars in cash on this first visit to New York. "Presently all the home boys' wives and sweethearts were wearing fresh diamonds and new mink coats," Damon noted. The floating card game was, naturally, financed by Rothstein, but that didn't keep a lot of the local talent from riding the Brain's coattails in the cleaning out of Nick the Greek.

To Rothstein, the half million or so of which he'd relieved the Greek was a tidy but not extraordinary sum. It resembled other large bundles he had won in the postwar years, some of them even larger. In one bet on one horse—Sidereal—in one race at Aqueduct on the Fourth of July 1921 he'd won just under a million dollars. Six-figure killings were all in a day's work for The Brain in those days. Indeed, considering he'd once been rumored to have staked 100 G's on a single roll of the dice, what is surprising is not that he outstayed Dandalos but that the Greek was able to outbid him even on a single throw. Rothstein preferred to take his victim in stages, coolly.

However, as Runyon pointed out from the advantageous viewpoint of fifteen years later, it was Dandalos who got the last laugh. Rothstein and his organization did not survive the twenties. The Brain, so scrupulous about collecting his debts, grew lax in paying those he owed others and ended up the main attraction in a quiet, discreet funeral. A decade later Dandalos was still going strong in card and dice action at Vegas. "He wins or loses sizeable sums," Damon reported at that time. "He is never without funds."

The World of Damon Runyon

The boys along Broadway agreed it was to Dandalos' credit that he bounced back from the New York debacle with his nerve intact. The story became part of his legend as handed down by Runyon, the Sir Thomas Malory of the betting kingdom.

> The Greek's losses were prodigious. No one knows but him just what they amounted to. However, it was freely predicted he would never again come back off the pasting he took that winter. If often happens there is a certain peak to a gambler's career that once passed he can never reach again.
>
> But here Nick is, still grinding along and all those high gamblers of that wild period are dead or dead broke. They tell me he plays against the house crap games in Las Vegas, bucking that house percentage that I never thought the Greek would go for. But perhaps it is the old story of "The only game in town."
>
> —"Two Gamblers"

Damon's stock of Nick the Greek stories was deep enough to tap for a column every now and then over the next two decades. Events in his personal life often gave him occasion to invoke this patron saint of the large plunge. Unlike the Greek, the Demon was not divinely guided in his bets. He could drop $10,000 in a month at Saratoga, in an evening at a prizefight, or over the two- or three-night spread of a card or dice game—and then, confident in his inconsistency, admonish his son, "Don't gamble!" His short stories, at a dollar a word, and his syndicated columnist's salary made these dubious pleasures possible.

Damon's was usually the unhappy plight of the man who changes his mind at the last minute and drops his interest in the long shot in order to take a large "safe" ride on the favorite— only to see the longshot come in by a nose. The longshot, of course, would be pulling in a fortune for some unsystematic guy who picked him off the form sheet on a hunch ten minutes before the race—like Mark Hellinger, the columnist and notorious short-end bettor, say—while Runyon, with all his "inside" conduits, was taking another sad fall. Damon would have lasted about two hours as a professional gambler, were that his only means of livelihood. Small wonder the image of a serendipitous player such as Dandalos, who always landed with his feet on the ground, should retain such perennial appeal for the newspaperman.

> I repeat some of my stories over and over not because I do not remember I have told them before but because I figure I may catch a new reader now and then who has not heard them, and this applies to my tale about the guy who has made a big bet at Nick the Greek in a stud poker game and then began shivering and shaking as Nick contemplated the situation at length.
>
> "Nick," he said, "if you call me I'll have a fit."
>
> "Go ahead," Nick said, pushing in his dough.
>
> The guy fell on the floor in his promised fit, sure enough.
>
> —"Friendliness Goes Out the Window"

Two High Shots

Damon, in his dreams, was that guy.

> I always recall vividly the thrill of taking my day's program to an expert, possibly some veteran turf-writer, or a famous brother sports columnist whose specialty was the ponies, like Damon Runyon, and asking him to mark it for me with his choices. I was always happy as a child with my marked program, especially before the races were run. —Paul Gallico

Gallico wrote with tongue in cheek, for after the races were over Damon's picks were rarely regarded as having been worth much. Nor were those of his fellow betting scribes like Bill Corum and Joe Williams considered to be of much value. Eventually so as not to lose face when his selections turned out to be so many armadillos and crocodiles and camels, Damon developed the habit of buying a $2 win ticket on every horse in every race, aside from his larger wagers. That way he could show off a stub that spoke in silent tribute to his handicapping genius—after every race! So much for the sarcasm of the Gallicos. What was the loss of a few thousand dollars in exchange for the ecstasy of the home stretch? "You cannot sit down for any length of time because you get too excited," Damon wrote in 1922, during the first week of his first season at Saratoga. "At the end of an imperfect day your dogs are squeaking loudly in your fancy sport shoes." The sight of a routine jockey, much less a Sande, "bootin' those babies home" was all the sustenance Damon needed even if the winners were only a now and then proposition.

Runyon bet as high on the fights as he did on the races, and with little more success. However, there were some notable close calls among the disappointments. In 1919 at Toledo Damon had taken a tip from his friend Jack Kearns and "laid the chunk" (several thousand dollars) on a Dempsey KO over Willard in the first round. Sam K. Harris, the Broadway theatrical man, took Damon's cash gladly and gave him 100–1 odds. But Kearns, who had $10,000 worth of the same action, must have known something. In fact, he later claimed that he had "weighted" his fighter's gloves (that is, inserted metal weights in them), a claim angrily disputed by Dempsey himself. In the days subsequent to the fight, Jess Willard grumbled about losing his title to a "bunch of gangsters." ("They really gave me a tough time. . . . You can beat fighters, but nobody can beat a bunch of gangsters, and that's what happened to me that day.") Heavy gloves or no, when Jack landed a punch that broke Willard's jaw near the end of round one, pandemonium broke out, Damon flung his hat in the air in a departure from his usual severe demeanor, and everybody in the big wooden bowl of a stadium figured the fight was over. No one had heard the bell that interrupted the referee's count at seven. The fight,

Damon with his horse All Scarlet at Saratoga in 1935.

or what there was of it, lasted two more rounds, and Damon went home a poor man temporarily. (Ring Lardner, who'd made an even worse bet—he'd picked Willard—got out of it with only a $600 dent in his pocket. But then to Lardner gambling was a joke, while to Runyon it was a serious endeavor; he lost grimly and with consistency and "class.")

In the thirties Damon owned a stable of fighters who were forever toppling over at the suggestion of a slight breeze in the auditorium or if the breath of someone at ringside grew too strong. His luck in picking fighters to finance was even worse than his luck in picking fighters to win. Among his stable of hungry but harmless heavyweights were such obscure contenders as Wyoming Warner, a crumpling cowboy; a Californian by the name of Hoffman who'd been in the Navy and was known as "The Sinking Sailor"; and, perhaps most inept, a large Louisiana youth named Napoleon Dorval.

Dorval was Runyon's biggest boxing gamble. Damon spent thousands paying the big Creole lad's bills, stuck his neck out in touting Dorval to his friends, and wagered heavily on him in every bout. The results were disastrous; on top of his cash losses, Damon had to endure the endless jokes of his sportswriting cronies, who were all too familiar with Napoleon Dorval's progress—or lack of same. Ring Lardner, sharpest of ringside wits, lampooned Dorval's training routine in a column that must have made Runyon squirm.

> Young Dorval is in training all the time. From 6 to 7 in the A.M. he does road work for a paving concern. From 7 to 12 he eats his breakfast, usually a wolf or bear and the inevitable sweet potatoes. From 12 to 1 he reads a sentence. From 1 to 3 he manicures himself all over. From 3 to 4 he practices expression, and from 4 to 5 cheek breathing. A good many boxers pick out the wrong features to breathe through, features that may get stopped up.

It was the same with Damon's horses. Those he bought were no luckier than those whose noses he bet on, although as he once pointed out to a friend (in explaining why he'd rather own Seabiscuit than Joe Louis), "you don't have to split the purse with a horse." The problem was largely academic; there were almost as few winning purses for Damon's racing properties as there were for his boxers. In his life he owned five thoroughbreds (All Scarlet, Angelic, Tight Shoes, Euclid, and Scribe), and they achieved various levels of distinction ranging from very little to none. The best of them, Tight Shoes, was a three-year-old in 1940 and, until turning up lame that year, looked like a plausible Kentucky Derby entry. The eventual Derby winner was a 36–1 shot named Gallahadion, to whose flowerlike moniker Mark Hellinger (way off in California) had taken a liking. To Bill Corum and Runyon and the other distinguished professors of the Sport of Kings, Gallahadion sounded like something off the back of a seed package. To their astonishment, Gallahadion paid $72.40. In Hollywood, Hellinger kicked his heels in the pure joy of the uninitiated. Damon Runyon sulked, wise to losing but unhappy in his wisdom.

When Damon went to the track, as often as not he came away with his pockets empty, a fact which as early as 1922 caused him to suggest half facetiously that a black flag with skull and crossbones be flown wherever horses were running for money. But what he lost in cash he got back in material. Like the colorful fight crowd characters (managers, rubdown men, promoters, ticket speculators) with whom he consorted at the gyms and arenas, the characters of the track populated his stories of the 1930s. The two-bit bettors and the high shots, the tinhorns and the touts Damon met at Jamaica and Pimlico and Hialeah enter literary history in "All Horseplayers Die Broke," "A Story Goes with It," "Money from Home," "Pick the Winner," "The Lemon Drop Kid," and other tales. All of Runyon's bettors have one thing in common: the knowledge of how to be graceful losers, developed over a lifetime cultivation of nonwinners. It's a similar knowledge which allows Damon to manage at least a small wry grin on the subject of his losing bets, once he gets far enough away from them to report them in his columns. This, however, sometimes takes years.

The World of Damon Runyon

I formed a coalition with Good Time Charley Friedman and launched a $40 parlay that was to run from Beaugay to True North to Pot o' Luck. The first two won and Charley was about to plunk the $112 that was in the b.r. on Pot o' Luck when along came a guy who said:

"Cancel the Pot. His trainer Ben Jones told a certain party that the horse can't pack his weight that far. Do me a favor and forget the Pot."

So we switched to the Jeffords entry and got differed out of over half a unit, or $500, when Pot o' Luck won. Good Time Charley sat as if stunned for a while and then delivered himself of a truism that I must pass on to posterity.

"I have often wondered why people go broke at the race track," Charley said. "Now I know. It is because they are always trying to pick something to beat the best horses."

—"Where to Find the Common Man"

Damon's sympathy with the horseplayers of his tales, who are always getting beat by a snoot, was born from experiences that were unpleasantly plural. No matter where he got his information, it was always wrong—even when it came from the "inside," as when he bet heavily on his friend Edward Riley Bradley's entry in the 1935 Kentucky Derby and, as one friend put it, "had his pockets cleaned of everything but his keys and handkerchief." No systems player, Runyon was willing to try anything. "I bet on favorites and long shots win, and I bet on long shots and favorites win," he wailed in a column called "No Justice." "All the time I get caught in the switches. I got four photo finishes last week. I went down and looked at the pictures and I don't see how the judges could split them out, they were so close. They could have called them either way. I don't know about that camera. It could be wrong . . . " That eternal conditional corrals the bettor's life. It is a hateful perimeter. "Why can't I win?" There's Warren Wright down there in his private box. He's got millions. "What does Warren Wright care about me?"

The losers complex, of course, binds Runyon with the rest of us and with Good Time Charley Friedman. The dream players, the Rothsteins and the Greeks, are beyond us permanently. Even so, like Hot Horse Herbie and Unser Fritz, we go on looking for The System because we are dreamers. Who do you like in the seventh? "A fellow has come up with a system for beating the races based on dreams. You dream about something and the next morning you look up the subject of the dream in this guy's book . . . " For a price, of course. Everywhere you look in Damon's racing stories, there is the teller of the tale. It was true in real life as well. Even his Florida chauffeur, Horse Thief Burke, was formerly prominent in the ranks of the National Turf Advisers ("libelously termed 'hustlers' by the race track fuzzes, or cops").

Two High Shots

> My friend Horse Thief Burke would give a mark, or customer,
> a horse in the morning predicted on a nightmare, but if that partic-
> ular horse was not in the race, Horsie would have another on tap.
> One thing about Horsie, he never ran out of horses . . .
> —"Just Dreamers"

In Damon's tales the prince of the touts is Hot Horse Herbie,
who has a little of Horse Thief Burke in him, a little of Runyon,
and a dash of Lou Clayton and a Hialeah handicapper or two
thrown in. He is every tale teller you ever met. Like the rest of
us, it is only a little luck here and there that keeps him from
being a winner. Or picking one.

> In 1929 Hot Horse Herbie has a nice bet on Naishapur to win
> the Kentucky Derby, and he is so sure Naishapur cannot miss that
> on the morning of the race he sends Miss Cutie Singleton out to
> pick a wedding ring. But Naishapur finishes second, so naturally
> Hot Horse Herbie is unable to buy the ring, and of course Miss
> Cutie Singleton does not wish to be married without a wedding
> ring . . .   —"Pick the Winner"

So reality punctures another fairy tale. Damon too had a nice
bet on the 1929 Derby, on Minotaur, and he advised his readers
a day ahead of time, which is not quite so radical as shopping
for a wedding ring, but it will do. The next day he retracted his
good words and called Minotaur an armadillo. Even Hot Horse
Herbie had made a better pick, as Minotaur was completely out
of the money. (Clyde Van Dusen, the horse, won.)

Minotaur might not have been carrying a wedding ring on his
back, but he at least could have helped Damon pay off the bills
for the appendectomy he had undergone in the spring. As it was,
the cost of the operation gave him the excuse to work, and his
high-spirited romance with a young show girl gave him the inspiration. That summer of Minotaur—1929—he wrote and published
in *Cosmopolitan* the first two of his Broadway tales, "Romance
in the Roaring Forties" and "A Very Honorable Guy." The two,
plus "Madame La Gimp" and "Dark Dolores" later in the year,
went a long way toward taking up the slack his Derby bet and
his appendectomy had left in Damon's budget. He was now sup-
porting two households, Ellen's and his own, and was stretching
his newspaperman's salary to the limit with his expenditures on
nightclub life and the courtship of his future wife, on card and
dice games, and on fights and fighters and at the track.

It was a life style that would have made Hot Horse Herbie
nervous, but it suited Damon nicely, for it kept him busy and on
the move and in the company of others, where he was always
most alert. You can bet that the Broadway sporting crowd was
quite aware of his plunge on Minotaur (in the area of five figures)

and that everywhere he went the week or two following the Derby—particularly along Jacobs Beach—there was gentle kidding at his expense. The Demon was one of the boys, a player, and therefore more often than not a loser. All horseplayers die broke. Fortunately for Damon he used his typewriter and not his marked-up copy of the *Morning Telegraph* to stay alive.

> Getting back to the subject of systems for playing the races, I once made my selection of the probable winner of the Kentucky Derby by the simple device of closing my eyes and stabbing a pin into a list of the entries and choosing the steed whose name was impaled. I got the idea from a lady player who always picked the horse she played in the race by using the same method in her program.
>
> The list I employed was in a newspaper, and the name I pinned was Scapa Flow, and what happened to Scapa Flow in the Derby should not have happened to a poodle. I showed Major Bill Corum the newspaper list and the way I had daggered it after the race, deploring my foolishness in adopting such a method, but after examining the paper, the Major said:
>
> "Your system was 100 per cent right only you forgot to notice the other side of the paper. Your pin also pierced an advertisement for a bank on the next page, and look at the line it went through."
>
> The Major held up the paper so I could see the line which read: "Save your money." —"Just Dreamers"

But the humor came later. At the time of their humiliations Scapa Flow and Minotaur made Damon quite unhappy, as did dozens of other unsuccessful men and beasts on whom he lost money over the years. Like fellow columnist Hellinger, the exuberant short-ender who did a fandango in the ring when James J. Braddock stopped Max Baer and a highland fling in a similar spot when Max Schmeling knocked out Joe Louis, Runyon believed that though there is much pleasure in the world, and many thrills, the winning of a good bet is the most pleasant experience of all. "I have heard a big gambler say that next to winning a bet his greatest thrill is losing one," he wrote, "but I cannot go along with that philosophy. I hate losing. It makes me angry with the whole world."

When he lost at gin rummy, Damon on occasion threatened to fire Horse Thief Burke, if not to strike him physically. It was not poor Horse Thief's fault. Damon took pride in his cardplaying; he just did not care to lose, thank you. In one game of gin with horse-racing analyst Ken Kling, Damon grew so frustrated over a series of bad hands that he threw his cards in his opponent's face. Dead serious at play, when he went to work and wrote about cards he was often at his funniest. It was a subject he knew well.

Back in the Denver days apprentice newsman Runyon had been an all-night cardplayer and drinker. He brought the card habit

Two High Shots

with him to New York and in his early years as a sportswriter he spent long nights on the road playing bridge and poker with ballplayers like Christy Mathewson and long nights in New York at cardplaying clubs like Honest John Kelly's. Later, while living at the Hotel Forrest, he discovered klabriasch, or klab—or, as he calls it in his tales, klob—a card game imported from Eastern Europe via Germany during the first war. The game was enjoying a vogue in the United States in the twenties. Runyon learned it from clothing-store owner Dave Levy, made a close study of it, and used his klab experiences in several columns and stories. Educated Edmund, in "Breach of Promise," makes a fair living playing klob with Spanish John and Little Isadore, but Damon himself was never fortunate enough to find such inexpert partners. It was not until later, when he went to Hollywood in the forties to become a movie producer and instead became a gin rummy bug, that he found a game he could call his own.

Gin rummy was what Damon liked best about California. He had picked up the game in New York, where he first saw it played by columnist Louis Sobol and Broadway physician Leo Michel in 1940. When Mayor La Guardia's proscription of public cardplaying made restaurant gin a no-no in that city, Runyon proclaimed it a tragedy, since cards and conversation seemed to him to go perfectly with civilized dining. In California there were no such annoying laws. There Damon became sufficiently adept at gin rummy to dominate the play at the table that was kept for him at Mike Lyman's place on Vine Street. A regular crowd gathered at the table to hear the Runyon small talk. Damon passed along the Broadway anecdotes that delighted his California friends, sipped coffee, and smoked cigarettes between hands.

When he returned to New York and was asked to stash the cards one night because of the LaGuardia ban, he complained in his column, striking a rare note of political crusade on behalf of his favorite game. "Banning gin rummy from the New York cafés removes a homey atmosphere that was long the great characteristic of the taverns of Southern California," he wrote, listing as examples Lyman's and Prince Mike Romanoff's, Dave Chasen's in Beverly Hills, and Billy Wilkerson's La Rue on the Strip. All were places where he had passed many an interesting hour in the elegant semidarkness playing gin rummy and chatting with the local sharps. The game kept Hollywood from boring him to death of an evening, and better still, his winnings paid his coffee and pastry tabs.

Damon emerged from Los Angeles with tales of the stud poker and hearts and roulette games of the movie mob, but it was the gin rummy players that he packed in mental ice and shipped back East for use in his last stories. The most picturesque of them was

The World of Damon Runyon

Sergeant Fortescue Melville Michael O'Shay, a.k.a."The Lacework Kid," who stars in the tale of that name. The Lacework Kid is a former rider of the tubs (a card hustler on ocean liners) who winds up playing gin rummy in a prisoner of war camp. (He gets there by a twist of circumstances that is pure Runyon.) Before he picks up gin rummy in the camps, bridge is the Kid's specialty, and he is quite a hand at it.

> He has long slim white hands like a society broad and in fact there is no doubt that his hands are the secret of The Lacework Kid's success at his trade of card playing as they are fast and flexible and have youth in them, and youth is one thing a good card player must have, because age is a drawback in everything in this wicked old world.
> It is really a beautiful sight to watch The Lacework Kid handle a deck of cards because he makes the pasteboards just float together when he is shuffling and causes them to fall as light as flecks of foam when he is dealing . . .

To the aging Runyon the grace and dexterity of The Lacework Kid was a nostalgic image of youth, as Billy Budd was for Melville. Not surprisingly Damon's romanticized hero is a card sharp. Melville saw innocence as tragic, Runyon saw it as comical.

> "I can teach any dumb animal to play gin rummy if I can get it to hold ten cards."   —"The Lacework Kid"

Gin rummy is a conversational game not usually played for high stakes, and great gin rummy players are seldom noted as high shots. When one such animal showed up on Damon's beat, it stirred his bardic instincts. Runyon first heard of Ray Ryan one winter in Hot Springs, Arkansas. Hot Springs, with its baths, was a great hangout of the mobsters and the sporting crowd. Damon stopped there in January or February most years to see what was doing and to get a little writing done. This particular time he got wind of a gin rummy player who was "winning or losing one hundred G'ses like they were pretzels." Ray Ryan, the grapevine said, was an oil man with a fancy for gin stakes in the upper zone.

News of the gin-playing high shot whetted Runyon's taste for characters, and when he got back to Broadway he bounced Ryan's name around. It was a kind of game of Damon's; sometimes it took him years to build up a composite portrait of a life that interested him. His mind was like a great garage or hangar, littered with the models and archetypes of sporting men's histories he'd collected over the years. He was continually adding details and new touches.

> "Do you know a chap named Ray Ryan?" I asked Benny Davis, the song writer, rotund, dapper, whose "Margie" is still played by bands to symbolize an era in the U.S.A.

Two High Shots

> "The first day Ray Ryan got to Miami Beach last winter he ventured so far out in the surf that the life savers had to go out after him," said Benny. "The sports along the beach were making book on the result. They were laying eight and taking two."
>
> "Then you know Ray Ryan?" I said.
>
> "Know him?" said Benny. "I'm just telling you. It was a photo finish but the life savers made it."
>
> "I hear he plays high gin rummy," I said.
>
> Benny, who has some local note as a gin rummy player on his own account, eyed me meditatively for several minutes, then he said:
>
> "Is the Empire State Building high? Is Pike's Peak high? Is the stratosphere high?"
>
> "I understand it is," I replied. "I mean the stratosphere."
>
> "Ray Ryan plays much higher gin rummy," said Benny Davis. "Much, much higher. And a nice fellow with it. He plays the highest gin rummy of any man since the game was invented."
>
> —"Two Gamblers"

Benny Davis' testimony confirmed what Damon had heard about Ray Ryan. Here was a guy, Runyon proposed, who obviously was to his game and his generation what Nick the Greek had been to poker and dice a generation earlier. Ryan was clearly a legend in his own time. Whereas gin rummy was considered by most professional cardplayers a difficult and chancy way of making a living, the far-famed Ryan must be "a man who gets a thrill out of the sheer gamble of the game." It followed, Damon reasoned, that such a man must be a lover of risks.

> Ryan is said to be a good steady gin rummy player but the margin between skill and luck is not great. Given equal cards the better card player is apt to win, but I think the real advantage in high stakes gin is with the player who best carries weight, which is to say who plays just as calmly for two dollars a point as he would for a penny a point. I know men who will beat for better card players at gin if the stakes are high enough just on superior courage, and courage is said to be Ryan's strength.

There is a gentle air of self-parody in Runyon's elevation of Ray Ryan to the cardplayers' communion of saints. Ryan's story, like those of all Damon's "characters," was an amalgam of fact and afflatus. Informal press agentry in the gaming world did more for the vaunted histories of big gamblers than the gamblers ever did for themselves. Incidents generated distortions that generated myths. The point of it all was simply a good story, so no one minded an occasional falsehood. Besides, would the man who wrote "Margie" be capable of a deliberate deception?

> I have always thought it rather curious that a man who may gamble into the millions in Wall Street or even in business attracts little attention, but when you point out a high player at cards or some other gambling game, all necks are craned for a peek at

him. And always when a figure like that of Ryan appears you get a lot of fiction and a modicum of fact about him.

There is usually a bearing down on the romantic side, if possible, and maybe much of what I relate here of Ryan can stand revision.

"The experience in the surf did not bother Ray Ryan," said Benny Davis. "He is a cool hand. As soon as he ungargled the salt water, he played a gentleman gin at ten dollars a point and blitzed his opponent six times hand running. Somebody told me he was going to California. If he did, maybe that earth shake out there we read about the other day was just Ryan beating The Greek at gin."

—"Two Gamblers"

In canonizing the likes of Nick the Greek and Ray Ryan, Damon added his own chapters to the mythology of the Gambler's Dream. Like many a part-time player, he lived vicariously through the exploits of the great high shots. The difference was that beyond merely contributing to the perishable word-of-mouth legend, Runyon used the comparative immortality of print to glorify these heroes, and so became their permanent laureate.

14

Damon and "Mr. Brown"

Arma virumque cano . . .
("Of arms and the man I sing . . .") —Virgil, *The Aeneid*

"Gee, what an experience I had!"
—Charlie "The Bug"Workman, killer of Dutch Schultz

"Grand opera is the berries." —Al Capone

*During the last score of years Runyon has studied and writ-
ten about the racket game and the racketeer. He has watched
them both grow to a stupendous menace . . .*
*Runyon knows his racketeer—and his daily stories will in-
terest and impress you. They will convince you that the racketeer
must go . . .*
—promotional blurb in the Hearst papers, May 1933

The Broadway columnists of the twenties and thirties—Walter Winchell was the first and most influential of the breed, Mark
Hellinger his most successful follower—cultivated extensive underworld connections. It was a symbiotic relationship. The columnists used the hints and tips provided by the gangsters as the
"scoops" and "items" which gave their work an aura of inside
knowledge that appealed enormously to readers. The fact that a
Winchell could predict the execution killing of Vincent Coll or
take part in the surrender of Lepke Buchalter lent credibility to
his work and consequently boosted the circulation of any paper
he worked for—which in turn made Winchell a rich man. The
gangsters and racketeers, most of whom had sizeable egos, were
gratified to see their names in print, particularly when the reference was positive, which was almost always the case (the columnists weren't *that* crazy). The big-time hoods basked in their notoriety, especially in the days of Prohibition when the publicity was
good for their nightclub businesses—and what was good for their
nightclub businesses was good for their liquor-importing concerns.
They too became rich men, richer (*much* richer) than the Winchells and the Hellingers.

Nevertheless it was always an uneasy alliance on both sides.
For twelve years Winchell lived in the same building as Frank

The World of Damon Runyon

Owney Madden

Costello, an underworld "don" he greatly admired; the columnist was slipped many an item (the Lepke surrender story being the biggest) through the Costello pipeline. The two men knew each other well—even resembled one another, down to the tilted grey hats—and often when Costello wanted to speak to his enemies or the law he did it through Winchell's column. Another pal of Walter's was Owney "The Killer" Madden, a onetime Hell's Kitchen roughneck who'd done eight years in Sing Sing before a quick rise to the top of the Manhattan liquor trade. When Winchell was still cutting his teeth at the *Evening Graphic* Owney approached him one day in a barbershop and said, "I like your stuff, kid." Thereafter the two were constantly seen together in public, in nightclubs and restaurants, and at the Garden on fight nights. (Madden was also a chum of Hellinger, whose columns made him out to be as innocent as a lamb; in 1929 Hellinger's private intercession with Madden put an end to Legs Diamond's plan of extorting $50,000 from Al Jolson.) But the very intimacy of the relations between the mobsters and the Broadway columnists was a source of nervousness for both parties.

Damon and "Mr. Brown"

Winchell's right-hand man, Herman Klurfeld, later recounted how nightclub hostess Texas Guinan introduced Walter to the underworld. "Its rulers courted him, appointed themselves his bodyguards, believed it was a mark of distinction to be in his company, and hoped he would mention them—or their girls—in his column." And yet, looking back on the period from the vantage of the fifties, Winchell told Klurfeld that he had never felt relaxed around the hoods. "The mobsters were wild," Walter admitted. "They could be as polite as headwaiters one minute and kill you the next." More than once, Winchell said, he'd feared that items in his columns might get him "taken for a ride." The columnist told Klurfeld he'd "secretly despised" the very hoods he'd associated with most closely.

There was an underlying tension between the gossip columnists and the gangsters from the start, caused by a basic misunderstanding of the columnists' function. The gangsters saw the Broadway scribes as their private corps of press agents. The columnists saw themselves as reporters. The gangsters had secrets they did not want exposed; there were certain lines the columnists were not allowed to cross, certain scoops they could not think of printing if they valued their health or that of their families. It was as simple as intimidation, though the columnists liked to think of it as "friendship." They were allowed access to gang circles only on the gangsters' terms: give us a favorable press or make yourself scarce. The columnists stayed and did not rock the boat with any unwise items that might cast the gang boys in an unfavorable light. Hellinger's biographer, Jim Bishop, said the columnist recited the hoodlums' "benefactions to the poor endlessly. One supported a widow and three children. Madden was a soft touch for any bum on Broadway. The Dutchman was nutty but he had a regiment of unemployed family men on his payroll. Zwillman helped more poor people than a charity organization . . ."

The appearance of sentimentality and naiveté was self-imposed; the gossip columnists wore blinders of their own making. There were doubts on both sides, theirs and the gangsters, as to who was the user and who was being used. No doubt there were many unpleasant moments for the columnists. Winchell was always being "summoned" here or there by the mob. In 1929 he got a call from Capone in Florida. He caught the first train to Miami and met with the Big Fellow at his Palm Island estate. Scarface—known to his Florida neighbors as "Mr. Brown"—had a grumble about the newspapers. He griped to Winchell about "phony inside-stuff writers who claim to know me." One British reporter had called Big Al "America's Nineteenth Amendment." "There's lots of grief attached to the limelight," the Big Guy complained. (This was just dawning on him around that time.) He

The World of Damon Runyon

demanded his tribute of respect from the scribes, and Winchell was delegated to make the commandment known. Having spoken, the big boss expected to have his words inscribed on graven tablets, à la God giving orders to Moses.

Walter showed deep sympathy and promised to do what he could.

And, of course, he did. Who needed a broken head?

Damon Runyon was closer to the figures of the underworld than were any of the gossip columnists, and he made them the central characters of his fiction. But for several reasons he had none of the anxiety problems the gossip columnists suffered in this regard. His column was that of a reflective essayist, not a gossip-monger; he did not comb the Broadway beat for one-line scoops and hot items to be shoveled into print the next morning. He avoided "scandal" news and kept private what was clearly private. He was on the lookout for stories that would make his readers laugh or cry, not scoops that would shock or titillate them. When he spoke of underworld characters in his columns, it was often cryptically, as many a columnist will make oblique references to his family and friends.

Runyon did not trade on the celebrity of his gangster friends or exploit it; nor did he feed their vanity with streams of name-dropping patter, à la Winchell, or blatant, undeserved paeans, à la Hellinger. He kept a storehouse of Broadway histories in his head and was always adding to it. The gangsters he wrote of in his tales could recognize themselves there, if they cared to look, but as a rule the reading public recognized little.

It was *types* Damon was after, not individuals. He was interested in paradigms and parables, stories that held a general human truth, not Broadway's dirty laundry. He found his life's work in the gangsters' life stories. But it took a process of imagination to adapt the human realities into the art of the tales, and it was this process that kept Damon at a safely objective distance from the mugs themselves. What he made of them in his parabolic fictions was often something quite different from the real-life prototypes he used as models. There was no question of simply slinging paint onto the canvas, or items into print, like spicy candid camera exclusives.

The mob boys knew Runyon was something different. Being fairly alert men, they were able to sense that he was interested in them in some way that went beyond the peek and tell of the gossip columnists. Perhaps they were flattered by his sincerity, perhaps not, but they definitely acknowledged it. Runyon advanced to a position of trust and respect with killers and the employers of killers as well as with gentler but equally "illegal" men. It is

Damon and "Mr. Brown"

possible that he shared something of the outlaw's mentality himself, making for a natural familiarity (as in the old saying about birds of a feather). At any rate the denizens of the underworld accorded him a position of esteem that was enjoyed by no other writer. "Enjoyed" is probably the wrong word; most writers would not have wanted to walk the same side of the street with certain guys whom Damon knew well, much less look upon them as pals.

Damon *did* look upon many of the crooks and mugs he knew in just that way, and vice versa. The outward signs of this, on his part, are everywhere in his writing and recorded conversation. On the part of the crooks and mugs, the testimony of affection is just as strong. The "boys" threw dinners in Runyon's honor (there was one notable bash at Miami in 1934); made offers to "silence" critics of his work (Damon once had to constrain his mob friends in print lest they inflict bodily harm on a New York *Times* critic who'd blasted a Runyon film production); and when he died, they contributed lavishly to the cancer foundation established in his name (Frank Costello donated $25,000, Bugsy Siegel $8,000, and even Joseph "Socks" Lanza, working his way through Sing Sing, sent $250). Damon's sympathetic alliance with the underworld was too strong to have been the result of accident or calculation on either side. He and his mobster friends had certain common attitudes about life, and they had roughly compatible philosophies. The Runyon-underworld match was one of those rare marriages of natural outlook that cross over the lines of vocation and social class because they are forged in the heavens— although in this case it might have been in the neighborhood of one of the darker stars.

As a ragged, motherless lad in the dusty streets of Pueblo, Damon's instincts had always driven him to admire those characters whose company was exciting and whose stories were full of color and action and life—even when they were not "good" men as such. The old Indian fighters he saw in the saloons his father frequented were images of the same rough, inventive individualism he was to encounter later in the dives of Broadway. The attraction was the same for the man as it had been for the boy; for better or worse this was his destined spiritual fraternity, the brotherhood of outlaws.

When Prohibition ended, the nationwide crime wave didn't, to the understandable displeasure of the majority of the American people. The public mood on this subject struck William Randolph Hearst—who was perennially unhappy with the circulation totals of his pet paper, the New York *American*—as a potential to exploit. (It was no upset; everything struck Hearst this way.) There was hay to make on the crime issue, he was sure, and he decided to splash the *American*'s pages with a blockbuster exposé on the crime wave, hopefully spilling a little black ink on the auditors' reports in the process. Naturally Hearst chose ace reporter and crime scholar Damon Runyon to carry the banner in his war on the underworld. Damon would write a series of crusading articles.

The results were curious. Professor Runyon made three or four quick passes with his fine-bladed irony, then dropped that and occupied himself with laying a smokescreen of humorous remarks about Abba Dabba Berman and Petunia Jones. In his most serious moment he opined that Al Capone's entire career in crime was as nothing compared to those of the "racketeers" of Wall Street and of such government administrations as Harding's. "Mr. Capone," he wrote, "made a racket of an entire city, which still leaves him a small timer alongside of those who made a racket of a nation." When it came to ethics, Professor Runyon saw little difference between the behavior of gangsters and that of elected officials and the high moguls of the world of finance.

His experience certainly provided ample support for such a view. As a reporter he hadn't been able to help noticing that dishonesty was a quality evident at all levels of society, not just among the criminal class. He knew that the underworld bosses worked hand in hand with politicians—like Tammany Boss Jimmy Hines, who was in cahoots with such operators as Owney Madden and Dutch Schultz. (Hines protected and shared the profits of Madden's laundry and coal rackets and Schultz' Harlem numbers game.) He had seen the "Poker Cabinet" of Harding (bootleggers, swindlers, con artists, and bag men) in operation. He had covered the Hall-Mills trial, in which a heavy-handed tilting of the tables of "Jersey Justice" won a surprising acquittal for the Hall-Stevens clan—among whom were a member of the New York Stock Exchange and shareholders of the Johnson and Johnson pharmaceutical firm. He had covered the Sacco and Vanzetti executions, heard how the judge had referred to the condemned men as "those anarchist bastards," and noted the official acquiescence of the governor of Massachusetts and the president of Harvard in the death verdict. "They're frying Sacco and Vanzetti in the morning," the first sentence of Damon's story had run. In its linking of underworld jargon with "legal" reality it was as politically indicative as any sentence he ever wrote. It was also the only one ever to be censored by an editor; Edmond Coblentz, then editor of the *American,* "killed" Damon's story, with its bitter lead, and substituted a wire service account.

Damon had also been privy to *American* reporter Nat Ferber's inquiry into the secrets of the Wall Street "bucket shops," which with the backing of the ubiquitous Arnold Rothstein had swindled unsuspecting investors out of millions. (Ferber recalled that when he had finally cracked the bucket-shop story and drawn the connection between Rothstein and the brokers, "Damon Runyon came up grinning, as if to say, 'I told you so.'") He had attended the Senate Banking Committee hearings, learning of the methods of such King Midas types as J. P. Morgan, who paid no American taxes, pulled off all kinds of funny-money deals, shared inside financial tips with a "preferred list" of special chums—and maintained a lily-white public reputation. ("If Mr. J. Pierpont Morgan should fall into a barrel of onion soup—may the fates forfend!—the chances are that he would come up with a rose in his hand," Runyon sneered in his report from the hearings.)

Damon's friend and disciple Bill Corum called him the D-Man—an echo of G-Man, then the popular term for federal investigators—in honor of his hardheaded pursuit of and respect for facts. In the ten years prior to his backhanded treatment of the Capone trial, Damon's frequent pursuits had netted more than enough facts to clinch his case on the subject of the law—which was that the world within its boundaries was no more honest than that without.

In one column the spinner of Broadway tales made a rare statement about his own work.

> Damon Runyon is not a humorist per se. He is more of a dramatic writer, but in a simulation of humor he often manges to say things which if said in a serious tone might be erased because he is not supposed to say things like that. By saying something with a half-boob air, by conveying an air of jocularity, he gets ideas out of his system on the wrongs of this world which indicate that he must have been a great rebel at heart but lacking moral courage . . .
> He has one not easily acquired trick which is conveying a thought for indirection. He makes it appear that he is not personally responsible for the thought, but there it is. This has something of the form and something of the effect of dropping rumors on someone where it will do the most harm . . .

When Runyon covered the Hall-Mills or Snyder-Gray or Lindbergh trials, he wrote "straight"—penetrating, accurate, thorough, nonironic chronicles. He was praised for the solidity of his reports, which in pretelevision days were the closest available thing to a total "picture" of the news. But when he covered the 1929 Arnold Rothstein murder trial, or Al Capone's income tax evasion trial in Chicago in 1931, he used "indirection" and adopted a "half-boob air" and "an air of jocularity." The difference was simple. Rothstein and Capone had been his personal associates, and though Damon privately suspected that each had been victimized (Rothstein by an execution plot, Capone by the federal government's persecution tactics), he refrained from approaching these issues in print for the same reason a man does not discuss family

"Mr. Brown" (Al Capone)

matters in public. The subjects were too close to home.

Two years after his reportorial tour de force at the Hall-Mills event, Damon opted for a disguise of nonchalance at the Rothstein trial and tiptoed his way through it. His irony became a high-wire act. He noted casually that despite Rothstein's celebrity, most of the jurors had sworn never to have heard of him. He reported

Damon and "Mr. Brown"

without comment the sight of the prosecution witnesses hustling across town to place bets with their bookies during recesses in the trial. He pointed out that only George McManus (of the four men indicted) had been brought to trial, "probably for the reason he is the only one handy." The "air of jocularity"was never more evident in a Runyon news piece.

Damon knew more about the Rothstein killing than he could afford to say, so he limited himself to cynicism, oblique smirks, and humorous noodlings around the issues, as he was to do three years later in the crime series assigned by Hearst. His writing took on not only a "half-boob air" but a gingerly quality, the tone of a guy who would just as soon change the subject. His printed remarks on the demise of Abba Dabba Berman (in the 1935 execution killing of Dutch Schultz) were similarly evasive, for the same reasons. Ditto his reports on the tax evasion trial of Al Capone.

Al had been a friend of Damon's for years. They had seen quite a bit of each other in Florida, where Damon vacationed often in the late twenties and where Al had a big mansion on Palm Island overlooking Biscayne Bay. (It was quite a palace, complete with scrolled balconies, minarets, turrets, cupolas, and spires, and Al filled it with constant social life.) They bumped into each other more than once in prizefight camps, such as before the 1927 Tunney-Dempsey rematch in Chicago. Both the writer and the mob boss were notable Dempsey backers. Damon had written Jack's life story *twice* and had given him a nickname, the Manassa Mauler, that was now familiar from coast to coast. At the Chicago fight Al demonstrated his support for the ex-champ by donating plenty of goodwill, plus select security troops, to his Lake Villa training camp. Capone also noticed Runyon at Lake Villa. He was quite a man for quick judgments, and it did not take long for him to reckon this sharp-tongued, dudish columnist as the classiest (and canniest) of Jack's army of journalistic admirers. Runyon, who liked colorful people, was captivated.

In 1929, on the occasion of the Stribling-Sharkey fight at Miami Beach, Al threw a big blowout for the visiting press at his Palm Island villa, and it was Damon he picked to carry the invitation to the writing mob. Sixty scribes and their escorts were to be on hand, Al decided. He figured the party would be a good way to build up his newspaper image, which had never been anything he had been tempted to write home about.

Runyon carried the Big Fellow's invitation (or summons?) to Nat Fleischer, who was handling publicity for the fight. (The promoter of the fight, Nat's Madison Square Garden boss, Tex Rickard, had just that week given up the ghost to a ruptured appendix.)

Nat saw to it that word got around. A Capone invitation was something special; you did not ignore it. Nat rustled up the sixty scribes in an afternoon.

When Runyon, Pegler, Gallico, McGeehan, Sid Mercer, and the other writers arrived at the Capone estate, they were shaken down for weapons, then ushered inside and given the run of the house. There were a dinner-jacketed dance band, several strategically located tables loaded with real, uncut imported liquor (a rarity in that period), and a vast spread of first-class eats. Capone's gorillas, acting as waiters, were on their best behavior. Grantland Rice, who wasn't there, was told by someone who *was* that it was "a demure cocktail party" and that "Scarface was strictly Emily Post."

The host took Damon and several of the other scribes to the basement to view his booze stash. The Capone wine cellar was a subterranean maze of dark aisles that seemed to go on for miles. While the scribes wandered along, peering at ancient labels whenever Al pointed out a particular vintage, a stir was occurring upstairs. Somebody's female companion, suffering from overexposure to real champagne after not being around the stuff for years, passed out on a couch. There ensued a great bustling as the gorillas rushed to reconceal the sawed-off shotguns they'd hidden behind the sofa cushions, which the young lady's collapse had disarranged. During the excitement the guests had a chance to roam at will among the mansion's twenty-five rooms unmolested and unnoticed. Around this time, a diamond ring mysteriously disassociated itself from a jewelry case in Mrs. Capone's bedroom and apparently vanished into thin air, although this is hard to say because there was never any search of pockets.

Whoever made off with the ring accomplished the job just in the nick of time, for in the wake of the young doll's fainting act Mrs. Capone went to her bedroom for a cosmetic repair, saw her jewel case open, looked inside, and shortly afterward blew the whistle. No sooner had the disappearance of the ring been announced than half the writers were on their way to the parking lot. No one tried to stop the hastily departing guests. There were some disapproving glances from the gorillas, but that was all.

Damon was left to make excuses on behalf of his friends to the wounded host, who turned out to be extremely understanding about it all. When Gallico and Pegler hinted in their papers the next day that one of their colleagues had lifted a ring at the party, Capone quickly scotched the story by reporting that the ring had been found. It hadn't, but admitting its disappearance would have meant a significant loss of underworld face for the Big Fellow. After all, the actual embarrassment of getting heisted by some

Damon and "Mr. Brown"

two-bit scribe was nothing compared to the potential humiliation of letting it get around!

The Big Guy did not hold Damon responsible for this peccadillo any more than he himself would have expected to be blamed for the rash act of one of his associates. (Could Damon help it if he had crude friends?) Al was ready to forgive and forget. He liked Runyon best of all the scribes because Runyon had class and knew how to keep his mouth shut. Despite his profession, Damon was a guy whom "Mr. Brown," with his love of good manners and his live-and-let-live philosophy, could appreciate.

At the fight a few nights later Al was the life of the party, spreading C-notes among the hired help with the insouciance of a man passing play money. He was escorted by a crew of thick-necked bodyguards to ringside, where his seat was dusted off by no less an usher than Jack Dempsey (who'd stepped in as promoter when it turned out that Tex Rickard's successor, a nice guy named Bill Carey, couldn't promote free water in a desert). Westbrook Pegler described the ex-heavyweight champ's stooping to mop the boards upon which the imperial posterior would be deposited, and the mob boss' graceful bow of acknowledgment, as "a gesture of good fellowship and an exchange of amenities between two professions having much in common."

Withal, Capone's social behavior before and during the match was a miracle of decorum and restraint, especially considering the timing. The Stribling-Sharkey bout occurred on February 27, 1929, just thirteen days after seven men (five of them members of the Bugs Moran mob) had fallen in a bloody pile on a garage floor on North Clark Street in Chicago, victims of an epidemic of hot lead. Bugs Moran, the apparent intended target, was known to be Al Capone's principal gangland rival. "Only the Capone gang kills like that," Moran told the newspapers on the evening of St. Valentine's Day. It did not require a Sherlock Holmes to connect "Mr. Brown" with the mass killing.

While Capone wined and dined the scribes on Palm Island, the Chicago police moved in on some of his boys back home. The night of the fight in Miami they picked up Machine Gun Jack McGurn, one of Al's top shooters. Machine Gun Jack told the law he'd spent St. Valentine's Day in bed with his doll, like any right-thinking guy would do.

Suspicion turned to two other Capone men, John Scalisi and Albert Anselmi, but a few days later these characters were merely a memory and a note on the police books. Al had sent word from Florida that Scalisi and Anselmi were to be given a special heroes' banquet. Accordingly, the pair were honored at a private spaghetti-and-vino feast, at the high point of which their heads were bashed

Machine Gun Jack McGurn and his doll.

in with pistol butts by a couple of their fellow thugs.

Al was unhappy about the degree of heat the St. Valentine's Day murders were generating; he could feel the warmth all the way down in Miami. He had plenty of reason to be worried. Chicago would never again be a place the Big Guy could call home.

The underworld chiefs of the other cities had been disturbed by the accelerating violence in Chicago, where soldiers of the rival mobs were dropping like flies. Sides were being drawn across the country. The situation was tense, and Al himself was growing nervous. The publicity he was getting irritated him, worse than a million British reporters. From Florida he made contact with Frank Costello, the top man in New York, and it was agreed that Don Francisco would preside over a peace conference in Atlantic City in early May. Damon, of course, heard all about it. His account of the 1929 peace conference can be found in "Dark Dolores," a tale published in *Cosmopolitan* in the fall of 1930.

In Runyon's version, as often happens, a doll steals the show from the guys, even though they are big shots. This time it's Dolores Dark, a show girl who lures her boyfriend's assassins to their deaths in the ocean as the climax of a complicated revenge plot.

The story begins with a conversation between the narrator and Waldo Winchester, the newspaper scribe, in which Winchester remarks that "It is a very great shame there are no dolls around such as in the old days to make good stories for the newspapers by knocking guys off right and left."

> "Why," Waldo Winchester says, "if we only have a Cleopatra, or a Helen of Troy, or even a Queen Elizabeth around now guzzling guys every few minutes, think what a great thing it will be for the circulation of the newspapers, especially the tabloids. The best we get nowadays is some doll belting a guy with a sash weight, or maybe filling him full of slugs, and this is no longer exciting."

Walter Winchell, the number one tabloid star, had taken his rapidfire gossip column from the *Evening Graphic* to the *Daily Mirror* the year before Damon's tale was composed. (The Winchell column was one of the great and coveted weapons in the New York circulation wars, which sometimes rivaled those of the underground for intensity if not bloodshed.) The dolls using sash weights (Ruth Snyder) and slugs (Mrs. Hall) had been antiheroines of the tabloids, whose sensational stories and photographs (some of the latter were faked) had convinced every American husband that the figure across the breakfast table contained unreckoned possibilities. Damon's grave and voluminous writing on both trials had briefly helped the *American*'s circulation to hold its own against the tabloids.

> Then Waldo Winchester tells me about a doll by the name of Lorelei who hangs out in the Rhine River some time ago and stools sailors up to the rocks to get them wrecked, which I consider a dirty trick, although Waldo does not seem to make so much of it. Furthermore, he speaks of another doll by the name of Circe, who is quite a hand for luring guys to destruction, and by the time Waldo gets to Circe he is crying because there are no more dolls like her around to furnish news for the papers.

Waldo's lament gets the narrator to thinking of the recent afternoon on which he is walking along Broadway thinking of not much, when he comes on Dave the Dude just getting in a taxicab with a suitcase in his duke, "and the next thing I know Dave is jerking me into the cab and telling the jockey to go to Penn Station. This is how I come to be in Atlantic City at the time of the peace conference. . ." Dave the Dude, a familiar figure from the Broadway series, bears a considerable resemblance to the Frank Costello of 1929: both are big-time bootleggers, fast men with a dollar, dapper, cocky, and tough. Dave the Dude's requests (like Costello's) are not to be taken lightly. So it turns out that although he has nothing to do with the peace conference, Runyon's narrator goes along with Dave the Dude just to keep him company—as who wouldn't, once asked?

> I am a guy who is never too busy to keep people company, and Dave the Dude is a guy who just naturally loves company. In fact, he hates to go anywhere, or be anywhere, by himself, and the reason is because when he is by himself Dave the Dude has nobody to nod him yes, and if there is one thing Dave is very, very fond of, it is to have somebody to nod him yes. Why it is that Dave the Dude does not have Big Nig with him I do not know, for Big Nig is Dave's regular nod-guy.
>
> But I am better than a raw hand myself at nodding. In fact, I am probably as good a nod-guy as there is in this town, where there must be three million nod-guys, and why not, because the way I look at it, it is no bother whatever to nod a guy. In fact, it saves a lot of conversation.

Damon, who at times seemed to be the only professional receiving set equipped with legs on all of Broadway, was notably adept at the nod. He once addressed this subject obliquely in a column, "Free-loading Ethics," in which he put forth a wry thesis on the importance of the occasional nod of the head in establishing both one's own intelligence and the "flattering clarity" of one's host's remarks. In fact Runyon spent half his waking hours hanging around restaurants, nightclubs, press boxes, city rooms, sports desks, lunch counters, gyms, racetracks, and other crossroads of human intercourse, just listening, putting in an occasional word, and nodding his head. He was one of the best nod men in the business. And in "Dark Dolores" it's nothing but his abnormal ear size that gets Damon's narrator into the act. For this guy, it is not unusual. Like his creator, the fictional character is a natural-born sounding board. The ability to listen is a ticket that opens many doors (not to mention a few worm cans).

> Anyway, there I am in Atlantic City the time of the big peace conference, although I wish to say right now that if I know in advance who is going to be at this peace conference, or that there is going to be any peace conference, I will never be anywhere near Atlantic City, because the parties mixed up in it are no kind of associates for a nervous guy like me.

Damon and "Mr. Brown"

Damon transfers the home town of the principals of the conference from Chicago to St. Louis in order to prevent a pat identification that might make innocent parties in the former city nervous, but his portrait of Capone as the head of the visiting party is clear enough. He gives the Big Guy the name Black Mike Marrio.

> This Black Mike is a Guinea, and not a bad-looking Guinea, at that, except for a big scar on one cheek which I suppose is done by somebody trying to give him a laughing mouth. Some Guins, especially Sicilians, can swing a shiv so as to give a guy a slash that leaves him looking as if he is always laughing out of his mouth, although generally this is only for dolls who are not on the level with their ever-loving guys.

As far as looks go, Black Mike is Scarface to a T.

In the annals of gang history the Atlantic City conference was a success. Damon didn't delve into the hard details in his tale (he had other dramatic fish to fry), but the business end of the affair went swimmingly. The representatives of the Eastern seaboard cities and the disputing Chicago groups settled all their differences and drew up new territorial lines and treaties that would be operative for several years. Spheres of influence were plotted, divisions of plunder mapped. The gang chieftains signed documents to make everything official, then decamped for their respective homes.

For "Mr. Brown" the trip home was longer than for any of his colleagues. In Philly he was arrested with his bodyguard on a concealed weapons charge on May 16, 1929. It led to the Big Guy's first imprisonment. He did a one-year hitch and, with time off for good behavior, was released March 17, 1930. When he finally got back to Chicago—nearly a year after he'd set out—he found sentiment against him running high. He was now Public Enemy Number One, no longer the Big Fellow, no longer as honored as he was feared. He still commanded the loyalties of his mob, but public feeling had turned against him.

At the beginning of the following year this feeling, and the growing pressure of the law, drove him from his adopted Midwestern home. He went to L.A. but was run out of town by the cops within twenty-four hours. When he showed his pretty face a few days later in the Black Hills, the governor of South Dakota called out the National Guard. The prospect of living as *persona non grata,* moving from state to state like some cheap hood on the lam, did not appeal to Al. He asked his lawyers to fix things up for him to return to Florida. They did, and he spent the spring of 1931 at his Palm Island place. Runyon, vacationing in Florida, ran into him there. It was obvious to Damon that this was not a relaxing holiday for the Big Guy. Al was anxious, fretful; he brooded like Napoleon in Moscow. By summer he was on his way to Chicago once more.

On October 6, 1931, the feds picked him up there on a tax evasion rap. He went on trial a week later, and Damon came to town to cover the story. He handled it much as he had the Rothstein murder trial two years earlier—with kid gloves. He stuck to the small points and let the larger issues of guilt and innocence slide by, like ships in the night.

The prosecution case, to hear Runyon tell it, was a fascinating course in the details of gangland affluence. It was brought to light that Capone (who was reputed to have made from $30 to $50 million off his various rackets since coming to power in the mid-twenties) had paid his Miami butcher $6500 for choice cuts over the last three years; had customarily spent $12 a pair for silk shorts, $30 for shirts, and $155 for tailored suits; and had dropped upward of 200 G's on the ponies alone over the past few seasons. (Elsewhere the Big Fellow claimed his total losses on dice and horses were somewhere in the $10 million range.)

This chronicle of extravagance gratified Damon, who was a great believer in free spending and fine things. His own suits and shirts probably set him back at least what Capone's did (on a considerably smaller income), and his ties and hats—which were made to order—would have made Al's look like bargain basement stuff. Damon was renowned as a head-to-toe clotheshorse of the first order. To the prosecution's inventory of the Big Fellow's wardrobe he listened with a competitive interest. But when it came to the figures on Al's gambling expenses, "Your correspondent cheerfully yields the palm he has borne with such distinction for lo these many years as the world's worst horse player to Mr. Alphonse Capone."

His coverage of the trial was entertaining but elusive. He did not reveal his suspicion that Capone was being railroaded by the government, punished for other sins. He swallowed his sympathies and trotted out an air of jocularity. Damon's favorite motto was "Get the Money," a personal axiom that often forced him into its obvious logical adjunct, "indirection" ("he must have been a great rebel at heart but lacking moral courage"). Damon settled for playing the Capone trial for laughs.

On October 18, 1931, federal judge James H. Williamson announced a conviction on five counts. Big Al was awarded a ticket to the big house at government expense, the first thing Uncle Sam ever gave him in his life. (Everything else he owned, he'd had to work for.) The man who had formerly been quoted so poetically—"Grand opera is the berries!"—was now in a darkly prosaic mood. Meanwhile he was out on bail while his lawyers went through their song and dance.

He returned to Florida for the winter to sweat it out. He saw Runyon and a few other close friends—and of course his mob allies—but that was all; there were no more all-night shindigs, no more open houses, no more champagne breakfasts with pretty show girls on his yacht. It was hard times that winter all over the country—and in Al Capone's heart.

For Damon it was a better time than for most men, a time of continuing prosperity, great activity, and change. *Guys and Dolls,* the first collection of his hugely popular Broadway tales, had just been published and was leaping off the sales charts, and he was selling new tales to *Cosmopolitan* and *Collier's* as fast as he could turn them out. He asked for and got a dollar a word for the 5,000-word stories. The motion picture companies were reading them with great interest, and offers from Hollywood would soon be coming in by the bunch. Accompanying this literary success was a new contract with Hearst that—in a year when, according to one historian, reporters with 20 years' experience averaged $38 a week—guaranteed Damon a base annual income of $25,000 for his daily column and one weekly feature. Not included in this figure were his syndication profits. (Since his pieces ran in all the papers of the Hearst chain and in dozens of other papers in noncompetitive cities, the syndication earnings added up to a sum at least equal to his base salary.) There was also a new magazine article contract from the Bell Syndicate. Damon's star as a writer had never been at higher ascendance, and despite the Depression he was on top of the world.

He had been estranged from his first wife, Ellen, for over a decade and formally separated from her for three years when, a few days after his return to New York from the Capone trial, she died of alcoholism in her rented house in Bronxville. Damon was living in his three-room penthouse suite at the Hotel Forrest at the time, following the Broadway beat by night, writing his columns and tales by the light of early morning, and sleeping well into the afternoon. He had neither the habits, the space, nor the inclination to make a home for his two teenage children, who were sent to Washington, D.C., to live with Ellen's sister. ("My sister and I both felt rejected by our father," Damon Jr. wrote twenty years later.) While his grief for Ellen was sincere, it did not prevent Damon from remarrying within months of her death. He wed the beautiful Silver Slipper show girl with whom he'd been in love for several years, Patrice Amati.

Patrice had been twice married. At the time of her marriage to Damon in 1932 she was twenty-five, less than half his age. Tall

The World of Damon Runyon

Runyon marries Patrice Amati, 1932 (Jimmy Walker
performs the ceremony).

and slender (nearly her new husband's height), she had the grace
of a dancer and dark, flashing eyes. She was gregarious, enjoyed
dining out, and spent long evenings on the town with Damon both
before and after their marriage. In New York they regularly went
for talk and a meal with friends to such spots as the swank
Colony—"an establishment infested largely by the Bong Tong,"
Damon wrote in one of his many columns about eating—and then
to the movies, followed by Lindy's or the Stork Club. "In ten years
of marriage we did not have more than ten meals at home," Patrice
later said.

For Damon life with his new spouse was to be quite different
from life with Ellen; henceforth his partner in life would actually
share a good deal of his time, and this was definitely a novelty.

The newlyweds occupied a lavish penthouse in the Parc Vendome, on West 57th Street, which was to remain their New York
home throughout the 1930s. But Damon soon decided that henceforth he would spend only the fair weather seasons in Manhattan.
Flushed with the new financial success his stories were bringing,

Damon and "Mr. Brown"

Damon and Patrice in Florida.

he bought himself and his bride a winter retreat. It was a large piece of land on Hibiscus Island, along Miami Harbor and across Biscayne Bay from the Palm Island estate of his friend "Mr. Brown." Another familiar neighbor was George "Big Frenchy" De-Mange, ex-con and former partner of Owney Madden in bootlegging, nightclubs, and other rackets. DeMange, whose local alias was "Mr. Fox," owned a house not far from Damon's on Hibiscus Island. The Runyon villa, put up at a cost of $75,000, had a red tile roof but otherwise was wedding-cake white—white from the typewriter keys to the telephone and dinner table. Damon and Patrice called it Las Melaleuccas.

The lanky, fourteen-year-old Damon Jr., now as tall as his father, had been mistreated in a parochial boarding school in the South where Ellen's family had placed him and was now enrolled by Damon in Riverside Military Academy, eighteen miles north of Miami. He visited his father and stepmother on holidays. ("There are more rules at your house than at Riverside," the young cadet's friends complained after weekend visits to the Runyon

The World of Damon Runyon

Big Frenchy DeMange

villa, where Damon's work regimen ruled.) Runyon's daughter Mary had—at eighteen and without her father's consent—just married a young Scripps-Howard newspaperman, Dick McCann. ("He is a mild looking youth of some 23 long, hard years," Damon had written to Agnes Fowler after meeting his prospective son-in-law, "a sportswriter, no less, and of the opposition, being one of Roy Howard's fledglings. Isn't that treason, or something?") Mary and her husband did not become part of the new Runyon household.

Damon wintered at the Florida house every year for the remainder of the decade. The life he found there with Patrice was at first idyllic. Damon loved Florida, "the land of sand in your shoes," where he and Patrice swam and sunned on the beach, alone or with visiting chums like Sid Mercer, Bugs Baer, and Gene Fowler. It was the closest contact with "nature" Runyon was to achieve in his adult life. He studied the fauna of the Florida littoral, writing columns for the *American* on jellyfish and poisonous Portuguese man-of-wars (one of which stung him), and was even inspired (mainly by Big Frenchy DeMange's pack of Great Danes barking at his heels) to take occasional sunset sprints among the palms.

Damon and "Mr. Brown"

He and Patrice went to the races at Hialeah and dined at the Hibiscus Island Tennis Club or, at rare times, in their own home.

Damon frequently expressed his contentment with the Florida life in his columns.

> It means the peace of Hibiscus Island when evening comes on, and the tide is in, and the Bay and the trees subside to a mere murmur, and the lights are twinkling in the houses across the water and there's a fat chicken frying in the kitchen, and the biscuits baking in the oven, and the radio is bringing into the white and quiet room the soft song of some sloe-eyed Señorita in a cafe on the Prado in Havana.

The greatest of the pleasures middle age (and his own efforts) had brought him was the company of the lovely sloe-eyed Señorita at his side, who shone like a dark jewel in his ivory and diamond castle.

There are few notes of discord or sadness recorded of these years in Damon's life. One is the touching recollection by Damon Jr. of hearing his father cry when the song "My Little Girl" came over the radio on a Miami station one evening in November 1932, slightly over a year after Ellen's death. For only the second time, Damon Jr. saw his father cry. (The other occasion had been the day of Ellen's death.) "My Little Girl," one of Ellen Egan Runyon's favorite songs from the year 1916, had been Damon's epistolary salutation to his wife over the years when his principal communication with her was from afar, as he traveled wherever his reporter's duties—and his loose feet—took him.

When Damon occupied Las Melaleuccas, his new neighbor and old friend, Capone, had only a few months of freedom left. The Big Fellow was not feeling expansive, but he invited Damon over now and then for a little quiet talk. Damon was one of the few writers Al could trust to listen to his problems and not spill them the next day in a gossip piece (perhaps the *only* one). In May the gang boss packed up his stuff, put everything valuable in storage, and closed the house. He gave Runyon his two prize whippets, which the writer kept as house dogs. Then "Mr. Brown" left Florida to take up residence in the federal pen at Atlanta.

Once Al was gone, his house stayed empty. Damon sat on his veranda and waved to the tourists who came by in boats, eager to get a look at the creamy villas of the big gangster and the big writer. When Damon waved, the rubbernecks waved back, delighted. Clearly this slim, dudish little man was not the big gangster, they decided. But the larger place across the way looked dead and forlorn, so they overcame their slight disappointment and made the best of things, shouting hellos at the big writer and snapping his picture to show the folks back home. In fact, Damon Runyon was big enough to merit a special postcard to the folks! ("Dear Mom, Dad, and Uncle Jim, Today we saw the famous author D. Runyon on his sun deck, he even waved to us!! Can you beat that? Wish you were here, xx, Bill and Marge.")

Now and then in his column Damon commented on how drastically the social life of his former neighbor "Mr. Brown" must have changed since his removal to Atlanta, but apart from such hints he never had another word to say about Al Capone—at least not for publication.

In 1934 Damon was passing through Chicago one day, on his way to cover a story. He had a few hours between trains, so he stopped at a downtown theatre where Walter Winchell was working as m.c. of a stage show. Damon didn't know it, but Winchell was receiving special "protection" in the Windy City. At the behest of Lucky Luciano, a chum of Walter's back home, there was a security force of mob boys on hand at the theatre to act as the gossip columnist's bodyguards for the duration of his stay. (Kidnaping was enjoying its finest hour as a profitable diversion for out-of-work hoods around this time, so Luciano's concern for his friend's welfare was at least marginally realistic.) Two of the protectors happened to be cousins of Al Capone. Unfortunately, however, they were not aware that the suspicious-looking, tight-mouthed guy in the expensive hat who turned up at the stage door was a friend of the family. One of the thugs, who as the story goes was a real starker, gave Runyon a little two-finger shove on the chest that pushed the frail (and greatly astonished) typewriter artist all the way out into the alley. "Mr. Winchell ain't seeing nobody," the mug said.

Only Damon's pride was wounded. He knew Al Capone well, and his brother Ralph Capone, but he had neglected to keep tabs on who was who among the in-laws.

The reception Damon got from the Chicago boys was pretty much the same one Westbrook Pegler got from the feds a couple of years later when he requested permission to go to Alcatraz— the top-security prison in California—to interview Capone. (Al had been transferred there from Atlanta in 1934.) Pegler tried and tried, and even though he was one of the most respected columnists in the country—and a "serious" one to boot—he was unable to get inside. Alcatraz was sealed tight around the Big Guy, and no one could get inside to hear (and record) his grumblings.

Pegler received a note of commendation from Runyon for his efforts. "Congratulations on the columns," Damon wrote, referring to his competitor's pieces describing the conditions of secrecy at

Damon and "Mr. Brown"

Alcatraz. "I don't make a practice of scattering rosebuds, but you're one bloke that's got 'em coming." Runyon and Pegler were never particularly close, but the Capone matter was obviously bothering Damon. It weighed on his mind, as did the death or incarceration of any of his pals from the old days, and by now they were dropping off right and left like leaves in autumn.

15

Fight Night at the Garden
with Jimmy Walker

Damon Runyon's favorite politician was Jimmy Walker. And Jimmy's favorite sportswriter was Damon.

It was a natural match. Never were two guys more devoted to a woman than these two were to a city. When New York City was still swift and beautiful and young enough to earn such affection, these two guys wore her around with them as close to the heart as the flowers in their buttonholes. While she stayed fresh, the show of feeling reflected only glory on both of them, and on her also.

Damon was taking Gene Fowler, who was new in town, for an informative, avuncular stroll through lower Manhattan one summer day in 1918. They'd been to the Polo Grounds and then ridden downtown in a taxi with Damon gesturing out the window and repeating, "Let it roar!" It took Gene a few minutes to realize that his friend and patron's "it" was just "the everlasting noise of the city."

They walked up Park Row, then paused on the steps of City Hall, where Damon declared there was someone he had to meet. After a few minutes a small, dapper man bounded up the steps. Runyon shouted "Jimmy!" and the two men greeted each other warmly, then conversed in whispered privacy for a moment before Damon turned and introduced the curious Fowler to State Senator James J. Walker. Gene, who missed the title in the traffic's roar, thought the small, dapper man to be "a song-and-dance crony of Runyon's from Broadway, perhaps the Palace Theatre." A couple of years earlier he wouldn't have been very far off target in that assessment.

Jimmy Walker went on to become not only mayor of New York but for many men (among them Fowler, who wrote Jimmy's life story lovingly in *Beau James)* the vivid symbol of the town in its greatest age. "Jimmy was of New York," the New York *Herald Tribune*'s great city editor, Stanley Walker, wrote, "and to the country he typified its gaudiness, smartness and insouciance to perfection." Less a politician than a kind of Broadway statesman, Jim had gone into the political racket only because it seemed to

Fight Night at the Garden with Jimmy Walker

Jimmy Walker

older men (including his father) the proper arena for a young Irishman with looks and brains and charm. In 1911 he was "drafted" to the state assembly by the Tammany Hall machine because he could think quickly on his feet, even though until then his first love had been songwriting. His greatest achievement in the musical field, a sentimental tune called "Will You Love Me in December As You Do in May?", became a standard that for several decades could be heard wherever late-night tipplers harmonized.

Runyon and Walker knew each other long and well. Now and then, as on that day in 1918 on the steps of City Hall, Jim did Damon a little favor—usually a matter of rescuing some friend of Damon's from hot water. (In that particular case the friend had been Wilson Mizner.) In return Damon gave Jim inside tips on the fights. Attending boxing events was always one of Jimmy's favorite forms of social recreation, and he liked knowing what was going on behind the scenes among the managers and trainers. Damon could always be depended on to fill him in. And for Jim the arch humorists of the *American,* Runyon and Bugs Baer, were the greatest newspaper writers in New York.

Walker was more than just a fan of boxing. With the help of a wealthy and influential lover of pugilism from Philadelphia, Jim in 1918 had overcome the opposition of his political patron Governor Al Smith and pushed through the New York State Legislature a boxing law which was to have an influence on the growth of the cauliflower industry at least comparable to that of the Declaration of Independence on the development of the American republic. His sponsorship of the boxing law (and of a bill that legalized Sunday baseball) permanently allied Jimmy Walker's name with ideas of sweetness and light in the minds of the New York sporting crowd.

On fight nights at Tex Rickard's new Madison Square Garden in the late twenties when Jimmy was in his heyday as mayor, he would arrive late—usually around 10 P.M., just before the top bout on the card—and make a grand entrance in the company of his show girl sweetheart, Betty Compton. (His wife, like Damon's, was always at home or away on vacation.) Betty, a pretty English girl, held tight to the arm of Jimmy, who was flanked by his fight-promoting office boys, Dan McKetrick and Jimmy Johnston (whom Damon called "Dapper Dan" and "the Boy Bandit" and Jimmy called "the Altar Boys"). On the way to his seat, Jimmy made a point of stopping at the press section to have a word with Runyon. Everyone in the area turned to watch, knowing that the grey-hatted and bespectacled front-row typist with whom the Mayor chatted was the ace scribe of the Hearst chain.

When the Garden public address announcer, Joe Humphreys, projected his electrifying tenor voice around the hall to herald the main event, Jimmy made like Fred Astaire and light-footed it through the ringside crowd to his seat. He needed no bodyguard. He shook the hands that shot out as he went by, tipped his hat and waved to his friends in the upper balconies, and got a cheer that drowned out even the stentorian tones of Joe Humphreys.

The fight crowds loved Walker for a list of reasons that included but was not dominated by his legislative works. Their affection went deeper than politics. He was their special man, their paragon; yet he was one of them, a player at life himself, a guy with whom the sporting crowd could identify. The cheer they gave him was strong and sincere. It made the white-hooded fighters turn in their corners and peer out from under their towels to see what celebrity had arrived. When they saw who it was, they too nodded in recognition and acknowledgment.

It is easy to see why Damon liked Jimmy Walker's politics: they were identical with his own. Both men were total pragmatists. In his political life Walker always went with the strongest pull, be it Tammany's, Smith's, the bootleggers', or the stockbrokers'. Damon, whom Hearst occasionally sent scurrying to a national convention to "scout" one candidate or to his typewriter to compose a eulogy of another (it was usually the likes of an Alf Landon he was assigned to praise), always responded to the pulse from the Clarendon or San Simeon as a compass needle responds to

Fight Night at the Garden with Jimmy Walker

True North. "Mr. Hearst giveth, and Mr. Hearst taketh away," was Runyon's tag line on the subject. When he spoke of the party line he always toed in his political reporting, it was usually with good-natured cynicism.

Both Walker and Runyon had populist instincts, but a common love of style and good living made them instincts neither could afford to indulge in adult life. Runyon kept his antiauthoritarian feelings at bay long enough to cash Hearst's paychecks, and he masked them in his "half-boob air" in his fiction and in sardonic remarks, just as Walker masked *his* in the joking repartee of the perennial wise guy. Damon wrote of hoboes, but during the Depression he had an annual income that approached six figures. Walker loved the "little man," on whose behalf he spoke out for the five-cent subway fare and the workmen's compensation laws, but in order to pay his way at the nightclub and the track he had to look sidewise while the big man dropped stock certificates and market tips and large checks in the pockets of his elegant striped pants.

Like Runyon, Jimmy Walker had seen too much of life—both the good side and the bad side—to allow him the luxury of being a political idealist.

Jimmy's New York State boxing commissioner was Big Jim Farley. Big Jim's job, it seemed, was to conscientiously look the other way as long as the cauliflower industry thrived. This both he and it did, throughout the middle twenties. It was the age of the Million Dollar Fight, a time of unprecedented prosperity for New York boxing.

As public interest and gate totals grew, however, so did honest sportswriters' concern about the integrity of certain bouts. W. O. McGeehan, "the Sheriff" to Damon and the other scribes and a foremost commentator of the time, wrote of the situation in 1927.

> Strange as it may seem when you consider the splendid type of businessmen associated with the business, many of whom would not climb a porch to get at the safe when there was any chance of jimmying the back door, many of the customers are beginning to suspect all has not been up and up in the business . . . These suspicions seem to have reached the inner councils of the New York State Boxing Commission, and I understand there is to be an informal hearing shortly to consider a few of the fights that have caused the customers to feel these unwarranted suspicions. This is in line with the boxing commission's policy in taking every precaution after the safes have been cracked. It is what is known as locking the barn door after the horse has been stolen.

Damon knew all about these matters; he had taken part in such highjinks himself on more than one occasion. Like the "dobie itch" he'd picked up in 1899 while soldiering in the Philippines,

The World of Damon Runyon

the "fixing" virus—endemic in the fight-promoting trade—was a bug Damon found it impossible to resist. If Big Jim Farley's boxing commission was neither overly scrupulous nor excessively diligent, it was just as well with Professor Runyon.

The arrangement of prizefights was an area of activity in which Damon frequently dabbled, sometimes independently but more often as the promoter of annual bouts for the benefit of Mrs. W. R. Hearst's pet charity, the New York Free Milk Fund for Babies. If some of the rumors about them are correct, the name was the most innocent feature of the Milk Fund bouts. They may have provided milk for babies, but the guys skimming the cream were no infants. Not that promoter Runyon had a hand in the till; he was merely in the middle of conflicting interests. The fans and Mrs. Hearst wanted honest bouts (though Mrs. Hearst wouldn't have known the difference); whereas the hoods who "owned" the fighters preferred scripted drama, an art form they considered superior for reasons having to do with the large bets they were in the habit of placing on the outcome. Considerable ingenuity was demanded of Damon, both in arranging the matches and in seeing to it that the correct party triumphed. The latter was occasionally a very touchy point.

The Milk Fund bouts were an aspect of Damon's job that he did not much cherish, but Mr. Hearst (who disliked boxing but found the promotion a useful sop for pacifying the public and his wife simultaneously) insisted the show must go on, year after year—and since Damon was the top boxing writer in the Hearst chain, the organizational chores usually fell to him. He was normally assisted by the current *American* sports editor or by fellow columnist Bugs Baer, for what such assistance was worth. The promoter's burden and responsibility were always Damon's in the end, as were the headaches and nightmares.

For the Milk Fund card in the winter of 1924, for example, Damon's original plan was to match the veteran Tom Gibbons, whom he'd seen take Dempsey fifteen rounds at Shelby the previous year, against the great black heavyweight Harry Wills, who'd been unable to get a crack at the title only because of the color of his skin. Damon "made a meet" with Eddie Kane, Gibbons' manager, and offered him a guarantee of $150,000. Kane turned the offer down, choosing to bypass Wills (who he knew might beat Gibbons' brains out) and go for Gene Tunney instead, a route Kane hoped would lead to another title shot at Dempsey. (Tunney stopped Gibbons, ending his career.)

Foiled on his first try and unable to locate a suitable "name" opponent who'd take on Wills, Damon shifted his attention to the middleweight division. He signed champion Harry Greb, "the Pittsburgh Windmill," a fighter he much admired, to oppose a

Fight Night at the Garden with Jimmy Walker

tough and popular challenger named Jack Delaney. But Delaney, a secret heavy drinker, canceled out at a late hour because of "appendicitis." Worried, Runyon hit the bricks again, canvassing the town for a middleweight. Finally he bumped into Mike Jacobs (with Damon's aid he would later become a kingpin among promoters) who was then managing an obscure English middleweight named Ted Moore. Jacobs let himself be talked into taking on Harry Greb for only $3500 because he knew his boy, Moore, could use the publicity. Damon, sensing Jacobs' willingness, had deliberately made his first bid an absurdly low one and was surprised and pleased to have it accepted.

He then went to Harry Greb, whom he'd promised 50 G's, and said he'd have to reduce that fee by two-fifths on the grounds that Ted Moore was no Jack Delaney. The battering puncher from Pittsburgh shrugged and stared at Damon with his glass eye and said okay to $30,000.

Harry Greb licked Ted Moore easily in the main event, and thanks to Runyon's sharp bargaining it cost the thirsty babies only thirty-three five. Damon had been able to sink the rest of the available capital into the preliminary fights, among them a light-heavyweight event featuring Young Stribling. That one turned out to be even more of a pain in the neck to promote than the Greb bout, and it ended embarrassingly for Damon.

Originally Damon had signed Stribling, one of the coming fighters and a kid with plenty of managerial "clout," to take on Paul Berlenbach, an ex-champ in the light-heavy class. But a week before the fight Berlenbach suffered vision impairment in another bout and had to be scratched. There was a frantic search by Runyon, *American* sports editor Slim Farnsworth, and a boxing-world ally, Herman Taylor, to find a substitute. Their hunt was unsuccessful until somebody thought of Tommy Loughran, a clever boxer who (it was assumed) couldn't "hit with" the bigger Stribling but might make a nice drawing card—and better still, might be available on short notice. Damon and Herman Taylor took a cab to Loughran's home and waited on the front steps until 11:30 P.M., when Tommy showed up. He was carrying his gym bag and walking slow.

"Hello, gents," he greeted the familiar fellows camped on his steps. "What can I do you for?"

"How would you like to box in New York tomorrow night?" Damon asked.

"I just went six rounds in Philly," Tommy said, tilting his head toward the streetlight and pointing out the contusions under his eyes.

"The offer still goes," Damon said.

"Okay," Tommy shrugged.

"Don't you even want to know who you're fighting?"

"Nah," Loughran said. "What difference does it make? Sure, I'll box."

"Maybe when you find out who it is you won't want to," Damon said, deadpan. He knew Tommy was one boy who feared nobody.

"Mister Runyon," Tommy said, "I can beat anybody in the world. Who have you got for me?"

"Young Stribling."

"Is that all?" the confident Loughran laughed.

Tommy wore his bravado well and would eventually justify it with his ring performances. He had just turned twenty-two, but he would later whip the likes of Mickey Walker and Max Baer and win a reputation as one of the master boxers of all time. Now he one-stepped past Herman Taylor and Damon and sprang up his front steps. "Come on inside, boys, and tell me all about it."

When Damon told Tommy about the flat fee of five G's that was in it for him, the deal was clinched. It was to be a six-round bout. If anything was said on the subject of tanks or water, Tommy was too busy thinking about the five G's to hear it. He had no thought about taking a dive with Young Stribling.

The Loughran-Stribling event came early on Damon's card, and the latecomers were still in the aisles when Tommy charged out, caught a thumb in the eye, wiped the blood away, and lit into Stribling with a fury that surprised those accustomed to his normally workmanlike style. Damon, in the press section, interrupted his running account to remove his glasses and de-fog them with two swipes of his silk handkerchief. Was he seeing things? Stribling was supposed to win and Loughran was taking him apart.

The crowd was on Tommy's side all the way, and it was all Tommy's fight. It was the best the stunned Stribling could do to remain upright, but when the bout was over the decision went to him, as if by foredestination. The crowd blew up. Curses and hard objects were hurled. The demonstration of popular displeasure lasted fifteen minutes, and New York's finest had to be called out to clear the ring so that Joe Humphreys could announce the next bout, which was to be a match between Gene Tunney and a spaghetti-eater named Spalla. The crowd, ignoring the fact that Gene was a local boy from Greenwich Village, continued to protest throughout the Tunney-Spalla bout. Damon's fight night had turned into a fiasco before his headliner, Harry Greb, had even had a chance to take off his monogrammed bathrobe!

In the locker room with his handlers Tommy Loughran laid down his beef. What was with those judges, boys? Did anybody know what was going on? Heads hung low around the room and nobody spoke until Herman Taylor stuck his head in the door.

Fight Night at the Garden with Jimmy Walker

He looked the scene over and shook his head, then took a tentative step inside.

"What happened?" Tommy asked him.

"Damon promised the decision to them, Tom," Herman said, not very loudly. "It was part of their guarantee, you know?"

Tommy looked away. He understood.

"I don't care about it, Herman," he said.

What went wrong in the Loughran-Stribling bout?

Either Tommy's enthusiasm blunted his understanding of Damon's offer or he had missed his cue. The decision had to go to Stribling because Stribling's backers were building him into Something Big. Damon's guarantee of the verdict had no doubt been part of the original bargain. The Stribling group was doing what came naturally in the management trade, especially in the upper weight classes. The formula was simple: first, find a likely-looking newcomer, then, in Runyon's words, "send for a sure-footed, over-size waterman (which is to say a big diver), to chuck out his chest when presented to the assembled throng, make enormous gestures, and then take a header into the wash bowl at the flick of an eyelid. . ."

What came next was to be expected. Damon described it in "Lost Art of Diving," a column that contained his wise-guy's blueprint for the engineering of a ring career (circa 1925–1935).

> This would be followed by an uproar from the crowd, some booing, some cheering. The boxing writers would belt blazes out of the performance and perhaps there would be an investigation by the boxing commission, but the stranger would be made. His name would be in all the papers. A new star would be sparkling in the fistic firmament, if you want me to wax poetic about it.
>
> This is the way the thing was done in the good old days before the apprentice plumbers came in, in those times when tanking was truly an art that was so highly appreciated by the public that all the papers had to do to insure a sell-out was to proclaim the impending evening's fistic entertainment a palpable hippodrome. I tell you, the customers loved to see those tankers splash.
>
> All the heavyweights that amounted to anything in the good old days were brought along in this fashion though some of them may not have known it. I have no doubt Mr. Dempsey and Mr. Tunney were kept in ignorance of any vaudeville in which they played a part in the course of their respective risks by their managers, who perhaps feared that their principals might protest in the name of integrity if let in on the script.

The problem in the Loughran-Stribling fight was that Loughran, not Stribling, was insufficiently familiar with the script. But then, as a promoter of aquatic events, Damon was never the equal of some of his mob pals, who pulled off such delicate forklift operations as the hoisting into the heavyweight championship in

1933 of Primo Carnera—a stunt Damon much admired at the time and later committed to fiction in his tale "The Big Umbrella."

Primo, whom Damon at first described to readers of his column in rhapsodic terms that now seem more appropriate to a description of King Kong, was in truth an athlete of doubtful skills at best. But there was no doubting the fact that he was a financial goldmine, one that Runyon felt he had staked out personally.

Following Jack Dempsey's descent from the heavyweight throne in 1926 and the ascension of Gene Tunney, Damon—who disliked Tunney's gentlemanly style—fell into the habit of dispatching personal envoys far and wide to scout new heavyweight prospects. Considering it his duty as a sporting man to see that the title was not permanently annexed by poetry-spouting panty-waists, he constantly enjoined traveling friends to "keep an eye out" for prospective punchers. (Tales exist of Runyon bird dogs combing gyms and arenas as far as Hong Kong!)

In 1929 Damon advised his chum Walter "Good Time Charley" Friedman, then touring Europe, to be on the lookout for anything that looked large, unfriendly, and vaguely mobile. Good Time Charley came back with a likely candidate in tow, the six-foot-five, 270-pound Carnera. But before Damon could get out his wallet, all shares in the unknown contender's future had been sold. Damon's chagrin was intense, but he knew better than to squawk about it. Among the purchasers of Carnera Common were such solid citizens as nightclub entrepreneur "Broadway Bill" Duffy, who in his youth had been (in Paul Gallico's words) "convicted of a little al fresco burgling and sent away for a spell"; Duffy's pal Owney "The Killer" Madden; and the charming Madden's dear friend (and Damon's future Florida neighbor) George "Big Frenchy" DeMange. Later, when the group sent Carnera on his triumphant dramatic and pugilistic tour of the United States, there were local partners, like the chivalrous Maximilian "Boo-Boo" Hoff of Philly, who for a piece of the action was careful to see to it that his New York pals' fighters lost no bouts in his town.

The wholesaling of Primo Carnera left Damon privately despondent. For once his bird dog had turned up a very valuable hunk of hamburger, but the mob had beat him to the scent. In the early thirties he followed Carnera's career with the baleful fascination of the man who bought the winning sweepstakes ticket and gave it to a friend before the lucky numbers were announced. If Carnera was, as he wrote, "the largest cauliflower in captivity," then Damon considered himself the largest fool for not having gone to Europe with Good Time Charley when the big cauliflower was ripe for picking.

Damon should not have been so disappointed. The Carnera

story was in the end a sordid one. Primo's career made certain parties a lot of money but reflected glory on nobody; it ended in 1935 with the monolithic son of an Italian stonecutter half crippled and hospitalized after being deserted by his mob allies and beaten senseless by Joe Louis and several lesser fighters. The details are not very edifying, and in the version of the story Damon eventually wrote—"The Big Umbrella"—many of them were sea-changed in the interests of humor.

Damon's tale documents the prevailing method of making a nobody into a contender, occasionally—as with Carnera—a contender into a champ. "Spider McCoy" is the generic figure of the fight manager. For "Jonas" read Primo, who by an ironic transposition becomes in Damon's tale an "ex-king."

> The matches Spider accepts have his own personal supervision, and they are much better for Jonas than what the promoters might think up.
>
> These matches are with sure-footed watermen, who plunge in swiftly and smoothly when Jonas waves at them, and while everybody knows these matches are strictly tank jobs, nobody cares, especially the customers who almost break down the doors of the clubs where Jonas appears, trying to get in. The customers are so greatly pleased to be permitted to observe an ex-king in short pants that they scarcely pause for their change at the box-office windows.
>
> Of course Spider does not tell Jonas that these contests are dipsydoos and Jonas thinks he is really belting out these porterhouses, and as he is getting pretty nice money for the work, he feels very well, indeed. Anybody will tell you that it helps build up a young fighter's confidence to let him see a few people take naps in front of him as he is coming along, though Jonas is slightly bewildered the night at the Sun Casino when a generally reliable waterboy by the name of Charley Drunckley misses his cue and falls down before Jonas can hit him. The boxing commission is somewhat bewildered, too, and asks a few questions that nobody tries to answer, and Spider McCoy explains to Jonas that he hits so fast he cannot notice his punches landing himself, but even then Jonas continues to look somewhat bewildered.

In real life Primo continued to look somewhat bewildered throughout a ring career that for him was nothing but a long series of surprises: first, the shock of finding that his opponents fell whether he swung or not; later, when the fix was off, the shock of finding that no one was going to fall but him.

In the perspective of such large-scale corporate doings as the building of the $700,000 bionic boxer (despite their considerable expenses in payoffs, the mob "earned" that much off Carnera), Damon's gentle tugging of the strings in the Loughran-Stribling bout seems like child's play. Similar minor adjustments of destiny doubtless occurred with regularity in the middle echelons of the fight game and on occasion even in the top ranks. It was only natural, conditions being what they were, that the less credulous customers would now and then gripe about a match they thought was less than genuine. As a columnist Damon saw the critics' point, but as a part-time promoter he had to sympathize with the showman's sense of things as well. In the middle and late twenties he handled his Milk Fund duties as best he could and was in no hurry to complain about the lenient administration of Jim Walker's boxing commissioner, Farley.

A special aura was in time attached to Damon, among the writing crowd, because of his involvement in such matters. It was not exactly a halo. Ring Lardner, always quickest of the scribes to sniff out a fix (or imagine it, if there wasn't one), addressed a letter to the *American* in the wake of Damon's 1924 Milk Fund promotion. Ring was happy to provide nutritional assistance to babies, he announced, but as for the charity matches and those who engineered them—he named Damon and Bugs Baer—it was Ring's verdict that "they must have done a lot of wire-pulling to even be on parole."

In the late twenties other writers—the arch McGeehan for one—grew more and more cynical in their accounts of the pugilistic workings of "Sweet Charity." Apparently none of this gossip got through to Millicent Hearst, however, nor did it seem to bother the thirsty babies, for the annual bouts went on, and in 1933 and 1934 Damon and the Milk Fund had a finger in two successive heavyweight championship pies. Since the fighter involved in both cases was a property of chums of his, it was only natural that Damon would be involved. The matches in question were Carnera vs. Sharkey and Baer vs. Carnera. Neither bout contained much to praise in the way of art. One, in fact, was extremely dubious in other ways as well: Sharkey deserved an Oscar for his graceful dying fall in shedding the championship to the glass-chinned oaf Damon had once called "the great blood-sweating behemoth of the Alps." But a year later the high-principled Max Baer turned down the mob's payoff and disposed of Primo in two rounds that did indeed involve the sweating of blood—all Carnera's. Aesthetic or no, the two so-called fights deposited $56,000 worth of liquid calcium into the stomachs of the poor infants of New York. Jimmy Walker, like Mrs. Hearst, thought that was just swell.

Jimmy's first term, 1925 to 1929, was one long champagne party. His second term was the hangover.

In 1929 Damon's only bad guess was Primo Carnera, whom he picked as the heavyweight of the future. That (and the embarrassment of his own stable of fighters, all of whom ate better than they boxed) aside, all his 1929 hunches paid off. He backed Jimmy

Fight Night at the Garden with Jimmy Walker

Walker's re-election campaign with many a warm word spoken on his travels around town, and his friend won a second term handily.

Al Smith, who'd been nervous about the effect on the voters of the married mayor's public romance with Betty Compton, had his fears dispelled by the 1929 Walker landslide. Jimmy felt the results vindicated him; Smith was forced to agree. Jimmy and Betty were seen on the town more often than ever in the months following the election.

Damon remarked in his column one day in 1929 that the mayor, ever the dandy, was suddenly a solid influence in the world of fashion. Big Jim Farley, Runyon reported, had appeared in public in a pair of spats, "showing the insidious influence of Mayor Jimmy Walker." It was obviously a case of When in Rome with the farsighted Farley, who was eventually to parlay his gift for protective coloration into a long and varied political career in both parties. In the last year of the third decade of the twentieth century Jim Walker was definitely the man to imitate.

Then hard times brought doubt and suspicion to people's hearts. When over the next few years a judge named Seabury poked around in Jimmy Walker's affairs, bringing up difficult questions about how Jimmy managed to afford to live the way he did and about how he ran the city, there began to spread through Walker's own domain a vague uneasiness. One unprecedented afternoon at Yankee Stadium during the midst of the Seabury inquiries Jimmy was booed by a crowd that had once loved him as a mother loves a son. He made a speech, then, that brought the crowd right back, but it had been an unsettling experience. He began to have trouble with his health and was seen on the town less often by night. 1932 did not agree with him. Yet the mayor continued to be as charming and generous as ever with his old friends, as though for isolated moments it were the magic year of 1927 again and the serious events of the years since then had been erased.

When Damon Runyon prevailed on him to perform a marriage ceremony in that difficult year, 1932, Jimmy never hesitated. Whatever the circumstances, a favor to a friend was always a number one Walker priority.

The wedding took place in the apartment of Ed Frayne, a boxing writer crony of Damon's from the *American.* No one from either Damon's or Patrice Amati's family was on hand. The Mayor showed up a couple of hours late, and it was obvious he'd been drinking heavily. He chatted seriously with Damon for a while; after that his spirits seemed to revive, at least long enough to allow him to run through the formal ceremony with no slipups.

The World of Damon Runyon

Wedding reception for Damon Runyon and Patrice Amati at the home of New York *American* sportswriter Ed Frayne, 1932. Frayne is third from left, back row; Bill Corum, fourth from left; fight manager Jimmy Johnston, sixth from left. Same row, Hype Igoe is fifth from right; Jack Kearns is fourth from right; Bugs Baer on far right. Damon and Patrice, seated, center.

The old Walker charm had not gone; it was only wearing a little thin.

The mayor withdrew before the group picture was composed.

In the center of that photograph the severely elegant and grim-faced fifty-two-year-old groom sits arm in arm with his very beautiful and very grownup-looking fair-haired bride, who wears a long white dress and veil. The couple is surrounded by a small crowd of perhaps two dozen close friends, mostly writers and their wives: Bill Corum, Hype Igoe, Jack Kearns, Bugs Baer, Jimmy Johnston, all pals of Damon's from the old days. The only guy missing from the picture (and from the remainder of the wedding party, which moved on to Billy LaHiff's for its final rounds) was Jim Walker, who'd gone home early because he was feeling sad.

While Damon and Patrice honeymooned with their feet in the Florida sand that spring, Jimmy was up to his neck in trouble. He appeared at the Seabury hearings, and though he kept up a cocky front, he found the judge's questions impossible to repel with one-liners. The famous Walker wit, which in other precarious times had always landed him safely on his feet, didn't seem to be working. In the summer Judge Seabury recommended to Governor Franklin Roosevelt that the mayor be removed from office. Roosevelt summoned Jim to Albany for a somber interview.

Meanwhile Damon, who'd been bored to tears at the Republican convention that year ("It's Hoover and Curtis," he'd written sarcastically, "Herb and Charlie. Same old battery"), had also represented Mr. Hearst at the Democratic convention in Chicago. There he had looked on with greater interest as the absent Hearst's invisible directives—cabled from San Simeon—"swung" the California delegation to F.D.R., tipping the scales against longtime Hearst antagonist Al Smith. (Ever the maverick in his political sympathies, Hearst at this early date was actually pro-Roosevelt!)

On his return to New York, Damon followed through on his interest in F.D.R., which may or may not have originated from mere loyalty to Hearst, and registered for the election as a Democrat. It was a rare and uncharacteristic action he was never to repeat. Damon was rarely "serious" about his personal political impulses, and typically his commitment to Roosevelt proved fickle and wavering. (In later years Runyon needled Walter Winchell mercilessly about Walter's affection for F.D.R.; only in his moving—and justly famous—account of Roosevelt's funeral in 1945 did Damon again show strong admiration, calling the dead statesman "a kind man.") But the Democratic candidate interested Damon as a person, which Hoover clearly did not. Damon also trusted Big Jim Farley, who was managing Roosevelt's campaign in that season of strange bedfellows.

Runyon at the time was both aware of and increasingly concerned about the pressure that was being put on F.D.R. to "deal with" Jimmy Walker. Yet he had seen Jim come through a lot, and he had faith in his friend. He hoped for, and in his heart expected, an imminent public response from the mayor, clearing his good name. That, Damon figured, would be followed by an official withdrawal of the charges, making everything as good as new and soothing the hurt feelings the Seabury-Walker affair had caused in the Big Town.

It did not work out that way. On September 1, 1932, Jimmy Walker and Betty Compton sailed for England. Jim had resigned from office.

In Europe Walker obtained a divorce from his first wife, and he and Betty were married in Cannes. He lived for the next few years in informal exile. Damon was shocked and greatly saddened by this loss of a friend, and these feelings preyed on him for months. Since he could not bring himself to write of them lightly, he did not mention Jimmy Walker in his column again for a long while.

However, in his holiday story for *Collier's* for 1932, "Dancing Dan's Christmas," he sent his chum in Europe a little message that harked back to the loyalty and fellowship and good cheer of the old days. In Damon's tale the narrator makes a point of mentioning that he does a first rate job on his rendition of "Will You Love Me in December As You Do in May?" The right readers would know whose song *that* was. It was Damon's way of telling Jimmy; who would read the piece in England, that in his case it was anything but out of sight, out of mind.

Walker eventually returned to the States—he and Betty were divorced in 1941—and once again he and Damon saw each other on fight nights and at the sporting crowd's favorite eateries and watering spots. Of course it was never again the same for Gentleman Jim, who seemed to have lost much of his buoyant spirit to the rigors of self-exile. But then it wasn't the same for Damon either, or for anyone else. There was another war, an unrecognizable one, and the young went off to it, but on Broadway time went on in a way that had started to look meaningless to many of the Old Guard. Jimmy Walker died on November 8, 1946, but Damon's doctors would not allow him to attend the funeral because at the time he was himself mortally ill. Thirty-two days later he followed his pal Jim into the big Garden in the Sky, where no doubt the times were always ripe and every night was Fight Night.

16

Hollywood Gold with a Black Lining

You will hear that money is not everything, and that is true enough. It is only 99 per cent of everything, and if you do not believe that, there are millions of elderly persons in this nation that you can ask.

Get the money. Get rich if possible, my boy. It is my observation that the rich have all the best of it in this nation, and my studies of American History fail to disclose any time when this same situation did not prevail.

—*"Magnificent Mammon," a late Runyon column*

I think my greatest misfortune was in getting caught in a current that demanded a certain standard of living and it took money to meet that standard.

I would have been better off if I had remained a struggling and obscure fellow of no great means in a small community where I might have found peace and contentment in plain living and spiritual considerations instead of becoming a big town by-line writer always fighting to keep up there and to make money.

" 'And what good came of it at last,' quoth Little Peterkin."

—Letter written by Damon Runyon to his son a few months before his death

What one writer has called Damon's "great splurges of fiction" in the thirties—his short story binges—went only part of the way toward earning him the kind of money he needed to live in the grand style he desired. A taste of high living whetted his appetite for more of the same. Elegant houses and apartments, fine jewelry for Patrice, expensive clothes for himself, costly dining and gambling habits, and the upkeep of dozens of such luxury items as hunting dogs, racehorses, and prizefighters—with such expenditures, the Runyon budget often entered the sphere of higher mathematics. A princely life style like that espoused by Damon in the thirties was out of the range of even a best-selling story writer and syndicated columnist. Damon's motto became "Get the Money." When he began to look around for alternative sources of income, he turned naturally to the movies, which was where the money was. Or, more accurately, the movie companies turned to him just when Damon was most willing to cash their checks.

Damon's involvement with moving pictures originated around 1930, when he became an intense cinema fan and began seeing at least ten films a week. After his marriage in 1932, he and Patrice attended nightly double features—a habit that Damon was to keep up, with or without his wife, throughout the decade. He was an authentic "movie buff," catching every new picture that came to town and seeing his favorite pictures anywhere from twice to a dozen times each. The influence of movies on his writing, especially his fiction, was direct—and vice versa. Both Runyon and the Hollywood producers were looking for the kind of "make 'em laugh, make 'em cry" story ingredients on which popular artistic success is always based. When Hollywood began to reciprocate Runyon's interest in movies with fat checks for his services, it had become a natural marriage of intention. Fiction writer Runyon and the movies always had the same thing in mind, and that was to entertain.

The first sale of a Runyon fiction property to a film company had occurred in 1927 with the purchase of "The Geezer," an unpublished story, by Universal Pictures. Universal's payment of $5000 for the rights—that was nearly a quarter of Damon's annual reporter's salary at the time—came as a pleasant windfall; but he regarded it as just that, an isolated stroke of good fortune rather than the beginning of a profitable career. Five years went by, and he had developed a whole new fiction style, by the time he cashed his next check from Hollywood. That one was followed shortly by many, many more—enough to make it possible for Damon in an austere decade to go first class all the way.

With the growing popularity of his fiction (and the earnings therefrom), Runyon in the mid-thirties was one of the two or three wealthiest working newspapermen in the country. Like his Hearst colleague Walter Winchell, Damon was then pulling in approximately a quarter of a million dollars a year. Only Mark Hellinger was making better money.

The source of Hellinger's bonanza was Hollywood, where within a few hard-working years of his arrival in the first years of the decade he'd become an acclaimed producer (his credits eventually included such films as *Brother Orchid, High Sierra, Brute Force,* and *The Naked City).* From the first, Runyon's awareness of Hellinger's lucrative film career contributed to the growth of his belief that he too could "make it in the movies." The screenwriting success of his former Hearst protégé, Gene Fowler, was equally well known to Damon though less tantalizing; while Damon knew Fowler to be a writer worthy of applause, he had no

Hollywood Gold with a Black Lining

Walter Winchell and Gene Fowler in Hollywood, 1933.

such feelings about Hellinger, who came from a later generation of scribes and had displayed, in Runyon's opinion, no unusual skills. If Hellinger could make it big, Damon figured, he himself should be able to make it even bigger. "I can do anything that Hellinger can do and do it better," he had always said.

Ironically, the movie debuts of star columnists Runyon and Hellinger occurred on the same occasion in 1930. Hellinger, a handsome and self-confident man who had daydreamed of being an actor, was asked to appear in a short comedy feature, *The Round Table.* The picture, a flimsy spoof of the Algonquin Hotel cardplaying wits, was directed by Wallace Sullivan, written by Murray Roth, and filmed at the Warner Brothers studios on Long Island. Hellinger, Runyon, and actor DeWolf Hopper (a former vaudevillian and longtime Polo Grounds chum of Damon's) were its "stars." One day during the filming Hellinger and Runyon went to lunch wearing full makeup and were accosted by a youthful movie fan who yelled to his friends, "Look! Actors!" Hellinger, flattered, gave the kid two bucks. Damon, equally pleased to be mistaken for a bona fide cinematic artist and never to be outdone in gratitude, peeled off *three* singles and handed them to the boy. (The film, released by Vitaphone Pictures late in 1930, had a very limited run and convinced reviewers that Runyon and Hellinger were best advised to stick to the writing racket.)

Guys and Dolls, the first collection of Damon's Broadway tales, was published by Frederick A. Stokes in 1931. A year later the William Fox Studios bought an option on the thirteen tales in that volume for the penny-ante price of $1000, which gave Fox the right to purchase the stories for film use for $15,000. Their readers, however, rejected the book as "uncommercial," and the rights reverted to the author. It was a rare but fortunate rejection for Damon; within months he was selling the individual tales for sums that, while small compared to the ultimate earning power of the films they generated, added up to considerably more than the Fox deal would have paid. "Madame La Gimp" was bought by Frank Capra for Columbia Pictures in 1932 for $3500. (When Capra, in his autobiography, recalled paying Runyon "a measly $1500 for 'Madame La Gimp,' " he was using the correct adjective—it was, after all, one of Damon's finest stories—but he was off by two units in his memory of the actual price.) The ensuing motion picture, *Lady for a Day,* was a box office smash that won Capra an Oscar for best director. When in 1960 Capra bought the rights to the story back from Columbia for his own remake, *Pocketful of Miracles,* it cost him $225,000.

Damon of course never got another penny after his original sales of the early stories, but even those sales added up to a tidy amount. Before long he would be getting better contracts that included the ever-popular "percentage of the gross," and in time he would be able to demand large advances for little more than a story idea. Within ten years of his first toe-wetting in the movie business he would be making several thousand dollars a week as a studio consultant and as much as $100,000 for the casual promise of a single script. By that time the name Damon Runyon would represent a very valuable commodity around the Hollywood lots, and only a fatal illness would stand between Damon and the truly grand life of a top independent producer.

Between 1932 and 1940 Damon sold thirty-four stories to *Collier's* at prices up to $5000 apiece. In the same period he sold twelve stories to *Cosmopolitan* and two to the *Saturday Evening Post* at similar rates. Damon's decisions about where to send his manuscripts were made on an exclusively economic basis. The stories had been written to Get the Money, and that they did, since Damon sent them only to the top-paying fiction outlets in the country, magazines that paid up to a dollar a word. The editors and publishers of these magazines found Runyon's stories to be well worth Damon's price; the words Damon Runyon on the cover could be counted on to increase sales of a single issue by fifty or sixty thousand copies.

The shock waves of public response to the early Broadway tales did not take long to reach the Hollywood production offices. Story material of any kind was in great demand. In the middle of an era of hard luck, the movie business was expanding and new stars were turning up at every corner. The people wanted distraction from their troubles, entertainment and fantasy and glamor, and the movies gave them these things. Hollywood had its stars but desperately needed "vehicles"—scripts, stories, ideas, *anything* that would keep the stars shining in the limelight, the production wheels rolling, and the box office cash registers ringing. The kind of thing Damon was turning out was just what the doctor ordered as far as the film companies were concerned. His stories had fresh new comic dialogue, original characters, a strong and colorful setting, and more than a little sentiment. They had all the virtues connoted by the word "popular," as Damon had intended; magazine circulation figures proved it. This stuff of Runyon's was something the big boys in Hollywood *had* to have, and they soon went to work on the business of acquiring it—and him.

In 1933 Damon made his first big movie killings. Any doubt that remained about the value of Runyon properties was removed by the success of *Lady for a Day.* That year Damon collected 10 G's from Twentieth Century Pictures for "The Old Doll's House" (which became *Midnight Alibi* in Hollywood). His total proceeds from motion picture sales for 1933 exceeded $30,000. The following year the figures were about the same. On the sale of "Three Wise Guys" to MGM in 1934, Damon picked up $15,000. Added to the $5000 *Collier's* had paid him for the story as a Christmas issue commission a few months earlier, it meant he had turned a neat profit of twenty units for a few days' work at the typewriter.

These figures were very much to Damon's liking—and were somewhat shocking to his press box cronies, to whom he broke the news of the MGM sale one day in the spring of 1934 when he turned up at Ebbets Field to write a story on an old favorite, Casey Stengel, now managing the Dodgers. Following Damon's announcement, soft "oohs" and "ahs" rose into the vernal air of Flatbush, and a moment of silence was observed in which everyone paused to study the clouds floating westward overhead.

Damon soon imitated those clouds. In that same year he was called to Hollywood to assist on the screenplay of "Little Miss Marker," a story he'd written as a Shirley Temple vehicle. Damon's sentimental tale was ideal for Miss Temple, who was then at her cutest. (The picture set her star on the rise.) For his consultant's services he was paid $2000 a week. By the time he got back to New York a new collection of Runyon tales, *Blue Plate Special,* was on the stands and selling briskly.

That August Damon and Patrice went to Saratoga for the month-long race meeting. August Saratoga had been a Runyon habit since 1922. It was one of Damon's favorite places, though his first wife, who'd loathed racetracks and racing types, hadn't enjoyed herself there and had refused to return after a first visit. Patrice, a horse lover, found Saratoga agreeable and then some. She had already talked Damon into starting a Runyon stable. Their first horse, Angelic, was running at Saratoga that August, and in the evenings Damon and Patrice strolled to their stable with trainer Hirsh Jacobs to see the big thoroughbred filly whose room and board bills the Runyon articles and columns and tales and scripts were paying. Resplendent in the scarlet and orchid Runyon racing colors, Angelic placed solidly out of the money all month but managed to look good doing it. After all, at Saratoga, where the Vanderbilts and the Whitneys played, class counted almost as much as winning—and now, for the first time, Damon could afford the former comfortably and sit back and appreciate the latter when it came. (His bookie, however, would not accept class as a marker, and Damon spent plenty of postracetrack afternoons with the pockets of his fancy striped pants turned inside out.)

That fall Damon covered the World Series as usual (Detroit and St. Louis), then returned to his Parc Vendome suite in New York to begin collaboration with Howard Lindsay on a play, *A Slight Case of Murder.* Their script was a development of a story idea Damon had never used. He and Lindsay worked intermittently in New York and at the various other stops on Damon's late autumn itinerary, including Pennsylvania (where Damon went at Thanksgiving to exercise the hunting dogs he kept at the farm of his pal "Baron" Jimmy Daugherty, the former boxing referee who'd been in the ring that hot July 4 at Shelby), Maryland (where Damon wanted to do some duck shooting), New Jersey (where Damon covered the trial of Bruno Hauptmann, accused kidnaper of Charles A. Lindbergh, Jr.), and finally Florida (where Damon and Patrice were wintering, as was their custom). With their toes in the Hibiscus Island sand and thick sweaters on their backs (it was a cold spring in Florida), Runyon and Howard Lindsay put the finishing touches on their underworld comedy early in 1935. That fall it opened for a successful run in New York, and within weeks of the first night Runyon and Lindsay had signed away the film rights to Warner Brothers for $50,000 plus a small piece of what turned out two years later to be a sizeable gross.

A third collection of Runyon tales, *Money from Home,* appeared in 1935. Damon's stories were as hot as ever at home and warming up overseas as well. (There was great demand for the London edition of *Guys and Dolls,* which within two years would be followed by three more British volumes.) Damon signed a contract with Frederick A. Stokes, publisher of the three American collections of stories, to produce more of the same and a novel. The latter he never got around to writing; he believed there was no real money in novels. A born newspaperman, Damon never felt secure straying beyond the 5000-word limit. *Inside* that range, though, he now knew he had a form—the twist-ending tale—of which he was the primary living master. The movie producers agreed with him; Hollywood's interest in Runyon material was reaching a peak after the box office achievements of *Lady for a Day* and *Little Miss Marker.*

In 1936 Sam Goldwyn sent an ambassador to solicit Damon's services. Sam wanted a story for an Eddie Cantor picture. "I need thinking money," Damon told the underling who'd been sent to enlist him. "My mind doesn't work very well until I see a check." The emissary repeated Damon's words to Goldwyn, who offered to put the famous story writer's mind to work to the tune of $5000. Runyon came up with a three-paragraph "idea" involving Cantor as a Broadway hotel desk clerk who owns a trained seal. This monumental piece of thinking appealed to Sam sufficiently to shake another check out of him, this time for 15 G's for Damon to work on a "treatment." The film was never made, but nobody in Hollywood ever asked Damon for the money back. He always did what was asked of him and kept his money.

Often Damon's work was treated in a cavalier or heavy-handed way by the studios once they'd paid him for it. Damon tried not to let this annoy him. It was sometimes a difficult task, particularly when the sensitive area of dialogue was involved. More often than not, Damon's ear-perfect dialogue was amended or even thrown out altogether by the screenwriters who adapted his stories and treatments. This was the case in *Saratoga Chips,* a film made from Damon's tale "That Ever-Loving Wife of Hymie's." Damon and songwriter Irving Caesar were paid $25,000 to go to Hollywood and collaborate on a movie script based on the tale. The two men worked hard—and, Damon thought, fruitfully—during the winter of 1936, but the final Twentieth Century Fox product contained very little of the bright Broadway talk they had written. Damon resented what he regarded as thoughtless and roughshod treatment of his work, but he took the Studio's money and did not complain.

The following year, Fox hired Runyon and Caesar again, this time to prepare a script about the horseplaying life. They wrote *Straight, Place and Show* on a month-long retreat at Hibiscus Island in the winter of 1937. When the film appeared in 1938, not a scene or a line of the Caesar-Runyon script remained intact. Irving was unhappy, but Damon persuaded him not to complain to Fox until the box office verdict came in. "Suppose the movie is a hit," he told his tune-writing partner, "then are you going to squawk?" When the film turned out to be a solid box office success Caesar had to agree with Damon, who despite his hurt feelings believed that the results showed Fox had been justified in butchering his script.

This was neither false modesty nor the pose of an embittered artist; it was a Runyon tenet, developed early, to respect the evidence of the dollar over all other types. "An old rule with me is never decry a success," he once wrote in a column. "I think I am one of the few who stick to this rule faithfully. It is much more fashionable to use the velvet knock on success—animal, vegetable or mineral—which is to say, boosts with reservations. The good old 'yes, but' method." Damon did not put the "velvet knock" on *Straight, Place and Show* even though his work had been thrown out. Later he was much less happy with unfaithful script adaptations that turned out to be failures, but this time he was all smiles. Even if he didn't have a piece of the gross, he was glad to be connected with a winner.

"Never knock a winner" was a Runyon axiom. It was a rule he held firmly and expressed many times in various forms, often for the benefit of his column audience. That audience now numbered about fifteen million, for his columns were syndicated in all the Hearst papers and in many others that, like Runyon himself, "went with a winner." Damon expounded a philosophy he knew these readers would understand. It was a belief that informed all his writing and movie work in the thirties. It was simple: go for the jugular. Find the common denominator, the human norm, and give it back a reflection of itself. This was Damon's goal: the accurate mirroring of common human feelings. It was a democratic aesthetic that also happened to prove economically sound. Popular success, in Damon's mind, was the only determinant of artistic quality. And that, in turn, led to money. He spelled all this out a few years after *Straight, Place and Show* in one of his most famous columns.

> My measure of success is money.
>
> I have no interest in artistic triumphs that are financial losers.
>
> I would like to have an artistic success that also made money, of course, but if I had to make a choice between the two I would take the dough.
>
> I have learned that when you carry your money to the bank the teller does not hesitate before accepting it to inquire:
>
> "Brother, was the enterprise from which this money came of artistic merit or just a commercial winner?". . .
>
> It makes me laugh when I hear someone say of a motion picture: "It isn't a good picture, but it will get the money."
>
> If it gets the money it is a good picture in my book, even though I may not like it myself. Oh, sure, I know this is a sordid attitude. I will abandon it as soon as the world arranges a system of compensation in luxury for an artistic failure equal to that which derives from a commercial success.
>
> What is merit, anyway? Is it not something that the most people approve? Or is it something that just a few persons fancy? I would say the former.
>
> I know of newspapers that many so-called expert newspapermen consider far below perfection in every detail yet that have greater circulation than newspapers deemed by these experts first class in every department of the newspaper-making technique.

Hollywood Gold with a Black Lining

> Who are the better judges, the public or the experts? I say the
> public.   —"Get the Money"

Damon got the money because the public judgment of his
work—columns, stories, movies—was nearly unanimous. People
liked it and bought it. When Pocket Books brought out a twenty-
five-cent edition of *The Best of Damon Runyon*—selected tales—
in 1938, it quickly sold over a million copies. (The same thing
happened four years later with *Damon Runyon Favorites,* another
paperback selection.) By Damon's measure of success, if not that
of the literary critics, his work was coming along just fine. The
audience approved it, and Damon acknowledged no other confir-
mation of genius. It was a personal "yardstick" he had picked
up in his salad days from the great masters of the School of Broadway realists.

> I suppose my yardstick is somewhat similar to that of Mr. Al
> Weill, a rotund fight manager whose daily menu was always evi-
> denced by the grease spots on his waistcoat and who thus became
> famous in pugilistic circles as "The Vest."
> I once told Mr. Weill about a fistic encounter I had witnessed.
> "Al," I said, "you never saw such a battle! It was ferocious from
> gong to gong! First one guy was down, then the other! Biff! Bang!
> Bop! You could scarcely distinguish their features for blood! One
> guy's eye was hanging out on his cheek! The other guy's nose was
> spread all over his kisser! There was blood everywhere! Oh, what
> a fight! The referee kept slipping in the gore on the canvas! What
> a Pier 6 thing it was, Al!"
> "Is that so?" said Mr. Weill, chewing a big cigar meditatively.
> "How much was in the house?"   —"Get the Money"

In the thirties Damon's fiction writing and movie work took
time away from his columns, but he managed to maintain a regular platform somewhere in the paper every day. In 1936, when
Arthur Brisbane died, he took over Brisbane's public affairs column and left his sports page spot in the *American* to Sid Mercer.
But it took Old Man Hearst only two months—and two or three
dozen Runyon wisecracks—to decide that his ace reporter and essayist was not cut out for the grimly serious chore of editorial
commentator. So Damon went back to writing a daily personal
column, now located in a new spot in the feature section. His
column, a general-interest forum, was headed "The Brighter Side"
in keeping with Hearst's belief that readers of features wanted—
and deserved—a cheery note to start the day off.

Damon had now written for the New York *American* for twenty-
seven years. The paper had been having circulation problems
since the birth of the tabloids in the twenties and had lately become known along Park Row as "the vanishing American" in
honor of its doubtful future. When on June 23, 1937, the *American*

finally folded and was merged with the *Journal* as the *Journal-American*, Damon and his column were moved to Hearst's tabloid paper, the *Daily Mirror.* Henceforth Professor Runyon's opinions rubbed shoulders with Walter Winchell's gossip column. It was all the same to Damon; he still cashed the Old Man's checks every month. ("The Brighter Side" remained a constant in the *Mirror* until 1944, when the daily Runyon column was shifted to the *Journal-American.*)

During these years Damon continued to pursue his newspaper work in other areas. He covered top sports events like the 1938 Joe Louis-Max Schmeling fight for International News Service, the Hearst news syndicate. He invented a Flatbush couple named Joe and Ethel Turp and featured them in a successful series of comic sketches in Brooklyn vernacular which appeared in the Sunday features section of the Hearst papers. He was constantly busy, always on the move. In New York he and Patrice dined out every evening. Afterward there were films to see and late-night restaurants for coffee and talk with friends. There were winter trips to Florida every year and "work vacations" in Hollywood that grew more frequent.

By the late thirties Damon was very much the coming man, on top of his many worlds. He was doing exactly what he wanted to do in life and was being paid handsomely for it. Thus it came as an annoyance when in the winter of 1938 his throat began to bother him—health problems were the last thing he needed when things were breaking so well.

It was not the first time Damon had had trouble with his throat. In 1931 Dr. Jules Lempert (an otologist who was Mark Hellinger's personal doctor) had removed Damon's tonsils and warned him of future complications in that area. Runyon had continued to go through three packs of cigarettes a day, and by 1938 his Miami physician was admonishing him sternly about his heavy smoking. But the specific inflammation passed, and Damon, relieved, forgot about it and continued to chain smoke; he had never given a serious thought to stopping.

Cigarettes and coffee were essentials of the Runyon style, especially over the quarter century since Damon had last taken a drink. The two stimulants he consumed with abandon were, as Damon probably realized, surrogates for the alcohol he craved. But if that was true, and if Damon knew it, the knowledge only made the transferred craving all the more difficult to conquer. Damon knew he could not drink because once started he could not stop. Coffee and cigarettes made it possible for him to live without drinking, but instead of bringing the release alcohol brought, coffee and cigarettes brought mental tension. They fueled his work instead of impairing it as booze had. Moving into his sixties, Damon was drinking forty to sixty cups of hot java daily and suffering no apparent disagreeable effects. And he smoked one cigarette for every cup of coffee he drank.

In 1939 Damon spent several months in Hollywood, his longest stay yet. He and Patrice occupied a cottage at the Beverly Hills Hotel while Damon worked at MGM. Louis B. Mayer had paid him $5,000 for a one-page sketch from his Hearst Sunday feature series on the Turps, and the studio now put him to work as an advisor in the preparation of the screenplay. The film was *Joe and Ethel Turp Call on the President*. As was the case in most of his movie jobs, Damon's responsibility was to provide an original plot, dialogue, and advice on characters. His story ideas were always subject to revision by the studio producers, to whom Damon deferred gracefully when it came to cinematic plot mechanics, and his dialogue was usually reworked by professional screenwriters like Earl Baldwin (who'd written the screenplay of *A Slight Case of Murder* for Warners) or Leonard Spigelgass.

Spigelgass had assisted Robert Riskin in mining the *Lady for a Day* screenplay out of "Madame La Gimp" and had himself written the screen adaptations of two other Runyon tales, "Little Miss Marker" and "Princess O'Hara." (Only the first two Spigelgass jobs had met with Damon's approval, for only the first two were box office smashes.) In 1940 Universal Pictures bought Damon's stories "Butch Minds the Baby" and "Tight Shoes" (for $10,000 plus a third of the gross) and sent Spigelgass to New York to get Damon's advice on the two screenplays.

It was Spigelgass' introduction to the milieu of the Broadway stories and his first meeting with their creator, whose appearance came as a shock. Influenced by some of the Hollywood casting for Runyon films, Spigelgass walked into Lindy's his first night in New York and looked around for a Broderick Crawford or Bill Bendix type. Instead the slender Damon, elegant in a Glen Urquhart plaid suit and Charvet necktie, rose from the table at which he and Patrice and several friends were dining, greeted the screenwriter politely, and invited him to sit down. Spigelgass felt very much the outsider. And he sensed a coolness in Damon's friends, who were clearly apprehensive about having their Broadway laureate whisked off by Hollywood as Hellinger had been.

The first few hours of the Runyon-Spigelgass encounter were a standoff with tight mouths on both sides. After dinner Damon took his California guest home to the Parc Vendome. Spigelgass, who'd been expecting some jazzy decor out of a George Raft picture, was set back on his heels by Damon's grandiose Louis XVI study. Feeling Damon's "cold and inquiring" blue eyes on him, the screenwriter caught his breath and after a period of throat-clearing launched into his ideas about "Butch Minds the Baby." Suddenly Damon warmed up; Spigelgass had hit the right chord in his approach to "Butch," and from that point on his host was no longer the remote author but a most helpful (and authoritative) Broadway guide.

Although Damon agreed to contribute the odd line of dialogue and a word or two on the characters, it was his Cook's Tour of the nightlife of New York that Spigelgass found most useful when the two men later sat down to write the screenplay. For several nights Damon took the Hollywood writer along on his usual rounds. They ate at the old Lindy's across from the Brill Building on Broadway (between 49th and 50th Streets), took in a couple of movies, then crossed Broadway again to sit and talk and drink coffee at the new Lindy's on 52nd Street until dawn. One evening they dropped Patrice at home and followed a floating crap game that introduced Spigelgass to a cross-section of Broadway gamblers. The game crossed Manhattan, in a winding route of upstairs haunts and secret passwords that left the screenwriter's mind reeling, and ended up in the grey light of dawn in the Bronx.

Another night, as they sat in the new Lindy's chewing the fat on the subject of the *Butch* screenplay, Spigelgass picked up on a couple of Runyon neologisms which he thought he might be able to use. One was "mooley" (denoting a mental lightweight), another was "komoppo" (a faded blonde—from "kimono" plus "mop"). The screenwriter noted these and several other colorful terms, and when a few months later the two men were at work on the screenplay in California, it was agreed to include komoppo, mooley, and the rest in the script. This minor experimental gesture got them in trouble with the movie censors at the Hays office. After the Hays board inspected the script of *Butch,* Damon got a summons. He was questioned about his coinages, which the board suspected were obscenities, and was asked to reveal "of what language they are a part." "I made them up myself," the author replied. The censors did not smile, but they approved the *Butch* screenplay.

When Spigelgass' New York visit ended, Damon agreed—for a nice price, of course—to accompany him to Hollywood to put in a couple of weeks of work on the Universal Pictures productions of his stories. The screenwriter was astonished by the treatment he and Damon received along the way. On their first night out of Grand Central on the Twentieth Century Limited they were served a special dining car feast that included such delicacies as caviar, wild geese and turkey, and three kinds of paté—all gifts put on board by New York pals of Damon's. In Chicago the next day they were met at the station by a sporting delegation and given a royal escort to the Blackstone Hotel, where a luncheon was held in their honor. It was the same thing all the way to California; Leonard Spigelgass was often left speechless by the local receptions Damon got—even in the New Mexico desert, where Runyon fans waited at whistlestops and waved and held up copies of his books as the Super Chief roared past!

Damon's couple of weeks in Hollywood were to stretch into several years. In 1940 he worked at Universal under Carl Laemmle. In 1941 he sold "Little Pinks," a new story, to RKO for $15,000, and in August he signed a contract as a writer-producer for that studio at a salary of over $2000 a week. He stayed with RKO for five months, collaborating with Earl Baldwin on a screenplay for a story he had sold to the studio earlier ("The Snatching of Bookie Bob") and with Spigelgass on a script for the "Little Pinks" film. The latter was to be called *The Big Street,* and it would provide Damon with his first crack at producing.

Inspired by the expanded duties and responsibilities of his new role, Damon worked harder on *The Big Street* than he had on any other movie. One of his first acts as producer was to insist that director Irving Reis fly to New York with him. As he had done with Leonard Spigelgass, he escorted Reis around Broadway personally, giving the director a crash course in the ways of the street their picture was all about. "Good night, Irving," Damon said with a wry smile at the completion of their evening on the town. "I think you can direct the picture now." The next morning the two men flew back to California and went to work on filming *The Big Street.*

Damon saw his picture in RKO's screening rooms more than a hundred times before its release. Its sentimental story and the performances of Henry Fonda and Lucille Ball in the leading roles seemed to affect him each time as deeply as on his first viewing. In more than one screening session he was moved to tears by his own picture, a fact which his repertoire of fake coughs and simulated nose-blowing could not conceal from Reis, Spigelgass, and the studio technicians.

Happily for Damon, the public agreed with him about the appeal of *The Big Street.* Although the picture received only mixed reviews (*Time* called it a "pleasant bit of paranoia that cannot possibly displease anyone but may baffle some cinema addicts for a while"), it quickly took off at the box office. Obviously those who bought tickets had fallen for Runyon's odd characters and surprising plot and didn't mind the maudlin passages. Damon had scored with the only audience that mattered to him. Even the *Time* reviewer saw that; "Runyon sees every scene through the lay eyes of the average audience," the anonymous critic admitted. That hit the nail on the head. *The Big Street* was a big money maker in 1942.

The success of *The Big Street* led Damon to greener pastures. He left RKO after less than six months and signed on at Twentieth Century Fox, where he worked at a fat salary for the remainder of his stay in Hollywood, nearly two years. For Fox he did several writing and production jobs, usually working as a consultant on big commercial vehicles. Many of them were large, creaking productions which could have been "saved," artistically speaking, only by a total overhaul, but Damon was asked only to provide an occasional high-priced oiling of the joints. One example that will be familiar to late-night movie fans of the present day is *Irish Eyes Are Smiling.*

Irish Eyes was a routine piece of sentiment, the kind of thing generally considered by the studios to be suited to a wartime audience that was tiring of gangster and "tough guy" pictures. The film's basic idea, a musical comedy about the life of the fellow who wrote the title song, was neither Runyon's nor much to write home about. Damon did what he could to throw in some interesting characters and funny lines—Monte Woolley may have been a Runyon casting suggestion—but overall, *Irish Eyes* came out a real cream puff; even Damon thought so. Well, wasn't that exactly what Fox had asked for? Who needed a "tough" vehicle for the likes of Dick Haymes and June Haver? On *Irish Eyes,* as on all the other pictures whose production he assisted for Fox, Damon did his job, stayed within his budget, and—unlike a lot of producers—didn't ask for or expect the impossible. ("The impossible," in *Irish Eyes'* case, would have been equal to "a first rate picture.")

Irish Eyes won no Oscars, but it made Fox over a million dollars—in view of which Fox quickly signed Damon to produce the movie of "The Bloodhounds of Broadway," one of his early tales. The money was good, and the opportunity—to turn one of his favorite stories into film—was one of which Damon had often daydreamed. He was at work on *Bloodhounds* in 1944 when his career in the town where dreams are made was stopped short. Just as Damon was reaching out to take the fruits of his long labors from the bright tree, his arm was grabbed by a shade.

Damon and Patrice's first home in California was a large one-story house on a shady street in Beverly Hills that Damon rented after going to work for RKO in 1941. There Damon attempted to reproduce his New York life style. He kept the shades drawn all day, rose late, dressed in suits, wore topcoats in the evening, and did most of his living by night—or tried to. But he was soon made aware that this style was not suited to the climate of California or to the working habits of Californians. The weather was too warm for suits and topcoats. Studio schedules, unlike those of New York morning newspapers, called for a nine-to-five day or something approximating it. Mark Hellinger (as his biographer, Jim Bishop, describes) had gone through the same educational process a few years before Runyon.

> This was Hollywood. He would have to learn to get to bed by eleven each night and be up before seven. That was the great big unbreakable rule in Hollywood. No one in Hollywood, they pointed out, went out whooping it up on any night but Saturday, because Sunday was the only day for sleep. The rest of the week was sheer murder. Of course, a producer could have dinner out with his friends. That was all right. But the party always broke up by ten or so. And everybody went home to bed.

Damon, never as engrossed in the studio routine as Hellinger was, managed to maintain in the face of the barbarism of Southern California certain bastions of "civilized" behavior. Insisting that he had "a mole's dislike of sunshine and fresh air," he did all his work by artificial light. "I've been breathing the air of jernts of all kinds all my life and prefer it to the open air," the erstwhile denizen of Broadway wrote in a column that showed how far he was from home.

Working on the set, Damon often wore an ankle-length topcoat made of heavy suede. Even so he often complained of drafts, and he made a public joke of his fear of colds. In his first year in Hollywood he wrote several columns on the subject of hypochondria, including himself among such well-known victims of the condition as Al Jolson, Irving Berlin, and the renowned Carl "Junior" Laemmle. Laemmle, then Damon's boss at Universal Pictures, had (as Damon told it) once departed from a football game in Los Angeles at halftime because of a draft, even though he was "bundled up like an Eskimo" at the time. (The "draft" had been caused by director Mervyn Le Roy, who had been sitting behind Laemmle and blowing small gusts down the back of Junior's neck.)

Damon had to adjust to early rising on days when his presence was required at the studio, and this took some doing. Coffee helped, but morning coffee usually required that a little sleep precede it, as a sort of booster. Sleep was something one did at home, and Damon was not used to spending evenings at home.

Not that Hollywood offered nocturnal activity as rich and varied as Broadway's. But the D-Man was always able to track down the best dining and sporting locations in any town, and Hollywood was no exception. By 1942 he had developed a string of restaurant hangouts to substitute for Lindy's and the Stork Club. His early favorite was Mike Lyman's place on Vine Street, where he soon became the acknowledged champion player of "the gin rummy

The World of Damon Runyon

capital of the world." A circle of disciples soon gathered around Damon, to play gin with him and hear his stories of Broadway and the horseplaying and fight rackets. It was not like New York, where Damon had let his table partners do most of the talking; at Lyman's he was the star and his listeners deferred to him.

After Damon had been a fixture at Mike Lyman's place for a year or so, the proprietor—who'd been a participant—closed down the gin rummy games. Damon later speculated that Lyman had "examined his books and found that he was losing more at gin than the joint was taking in." Columnist Runyon soon let his readers know he was finding other taverns that were conducive to gin rummy and good company, like Billy Wilkerson's La Rue on the Sunset Strip and Dave Chasen's place in Beverly Hills. There was also Prince Mike Romanoff's, which in his last two years in Southern California became Damon's second home.

Damon and Prince Mike grew close. The Prince was a kind but occasionally combative soul whose fights, his New York friend wrote, "seldom last long enough for anyone to see them." (Romanoff's unfortunate tiff with race car driver Barney Oldfield—"an outdoors event [which] came up over a kissing of auto fenders"—inspired the hilarious Runyon Column "Café Gladiators.") Prince Mike was a lover of art and literature and enjoyed chewing the fat with Damon about the Finer Things. It turned out the Prince and Squire Runyon shared a common enthusiasm for the paintings of Gustave Moreau, no less, and in their nightly discussions they kicked around such names as Kafka, Spengler, Hesse. Clearly Damon was far from home.

Before long Damon had quite a few friends in Hollywood. Aside from his gin rummy set, there were other lovers of chance—some of them familiar faces from earlier days—whom he ran into at gambling clubs like the Clover on Sunset. There was also the movie crowd, whom Mrs. Runyon at least found more congenial than the gamblers. Many of the film stars were old-time stage artists whom Damon had known for years.

George Burns and Gracie Allen became particular friends of the Runyons. Burns, a pal since the days of vaudeville and the "real" Broadway, was Damon's favorite party humorist. "I am a tough one to make laugh," the deadpan Damon wrote in a column ("Burns the Devastating"), "yet there is one man who utterly devastates me when he opens up his bag of tricks at a private gathering. He has me laughing up and down the scale . . . I am speaking of George Burns." Damon claimed to be Burns' greatest audience, with the twin exceptions of George's wife Gracie (who didn't count) and Jack Benny.

> [Benny] literally falls right on the floor laughing at George. What appeals to Jack about George's performance is the seriousness with

which George goes about it. He works like a dog. He loves to be "on," or the center of attraction, all the time and is a bit inclined to resent the attempts of others at entertainment.

He is pretty cunning about it, and his long experience enables him to outmaneuver the average rival for the spotlight. I saw him one night against Eddie Cantor, Lou Holtz, Jack Benny and Danny Kaye, all on the floor of a living room at a Hollywood party at the same time, and George was out in front all the way. He would not work as hard on the stage for a large salary as he does for nothing at a party.

One party at which the great funnyman worked for nothing was one he and his wife threw in Damon Runyon's honor at their Beverly Hills home. Burns, who always took over the entertainment duties at his own soirées, on this occasion sang one number after another, threatening to monopolize the entire evening without challenge until Al Jolson rose from a sofa and butted into the vocalizing. While Jolson was said to be as hard to shut out of an evening's entertainment as the Yankees were in a ballgame, Burns was more than a match for him. The host simply raised his voice to drown out that of his guest. The "Mammy Man," as Runyon called his pal Jolson, left the party in a huff.

Over the next several years, every time Damon ran into Al Jolson he ribbed him about the time he had been upstaged by "Burns the Devastating."

The Runyons had many mutual friends in Hollywood, and in their first two years in town they were seen often at parties. But as the years went by the nights Damon went out alone to play cards began to outnumber the nights he spent with his wife. Patrice was developing her own interests. This was inevitable; while Damon was in his sixties, she was still a young woman. Obviously, there were activities that were better suited to her than all-night card games. Left alone, Patrice did not turn to drinking, as had Ellen Egan Runyon twenty years before. A more modern woman, she had more modern interests.

She learned to fly, and she flew B-17s for the Army. Although her husband's age and work habits prevented him from participating in the war effort, no such barriers existed for Patrice. She went to flying school, became a pilot, and—while Damon was playing gin at Chasen's and Romanoff's—spent her time ferrying bombers back and forth between California and the East Coast.

Pearl Harbor had come too late for Damon to get involved; he was too old to fight and too busy with his lucrative movie career to think of going overseas as a correspondent. He remained in California and wrote occasional columns of comment on the new kind of soldiering, which he failed to comprehend. This was evident in his remarks after Drew Pearson broke the story of the soldiers slapped by General Patton in Sicily. Damon, who had ridden with "Black Jack" Pershing in Mexico and dined with him at his European command post during the 1919 Allied Occupation, was outraged by Patton's act. "It is my opinion," he wrote, "that had any officer smacked a private in World War I he would have been 'busted' by old man Pershing quicker than you can say scat and that goes for Patton although he knew Patton from the days along the Mexican border and liked him."

The only real effect the war had on Damon's life was in the high toll charge he now had to pay for wiring his columns back East. Before Pearl Harbor he had mailed them, which was cheaper but took several days. Although he did not appreciate the extra toll expenses at the time, the service was worth the cost, since the telegraphed 1942 columns regained an immediacy that had been missing in those sent by mail in 1941. The 1942 columns read like personal news, not history—a fact that Damon's audience (and Mr. Hearst) noticed immediately. In 1942 the Runyon column caught fire across the country, picking up new syndication outlets every day. Columnist Runyon was "hot." The next few years he was to grow more so.

In 1943 Damon and Patrice moved to the rented Holmby Hills residence of comedienne Gertrude Neisen. He grew fond of Miss Neisen's Angora cat, Sheba, and at the same time acquired another pet, a cocker spaniel. Nubbin was a particular favorite of Damon's; he was considerably affected when it died after he'd owned it less than a year.

Nubbin's mortal problem was tonsils, which struck Damon as sadly ironic since he himself had had trouble with his tonsils— and had in fact been bothered by a nagging sore throat during the months preceding the dog's demise. Damon still smoked three packs of cigarettes a day. His voice had become so hoarse that old friends like Agnes Fowler told him they couldn't recognize it. He hesitated about seeing a doctor, but when he took the sick Nubbin to a veterinarian, Dr. Eugene Jones, he mentioned his own problem in passing. Dr. Jones offered to take a look at Damon's throat. "Why not?" Damon said with false joviality. He tipped his head back, opened his mouth, and said ah.

What Dr. Jones saw made him suggest that Damon see a specialist immediately. Damon did not. But he felt tired and run down, and his sore throat got worse. He made vows to consult doctors, reneged, procrastinated, and began to suffer in earnest. So too did his work—but only in quantity. The quality of his columns remained what it had always been and if anything increased. But the columns became irregular, brightening Mr. Hearst's pages only three or four mornings a week instead of five. He apologized to his readers and explained that on some days he "had nothing to say." In fact he was now physically incapacitated. He had in mind much to say, but a large shortage in the body department prevented his saying it. Some days a mere 750 words was more than this former Iron Horse of Journalism could produce. His fiction writing ground to a halt, and he became a missing person at the studio.

Damon finally gave in to the proddings of his wife and friends, flew to New York, and on April 13, 1944, consulted a throat surgeon, Dr. Hayes Martin. Dr. Martin hospitalized him on the spot. After a week of tests, surgery was performed on April 10. Damon's sore throat, Dr. Martin discovered, was the result of a cancerous larynx. The organ was removed in that day's operation and in a second exactly six weeks later.

Damon was kept in the hospital until June, when he was allowed to return to California. There his condition continued to deteriorate. The pain in his throat made studio work impossible. The Runyons vacated the Neisen house in Holmby Hills before Labor Day. Most of their belongings were shipped to the house in Florida, to which Patrice now returned. Damon flew to New York and was hospitalized again on the next to last day of September 1944.

On October 2 Dr. Martin operated again, this time removing the lymph glands on the left side of Damon's neck. The cancer, it was now clear, was spreading. When Damon came out of the anesthesia, he asked Dr. Martin to give him the "lowdown." The surgeon told his patient gently that it was now "simply a question of management." The meaning was clear. "A matter of time" were the words the doctor hadn't said, but Damon understood.

This time he stayed in the hospital until December. Working from his bed on a typewriter propped on a table in front of him, he resumed his daily column in November. Ironically, it was still called "The Brighter Side," even though Damon understandably now turned toward topics that belied the cheerful heading. He reviewed his life and wrote of his death, which was now no stranger. "Why me?" he wailed in anguish one day. On another, November 18, he wrote "Death Pays a Social Call." Despite the gravity of the subject, Damon's prose glittered.

> Death came in and sat down beside me, a large and most distinguished-looking figure in beautifully tailored soft white flannels. His expansive face wore a big smile.
>
> "Oh, hello," I said. "Hello, hello, hello. I was not expecting you. I have not looked at the red board lately and did not know my number was up. If you will just hand me my kady and my coat I will be with you in a jiffy."
>
> "Tut-tut-tut," Death said. "Not so fast. I have not yet come for you. By no means."
>
> "You haven't?" I said.

The World of Damon Runyon

"No," Death said.

"Then what the hell are you doing here?" I demanded indignantly. "What do you mean by barging in here without even knocking and depositing your fat Francis in my easiest chair without so much as a by-your-leave?"

"Excuse me," Death said, taken aback by my vehemence. "I was in your neighborhood and all tired out after my day's work and I thought I would just drop in and sit around with you awhile and cut up old scores. It is merely a social call, but I guess I owe you an apology at that for my entrance."

"I should say you do," I said.

"Well, you see I am so accustomed to entering doors without knocking that I never thought," Death said. "If you like I will go outside and not come in until you answer."

"Look," I said. "You get out of here and stay out of here. Screw, bum!"

Death burst out crying.

Huge tears rolled down both pudgy cheeks and splashed on his white silk-faced lapels.

"There it is again," he sobbed. "That same inhospitable note wherever I go. No one wants to chat with me. I am so terribly lonesome. I thought surely you would like to punch the bag with me awhile."

I declined to soften up.

"Another thing," I said sternly, "what are you doing in that get-up? You are supposed to be in black. You are supposed to look sombre, not like a Miami Beach Winter Tourist."

"Why," Death said, "I got tired of wearing my old working clothes all the time. Besides I thought these garments would be more cheerful and informal for a social call."

"Well, beat it," I said. "Just Duffy out of here."

"You need not fear me," Death said.

"I do not fear you Deathie, old boy," I said, "but you are a knock to me among my neighbors. Your visit is sure to get noised about and cause gossip. You know you are not considered a desirable character by many persons, although, mind you, I am not saying anything against you."

"Oh, go ahead," Death said. "Everybody else puts the zing on me so you might as well, too. But I did not think your neighbors would recognize me in white, although come to think of it, I noticed everybody running to their front doors and grabbing in their 'Welcome' mats as I went past. Why are you shivering if you do not fear me?"

"I am shivering because of that clammy chill you brought in with you," I said. "You lug the atmosphere of a Frigidaire around with you."

"You don't tell me?" Death said. "I must correct that. I must pack an electric pad with me. Do you think that is why I seem so unpopular wherever I go? Do you think I would ever be a social success?"

"I am inclined to doubt it," I said. "Your personality repels many persons. I do not find it as bad as that of some others I know, but you have undoubtedly developed considerable sales resistance to yourself in various quarters."

"Do you think it would do any good if I hired a publicity man?"

Hollywood Gold with a Black Lining

Death asked. "I mean, to conduct a campaign to make me popular?"

"It might," I said. "The publicity men have worked wonders with even worse cases than yours. But see here, D., I am not going to waste my time giving you advice and permitting you to linger in my quarters to get me talked about. Kindly do a scrammola, will you?"

Death had halted his tears for a moment but now he turned on all the faucets, crying boo-hoo-hoo-hoo.

"I am so lonesome," he said between lachrymose heaves.

"Git!" I said.

"Everybody is against me," Death said.

He slowly exited and as I heard his tears falling plop-plop-plop to the floor as he passed down the hallway I thought of the remark of Agag, the king of the Amalekites, to Samuel just before Samuel mowed him down: "Surely the bitterness of death is past."

In the obscure hours after his "sentence" had been passed on to him by his doctors, Runyon had by an effort of sheer will turned the wall of sightless darkness that now lay before him into a clarity of prose that dazzled. This was Damon's pinnacle as an artist, and it had nothing to do with dollars and cents. A man who had seen through to the other side of his own life and come back to tell of it with accuracy and high humor, he was now prepared for anything.

In a mid-1944 Hearst reorganization of personnel Damon's column had been shifted from the *Mirror* to the *Journal-American.* The columns he wrote for that paper between November 1944 and the end of his life contain a new quality of feeling. By this time his horizon, beyond the present moment, consisted only of death, but the prospect seemed to inspire him to strive all the harder to make his writing vital and alive—as if manufacturing lively prose out of the wooden mass of language were somehow a way of creating and extending life itself. Formally, the late columns are in the classic Runyon mold. The style is as spry as ever, the thought transparent and exact, the philosophical drift stoical and laconic. What is new is the overriding emotion, the nostalgia for life, and—despite an occasional outcry of pain—the tolerance of suffering. Damon did a lot of belated accepting in these last years, and it shows in his work: the acceptance not only of physical agony but of the human race, of fate, and ultimately of life itself. Like many men, he held most dearly to it when he knew he was about to lose it. Unlike most men, he was able to express this to others in a way that was both clear and permanent.

Runyon's final columns are one of the delights of our literature, pieces sometimes as free-roving, conversational, and bright as the essays of Addison, sometimes as intelligently reflective as those of Montaigne, and now and then as painfully self-exploratory as those of Pascal. If the art of the essay—a form defined perfectly by one great practitioner, Samuel Johnson, as "a loose sally of the mind"—has reached greater sophistication in this century, it is hard to see where.

For his old crony in the writing racket, Bugs Baer, and for many other readers including this one, Damon's late columns in the *Journal-American* are the best things he ever wrote.

In March 1945 there was another operation. Out came Damon's trachea. There followed x-ray and radium treatments. In one stretch Damon spent thirty-five straight days under the invisible beam of the cobalt gun. His skin was scorched from his chest and neck. During therapy he slept fitfully at the hospital by night— the adjustment to nighttime sleeping was one Damon could never accomplish, even with the use of drugs—and lived by day in his rooms at the Hotel Buckingham on 57th Street, west of Sixth Avenue.

He was out of the hospital again in April, and when in the second week of that month President Franklin D. Roosevelt died of a cerebral hemorrhage, Damon insisted on covering the funeral for the *Journal-American* and International News Service. His doctors said no, but when Damon stated his intention of going anyway, they relented on condition that he take along a hired nurse. Reporter Runyon went to Washington, followed the president's cortège through the streets, and filed an account that appeared under his byline in Hearst papers across the country on April 15, 1944.

Damon's elegiac tribute to Roosevelt (and clearly, in a private sense, to America) was as eloquent a news story as he ever wrote, and it is justly famous. In personal terms the story was also one of the most expensive he'd ever written. The strain of the trip left him too tired to go "around and about" for several weeks. But the story itself shows no sign of debility. It captures the quiet gravity and stately rhythm of the funeral parade in prose that has similar qualities. The piece also contains an autobiographical touch that adds to its eloquence. The cynical Demon, who a few years before had snickered behind his hand when Winchell and other friends praised F.D.R., here abandons his "half-boob air" and puts words into the mouths of his characters that express only openness and compassion.

> Hundreds of thousands of the people of Washington packed the sidewalks along Constitution and Pennsylvania Avenues, and watched the passing of the mournful troop.
> At the corner of 12th Street and Constitution Avenue stood a well-dressed, confident-appearing man, a prosperous businessman, perhaps, with a boy in his mid-teens but tall for his years. He could look over the heads of most of those wedged in 10-deep ahead of him.

Hollywood Gold with a Black Lining

"I remember his smile, father," the boy was saying, "I mean I remember it from the pictures of him in the newsreels. It was such a wonderful smile. It crinkled his face up all around his eyes."

"Yes, he smiled a lot," the man said. "I used to say he smiled to think of the way he had fellows like me over a barrel. I hated him.

"I hated him most of the 12 years he lived in this town. I mean I hated him politically. Now I wonder why. He only did the best he could. No man could do more."

Against a sky of crystal, flocks of silvery planes roared overhead at intervals, gleaming in the sunlight. But when the noise of their motors had died away the city seemed strangely quiet.

"Yes," the man said, "he was a kind man. He was kind to many people. I used to say I hated him when he was alive but now it is difficult for me to pick out any reason why. How could I hate a kind man?" —"A Great Man Passes By"

Damon went into the hospital again in October 1945 for surgery to complete the removal of his vocal chords and windpipe. There was now nothing left to take out, but the disease galloped on. His doctors agreed that further irradiation or surgery would only be unnecessary cruelty. When Damon was discharged from Memorial Hospital at the end of October it was for the last time. For the time being he became an outpatient; his next overnight visit, fourteen months later, was to stretch into eternity.

The body Damon was left with in the interim was not exactly what the doctor ordered, as the saying goes—yet, literally, what else was it? The surgeons had put a metal pipe in his throat to conduct food and drink from his mouth to his stomach. Another surgically implanted tube emerged from beneath his clavicle on the left side, its purpose to admit air to his lungs. The end of the tube protruded several inches beyond the skin of his neck. It was covered by a gauze bib that prevented foreign objects from tumbling into his chest cavity by accident.

The throat pipe left a metallic aftertaste in Damon's mouth, but otherwise it suited its purpose. It did not, however, permit speech, since there was no vocal mechanism left. The best Damon could do was to emit rough croaking sounds, which were then mouthed into words. Except on rare occasions, he avoided attempting to speak by this method, which he found ineffective as well as grotesque. Instead he developed the habit of carrying a notepad and pencil at all times; whenever he had something to say, he scribbled the words on his pad, tore off the page, and handed it to the person with whom he was "talking." This kind of "conversation" made it possible for him to maintain most forms of social life. (He could not of course use the telephone.)

It also created certain problems, which Damon took somewhat more seriously in real life than he did in a column called "Passing the Word Along." (Joe Connolly was the general manager of King Features, the Hearst feature-article syndicate that distributed Damon's column around the country.)

> I carry a pad of paper in my pocket and when conversation is indicated I jot down my end of the gabbing on paper and pass it on to my vis-à-vis who takes a glaum at the chirography, crumples up the slip of paper and casts it aside, nodding his head or muttering a noncommital um-huh because he can not read it any more than I can after it is two hours cold.
>
> The forced practice has produced a headache for me as this morning I was waited on by four guys who were all mighty belligerent. I mean they all wanted to place the sluggola on me. They wanted to bash out my brains, if any. I mean they were sizzling.
>
> The first one to appear we will call Pat, though his name is really Pete. He had a piece of paper in his hand that he handed to me, saying, truculently:
>
> "What does this mean?"
>
> The paper had obviously been wadded up and smoothed out again and I could not decipher the writing, though it looked familiar.
>
> "Who wrote this?" I asked Pat (in writing).
>
> "You did," he said, fiercely.
>
> Then it dawned on me that it was indeed my own writing and I read it better.
>
> "Pat is a louse," the writing said.
>
> I tried to remember when I had written it. It could scarcely have been at the editorial council in Joe Connolly's office because insects were not discussed, only a few heels. As a matter of fact I did less talking in Joe Connolly's office than anywhere else in town because when I walked in he had a great big pad of foolscap lying on his desk and I felt insulted. It was a hint that I talk a heap.
>
> It might have been in Lindy's late at night when I had a meeting with Oscar Levant and Leonard Lyons, but it comes to my mind that we did not get as far down the alphabet as the P's. We quit at the O's because I ran out of pad paper and Lindy commenced to get sore at the way I was working on the backs of his menu cards.
>
> I was busy writing out a denial for Pat when Joe and Ike and Spike, as we will call them, came barging in and each of them had a crumpled slip, and were so hot that taken jointly you could have barbecued a steer on them. I read one slip that said Mike would rob a church, another that stated that Ike would guzzle his grandmamma if he thought it would help him while there was still another that I would not think of putting in a public print. I did not realize that I knew some of the words.
>
> I think if there had been only one present he would have belted me but the four being there at the same time complicated matters because each one knew the others are copper hollerers or stool pigeons, which is what I had in mind in my writing, and would belch to the bulls if a murder or mayhem came off.
>
> So they finally left muttering they would see me later and I was taught a lesson about leaving written testimony scattered around.

After a few not-so-funny episodes on the order of the Pat/ Pete embroilment, Damon began to make a point of retrieving his notes as soon as he'd written them, balling them up, and dropping them in his pocket to destroy later. The small blue sheets, with the monogrammed SAYS DAMON RUNYON logo—many of them containing incriminating evidence of Runyon "knocks"—were floating all over town by that time. To Damon, who'd always been famous for his reticence, that felt like asking for trouble.

17

The Biggest Deadline

I once asked my father about our ancestors. Said he, "We come from a long line of Huguenot horse thieves who were run out of France by posses." It was his way of dismissing pretentions about family. —Damon Runyon Jr., *Father's Footsteps*

In the last two years of his life Damon made attempts to piece together what remained of his family. His own father's lonely passing—in a tuberculosis sanitarium in Arizona in 1911—was an event the young baseball-writing Runyon had had little time to mourn. Only now, in his terminal illness, did his thoughts return repeatedly to the barren circumstances of his father's death. His mother and sisters, long since lost to him, were by now unclear images in his memory. His first love, Ellen, was sadly gone. He had grown estranged not only from his present wife, Patrice (whose life was expanding toward other friends even as his own was narrowing), but from the two children of his first marriage.

Family to Damon had meant only regret and pain, the majority of his experiences in that area having been failures; he had for some years displayed a distaste for the subject that often shocked his friends. Since his separation from his first wife in the late twenties he had had only limited contact with his children. In the early 1930s Damon Jr. had spent his vacations from Riverside Military Academy with Damon and Patrice in New York and Miami, but when in 1937 the boy chose to leave school and go into newspapering, Damon was hurt and infuriated. He had promised his son the proverbial "best education money can buy" and had looked forward to sending him to an Ivy League school to obtain the kind of degree and "polish" only the rich could afford. In his anger he cut off relations with his son for several years. In 1944 his daughter, Mary, a gentle, vulnerable young woman whose life since childhood seemed to have been fraught with difficulty, suffered a nervous breakdown. Meanwhile Damon Jr. wandered from one newspaper job to another, carrying his father's name (a valuable credential) and his father's predilection for alcohol (a ruinous burden).

The problems of his children had concerned Damon only remotely until his own life was threatened by cancer, at which point there was an awakening of feeling on his part. It led him first to bring Mary to New York to live with him at the Hotel Buckingham for a while in the summer of 1945 and later to pay for her care in a sanitarium in Ohio. It also led him to re-establish relations with his son, who visited him in New York in October 1944, shortly after the second round of surgery had revealed Damon's destiny. Damon Jr. came again to visit for a few days in 1946. Over this period the two communicated by mail—a rare correspondence for Damon, who disliked writing for anything but money—and in December 1946, when Damon was on his deathbed, the son returned to New York to be at his father's side.

The relationship of father and son over the years is described in the late Damon Runyon, Jr.'s poignant memoir, *Father's Footsteps,* published in 1954. In this book Damon Jr. revealed an attitude toward Damon's Broadway circle of friends—the horseplayers, bookies, touts, pugs, chorines, card sharps, and hustlers—that provides an interesting reflection of Ellen Egan Runyon's attitude. Ellen, whose dream was of a house on Fifth Avenue, a life on a high and well-mannered plane, and a husband who came home nights, bore a permanent grudge against Damon's crude-talking, shady-looking colleagues of the nightspots, gyms, and tracks. She refused to entertain her husband's "low-life" friends in her house, and she looked with disdain on the string of tin-eared and pug-nosed chauffeurs with which he provided her. (They were selected from his personal stable of heavyweights, all of whom could drive better than they could punch.) Fascinated as a boy by his father's friends, Damon Jr. was later to share his mother's distaste for them, and on his final trip to New York he found himself and Damon's longtime Broadway cronies—who resented the intrusion of this "outsider"—in openly adversary roles.

During the last two years of his life the always active Runyon was around and about more than ever. Preferring physical fatigue to hours of staring at the wallpaper in gloomy insomnia, he retired to his hotel room only when his legs would no longer hold him up. Most days he went, as he had in earlier New York years, to Nat Lewis' clothing shop on Broadway between 47th and 48th Streets, and strolled through from the Broadway door to the Seventh Avenue door, buying new items for his wardrobe. His purchases had always been numerous and extravagant; his collections of robes, topcoats, sweaters, hats, shirts, and shoes were legendary, and these were largely amassed in daily buying sprees at Nat Lewis' shop. Damon had been known to walk in and, in one typically nonchalant splurge, throw down a thousand dollars for such essentials as a set of eight Malacca canes with ram's horn handles.

(When Runyon found an item he liked, one was never enough; he always had to have extras to give to friends.)

Squire Runyon was a believer in the adage that clothes make the man. He had once possessed a large glass case containing over 1200 beautifully tailored suits, and he had been famous for changing his entire outfit—from his necktie to his typewriter case—as many as four times a day. Now in his dying years he bought more clothes and accessories than ever before, spending by one estimate $30,000 at Lewis' shop in 1945–1946. Most of these latter-day buying sprees seemed to spring from pure impulse, since Damon had never had less need for an expanded wardrobe. In fact he now began to give away his purchases, along with the contents of his clothes-closet. He presented unsolicited gifts to friends, acquaintances, total strangers. "What good is it going to do me?" Damon would reply whenever any of the objects of his generosity balked at accepting some particularly valuable item.

He sent several trunks full of expensive clothing to Damon Jr. in Cincinnati, where the younger man was working as a reporter and was active in Alcoholics Anonymous. "The thought occurred to me that in your A.A. work you may occasionally have to outfit some bloke and perhaps you can make use of these garments," Damon wrote. The trunks contained such high-class articles as tailored topcoats from Abercrombie's. There must have been some very well turned out winos in the Ohio River valley in those years.

His compulsive clothing purchases apart, Damon's expenses remained high even after he had left Hollywood and his $10,000-a-month producer's salary. He insisted on spending money, even if (or possibly *because*) it meant he would have to push himself to earn more. He liked to believe he could continue to support himself in any style he chose. But his illness had made this an illusion.

In June 1945, four months before his sixty-fifth birthday, Damon managed to turn out two 5000-word stories for *Collier's,* which for years had been begging him for more Broadway tales. Perhaps the stories didn't measure up to his earlier standards, but one of them, "Blonde Mink," gave inklings of what was going on inside Damon's heart at the time, behind the facade he kept up for the benefit of his friends. Patrice, with whom he was still in love, and whose companionship he sorely missed, was living alone at the Runyon villa in Florida. "Blonde Mink" told of the callousness and disloyalty of a beautiful woman who disregards her dying husband's last wish and buys a mink coat with the money he gives her to purchase his gravestone. The twin obsessions with death and the loss of his wife—from whom he was now formally separated—showed through every line of "Blonde Mink."

The Biggest Deadline

The sale to *Collier's* brought Damon cash—$10,000—and, he wrote his son at the time, he could use it.

> I have to keep plugging away at an age when I thought I would be in retirement, because my illness practically broke me. I went to Hollywood at a salary of over $2,000 a week largely as a matter of satisfying my vanity—I thought it was wonderful to command that kind of income at sixty-three—forgetting that it only added to my normal income and increased my taxes.
>
> Well, the upshot was the government taxes took most of it, and when I became ill and the big money was shut off entirely the doctors and the hospitals cut up what was left. I am now living not only on borrowed time but practically on borrowed money. But having seen others similarly afflicted I know that I have no kick coming.

Damon's money worries were not as serious as he made them out to be. He still had his reporter's and columnist's salaries, and now and then there was a windfall from a film company that wanted a one-paragraph "idea." Fiction writing was a greater chore, however. "I have an offer from *Cosmopolitan* magazine of $5,000 per story for twelve stories per year," he wrote Damon Jr. in October 1945, "which strikes me as a trifle ironical as it comes at a time when I could not possibly muster the physical energy for even a third that much, while in the period of my greatest activity, when I might have been able to do it they paid no attention to me." The last was an exaggeration, but Damon's general sense of the matter was correct. Hearst, *Collier's, Cosmopolitan*—all wanted more Runyon material and were willing to pay as well or better than ever before to get it. But Damon could not comply. He *wanted* to work on fiction, but the energy was lacking. He promised himself he would get to it tomorrow. There was a growing temptation to drift, to let things go. As he wrote his son, commenting on his weight—he'd put on quite a few pounds, sometimes wolfing down two and three dinners an evening even though he could barely taste the food—"I suppose I should go on a diet, but why? Where am I going?"

After the two operations in 1945 it was clear to the surgeons, and to Damon, that nothing more could be done for him except to ease his passing. To this end medications for pain and sleep were prescribed, but Damon quickly found another specific—human company—more effective in relieving his suffering. He arranged his habits to avoid being alone. By day he saw much of his agent, Paul Small, and a fight manager friend, Eddie Walker, who visited his hotel and dined with him daily. Without Patrice the tag end of evenings were a problem Damon staved off by staying out later and later at night. He stopped going to the movies— the darkness and silence of the theatre had begun to terrify him—

and instead passed the small hours of each morning in the secure company of friends at the Stork Club. He and Walter Winchell became particularly close.

The two men had known each other for some twenty-five years, ever since the days when Winchell, a young gossip columnist for *Vaudeville News,* lived with his wife and infant daughter above Billy LaHiff's Tavern, a favorite hangout of Damon's. (Damon had once persuaded LaHiff to reduce the struggling Winchells' rent on the grounds that their baby carriage, parked in front of the place, was "the only touch of respectability there is to this joint!") In the twenties and thirties Damon had often ridiculed the gossip columnists ("gossip columns are for women only," he'd once said), and his portrait of Waldo Winchester in the Broadway tales contained arch passages that may or may not have gone over Winchell's head. But when, after his 1944 operations, Damon began to frequent table 50 in the Stork Club every night, of all the table's regulars—Walker, agents Small and Irving Hoffman, Broadway jeweler Charles "Chuck" Green, columnists Leonard Lyons and Louis Sobol, sportswriter Jimmy Cannon, and host Sherman Billingsley—it was Winchell with whom Damon found himself constantly identified. At first he resisted Winchell's invitations to join him in his dawn patrols of the streets in pursuit of police calls, calling Walter's jaunts "little boy stuff." But when finally he gave in and went along once for the ride, he found himself fascinated. He was also delighted to have such vocal company. "Walter and I make the ideal companions," Damon quipped in a note to a pal. "He loves to talk, and I can't do anything but listen."

The Winchell-Runyon match was indeed ideal. Although both men were accustomed to regarding themselves as "the best" at their common calling, a remarkable noncompetitiveness marked their relationship. Considering that they spent approximately one-third of every twenty-four hours in each other's company for nearly two years, their disagreements were surprisingly few. One concerned Roosevelt, whose policies and character Damon often flayed in snide notes passed across the gleaming white tablecloth of table 50 in the months before Roosevelt's death. Walter, whose reverence for F.D.R. amounted to a religion, finally lost his temper. When Damon saw he'd gone too far, he apologized, explaining that he was never serious in his political comments, and Walter was assuaged. (Later, when Walter first told Damon his opinion of Truman, Damon scribbled, "I would rather meet a heavyweight champion than a president any time!") Winchell, whose ego bruised easily, once absented himself from table 50 for a week after Runyon had ribbed him in several notes about the illiteracy of radio audiences. Walter was easy to offend on this subject, and he nursed his hurt feelings until Damon wrote him a graceful

The Biggest Deadline

note of reconciliation and left it in his hotel mailbox. After that they were closer than ever; Damon's note had clearly touched the large, soft heart that beat inside Walter's thin skin.

Their friendship flourished; those who knew them began to call the pair Damon and Pythias. Winchell's longtime aide and eventual biographer, Herman Klurfeld, said later that in 1945–1946 the two men were "inseparable." It was obviously a relationship born not only from affection but from mutual respect. Walter had long admired Damon's achievements and considered his friend to be a great newspaperman. (In the foreword to Runyon's 1934 story collection, *Blue Plate Special,* he had called Damon "our idea of a big-time, first-rate Grade-A reporter" and "the most exciting and spellbinding of historians.") Walter had worn out several copies of a clipping of a laudatory column Damon had written about him in the *American;* he carried the story in his pocket and pulled it out for display on the slimmest of pretexts. Klurfeld, who recorded this and other demonstrations of Runyon's respect for Winchell, felt that the two columnists had much in common. "Both men," he wrote, "were sentimental cynics whose formula for success was 'Get the money' . . . They were both denizens of Broadway whose unique journalists' styles had elevated them to Hearstian heavens."

Certainly Damon respected Winchell's success, and vice versa. Once, when Damon Jr. (then a $25-a-week copyboy) criticized Winchell's column, his father told him, "That fellow you are knocking makes $250,000 a year. How much do you make?" Indeed, after Mark Hellinger, no newspaperman of their time had done a better job of getting the money, a fact of which both men were justifiably proud. Both had risen to the top from humble origins. One night in the Stork Club Damon astonished Walter by throwing to the floor a check for $100,000 which he had just received from Sir Alexander Korda. (The check was payment for Damon's simple verbal promise of a script for a Bing Crosby film.) "Why did you do that?" Walter asked. "To see if it would bounce," Damon wrote gleefully on his notepad. The joke delighted Winchell, one man who surely never envied Damon his success. Walter had his own.

In time Damon grew to enjoy the fast-talking, reckless-driving gossip columnist's company wholeheartedly. On one occasion he wrote, "I know of no man who's more entertaining than Walter when he is in the mood, nor one who has a greater store of experience from which to draw." When certain of his old friends questioned this new alliance, Damon justified it in terms that were familiar and inarguable: "When a guy's got class, I got to go with him." And go with Winchell he did, from one day's night into the next day's morning.

Winchell was known as the "cops and robbers columnist" because of his habit of filling his daily space in the *Mirror* with reports of his predawn drives through the streets of the city. His car was equipped with a powerful radio that received the police calls he navigated by. As he drove, he talked. After one such ride in Walter's car, Damon opined in print that "Winchell likes to talk more than any other man alive." (As was his custom when making sweeping statements, Damon had to include a few qualifying exceptions—in this case the verbose ex-*World* editor Herbert Bayard Swope and the garrulous former Michigan football coach Fielding Yost—but he concluded that "Winchell could have spotted Yost six all-American elevens and Swope an encyclopedia and still out-talk them both.")

As potent a conversationalist as Walter was—and although Walter was thirteen years his junior and in good health—Runyon the listener could outlast Winchell the talker on any given night's ride. "Winchell kept me out until broad daylight two nights hand-running," Damon said one day in his column. In fact it was the other way around; it was *Damon* who did not want to go home. Winchell, often exhausted, kept going only to satisfy his friend, who now feared being alone more than anything. Their rides often continued well into what Damon called "the tubercular light of morning."

The street life Walter and Damon observed on their 4 to 6 A.M. drives was the source of dozens of vivid columns by both writers. Often Walter cruised through Harlem, where the dawn's early light was particularly garish. One night he and Damon happened onto a death struggle between a legless derelict and a "chattering Latin" on a Harlem street. Taunted and kicked by the Hispanic youth, who'd been drinking, the legless man—whose upper body was as powerful as an athlete's—had in Damon's and Walter's presence grabbed the heckler and begun throttling him. The lit stub of a cigar still smoking in his lips, the legless man smiled up at the columnists in their car even as his strong hands worked on his struggling victim's throat. "Watch him go to sleep," he told them, as he tightened his grip. Walter wanted to get out of the car and pull the two men apart. Damon restrained him. "I've never seen a man choked to death before," he scrawled on his notepad. So the two friends sat and watched. At length the Hispanic youth broke free of the stranglehold and fled, the legless man hopping along on his hands and stumps in hot pursuit. "The fight between the legless man and the chattering Latin," Damon wrote when he got back to the Buckingham, "was the most bizarre incident I ever witnessed in all my many years on Broadway. The telling really calls for a Zola, not a Runyon . . ."

The Runyon-Winchell nocturnal excursions often took the two

The Biggest Deadline

Damon Runyon, Walter Winchell, and Sherman Billingsley at the Stork Club, 1946.

men the full length of the city, from midtown to Harlem, then all the way down to the Lower East Side, where Damon liked to stop in at Ratner's for coffee and blintzes around dawn. The columns Damon wrote about their trips were filled with urban "soul." He became a collector of the dark lyrics of the streets, the wild 4 A.M. outcries of those frightened or in pain—or worse, frightened and alone. It was material that suited his own state of mind as perfectly as kites and balloons suit a child's. In his last year or two on the planet no subject matter could be too "earthy" for Runyon. He wrote haunting columns on such subjects as the voices of women in the night.

> The women of the lower East Side of New York when in pain or fright cry out "Oh-h-h, Oh-h-h. Oh-h-h," subdued and wailingly.
>
> The women of midtown, the so-called Roaring Forties, taking in the Broadway night sector, cry more shrilly and sharply from the head, "eee-eee-eee-eeee," the tonal quality being more characteristic of women of the United States generally. I mean thus do women cry in Pueblo, Colorado, or Los Angeles.
>
> The women of Harlem cry "ooo-ooo-ooo," long drawn and throaty and eerie when it rises out of the quiet night. There is great pathos in the cry of the women of Harlem; there is high bloodcurdling alarm in the swift shriek of the midtowners; and vast distress in the low moan of the East Side.
>
> You note these things riding through the streets of the big city in the early hours of the morning with Winchell . . .

The World of Damon Runyon

Darryl Zanuck, once Damon's boss in Hollywood, was so attracted by these columns that he joined Damon and Walter on their prowls one night and in the morning proposed that the two reporters collaborate on a film script based on their "dawn patrol." It would be "a sort of *Grand Hotel* of New York," Winchell hinted in his column. Zanuck reportedly had told the two men to "name their price" for such a script. Damon, naturally, was interested, and he came up with a title, *Proceed with Caution*. But things never got past the talking stage; for Damon—the "brains" of the team—it was much too late to take on any grand projects. He had too little time and strength left.

The table talk at the Stork Club, where Winchell and Runyon continued to spend the earlier parts of their evenings, was usually lively and entertaining. When it wasn't, Damon often showed his impatience by shaking his head, tapping on the table anxiously (as though he were beating out sentences on a typewriter), or scribbling hasty notes in block capitals, as once after a wordy Winchell monologue when he wrote, WALTER, YOU'RE FULL OF SHIT. (Another time, when Damon was trying to get a point across to Mike Todd, the producer, he resorted to block capitals so big he could only fit one word on each page. "Damon, stop shouting!" Todd finally replied.)

The talk at table 50 was more often fast and sharp—waiters called the table "the blasting block"—and critical opinion was never suppressed. Women were frequently the subject of debate. Each female to enter the club got the once-over from all eyes at table 50 and was discussed at length. Only coffee was served at the table, so there was no boozy weeping, yet difficulties with women often reigned as the topic of conversation. Winchell, who fancied himself a great lover, often had a tale of woe to tell of his various amours around town. (One of Damon's first Broadway stories, "Romance in the Roaring Forties," had described Waldo Winchester's fling with a mobster's doll, and it was known on the q.t. that Winchell himself had once had a brief, nervous affair with a "private" doll of Frank Costello's.) A table 50 maxim held that "It's the man who pays," and Winchell was one night expounding this truth to Sherman Billingsley as the two commiserated over the infidelities of their current paramours. Damon too had problems along the lines his friends were describing; Patrice had been seeing a younger man in Florida. The fact that his wife's new beau was more than forty years Damon's junior must have made the situation particularly galling for him, but he did not talk about it. He didn't believe in making his love troubles public. As Walter and Sherman continued to fret, Damon grew more and more agitated. Finally he pulled out his gold pencil and scrawled a note in large caps: DON'T WORRY, BOYS. NO ONE EVER RUINED A GOOD CUNT BY FUCKING.

Damon's wisecrack quickly broke up the Winchell-Billingsley sob session, as he'd intended. The table 50 chat turned to brighter subjects—like that blonde who just walked in the door.

Not long after this incident, on June 11, 1946, Patrice obtained a divorce from Damon on grounds of "desertion." It was one of the truly dark days of Damon's life, but he refused to show his feelings in front of his friends, all of whom were aware of what had happened. His face seemed tense and grave, his blue-grey eyes cold behind his metal-rimmed glasses. When he at last let out a tired sigh and wrote "What a day!" on a note page, his table-mates were moved to silent nods of compassion. Sensing their sympathy—or pity—Damon quickly amended his first note with a second. "Yes, what a day," this one said. "My horse Scribe came in at Jamaica—paid $10.20!"

Damon's spirits were at a low point after the divorce, a "legal hurricane," his son called it, in which Damon had "lost all the family property." He had simply given Patrice most of what he owned, including half of the earnings from his writings. (Later, in his will, the remaining half went to his children and a grand-child—Mary's daughter.) Patrice had promptly remarried. "Pat has married a guy twenty-four years old," Damon wrote in a note to Bill Corum. "Hah! She'll come back to me." Despite his public bravado, Damon was left brokenhearted. He still loved his former wife deeply; she had divorced him when he was desperately ill, and now at last he was in real need of money.

In order to go on he had to work. The ability to earn money through his work had been something Damon took for granted, like breathing. Now nothing could be taken for granted. *Cosmopolitan* had assigned him a three-part story, but he did not have the energy to begin it. He complained to Damon Jr. in a letter that he was "inordinately tired all the time" and "sleeping most of the day." Still, he said, he was "up and around," which meant those long nights on the town that ended—as they had for forty years—with mornings at the typewriter. Before collapsing into bed after his drives with Winchell, Damon still went to his worktable and tapped out his 750 words, if he had the strength. If he did not, there was always tomorrow's column to think ahead to, or perhaps a news story. Despite the tiredness and the "terrific" pain that he admitted to his son was now attacking his rib cage, Damon worked on conning news assignments out of his editors as often as he could, to prove to himself that he could still perform on the "front lines"—and to stay on the payroll. Up to the last months of his life he was actively earning the $35,000 reporter's salary he was paid by International News Service. That summer of 1946 he contributed to the Hearst papers taut, present-tense accounts of Joe Louis' title defenses against Billy Conn and Tami Mauriello.

The Conn fight occurred only eight days after his divorce, but you wouldn't know that the man who wrote it was suffering mightily. It is clear, bright, effective prose in the vigorous present-tense reporting style Damon had developed years before. " 'Old Steady,' Joe Louis, patient and plodding as a school master, knocks flashy Billy Conn out in the eighth round last night at Yankee Stadium to keep his title," Damon's story began. It went on for two entire columns. The sheer physical exertion of writing it took much of what remained of Damon's strength and left him flagging. He did not appear in the *Journal-American*'s pages again until the end of July. Then he felt well enough to cover the Louis-Mauriello fight on September 18, again in Yankee Stadium. "Thank goodness, Joe Louis makes it quick and merciful knocking out Tami Mauriello in two minutes and nine seconds of the first round of his twenty-third defense," went Damon's lead. Once again his story is a model of brisk, accurate reporting. The last big sports story Damon ever wrote, it seems much too full of life to have been produced by a dying man.

That summer Damon Jr. came to visit and stayed with his father at the Buckingham. One evening Damon took him out to the old Lindy's for dinner and then down the block to Madison Square Garden to catch the weekly fight card. After the bouts they stopped off at a nightclub across the street from the Garden, the Carnival, where Milton Berle was playing. During the show Damon Jr. watched his father ogle a pretty teenage girl at another table. Then they adjourned to the old Lindy's, where Berle dropped in to say hello to Damon. By means of a note, Damon informed the comedian that his act had contained too much "blue" material. Berle seemed excessively upset by the note. Was it that his father's comment had bothered the comedian, Damon Jr. wondered, or was it simply that his father was dying and Berle, like all his friends, knew and was affected by it? The younger Runyon, exhausted, went off to bed while his dying father continued on to Toots Shor's and then back to the Buckingham with friends for a marathon postdawn session of gin rummy.

A few days later father and son had a final heart-to-heart "talk" concerning Ellen Egan Runyon. Out of the blue, Damon had suddenly passed his son a note reading, "Why did your mother drink?" The question, bringing into the open an issue the two had never discussed, touched Damon Jr. deeply. He replied at length that he did not blame his father for his mother's unfortunate fate. Damon listened and when his son was finished remained silent briefly. Then, according to Damon Jr., his father "gestured with hands outward and palms up, meaning 'That's that.' "

Damon had by this time taken to sleeping at odd hours—whenever the gift of Morpheus arrived—and it was in the midst of such a midday slumber that Damon Jr. prepared to leave for home. As the son was about to go out the door, the phone rang and he was forced to rouse his father.

> I carried on the conversation for him and then came the moment he had tried to avoid. I knew how it was with him, because it was the same with me, so I didn't make a production of it.
> "So long, Dad," I said.
> His lips formed the words, "So long, Son."
> He broke but a little—he put his arm around my shoulder and squeezed.

It was the last time Damon Jr. would see his father conscious.

Damon had by now begun to come apart—if only a little at a time—in front of the Stork Club friends with whom he'd always maintained a hard-boiled exterior. He tried to keep his chin up and his mind on the conversation, but life was escaping him. As the dog days of summer came and went, his table notes grew scarcer. He sat and listened to his friends' conversation but seldom commented; the physical act of writing tired him too much. On August 10 Winchell and the table 50 crowd were discussing the ad that agent Ben Piazza took out in *Variety* every year on that date to commemorate the death of his (and Damon's) friend, sportswriter Paul Armstrong. It was remarked at the table that even though Armstrong was thirty years in the ground, he was not forgotten—"That's real gratitude," someone said. Damon nodded sadly. "When I'm gone," he slowly wrote on his pad, "I hope some one remembers me even a little while." His eyes, the others saw, were moist.

Damon still had a contract with Twentieth Century Fox and had been expected on the Fox lot in Hollywood on August 1 to work on *The Bloodhounds of Broadway,* but he hadn't made it. In September he explained to his son that he had to "stick around here a while to pick up some loose ends of the divorce" and that perhaps he would finally "decide not to go" back to Hollywood at all. "It is too far from the doctor," he wrote. By this time it was all he could do to cope with his obligations at home. He confided to Damon Jr. that even keeping up with his daily column was more work than he could handle. What complicated matters was that the public demand for the Runyon column had never been greater. "Of a sudden my column took fire with the boss people, including Mr. Hearst, and he is prodding the editors to be sure and get it in the papers, which only makes it necessary for me to keep on a regular schedule instead of doing it when I felt like it," he wrote Damon Jr. on September 6, 1946. "Newspaper work is, of course, not of great importance to me now and sometimes I wonder why I keep at it. I am commencing to think it is force of habit . . ." A week later he was back in harness as a reporter at the Louis-Mauriello fight.

By October there was no longer thought of following the sports beat; the World Series came and went, and Damon was sicker. He had bills to pay. "My divorce cleaned me out pretty well but all I need to raise money is a little health and time and a typewriter and given that I will be back fast," he wrote his son. "I don't waste time contemplating my sad state and never will." This was so much whistling in the dark; Damon's real feelings came through in other sentences in the same letter. "I have no one to help me in any way save when a good soul drops around out of the goodness of his heart, no one to aid and comfort me. I have no permanent habitation, no possessions any more save a few clothes, and most of those were stolen the other day by a thief." For him it was an uncharacteristically weepy tone. The bright facade was crumbling; Damon was breaking down. He responded bitterly to some petty complaints in one of Damon Jr.'s letters.

> I notice you do a lot of thinking about yourself and your problems. Sometimes when you are in a mood for thought give one to your old man who in two years was stricken by the most terrible malady known to mankind and left voiceless with a death sentence hanging over his head, who had a big career stopped cold, and had his domestic life shattered by divorce and his savings largely dissipated through the combination of evil circumstances.
>
> All this at sixty-five years of age when most men's activity is completely ended.
>
> Try that on your zither some day, my boy, especially when those low moods you mention strike you.

Late that autumn Bill Corum, in the twenties and thirties Runyon's roommate on hundreds of road trips on the sports beat, came to visit him one day at the Buckingham. It was late afternoon of a grey day at the end of November. Damon was already up, had read the papers, and was sitting forlornly in a chair when Corum came in. For a while they managed to make conversation, then Damon's face—thinner now, Corum noticed—grew drawn and tight. The sick man turned his chair away from his friend, moved it to a corner, sat down, and began to weep. Disconcerted, Corum waited and smoked. After a time Damon got up and crossed the room to his bed, lifted the corner of a colored cloth on the bed-table, gazed for a moment at what was concealed there, and then returned to his chair.

Later, when Damon had stepped out of the room, Corum's curiosity got the best of him and he lifted the cloth on the bed-table. Beneath the cloth was a full-length photo of Patrice, placed directly under the bed-light, where Damon could lift the cloth and look at it even when he was in too much pain to get out of bed.

The man who in his wild Denver youth had been called the Demon was now living quietly in his own personal hell, existing from day to day on prescribed dope and the few shreds of dreams that remained to him. He held tighter and tighter to them as his time dwindled.

November, a bleak month in which his confinement prevented him from attending the funerals of two old friends, Sid Mercer and Jimmy Walker, came and went for Damon with terrifying speed. He was rarely fully conscious, and when he was, it was only to notice that two or three pages had disappeared from the calendar since the last time he had looked.

Two or three weeks after Bill Corum's visit Damon was down to 100 pounds (from the bloated 195 he'd weighed a few months earlier) and was wobbly on his feet because of all the medication. Cancer had eaten his chest and stomach and was now working on his liver. By this time he'd stopped going out at night and was even having a hard time getting down to the car that the faithful Eddie Walker or one of his other friends provided every day for his visit to the doctor.

One day, when Damon felt or imagined a return of strength, he did go out, strolling to Columbus Circle with his old pal Mike Jacobs, the fight promoter and manager of Joe Louis. (Damon's columns—and his assistance in getting Joe his first big fight, the Milk Fund meeting with Max Baer in 1935—had helped considerably in the building of Louis' career.) Jacobs was now planning a new stadium to compete with the Garden. He and Damon were senior partners in the Twentieth Century Sporting Club, under which aegis Jacobs proposed to launch the venture. The idea of a grand new sporting coliseum in his town kindled a last spark of enthusiasm in Damon. Excited, he went home and wrote a column about the Jacobs plan. Pain or no, he still clung to life jealously.

There were to be no more strolls or columns. On December 6 Damon was too ill to visit his doctor. The surgeon paid a house call and after examining his patient told Paul Small—who with Eddie Walker was now constantly at Damon's side—that a return to the hospital would be necessary. He gave Damon injections of morphine, then Small and Walker and the hotel bellboys helped the columnist make it to the elevator and from the elevator to a taxi. After speaking with the driver, Small got in beside Damon and told him that they were going to take a ride around town to see the sights.

Damon was woozy enough to accept this explanation without protest until the cab pulled up at Memorial Hospital. The sight of the white-coated attendants approaching the taxi suddenly brought his mind into focus. He panicked. He did not want to go into the hospital, for that meant he would now surely die. His hands moved frantically over the robe that covered his lap. They found his notepad and pencil and closed around these objects that were his voice. "What's this?" he scribbled in large wild letters. A doctor opened the door of the taxi and tried to explain the situation in a kindly way, but Damon wanted none of it. He mouthed and croaked his angry resentment. "Where is Walter?" he was trying to say. "If Walter were here, he wouldn't let you do this to me!" (Walter Winchell had left on his annual Florida vacation a month before and since then had been making daily telephone calls from Miami to the Buckingham to inquire about his friend's condition. In his drugged state Damon now remembered none of this.)

Damon did not resist the attendants; he was too weak, and what was the use? They wheeled him inside to the room that was waiting, and sat him on the bed. Damon's head began shaking from side to side, as it did when he meant to say no. Paul Small asked what was the matter. Damon beckoned for his notepad, and it was handed to him. "This is not as good as the old room," he wrote in feeble, tilting script. Small looked at the note, then back at Damon, puzzled. Squire Runyon waved a frail hand in the direction of the room's only window, which faced another wing of the hospital. Then he picked up his pad again and committed to it the last of the eighty million or so words he'd written for public consumption in the sixty-six years of his life.

"The old room had a nice view," he wrote.

Paul Small nodded sadly in sympathy. Then Damon was undressed and laid on the bed. His bones were light, like a puppet's, and his thin hands were whiter than the white sheets.

The next day Damon managed a final private note to his son, instructing him to see to it that "Alfred Damon Runyon" was carved above Ellen Egan Runyon's name on her tombstone in Woodlawn Cemetary. The note also contained a special wish as to the disposal of his body, which his son was instructed to keep private until the proper time. Damon also scrawled a last message to Patrice, whose picture had come along with him to the hospital and was now at arm's reach on the table beside the bed. That evening his physical anguish increased, and he lapsed into a coma. Three days later, at 6:10 P.M. on December 10, 1946, he stopped breathing.

A few days after Damon's death Walter Winchell went on the air to say a few choked-up words about his dead friend and to ask "Mr. and Mrs. North America" to send in "a buck or so" to start a Runyon Memorial Fund to fight cancer. At the time it was considered bad taste even to refer to cancer as cause of death in news stories, but Winchell did so because, he later explained, "when Damon was released from the pain he never talked about, I had to say something, if only to get it off my chest." Within days donations had come in to Winchell from Bugsy Siegel and Bernard Baruch, from Frank Costello and the candy vendors at the Garden, from Bronx school kids (9000 pennies) and Broadway cabbies, and even from Bowery panhandlers, who turned over to the fund one entire day's take. Money came in from Socks Lanza, dying of cancer in Sing Sing, and from a soldier stationed in the Panama Canal Zone, whose wife had been killed by the disease. A former Hollywood starlet turned hooker went out "moonlighting" for the Runyon Fund and sent Winchell all her profits. Over the next two and a half decades the "buck or so" grew until $32 million had been collected in Damon Runyon's name for use in cancer research. Newspapermen suffering from the disease were treated free of charge through the auspices of the Runyon Fund. That provision would certainly have pleased Damon. As well as any man, he had known what it was to turn out good copy under the pressure of the biggest deadline of them all.

In compliance with the special wish expressed in Damon's last note to his son, his ashes were strewn over Manhattan Island by Captain Eddie Rickenbacker. Damon, who seemed to have known *everybody,* had ghostwritten some speeches for the World War I air hero way back in 1919. Now, a week before Christmas 1946, Rickenbacker got a chance to repay Damon in services. He took off from LaGuardia, flew north, and banked over Woodlawn to move down the Hudson. At the Statue of Liberty he turned again and steadied his Eastern Airlines twin-engine transport on a northward course over Manhattan, angling uptown. At Times Square, on a sign from Damon Jr., the urn containing the ashes of the self-appointed laureate of the Big Street was tipped out the window by the former flying ace. The mortal remains of Damon Runyon became at that moment a part of the great atmosphere of Broadway. They fell in a compact mass for a second or two through the chill grey sky, then dispersed into the wind.

Postscript

An inveterate gambler, Damon in his lifetime had put money on almost every big sporting event he'd covered—and some that were not so big. In death he became himself the subject of his own last wager. It was an ironic bet he'd placed in one of his last columns, "Shall I Return?"

> I have bet practically all my life.
>
> I will continue to bet until I die.
>
> In fact, you might say I will be betting after death, as a wise guy recently laid me $1,000 to $10 that I will not return from that bourne that is popularly supposed to permanently detain all travelers.
>
> Most persons will no doubt say that I have a bad bet. I think I have a good one. In any event, could I resist the price?
>
> It all started at a sidewalk session at Broadway and Fiftieth when the name of a departed brother came up and someone recalled that he had promised to return after death and visit his old friends.
>
> "So will I," I remarked, sociably.
>
> "You will?" said the wise guy, emphasizing the "you" as much as to say no matter who might return I am least likely to enjoy that privilege.
>
> "Yes, I will," I said, stiffly.
>
> "I would like to lay you ten thousand to a nickel that you don't," said the wise guy.
>
> At these words, everyone present turned around and scrutinized all persons nearby lest some of them be coppers.
>
> "You have a wager," I said to the wise guy after noting that the coast was clear.
>
> He quickly reconsidered.
>
> "No," he said, "that would be too far out of line. I might not be able to pay you off if you won. Let me do a little figuring on this proposition."
>
> So he outs with a pencil and an old envelope and did some calculating. Then he went into the corner drug store and made a telephone call, possibly to his lawyer to see what he thought of the bet. When he came back he said:
>
> "The best I can offer you is a thousand dollars to ten."
>
> "Set!" I ejaculated, the laconic Broadway binder of a speculative deal.

History does not record the outcome of Damon's wager, but if in fact he returned to collect, it might have been in the form Slats Slavin took when he came back from the dead in "Blonde

Postscript

"The Demon"

Mink." That party was seen to reappear by Julie the Starker, who was interrogated later by the tale's narrator.

> "You state that you see the late Slats walking around and about. Do you see him all pale and vapory?"
>
> "Well," Julie says, "now you mention it Slats is a little on the pale side of what he used to be. . ."

Slats' ghost had matters of its own to tend to, such as providing Julie the Starker with a tip on the horses in return for Julie's assistance in evening up the score with Slats' onetime doll, the beautiful but faithless Miss Beatrice Gee.

Damon, according to his last remarks on the subject, had no such vindictive plans on his agenda for the afterlife. On this point our information comes from Damon Runyon, Jr., to whom his dying father once expressed the hope that when he "woke up dead," he would "find himself in a big poker game with his departed pals—'Tad' Dorgan, Sid Mercer, Matty Mathewson, Hype Igoe, and all the rest."

Runyon told his son he did not care how the cards went, or what the stakes were, so long as his friends held a seat open for him.

How could they have done less?

Appendix: Runyon at Work—
A Composite Portrait

My father was an agony writer. That is, writing was a heavy labor for him and each word hit the paper bathed in sweat. Writers vary in this respect. At the other extreme, according to legend, was Heywood Broun. It's said he used to knock out his daily column of 700-odd words in thirty minutes or less.

My father thought his whole story out long in advance so the actual writing was a mechanical process of polishing and retouching. For his short stories he resorted to longhand to write the first draft, sometimes doing this chore in bed, a way of working fancied by Mark Twain. The final draft was the result of several rewriting sessions at the typewriter.

It was heavy going not only for him but for the rest of us around the house since he became more moody than ever and was difficult if not impossible to deal with during these periods. The whole household had to function under a sort of quarantine of silence and any decisions demanding his attention simply had to wait for a spell of idleness.

—Damon Runyon, Jr., *Father's Footsteps*

The Runyon gospel of workroom privacy and the bare wall might seem inconsistent with his fondness for Broadway excitements, the roar of the town. Back in the 1920's he usually wrote his column "The Mornin's Mornin'" at home. However, many other assignments found him and his typewriter at public places. There, like other reporters of that age of hurrah and tumult, he had to forego the benefits of monastic peace. Hermits seldom appeared to advantage on Park Row.

More often than not, the working press was harassed from all sides, jostled, given scanty space in which to sit or write. In certain emergencies, a reporter had to fight both mankind and nature itself while trying to win a place beyond that door upon which some misinformed signpainter had put the legend: "Gentlemen."

I cannot recall, however, that occupational hardships, the sardine conditions of the press box, the hullabaloo of the crowd, or anything else bothered Runyon. He seemed well insulated at all times. He would find a place for his typewriter, a feat comparable to pouring a quart into a pint bottle. After a quick look-around

Appendix

and some grunted hellos he would sit down, unhinge the lid of his typewriter, then feed a sheet of pulp paper into the machine. He would glare at the blank copy paper as though it had just told him an off-color story, and puff the while on his cigarette. Now he would draw his hatbrim low over his spectacles, readjust his necktie, then . . . bingo!

Damon wrote with the forefingers, as did most other newspapermen. He typed rapidly, steadily, with the tempo of a woodpecker in search of breakfast. He seemed aloof and alone in the crowd. In some respects he seemed alone always, everywhere.

—Gene Fowler, *Skyline*

He detested being alone even for a snatched meal or even when writing. For a time he tried the solitary study for turning out his prose, but he always insisted he was happier at a typewriter in a jostling, noisy news room or at the crowded ringside table and press box. . . .

. . . He was a quantity as well as a quality producer and sometimes would let himself go for whole pages about a fight that had excited him or a cross-examination that made his pulse race. He did not churn the stuff out. He tapped delicately at the typewriter, rippling and riffling over the keys, a cigarette always dangling from his lips. Now and again he would pause and gaze around and upwards, trying out a phrase in his mind. He was a cool and calm customer at his job, though occasionally he would rip out the copy paper from his machine and throw the crumpled ball to the ground.

—Don Iddon, "Memoir of the Author," in the English edition of Runyon's collected columns, *Short Takes*

Runyon used to cover fights and did something you rarely see. He did the running on a fight on a typewriter. He wouldn't take notes and write after the round. He had an operator named Levitt, a postal telegraph guy who read over his shoulder all the time. And the big thing about Runyon in those days, he used to cover all the big murder trials that would bring the stars out. They would all use legmen. But he didn't. He did all his own work.

—Jimmy Cannon in *No Cheering in the Press Box*

Damon Runyon was another baseball writer who was frequently yanked out of sports to do a sensational trial. He wrote that stuff in court in longhand, and you never had to change a word. He would describe a woman on the stand as being a "frosty blonde." He used fine terms, and quick. A fellow had to be very much disinterested in everything not to read those stories from start to finish. He presented the case. You understood what it was about. He always checked with the attorneys on the few little technicalities so he would be all right.

The World of Damon Runyon

I knew Runyon better than any of the others. He would seclude himself and I think kind of feel sorry for himself. But I got acquainted with him. He sometimes would come down to Hot Springs, when the Babe was tubbing. He'd come down to write a few things about the Babe but mainly to get away from New York, to hole up in a hotel room and write short stories. And when he was writing these he was quite touchy. Well, I didn't care whether he was touchy or not. I used to kid him and try to get him out to play golf, for dinner, and finally one morning at one of the better hotels—we were eating on the veranda, having baked scrod. Lots of people wouldn't eat that fish for breakfast, but we did. He looked up at me and grinned and for the first time he seemed to mean that grin, and from then on we hit it off. We talked a lot about newspaper work, writing, baseball, books—everything—wherever we met, in New York or any place. He had been in the Spanish-American War, a drummer or something. He began picking up expressions, and he was one of the few fellows who could take the words of the mob and get them into print and make them sound right. He had a good ear for dialogue and that's how he wrote those short stories. Much of it is dialogue. He didn't invent those names. He just changed them. They all had screwy names.
—Marshall Hunt in *No Cheering in the Press Box*

In 1918 Damon speaks to Gene Fowler about his intercession with Jimmy Walker to obtain a street vendor's license for a long-time acquaintance named Doctor DeGarmo. A former card sharp on trans-Atlantic liners, DeGarmo had had his card-dealing career cut short by an accident that cost him his forefinger. (He had also been a track vet for a while, and remained an opium head ever since.) Doctor DeGarmo crops up in "Broadway Financier"—written a dozen years after the speech Fowler quotes—as Doc Daro, who is considered one of the highest-class operators that ever rides the tubs, until rheumatism ruins his shuffle. As Damon explains to his younger colleague—

". . . With the doctor's record he can't get a license unless somebody puts in the right word. And that's what I was talking about to Senator Jimmy Walker. I went to this trouble because it is an investment, as I said. And there is a story in Doctor DeGarmo, maybe several, and I am always looking for stories, for characters mostly.

"For it is characters that I remember from the things I have read," he went on to say. "I never got beyond the fourth grade. I learned geography by traveling hither and yon, and as a soldier. The best geography there is is the map of a man's life; not just anyone's life, but a special life like Doctor DeGarmo's. His life has a latitude and a longitude; and it has islands, like the ones that come up and then disappear when there is an earthquake

Appendix

under the sea. And the stories I mean to write later on will be good, because they'll have to be good, or I'll not send them along. I'll cash in on my investment in Doctor DeGarmo, and on my investment in a lot of other mugs of the Big Town.

"I invite you to do the same," he said. "And to hell with plots, because nobody remembers much about the plots of Dickens or Mark Twain. They remember the characters. . . ."

—Gene Fowler, Skyline

Bibliography

The following works were consulted. Not listed here but also consulted were numerous newspapers and periodicals, especially the New York *American, Journal-American,* and *Daily Mirror, Collier's,* and *Cosmopolitan,* in which individual Runyon articles, columns, and stories appeared. The list of books by Damon Runyon is partial—a basic listing—and includes only the original editions of the collections of his writing.

Allen, Frederick Lewis. *The Big Change.* New York: Harper & Row, 1952.

———. *Only Yesterday.* New York: Harper & Row, 1931.

Allen, Lee. *The National League Story.* New York: Hill & Wang, 1961.

Asbury, Herbert. *The Great Illusion.* New York: Knopf, 1927.

Bates, Ernest, and Carlson, Oliver. *Hearst, Lord of San Simeon.* New York: Viking, 1936.

Bendiner, Robert. *Just Around the Corner: A Highly Selective History of the 30's.* New York: Harper & Row, 1967.

Bishop, Jim. *The Mark Hellinger Story.* Englewood Cliffs, N.J.: Prentice-Hall, 1952.

Cahn, William. *Good Night, Mrs. Calabash: The Secret of Jimmy Durante.* New York: Duell, Sloan & Pearce, 1963.

Capra, Frank. *The Name Above the Title.* New York: Macmillan, 1971.

Carse, Robert. *Rum Row.* New York: Holt, Rinehart and Winston, 1959.

Churchill, Allen. *Park Row.* New York: Holt, Rinehart and Winston, 1959.

Cobb, Irvin S. *Exit Laughing.* Indianapolis: Bobbs-Merrill, 1941.

Cooke, Bob (ed.). *Wake Up the Echoes.* New York: Hanover House, 1956.

Corum, Bill. *Off and Running.* New York: Holt, Rinehart and Winston, 1959.

Creamer, Robert. *Babe: The Legend Comes to Life.* New York: Simon & Schuster, 1974.

Dempsey, Jack, with Considine, Bob, and Slocum, Bill. *Dempsey.* New York: Simon & Schuster, 1960.

Durso, Joe. *Casey: The Life and Legend of Charles Dillon Stengel.* Englewood Cliffs, N.J.: Prentice-Hall, 1967.

Bibliography

Einstein, Charles. *The Fireside Book of Baseball.* Vol. 2. New York: Simon & Schuster, 1958.

Farr, Finis. *Fair Enough: The Life of Westbrook Pegler.* New Rochelle, N.Y.: Arlington House, 1975.

Ferber, Nat. *I Found Out.* New York: Dial Press, 1939.

Fitzgerald, F. Scott. *The Great Gatsby.* New York: Scribner, 1925.

Fleischer, Nat. *Jack Dempsey.* New Rochelle, N.Y.: Arlington House, 1972.

Fowler, Gene. *Beau James: The Life and Times of Jimmy Walker.* New York: Viking, 1949.

————. *The Great Mouthpiece.* New York: Grosset & Dunlap, 1931.

————. *Schnozzola.* New York: Viking, 1951.

————. *Skyline.* New York: Viking, 1961.

————. *Timberline.* New York: Viking, 1933.

Fowler, Will. *The Young Man from Denver.* Garden City, N.Y.: Doubleday, 1962.

Freedland, Michael. *Jolson.* Briarcliff Manor, N.Y.: Stein and Day, 1972.

Frick, Ford. *Games, Asterisks and People.* New York: Crown, 1973.

Gallico, Paul. *Farewell to Sport.* New York: Knopf, 1938.

Giesler, Jerry, and Martin, Pete. *The Jerry Giesler Story.* New York: Simon & Schuster, 1960.

Heller, Peter. *"In This Corner. . . !": Forty Champions Tell Their Stories.* New York: Simon & Schuster, 1973.

Higham, Charles. *Ziegfeld.* Chicago: Regnery, 1972.

Holtzman, Jerome (ed.). *No Cheering in the Press Box.* New York: Holt, Rinehart and Winston, 1973.

Hoyt, Edwin. *Gentleman of Broadway.* Boston: Little, Brown, 1964.

Kahn, E. J. *The World of Swope.* New York: Simon & Schuster, 1965.

Karst, Gene, and Jones, Martin. *Who's Who in Professional Baseball.* New Rochelle, N.Y.: Arlington House, 1973.

Katcher, Leo. *The Big Bankroll: The Life and Times of Arnold Rothstein.* New York: Harper & Row, 1958.

Klurfeld, Herman. *Winchell, His Life and Times.* New York: Praeger, 1976.

Lait, Jack, and Mortimer, Lee. *New York Confidential.* New York: Dell, 1950.

Lardner, Ring, Jr. *The Lardners: My Family Remembered.* New York: Harper & Row, 1976.

Lewis, Mildred, and Lewis, Milton. *Famous Modern Newspaper Writers.* New York: Dodd, Mead, 1962.

Lieb, Fred. *Baseball As I Have Known It.* New York: Coward, McCann & Geoghegan, 1977.

————. *The Story of the World Series.* New York: Putnam, 1949.

Livingston, Bernard. *Their Turf: America's Horsey Set and Its Princely Dynasties.* New York: Arbor House, 1973.

Menke, Frank. *Pictorial Encyclopedia of Sports.* Cranbury, N.J.: Barnes, 1953

The World of Damon Runyon

O'Connor, Richard. *Heywood Broun.* New York: Putnam, 1975.

Reichler, Joe (ed.). *The Game and the Glory.* Englewood Cliffs, N.J.: Prentice-Hall, 1976.

Rice, Damon. *Seasons Past.* New York: Praeger, 1976.

Rice, Grantland. *The Tumult and the Shouting: My Life in Sport.* Cranbury, N.J.: Barnes, 1954.

Ritter, Lawrence. *The Glory of Their Times.* New York: Macmillan, 1966.

Runyon, Damon. *Guys and Dolls.* New York: Frederick A. Stokes, 1931.

————. *Blue Plate Special.* New York: Frederick A. Stokes, 1934.

————. *Money from Home.* New York: Frederick A. Stokes, 1935.

————. *Runyon a la Carte.* Philadelphia: Lippincott, 1944.

————. *In Our Town.* New York: Creative Age Press, 1946.

————. *Short Takes.* New York: McGraw-Hill, 1946.

————. *Trials and Other Tribulations.* Philadelphia: Lippincott, 1947.

————. *More Guys and Dolls.* New York: Garden City Books, 1951.

————. *A Treasury of Damon Runyon.* New York: Random House (Modern Library), 1958.

Runyon, Damon, Jr. *Father's Footsteps.* New York: Random House, 1953.

Sann, Paul. *Kill the Dutchman! The Story of Dutch Schultz.* New Rochelle, N.Y.: Arlington House, 1971.

————. *The Lawless Decade.* New York: Crown, 1957.

Seymour, Harold. *Baseball: The Golden Age.* New York: Oxford University Press, 1971.

Shannon, Bill, and Kalinsky, George. *The Ballparks.* New York: Hawthorn Books, 1975.

Smith, H. Allen. *The Life and Legend of Gene Fowler.* New York: Morrow, 1977.

Spigelgass, Leonard. *Hello, Hollywood.* Garden City, N.Y.: Doubleday, 1962.

Spink, J. G. Taylor. *Judge Landis and Twenty-five Years of Baseball.* New York: Crowell, 1947.

Swanberg, W. A. *Citizen Hearst.* New York: Scribner, 1961.

Tebbel, John. *The Compact History of the American Newspaper.* New York: Hawthorn Books, 1963.

————. *The Life and Good Times of W. R. Hearst.* New York: Dutton, 1952.

Thomas, Bob. *Winchell.* Garden City, N.Y.: Doubleday, 1971.

Walker, Stanley. *The Night Club Era.* Philadelphia: Lippincott, 1933.

Weiner, Ed. *The Damon Runyon Story.* New York: McKay, 1948.

————. *Let's Go to Press.* New York: Putnam, 1955.

Wentworth, Harold, and Flexner, S. B. *Dictionary of American Slang.* New York: Crowell, 1960.

Wheeler, John. *I've Got News for You.* New York: Dutton, 1961.

Yardley, Jonathon. *Ring: A Biography of Rand Lardner.* New York: Random House, 1977.

Index

Index

Index

Index

Index

Index

Index

Index